Writing the Oral Tradition

Poetics of Orality and Literacy

general editor
John Miles Foley

Writing the Oral Tradition

Oral Poetics and Literate Culture in Medieval England

— MARK C. AMODIO

University of Notre Dame Press

Notre Dame, Indiana

Manufactured in the United States of America

Library of Congress Cataloging-in-Publication Data
Amodio, Mark.
Writing the oral tradition : oral poetics and literate culture in medieval
England / Mark C. Amodio.
p. cm.—(Poetics of orality and literacy)
 Includes bibliographical references and index.
ISBN 0-268-02023-x (cloth : alk. paper)
ISBN 0-268-02024-8 (pbk. : alk. paper)
1. English poetry—Middle English, 1100–1500—History and criticism.
2. Written communication—England—History—To 1500.   3. Oral
communication—England—History—To 1500.   4. Oral tradition—
England—History—To 1500.   5. Oral-formulaic analysis.   I. Title.   II. Series.
PR317.072A47   2004
821'.109—dc22

2004023679

∞ *This book is printed on acid-free paper*

For my parents,

THERESA *&* ANTHONY

Contents

Acknowledgments

It is a pleasure to acknowledge the institutional and personal support I have received during the writing of this book. Thanks to its president, Frances D. Fergusson, Vassar College continues to be a richly rewarding place to think, teach, and pursue research. I am grateful to her and to this institution for supporting my scholarship in numerous ways, and I am especially thankful for the sabbaticals during which this book was written. Many of the ideas here were first road-tested in seminars at Vassar, and among the many talented students with whom I have had the pleasure of working, I would like to give thanks to Katrina Bartow, Rachel Becker, Jennifer Flynn, Marjorie Rubright, Matt Saks, and Samantha Zacher, all of whom helped me deepen my understanding of the often inchoate ideas I brought before them and their classmates. Among the audiences who heard portions of this study at various stages of its development, I would like to single out for special thanks those at the University of Missouri, Columbia in the spring of 2000 and at Smith College in the fall of that same year.

Bashir el-Beshti, John McBratney, and Michael Schoenfeldt have been valued friends since early in our graduate school days, and I owe them a deep debt of gratitude. My colleagues in the Vassar English Department have always been supportive of the medievalist in their midst, and I would like especially to thank Frank Bergon, Don Foster, Eamon Grennan, and Ann Imbrie. Among the many others who have contributed directly or indirectly to this project, Benjamin Bagby, Robert E. Bjork, Nancy Mason Bradbury, Joseph Harris, John M. Hill, Edward B. Irving Jr. (in memoriam), Seth Lerer, John K. "Monk" McDonough, Kim Montgomery, Joseph Falaky Nagy, Alexandra Hennessey Olsen, Joel T. Rosenthal, Lawrence Schek, and Vinni Genovese Schek deserve special thanks. John Miles Foley, Katherine O'Brien O'Keeffe, and Andy Orchard read the manuscript in its entirety and generously offered many suggestions for improving it. Their thoughtful and incisive comments not only helped me to rethink and substantially improve some crucial aspects of this study but also saved me from numerous minor as well as several major blunders. The infelicities of expression and factual errors that remain are, of course, entirely my own. I would like to thank Barbara Hanrahan, the director of the University of Notre Dame Press, and her first-rate staff for the care with which they treated this project from start to finish. Katrina Bartow, '03, and Jaji Crocker, '04, were my student assistants while this project was being completed and readied for publication, and I am thankful to them for all their help.

Randall Nakayama(†) was a gifted scholar and my chrerished friend for twenty-five years. May he be at peace

As the chapters that follow will make clear, the works of John Miles Foley and Alain Renoir have played a fundamental role in shaping my approach to the questions of orality and literacy in medieval England; what those chapters cannot reveal is how much their friendship over the years has meant to me and how deeply indebted I am to them for all their intellectual and personal guidance.

My wife Julie Hellberg, who cheerfully traded life in the Bay Area for life in the Hudson Valley, and our children, Min and Luc, daily bring great joy into my life, and it is for them that I do everything I do.

Finally, I dedicate this book to my beloved parents, Theresa and Anthony, who have always given me so very much.

～ The image on the cover is taken from London, British Library, Cotton Caligula A. ix and is used by the kind permission of the British Library. Some portions of this book are based on work that has previously appeared and I would like to thank the editors of *Oral Tradition, Poetica,* and *Studia Neophilologica* for allowing me to present here revised versions of material that originally appeared in the pages of their journals. My discussions of Beowulf's fight with the dragon in chapter 2 and Morpidus's fight with the beast in chapter 3 are drawn from "Affective Criticism, Oral Poetics, and Beowulf's Fight with the Dragon," *Oral Tradition* 10 (1995): 54–90. The discussion in chapter 3 of the *Brut's* syntax and lexicon is drawn from "Laȝamon's Anglo-Saxon Lexicon and Diction," *Poetica* 28 (1988): 48–59, and "Some Notes on Laȝamon's Use of the Synthetic Genitive," *Studia Neophilologica* 59 (1987): 187–94. My discussion of the Middle English lexeme *abelgen* in chapter 3 is drawn from "Tradition, Performance, and Poetics in Early Middle English Poetry," *Oral Tradition* 15 (2000): 191–214. "High Noon," lyrics by Ned Washington, is cited by permission of Warner Bros. Publications.

Abbreviations

ACMRS	Arizona Center for Medieval and Renaissance Studies
ANQ	*American Notes & Queries*
ASE	*Anglo-Saxon England*
ASPR	*The Anglo-Saxon Poetic Records*, ed. Krapp and Dobbie
BJRL	*Bulletin of the John Rylands University Library*
CI	*Critical Inquiry*
CL	*Comparative Literature*
CR	*Chaucer Review*
CSASE	Cambridge Studies in Anglo-Saxon England
CSML	Cambridge Studies in Medieval Literature
CUL	Cambridge University Library
DOE	*Dictionary of Old English*, ed. Healey et al.
EEMF	Early English Manuscripts in Facsimile
EETS	Early English Text Society
ELH	*English Literary History*

ES	*English Studies*
JAF	*Journal of American Folklore*
KCLMS	King's College London Medieval Series
MÆ	*Medium Ævum*
MED	*Middle English Dictionary*, ed. Stratmann
MLR	*Modern Language Review*
MP	*Modern Philology*
MRTS	Medieval and Renaissance Texts and Studies
NM	*Neuphilologische Mitteilungen*
NMS	*Nottingham Medieval Studies*
NQ	*Notes & Queries*
NLH	*New Literary History*
OED	*Oxford English Dictionary*, 2nd ed.
OT	*Oral Tradition*
PAPS	*Proceedings of the American Philosophical Society*
PBA	*Proceedings of the British Academy*
RES	*Review of English Studies*
SN	*Studia Neophilologica*
SS	*Scandinavian Studies*
TAPA	*Transactions of the American Philological Association*
TRHS	*Transactions of the Royal Historical Society*
TSLL	*Texas Studies in Language and Literature*
YES	*Yearbook of English Studies*

Preface

This book is a study of the oral tradition's influence on the vernacular verse produced in England from the beginnings of the Anglo-Saxon period in the fifth century C.E. through the close of the Middle Ages in the early fifteenth. It has become almost axiomatic to assert that some sort of oral tradition underlay the chirographic one that began its rise to dominance during the Anglo-Saxon period, but many questions about the medieval English oral tradition remain: we have yet to define it with any precision, we do not fully understand its tectonics or how it developed and was passed along through successive generations, and we have not yet fully charted its complicated situation in a cultural climate that was steadily becoming more and more literate. While this book will touch upon these and other matters in the following chapters, one of its primary aims will be to explore how what was once a living tradition articulated only through the voices of singers engaged in public acts of (re)composition comes to find expression through the pens of authors engaged in very different, private moments of composition.

   Throughout the medieval period, the vast majority of the population did not have access to the technology of literacy and so lived in what was a predominantly oral world, one in which orality and its attendant habits of mind not only played an important role in daily life but also exerted a powerful influence over the articulation of vernacular verse. The oral tradition's influence on medieval English poetry can be most readily apprehended in the *oral poetics* that infuses much of the poetry extant from the period. This oral poetics—a powerful, supple, and highly associative expressive economy—enables poets efficiently to bring worlds of traditional meaning(s) to their narratives by deploying a vast array of compositional devices, some as small and highly tradition specific as a single lexeme or phrase and others as large and widely shared among discrete traditions as story patterns.

One of the most important features of medieval English oral poetics— and something that holds true for most, and perhaps all, traditional oral expressive economies—is that it not only provides poets with the means of articulating verbal art but also figures centrally in that art's dissemination and reception. Beginning with the trips Milman Parry and Albert B. Lord made in the 1930s to what was then Yugoslavia and continuing to the present with reports from other distant and not so distant communities where verbal art continues to be produced and/or transmitted chiefly, and in some cases only, orally, fieldwork continues to reveal just how deeply intertwined the production, dissemination, and reception of oral poetry continue to be. That such a complete confluence of these three should be one of oral poetry's hallmarks is not especially surprising given that it depends fundamentally upon a poetics of presence that is necessarily intersubjective: in oral traditions, there can be no poem without a performer to give it being, however ephemerally, in her or his voice and without a listening audience to be its repository, however temporarily.

Many of the features of oral poetry that distinguish it and its specialized poetics from literate poetry developed in response to the demands placed upon oral poets. Repeated verbal formulas and set narrative patterns, to take but two examples, are extremely useful aids to oral poets, who, of necessity, (re)compose during performance. In addition to their obvious and important structural utility, though, the components of traditional, performative oral poetics have rich aesthetic dimensions. But how oral-traditional features linger following the advent of literacy and the development of a literate poetics and literate-based reception strategies and why they continue to appear in poems whose genesis is demonstrably literate—not oral—are questions that have yet to be answered satisfactorily. Why do literate poets of the Middle Ages deploy, for example, the same introductory phrase over and over when they are not under the pressure of composing during performance? How does their literate aesthetics come to accommodate, and in many instances embrace, the very different aesthetics discoverable in oral poetry? Does the physical act of inscribing a poem on the page instead of voicing it aloud necessarily signal a sea change in the processes of poetic production and reception? What is the relationship between the silent, static manuscript page, the most powerful witness to the fundamentally literate nature of our extant medieval English verse, and the dynamic oral poetics, the most powerful witness to the English oral tradition's continued presence and vitality, that vernacular verse everywhere evidences?

We will turn to these and many other questions over the course of the following chapters, but it is important to stress from the outset that this study acknowledges the textuality of the poems we will consider, the nonperformative nature of the oral poetics discoverable in them, the *authority* of the poets who composed (and in some cases inscribed) them, and the literate character of the culture within which vernacular poetry was composed and received throughout the period.[1] The English engagement with literacy in the Middle Ages was an enormously complex process that is difficult if not impossible for us to chart with any real precision given our great temporal and cultural remove, but it was not traumatic, and it did not result in the immediate jettisoning of compositional practices and habits of mind that had been in place for millennia; rather, orality and literacy as we find them in medieval England are integral, interrelated, and delicately balanced components of what is an extraordinarily rich, complicated, and dynamic cultural matrix. We will begin our exploration of medieval English oral poetics with a consideration of some of this matrix's fundamental characteristics and their cultural situation in Anglo-Saxon England.

The Medieval English Oral-Literate Nexus

~ The nature of the medieval English oral tradition and its relationship to the literate tradition that comes to supplant it during the period are complex and vexed issues that have been discussed and debated—often quite heatedly—for more than fifty years.[1] Until fairly recently, this discussion tended to be rather polarized, with oralists and nonoralists alike accepting that orality and literacy were opposing, perhaps even competing cultural forces whose interaction could best be understood in decidedly Darwinian terms. According to this view, while oral traditions were widely, and logically, held to have preceded writing in primitive societies, cultural evolution and advancement went hand in hand with the appearance and increasing importance of literacy and the written word's supplanting of the spoken word. As a result, oral traditions that had in some cases preserved and transmitted cultural praxes and mores for centuries were believed to lose steadily (often rapidly) both their cultural centrality and their specialized functions following the emergence of literacy in what had been oral cultures.[2] Once stripped of their raison d'être and culturally marginalized, the oral traditions simply disappeared altogether. It may be appealing to portray the movement from orality to literacy in terms of a new technology and its subsequent complete displacement of an older one—a model of change with which we are especially comfortable, given the frequency with which we encounter it in contemporary society—but in the Middle Ages the interaction of orality and literacy was not nearly so simple, sequential, and unidirectional as the *grand récit* of cultural development and progress has often posited it to be.

The Derridean postulate regarding the absolutely privileged position accorded écriture in the West notwithstanding,[3] anthropological and physiological evidence suggests that spoken language antedates all attempts to inscribe it physically through any sort of representational system. We can point with some confidence to the inherently sequential nature of orality and literacy in cultural development, but once we move beyond their initial point of contact we need to avoid casting their relationship in evolutionary terms. Doing so can only lead, and often has led, to the creation of a false dichotomy between orality and literacy, a dichotomy that reinforces the tendency of literate cultures to see them not as mutually dependent and enriching cultural components but rather as "two seemingly exclusive and sequential epistemes" whose conjunction has "been resisted (Augustine), negativized (Plato), deplored (Lévi-Strauss), elided (Derrida), with the result that the text has always been privileged over the voice."[4]

Orality and Literacy: The Great Divide

Early twenty-first-century Western culture is undeniably text centered. The world of the text and printed documents is one that we encourage our children to enter at as early an age as possible, and mastery of the textual technologies central to Western society is a sine qua non for success at all levels of society. From the scholars who must keep abreast of the veritable mountains of written material that daily arrive at their desks or computer desktops to those on the margins of society who must nevertheless negotiate an endless stream of paperwork in order to receive public assistance, our society, and in some sense our world, is text dependent. Given Western society's increasing reliance on texts since writing was initially introduced to it,[5] it is not surprising that the shift from an oral to a textual culture should be almost exclusively articulated in the positivistic, evolutionist terms of what has come to be known as the Great Divide model,[6] especially since the "rise of a more literate sector in culture"—the very sector in which the controls of society are invariably situated—attends "the large-scale shift from the oral to the written."[7]

The tendency among literates to cast orality and literacy as binary opposites is not a recent development but goes back at least as far as Plato, who unwittingly rejects nonliterate thought and discourse.[8] As Eric Havelock argues, Plato's opposition to the oral poetic experience arises from his "self-imposed task . . . to establish two main postulates: that of the personality which thinks and knows, and that of a body of knowledge which is thought about and known. To do this he had to destroy the immemorial habit of self-identification with the oral tradition. For this had merged the personality with the tradition, and made a self-conscious separation from it impossible."[9] Plato himself points to what he sees as the inherent conflict between the oral and the literate worlds when he has his Socrates proclaim to Adeimantus that poetry "and similar things" must be struck out from the republic because "the more poetic they are, the less they should be heard by boys and men who must be free and accustomed to fearing slavery more than death."[10]

From the Greeks onward, the dichotomy between the oral and the written world was inscribed and reinscribed into cultures that were acquiring (or in some cases reacquiring) literacy because in their attempts to distinguish themselves from their past, cultures habitually figure the traditional as the static other against which their own progress can be measured. That is, for societies to establish their modernity—and by definition, all societies see themselves as synchronically "modern"—they need something against which to measure the distance they have traveled.[11] But tying cultural advancement to the rise of literacy is a flawed strategy because many oral cultures manage(d) quite well without ever developing or becoming dependent upon a system of graphemic representation. Indeed, only a small percentage of "the tens of thousands of languages spoken in the course of human history . . . have ever been committed to writing to a degree sufficient to have produced a literature, and most have never been written at all."[12] The "strong thesis" in which orality and literacy were seen not just "as differing mentalities" but as entirely discrete and unconnected "states of mind and . . . stages of culture"[13] held sway for the better part of a generation because the radical differences between the oral world it so convincingly illuminated reconfirmed literate culture's view of itself as being quite separate from oral culture.

Primary Orality and Pure Literacy

Over the past fifty years, it has become increasingly evident that there are real and substantial differences between what we may reductively but conveniently label the "oral" and "literate" minds. Plato correctly identified oral

poets as the possessors of a radically different mode of preserving and transmitting essential cultural information, and there is not much doubt about the
threat their system posed to the one he advocated. Although he does not articulate it in such terms, Plato seems acutely aware both of the crucial weight that
written documentation must bear in the preservation and transmission of a
literate society's mores and of the challenge that oral poets pose because they
are able to "achieve the same result by the composition of poetic narratives that
serve also as encyclopedias of conduct."[14]

From Plato onward, literate cultures have tended to figure orality and
literacy as (largely) unrelated moments of cultural evolution whose contact
invariably spells the end of the former. However, a very different, far more
nuanced picture of the ways orality and literacy interact and intersect has begun
to emerge. As a result, we have come to see that orality and literacy exist along
a continuum whose termini, "primary orality" and "pure literacy," ought to be
recognized as the theoretical constructs they are and not mistaken for discoverable, accessible real-world states.[15] As theoretical postulates, the end points of
the oral-literate continuum retain considerable heuristic value for the investigation of human cognition and development, and with this in mind we now
turn to consider them. But as we do so, we need to guard against uncritically
accepting the notion of primary orality because it "is forever inaccessible to us
(if it is not merely mythical)."[16] And we need to keep in mind that the same is
true of pure literacy.

In a primary oral culture, one that is absolutely innocent of the technology of writing and of the specialized habits of mind that it entails, oral poets
serve as "[t]he repositories of learning, of the knowledge necessary for the
preservation of the fabric of society,"[17] and orally composed and transmitted
epic poetry serves as a tribal encyclopedia through which the culture's practices and mores are passed along to successive generations. Functioning as a
paideia, poetry in a primary oral culture accordingly carries with it a crucial
didactic burden that it loses only following the rise of print culture.[18] Instead
of being marked by the author's absence, one of the hallmarks of postoral literary production, oral poetry is marked by the poet's immediate physical presence. Without poets to give voice to and to embody it, there can be no poetry
in an oral culture. Similarly, because the poem an oral poet produces is not
entexted but exists only during the moments it is being publicly and commu-
nally articulated, oral poetry is inherently dynamic and ephemeral. Residing
only within the collective memory of those present while it is performed, an
oral poem leaves no trace once the final reverberations of the poet's voice die

out. Necessarily composed (and recomposed) under the exigencies of performance, the poetry produced within a primary oral culture is, therefore, highly
protean.[19]

At the opposite terminus of the oral-literate continuum lies a purely literate culture, one in which orality exerts no influence over the production or
dissemination of texts. Such a culture depends exclusively upon the technology of writing to preserve and transmit culturally essential knowledge, and
those who have no access to the literate world or who are unable to negotiate
it easily or competently find themselves socially and culturally disadvantaged.
Within a fully literate culture, both the production and the reception of texts
are intensely private, highly idiosyncratic, and highly unconventional (in the
most technical sense of the term) endeavors. In contrast to what we posit for
primary oral cultures, the paradigm for literary production in a literate culture is highly and consciously intertextual. The principal way meaning is gen-
erated is also sharply different in the two cultures. Oral poets have recourse to
a vast array of compositional devices, or "words," in John Miles Foley's specialized sense of that term,[20] ranging in size and complexity from single lexemes, to narrative themes, to entire story patterns, all of which function
metonymically to summon traditional meanings to given narrative moments.
Meaning in traditional verbal art inheres in and is inseparable from the highly
specialized idiom that constitutes the very fabric of the expressive economy
through which that art is articulated. The meaning of literate texts, by way of
contrast, is idiosyncratically conferred upon them by their authors.[21] Unlike
traditional oral poets, literate authors are praised for their originality, either
for the unique ways in which they produce original creations or for their additions to and novel reshaping of inherited materials.[22]

The reception of verbal art is also markedly different in the two cultures.
For members of an oral culture, it is an aural and necessarily communal experience,[23] while for members of a literate culture it is most likely to be a chiefly
ocular, private one. The responsive, frequently participatory group reception
of verbal art in oral culture is replaced in literate culture by the silent, personal
negotiation of a text. Writing, because it divorces words from their orality and
is predicated upon silence and absence, truly becomes a "technology of alienation" for both author and audience.[24]

But perhaps the most important difference between the production and
reception of verbal art in oral and literate cultures is that while orally produced
texts are rooted in a highly specialized, conventional idiom, one shared by both
poets and audiences, fully literate texts spring from the imaginative well of

authors who carefully mold their thoughts according to their tastes, inclinations, experiences, and abilities. From its beginnings in the writings of Parry, contemporary oral theory has emphasized the simultaneously determining and enabling nature of oral poetics, but until recently the mechanistic, structuralist features of oral poetics have routinely been stressed, with the result that the artistry and aesthetics of oral poetics have yet to receive the full attention they deserve.

In an argument that was greatly to influence the direction of the critical discourse concerning how oral poets negotiate their traditions, Parry claimed that "the mind of the poet (or poets) of the *Iliad* and the *Odyssey* was so thoroughly steeped in traditional formulae that he never once . . . created of his own accord an epithet revealing the personal stamp of his thought."[25] Similarly, Homer's failure to "personally invent [the traditional] ways of recollecting custom and usage" that are the essence of his poetry leads Havelock, another early and highly influential oral theorist, to conclude that we should therefore think of Homer

> as a man living in a large house crowded with furniture, both necessary and elaborate. His task is to thread his way through the house, touching and feeling the furniture as he goes and reporting its shape and texture. He chooses a winding and leisurely route which shall in the course of a day's recital allow him to touch and handle most of what is in the house. The route that he picks will have its own design. This becomes his story, and represents the nearest that he can approach to sheer invention. This house, these rooms, and the furniture he did not himself fashion: he must continually and affectionately recall them to us. But as he touches or handles he may do a little refurbishing, a little dusting off, and perhaps make small rearrangements of his own, though never major ones. Only in the route he chooses does he exercise decisive choice. Such is the art of the encyclopedic minstrel, who as he reports also maintains the social and moral apparatus of an oral culture.[26]

I quote this passage at such length because it neatly presents what was for a long time the prevailing view of how oral poets were thought to relate to their tradition. It also allows us clearly to see the problems that attend figuring the very stuff of oral tradition—its verbal collocations, metrics, thematics, and story patterns—as impediments that must be physically negotiated by the poet. The poet has very little influence over the impediments themselves and, to extend Havelock's metaphor, is little more than a housekeeper who may shift objects slightly as he goes about his duties but who is far removed from both the artist who created the objects and the owner who determined their positions in the room. Following the departure of the oral poet/housekeeper, the objects themselves remain unaltered, and their physical relationship to one another remains unchanged: the end table maintains both its accustomed shape and place, as do the couch, lamp, and so on.

But oral poets do not negotiate their way through a static tradition (some more successfully than others), a tradition that they know and can take in fully at a glance, and simply construct slightly different models out of the same store of preformed material. Rather, they relate much more dynamically to their tradition because they, in conjunction with the works of verbal art they create via their traditional, uniquely charged expressive economies, *are* the traditions. Each oral poem is at once an absolutely unique artistic creation (one that is neither reproducible nor recoverable) and a piece of its tradition, the whole of which is beyond the comprehension of any single producer or receiver of the poem. Traditional verbal art was long considered mechanistic because its oral poetics lends a veneer of sameness to it, but the traditional expressive economy through which it is articulated everywhere contains evidence of lexical, metrical, and narrative innovations. Whether they are ultimately attributable to, among other things, authorial (or scribal) error or experimentation, such innovations, as we will see in the following chapters, are the products of individual poets working within and hence constantly altering the tradition. These innovations do not reveal a given poet's incomplete mastery of his tradition's expressive economy but rather testify eloquently to the vitality and presentness of oral poetics. The poets working synchronically within the tradition need not be, and most likely were not, conscious or even desirous of implementing the changes evident in their work, although we cannot completely rule out that they might have been.[27]

Just as no single poet's abilities embrace the totality of the tradition, so, too, no single poetic creation can do more than suggest the tradition's vast diachronic richness or synchronic fluidity and flexibility. Far from being something that poets either skillfully thread their way through or clumsily collide into, a culture's oral tradition provides the background against which the aesthetics of individual creations must be judged because it is the tradition that provides the culture's verbal art with the broad contours of both their shape and meaning. *How* these works of verbal art generate meaning ultimately derives from idiosyncratic, tradition-specific features, but that they are expressed through traditional channels in no way limits *what* they mean.[28]

Traditional oral poetics is expressed through a specialized register, a remarkably economical, useful tool for expressing verbal art that no doubt developed as an aid to oral poets who had to compose rapidly during perform-ance.[29] The poets who engage this register are far from the mere mechanics lacking entirely in individual artistic achievement or genius that at one time they were thought to be, although one must readily admit that all oral poets are not equally gifted; some will necessarily be less talented than others at their craft, just as all literate authors are not similarly skilled.

For the literate poet, composition remains an exclusively private and internal rather than public and communal process.[30] Unlike their oral coun-terparts, who are unable to revise or correct metrical deficiencies or narrative infelicities because for them the acts of composition and presentation are simultaneous, literate poets have the leisure to dwell over every aspect of their creations. They can take as much time as they deem necessary to select and order their lexemes and to shape the content and arrangement of the narrative structures they employ. Literate authors can also go back and review what has been created and make any changes that seem desirable or necessary. They thus *authorize* and control the verbal art they produce in ways impossible in oral culture.

Literary reception in a fully literate society is an equally private and highly subjective endeavor. In some poststructuralist theory, the physical text itself is secondary to the more abstract, constantly shifting, and infinitely vari-able text that we as individual readers constantly write and rewrite: "[T]he text as an entity independent of interpretation and (ideally) responsible for its career drops out and is replaced by the texts that emerge as the consequence of our interpretive activities."[31] At this level of abstraction, we can see that the reception of verbal art in oral and literate societies is similar, for in a vital sense literature is only and always *within* the recipient in oral cultures in just the way fluid texts, for the active, participatory reader, are constructed by subjective criticism.[32]

The reader in a literate society plays an important, active role in "writ-ing" the "text" he or she reads[33] and thus plays a role in creating the "text" in just the way listening audiences in oral cultures are co-creators of the text they receive aurally, but the text produced within literate culture has an attendant physicality, and hence fixity, that oral texts lack.[34] As Stanley Fish has argued, readers perceive the text that their "interpretive strategies demand and call into being."[35] The text that we thus read/create is in constant flux, but the physical object that remains the source of the varied and various "texts" we (co-)produce remains a static monument. Whereas the "modern text is a radically immaterial object," the scribal, "chirographic text . . . has no existence other than a material one."[36] How the line "Æfter ðam wordum   wyrm yrre cwom" [After those words, the worm angrily came forward][37] fits into my reading of *Beowulf* has changed over the years and will no doubt continue to do so, but when I open my copy of Friedrich Klaeber's third edition of the poem, I should be surprised if I did not find it physically situated on page 100 at line 2669. Similarly, in London, British Library, Cotton Vitellius A. xv, the phrase appears as "æꝼꞇeꞃ ðam | poꞃðū pẏꞃm .ẏꞃꞃe cꝥom" on fol. 197ʳ and occupies part of the eleventh and twelfth lines of the manuscript page every time I examine it, as it does when I consult either page 124 of Julius Zupitza's facsimile of the poem or Kevin Kiernan's electronic edition of it.[38]

For the oral poet, one instance of a poem is equal to another, and performances of the same song by the same oral poet may show considerable variety, despite the poet's sense that he has told precisely the same tale in precisely the same words each time.[39] Because "words" in oral cultures are not understood to be spatialized and reified objects, as they are in literate cultures, the habits of seeing texts as fixed and viewing alterations and variations as deviations (at best) and errors (at worst) develop only after the arrival of print culture. Chaucer's well-known excoriation of his scribe Adam's sloppy practices would be meaningless in a preliterate society in which texts exist only *as* variants, not fixed, *author*ized, monolithic entities capable of being compared to a known, unvarying standard (either the author's own conception of the work or a written avatar that approximates the author's ideal) and corrupted in transmission:

> Adam scriveyn, if ever it thee bifalle
> Boece or Troylus for to wryten newe,
> Under thy long lokkes thou most have the scalle,
> But after my makyng thow wryte more trewe;
> So ofte adaye I mot thy werk renewe,
> It to correcte and eke to rubbe and scrape,
> And al is thorugh thy negligence and rape.[40]

Because of our own literate biases, modern readers tend to take this poem "not as [an] offhand, scribal entry" whose attribution to Chaucer is by no means certain "but as the epitome of Chaucerian making."[41] In depicting Chaucer as an author preoccupied with textual transmission and textual and authorial authority, this short poem crystallizes contemporary literate culture's own obsession with these very issues.[42]

There are profound differences between the so-called oral and literate minds and between the termini of the oral-literate continuum we have been exploring here, but the likelihood of discovering a culture that unambiguously evidences primary orality is remote given literate culture's relentless spread across the globe. The possibility of encountering an absolutely literate culture is perhaps even more remote because even those cultures that place enormous social and institutional weight on the written word are deeply and daily affected by oral habits of mind as their members slide easily and continually into, out of, and between literate and nonliterate modes of thought and expression. An equally important but often overlooked fact is that texts in a literate culture are not isolated from orality but are in every way surrounded and influenced by it despite their being produced in a highly intertextual milieu. Within a literate culture, the confluence of orality and literacy can be seen quite readily in the process through which children are taught to read, a process in which they are habitually encouraged to translate from the chirographic (the individual graphemes before them whose arrangement has led to momentary puzzlement) to the auditory (the sounds that the individual letters in a syllable combine to make); "Just sound it out" is a standard phrase of parental encouragement. Even in the scholarly world, one of the most self-consciously and most highly intertextual corners of our literate society, the oral infuses and shapes both works of verbal art and works that explicate them. Knowing that a critical essay will reach its intended audience through performance (a public reading at a conference) rather than visually (as words printed on the pages of a book or journal) leads to the adoption of different rhetorical strategies, ranging from the practical (avoiding certain words that the author has difficulty enunciating) to the more abstract (employing a less formal register and perhaps varying the paper's rhythm by including illustrative or possibly humorous anecdotes).

While it remains true that the theoretical discussion of primary orality and primary literacy contained in the work of, to name but a few, Eric Havelock, Albert B. Lord, and Walter J. Ong has revealed aspects of human cognition to which our literacy had blinded us, the poles of the oral-literate continuum surveyed above are far more useful for their heuristic than hermeneutic value. This becomes especially apparent when, as we move away from the purely theoretical plane upon which any consideration of primary orality must necessarily take place, we encounter enormous difficulties in simply defining the central term *orality,* let alone trying to understand how it functions within any given society. *Literacy* proves to be an equally slippery term: after detailing the chief characteristics of oral culture that have emerged in Ong's work, Katherine O'Brien O'Keeffe astutely observes that "[w]hile it would be possible to construct a complementary list to characterize literate thought, it is doubtful that any definition of 'literacy' which such a list might imply would command agreement in the Old English scholarly community."[43] This statement can easily be extended to the later Middle Ages as well, if not all the way to the modern era, because literacy continues to connote a broad spectrum of abilities, attitudes, and practices encompassing both highly valued mechanical skills and a complex (and shifting) set of ideologies.

Medieval literacy has remained an especially elusive and difficult concept for several reasons. First of all, our status as *homo legens* and our habit of imposing contemporary interpretive strategies upon the written remains of the past has led many myopically to assume that medieval habits of mind and procedure parallel our literate ones. As a result, it was long the practice to attribute to medieval culture modes of perception very similar to those that operate for us today. The problem here is not so much that we have privileged contemporary, literate texts over those produced within earlier stages of our culture but rather that we have habitually judged all texts against the standard of our tradition's idiosyncratic, literate poetics, no matter how impertinent that poetics may be to the texts at hand. Second, because literacy is so culturally central for us and because our literate interpretive strategies have proved so useful for so long, we rarely critically question the various ways they have handicapped us.[44] Finally, attempts to understand medieval literacy have understandably been "bedevilled by the difficulty of distinguishing between the modern 'literate' and the medieval *litteratus.*"[45] The standards one adopts for determining who in a given society falls within the ambience of literacy are extremely various and yield wildly different results. Should only those who can read *and* write Latin be included among the literate,[46] or should anyone with knowledge of Latin (be it reading or writing knowledge) be considered literate? And where do we place those skilled in reading and/or writing the vernacular but not Latin, or those who can read and/or write both Latin and the vernacular?

Even though we are not likely to reach a consensus on a quantitative standard for determining any given individual's literacy, the literate skills of those who produced our extant medieval English verse texts can tell us a great deal about the medieval oral-literate nexus if we take them as metaphors "for culture [rather] than as a condition of individual achievement."[47] Any inquiry into medieval literacy must take into account not only the wide variety of uses to which texts were put during the period but also the audiences for which they were intended, as well as the manner in which they were produced and received, because access to culturally essential knowledge and membership in a textual community were not restricted solely to those skilled in encoding and/or decoding written texts but were much more broadly available.

Textuality, Poetic Authority, and Literacy: Problematizing Oral Theory

This study thus follows a strategy that may appear to be paradoxical (if not in some quarters heretical): it accepts the physical nature of the evidence at hand and the concomitant validity of what has long been seen to be the crippling irony of the oralist position, namely that the medieval English oral tradition survives only in silent, written records produced by artists whose compositional practices mirror our contemporary ones. That one must acknowledge what appears to be an indisputable fact of literary history—that all the "oral" poetry from the English Middle Ages survives only in writing—testifies eloquently to the degree to which the theory of oral-formulaic composition articulated first by Parry and extended and developed by Lord has shaped the critical discourse on oral tradition. Perhaps more than anything else, more than the existence of indisputable written sources for many putatively "oral" poems, more than the implicit (or demonstrable) literacy of many medieval authors, and more than the presence of textual culture throughout the English Middle Ages, the undeniable textuality of the poetry extant from the period has proved to be a nearly insurmountable impediment to our understanding of medieval English oral poetics. The physical evidence offered by the poems has proved problematic because it contravenes one of oral-formulaic theory's most influential tenets: the absolute division between the world of orality and the world of literacy. Instead of confronting the evidence of the texts' physicality, oral theorists have tended to circumvent it by eliding the enormously complex processes that must have attended an oral performance's transformation into a written document. To cite just one example, in his early application of oral-formulaic theory to Old English poetry, Francis Peabody Magoun Jr. raises the issue of textuality only briefly and tangentially when he explains that "an oral poem until written down has not and cannot have a fixed text, a concept difficult for lettered persons; its text, like the text of an orally circulating anecdote, will vary in greater or lesser degree with each telling."[48] Perhaps because he subscribed to the dictum that "[o]ral poetry . . . is composed entirely of formulas, large and small, while lettered poetry is never formulaic,"[49] Magoun never engages the poems' textuality. For him, and for many others, the presence of a demonstrably high percentage of formulas is sufficient to classify a poem as unequivocally oral.[50] Recently, though, we have come to see that the textual materiality of our Old English poetic remains and the processes through which that poetry is physically encoded evidence the close, dynamic relationship between orality and developing literacy in the Anglo-Saxon period.[51] And even though they generally witness a higher degree of incipient textuality than do their Anglo-Saxon predecessors, codices that date from the post-Conquest period continue to offer important evidence regarding the later history of medieval English oral poetics. Rather than impeding the study of the English oral tradition and of its specialized oral poetics, the physical en-coding of medieval poetry, its spatialization on the manuscript page, and the development of such graphic cues as mise-en-page, spacing, capitalization, and punctuation prove indispensable aids to it.

How poets authorize their poetry has proved to be another problematic question for those investigating the medieval oral tradition, largely because oral-formulaic theory foregrounded the utilitarian and mechanistic aspects of a traditional poem by focusing on, for example, formulaic language and the structure of traditional thematics at the expense of its aesthetics. As Foley suc-cinctly observes, "Virtually from the time of Milman Parry's French theses, scholars have quarreled over whether the demonstration of the compositional role of *formulas* and *themes* makes the poet a prisoner of his compositional idiom and thus turns great poems into mechanical tours-de-force."[52] No such issue arises in discussions of literate texts' authority because they are produced by authors with literate sensibilities working within a culture where every text is the result of conscious manipulation and careful molding on each author's part. Wordsworth's well-known contention that the "successful composition" of poetry "takes its origin from emotion recollected in tranquillity"[53] captures the broad steps of the compositional process in which literate authors engage. Following the moment of inspiration, the literate poet drafts, revises, and pol-ishes his or her text until satisfied with it, a process that can occasionally take years, and only then is it published and disseminated (or not).[54] For the oral poet, the moments of inspiration, composition, and "publication" are concur-rent and ineluctably interwoven: they cannot be viewed as discrete components of the text-producing process. Even though the highly intertextual nature of composition in literate cultures ensures that "[a]ny text is constructed as a mosaic of quotations; any text is the absorption and transformation of another,"[55] the literate text stands as a unique and inviolable instance of authorial making despite its fundamentally patchwork nature.

Oral poetry, in contrast, derives its authority from a very different source. While it is necessarily performative and so depends upon a poetics of presence, its authority paradoxically *does not* derive mainly from the poets who articulate it. Just as meaning in traditional poetry inheres in the structures that constitute its expressive economy, so, too, does an oral poem's authority lie chiefly in the tectonics of the tradition itself rather than in the person of the poet. Oral poets are responsible for the unique shape they give to their traditional, inherited materials, but they stake no claim to any sort of originary status. Unlike their literate counterparts, who are forever in search of the new, oral poets are "bearer[s] of a past that is a common possession of all the persons active as poets or audience within a given tradition."[56] As such, they make no attempt to appropriate and so authorize the material they present as something uniquely of their own making. Nowhere among oral poets is there anything that parallels the proprietary impulse that is one of the hallmarks of their literate counterparts. Oral poets strive to make the collective past present once again in their necessarily anonymous acts of poetic making; they do not seek to fabricate wholly new matter that will be closely associated with their names.

Oral poets engage in a highly specialized, associative register that is shared deeply by poets and their intended audiences, and although this idiom enables the production of poetry and helps shape the contours of poetic articulation, it is broadly determining rather than absolutely deterministic. Far from being somehow restrictive, the constituents of oral poetics—its specialized lexemes, metrics, themes, and story patterns—are "responsive, echoic verbal instruments that in the hands of the talented poet can provide entry to the world and wisdom of tradition."[57] The protean nature of traditional verbal art reflects its expressive economy's suppleness. Each piece of verbal art produced within an oral culture is as authoritative as any other because no one instantiation of a poem represents anything but a thin slice of the tradition's vast, rich, and unchartable narrative possibilities.

Although the actual mechanics of producing poems orally are very different from those that attend the production of poems in writing, the stages of composition in oral tradition significantly parallel those in literate tradition.[58] Literate composition allows for more leisurely reflection, but the fact of oral composition in no way diminishes or limits the potential aesthetic accomplishment of orally composed poems. More pressure may be put upon oral poets who compose during performance (although they may not necessarily feel the pressure that moderns completely removed from the traditional oral mode of composition project back unto them), but the performance-based poetic idiom at their disposal more than adequately equips them with the tools necessary for fluent composition. The channels through which oral poets authorize their poetry have proved difficult for literates to comprehend in part because "[o]ral society has faith in one type of text, literate society in another,"[59] and in part because literates have been slow to recalibrate the literate interpretive strategies upon which they have relied for so long.

There can be little doubt that the cultural matrix out of which medieval English vernacular poetry emerges was a predominately literate one that relied extensively upon writing to transmit knowledge.[60] It would certainly be beneficial to know as much as possible regarding the practical literate skills of any individual or group of individuals, but the evidence so far adduced is sparse and accordingly holds little hope that we will ever possess a sufficiently detailed picture of literacy's praxis during the period. That "references to reading and writing, to the literacy of individuals, to basic education and book-ownership"[61] are rare (and rarely unambiguous) further complicates an already complex issue. Even such a seemingly straightforward account as Asser's discussion of King Alfred the Great's acquisition of English letters is open to question on almost every point.[62]

But rather than attempting to determine what percentage of the population may have arrived at some arbitrarily designated level of competence with written language, we will focus upon the social and cultural implications of its presence on the island as a way of establishing that medieval English culture was far from being the oral one it has been seen to be. Literate skills ranging from the simply pragmatic to those that rival or surpass the complex of activities that modern literates value and strive to attain remained the provenance of a tiny percentage of the society, but participation in the literate culture of the English Middle Ages was not limited to those skilled in graphemic inscription or to those able to undertake the private, readerly negotiation of a text.

The Diglossic Medieval World

The diglossic character of life in medieval England further complicates any discussion of the period's oral-literate nexus.[63] When Latin first came to the island following the establishment of Roman rule in 43 C.E., it came as the language of empire with well-established social, cultural, and political functions, as well as with the highly codified system of grammar and the fully developed system of graphemic representation that it had possessed since antiquity. Even during the years between the Roman withdrawal in 410 and the arrival on the Isle of Thanet of the Christian mission led by Augustine in 598—the so-called Dark Ages that separate the period of Rome's political hegemony from that of its religious hegemony—Latin culture continued to exert an influence on the island, as men such as Gildas and Patrick continued to produce sophisticated works that were presumably available to a contemporary audience sufficiently well educated in Latin to understand them.[64]

Because Latin's status as a prestige language was unchallenged in both the secular and ecclesiastical spheres throughout the period, its relationship to the vernacular is generally cast in terms of a simple and strict polarity, and it is sometimes thought to stand above and be thus isolated from and unaffected by the developing vernacular. Latin was the language of discourse among members of monastic and other religious communities, but it and the vernacular ought to be seen as deeply dependent alternative literary languages rather than as discrete, disconnected, and competing modes of expression.[65] Because there were no native Latin speakers during the Middle Ages, every Anglo-Latin scholar was by definition diglossic, as the very term *Anglo-Latin* suggests.

Although many examples could be easily adduced that point to the dynamic interaction of Latin and vernacular cultures,[66] there is intriguing, if not finally clear-cut, evidence suggesting that neither Aldhelm and Bede forgot altogether the tone and literature of their native tongue because "no one really leaves his cultural heritage completely behind, and the Anglo-Saxon monks, like the Irish, carried much of their native culture with them."[67] Whether or not we accept that Aldhelm was an oral poet who (re-)composed during performance, what emerges from the accounts of Alfred, William of Malmesbury, and Faricius is the picture of a man so steeped in literate Latin culture that he has been called "unquestionably the first and perhaps the most prodigious Anglo-Saxon man of letters."[68] He may also have been an accomplished vernacular poet. William reports in the *De Gestis Pontificum Anglorum* King Alfred's assertion that Aldhelm's vernacular poetry was unmatched [nulla umquam ætate par ei fuerit quisquam] (I, 336).[69] He goes on to cite Alfred's account of Aldhelm's public performances of vernacular poetry [vulgo cantitatur] (Aldhelm's own compositions?) within which he sprinkled biblical phrases

[Scripturarum insertis] (in Latin?) among the amusing phrases [ludicra verbis] (vernacular ones?) as a way of exciting his congregation's attention so that he could lead "the people back to soundness" (I, 336) [cives ad sanitatem reduxisse]. We must, however, proceed with due caution in assessing William's vague and perhaps apocryphal account of Aldhelm's performances, especially as we cannot check his account against that of Alfred's no longer extant *Handboc*.[70]

But despite the problematic aspects of William's account of Aldhelm's performance of vernacular poetry, evidence of his competence in vernacular composition can be found in what appears to be a most unlikely place: his surviving Latin poetry. The deeply diglossic nature of this poetry strongly suggests that "in ignorance of classical techniques of verse composition, Aldhelm resorted to techniques familiar to him from native English poetry,"[71] in particular alliteration and verbal formulas. What we witness then in his Latin poetry is nothing less than the transposition of native poetics to another key by the man who proudly considered "himself to be the first Anglo-Saxon poet to sing in Latin verse."[72]

Bede provides us with another example of an Anglo-Saxon highly trained in Latin who nevertheless switches with apparent ease between the two dominant expressive economies of his diglossic world. According to Cuthbert's account in the *Epistola Cuthberti de Obitu Bedae*—another source that must be approached with due caution—in the days preceding his death Bede "gave daily lessons to students, sang psalms, ruminated upon scriptural passages, recited a one-sentence Old English poem ('Bede's Death Song') on the theme of death, and dictated a translation from Latin into Old English of the Gospel of John and extracts from the writings of Isidore of Seville."[73] Somewhat earlier in his career, Bede's diglossia manifests itself in the Latin paraphrase of *Cædmon's Hymn* that he includes in the *Historia Ecclesiastica*.[74] Although the attribution to Bede of any extant Old English prose or poetry is fraught with problems, his surviving work and the various reports of his activities suggest that he remained closely tied to the vernacular throughout his life because "[e]ven a person who took a solemn vow to communicate solely in Latin would not have been free from the vernacular: his thoughts and his means of framing them would have been shaped partly by his vernacular."[75] Even Bede, one of the most accomplished Anglo-Latin scholars, presumably entered the community at Monkwearmouth at age seven speaking not Latin but his native vernacular tongue.

It is tempting to cast the relationship between Latin and the vernacular exclusively in terms of a conflict. After all, Latin served as the language of empire when it was initially introduced into the island, and it later served a related imperialistic function in the religious conversion that began in the late sixth century. The evidence of Latin loanwords in Old English emphasizes not the intercourse of the languages but their hierarchical relationship. A number of terms having to do with domestic life are borrowed early in the period, but by far the majority of the 450 or so Latin loanwords datable to the Anglo-Saxon period are for technical or religious concepts introduced by Latin culture because "[t]he many new conceptions that followed in the train of the new religion would naturally demand expression and would at times find the resources of the [Old English] language inadequate."[76] The same holds true for the more technical, intellectual terms that entered the vernacular during the post-Benedictine reform period of borrowings.

The examples of Aldhelm and Bede and the evidence of a text such as the Eadwine Psalter (Cambridge, Trinity College, R. 17. 1), however, suggest that in mapping the relationship between Latin and vernacular culture we should adopt a model that admits their interpenetration and constant, varied, and complex intersection rather than one that denies any sort of mutual inter- action and influence: "[W]e must avoid drawing hasty correspondences between vernacular, oral, and unlearned or between Latin, literate, and learned; for there were no absolutes. The vernacular was not always oral, the Latin not always literate. Even the most unlettered peasant was aware of the textuality of the culture around him; even the most literate Latin-writing cleric was steeped in both spoken Latin and spoken vernacular traditions."[77]

That the large majority of the population were not among the *litterati*— and here I apply this term broadly to those who could engage Latin literary culture and/or vernacular literary culture, whether as readers, writers, or both—has long been taken to signal their exclusion from the controlling cul- ture because it has often been assumed that as writing becomes more impor- tant as a means of preserving and transmitting culturally essential knowledge and as the controlling classes of society come to embrace more and more com- pletely the written word, oral tradition "*sinks* to the illiterate, i.e. the *disadvan- taged* in such a society."[78] The evolutionary model upon which this view is founded is accurate, but only to a degree. The function of poetry does shift once it no longer need serve as the repository of culturally significant infor- mation, as a tribal encyclopedia,[79] but its marginalization is neither so neat nor so absolute as this model makes it appear.

Anglo-Saxon Textual Culture

While most people in medieval England had very little direct intercourse with letters, their exclusion from the ranks of the *litterati* neither automatically situates them among the culturally disadvantaged nor establishes their culture's primary orality. Because reading and writing were skills possessed by only a few, the majority of the population had to rely on what they could take in aurally. But viewing this as proof that "[e]arly medieval European culture had been dominated by what might be termed 'primary orality'"[80] fails adequately to account for either the dynamic diglossia that characterizes the medieval cultural matrix or the various roles texts and textuality played in shaping and defining that matrix.

If we define a primary oral culture as one absolutely innocent of writing, in all its various manifestations—pictographic, logographic, syllabic, or alphabetic—and equally innocent of the specialized habits of mind that writing entails, the number of ancient, medieval, or modern cultures that unambiguously evidence primary orality will be small indeed. Although oral tradition played an important role in classical Athens, the considerable written records that have survived from the city preclude its being categorized as a primary oral society.[81] Nor can medieval England be so classified: the Romans who conquered the native Britons brought with them their highly developed literate practices, practices that largely faded into the background during the so-called Dark Ages but that nevertheless did not disappear without a trace. Indeed, evidence preserved mostly in "a considerable number of documents from south-eastern Wales from the mid-sixth century onwards" strongly suggests that "at least in some areas, Latin-using culture survived into the sixth century and may sometimes have been stronger than it had been in the days of Roman power."[82] The runic alphabet that the Germanic tribes brought with them during the Age of Migration offers further evidence that Dark Age Britain did not revert to a state of pristine, primary orality in the period between the departure of the Romans in 410 C.E. and the arrival of the Christian missionaries nearly two hundred years later. Even though the evaluation of both the cultural importance of runes and the extent of runic literacy in Anglo-Saxon England has been (and will continue to be) impeded by the nature and limited quantity of the documentary evidence available to us, the presence of a functioning, complex system of runology effectively establishes enough of a literate background for the Germanic invaders' culture to prohibit its being considered a primary oral one. The percentage of the population educated in encoding and/or decoding runes may have been quite small,[83] but as the Franks casket, the Ruthwell Cross, the runes carved into St. Cuthbert's coffin, rune-stones commemorating the dead, and wooden sticks that bear inscribed runic messages suggest, runes may have been widely known and may have had important social and cultural functions, even if few could decipher them.[84]

Although many contemporary literates consider literacy as the only way to engage textual culture—despite the many alternative avenues by which non-literates are able to negotiate their way into and through even the most fully text-based cultures[85]—emphasizing the textual nature of medieval English culture does not entail claiming a high degree of pragmatic, craft, or full literacy for a broad spectrum of the population. Even the most marginal members of medieval society were situated within a textual culture, whether or not they remained largely or wholly unskilled in its mechanics. While those skilled in the technology of writing were necessarily a part of literate culture, others who could not write or read participated in it as well; its scope was broad and people came into its ambience in a variety of ways. Medieval textual communities were not, unlike Fish's interpretive communities,[86] composed of only those with enough literate skills to be able to encode and decode written texts but included a wide range of people, from the illiterate to the fully literate. What was required for a textual community "was simply a text, an interpreter, and a public. The text did not have to be written; oral record, memory, and reperformance sufficed. Nor did the public have to be fully lettered. Often, in fact, only the *interpres* had a direct contact with literate culture, and, like the twelfth-century heretic Peter Waldo, memorized and communicated his gospel by word of mouth."[87] Through their situation in these textual communities, nonliterates were exposed to the texts underlying the oral (readerly) performances they attended as well as to the world of textual culture and to its modes of constituting and authenticating meaning.

Latin textuality was a chief constituent of the fabric of medieval life, but it was not the sole one. Standing alongside it, although certainly no rival to it in terms of prestige, function, or influence, was the tradition of English vernacular letters. Latin retained its priority in literature and remained the chief avenue for formal communications throughout the period, but the vernacular was already being used for documentary and literary purposes in the ninth century and there is evidence that it was so used several centuries earlier.[88] From the ninth century on, vernacular documents came increasingly to be used for recording complex transactions involving land and real property, and by the tenth century the vernacular had become "a medium of instruction in schools and was regularly used by draftsmen of leases and agreements and by the royal administration for sealed writs and lawcodes."[89] The wills that survive from Anglo-Saxon England provide a good example of one of the important uses to which the vernacular was put: fully fifty-three of the surviving fifty-eight are composed in English.[90]

Vernacular poetry, as well, is attested in writing from at least the eighth century, although most of our Old English poetry is found in codices that are generally accepted as having been copied during the tenth and eleventh centuries. Two eighth-century manuscripts of Bede's *Historia Ecclesiastica*— St. Petersburg, Russian National Library, Q. v. I. 18, and Cambridge, University Library, Kk. 5. 16 (the Moore MS)[91]—contain vernacular versions of the earliest extant Old English poem, Cædmon's *Hymn,* both copied by their original scribes.[92] We will never be able to determine whether the scribe who included the poem in the bottom margin of fol. 107ʳ of Q. v. I. 18 did so at the time he copied the *Historia* or whether he added it at a later date,[93] but its very presence in a careful copy of Bede's text bespeaks the regard in which scribe D held it, especially since it is one of only two pieces of significant scribal marginalia in the entire manuscript[94] and the only one in the vernacular. When and why this poem was inserted into the St. Petersburg Bede, why it appears as a marginal text in Latin manuscripts of the *Historia* copied as late as the fifteenth century,[95] and what its relation is to Cædmon's original poem are questions to which no simple answers will be forthcoming.[96] But its inclusion in some of the earliest extant Latin manuscripts of the *Historia* points to the complex cultural situation of vernacular poetry, a poetry constituted by the "interplay between the textual memory of an oral culture, known to us only as a dialectical inverse of textual culture inscribed as a trace or absence within a text, and the culture of *grammatica.*"[97] The well-attested, varied, and in many ways remarkable tradition of Old English vernacular prose writings further witnesses textual culture's vital presence throughout the period.[98]

Writing (both Latin and vernacular), although certainly a technology that restructures thought, is not the disruptive cultural force that many have taken it to be because "mere commission to writing entails neither the final fossilization nor the wholesale shift in poetics that earlier studies in oral tradition assumed as matters of course."[99] During the English Middle Ages, writing was introduced and developed within a society that already knew and had texts, whether runic, Latin, or vernacular.[100] The transition from a state of pure orality to a state of full literacy would be momentous and accompanied (and marked) by a number of dramatic and far-reaching cultural, technological, and cognitive changes, but during the Middle Ages such a radical transition did not take place because medieval English culture was never positioned at the originary, oral terminus of the oral-literate continuum and certainly never achieved (as no culture can) the culminating terminus of pure literacy, the point at which all commemorative activities are based exclusively on the written word.

Medieval English oral poetics survives the steady advancement of literate, textual culture and continues to figure prominently in much of our extant medieval vernacular poetry because the oral and the literate do not occupy discrete and conflicting cognitive spheres. Orality and literacy are parts of a subtle, complex, lengthy process of cultural change rather than sudden and (largely) unrelated moments of cultural evolution.[101] Because the transition from an oral to a literate culture is marked by continuity, not rupture, oral habits of mind not only persist within increasingly literate societies but retain much of their cultural centrality.[102] The technology of writing may reduce the "dynamism of sound to quiescent space,"[103] but this technology merely muffles rather than throttles the continued articulation of oral poetics. What emerge from the vernacular manuscript culture of the English Middle Ages are, to paraphrase a title of Foley's, texts that speak to readers and listeners who hear.

The trope of the talking book that Foley invokes in "Texts That Speak to Readers Who Hear" stretches back virtually to the first alphabetic inscriptions and witnesses the inherent interdependence of voice and text and the (perhaps originary) vocality of writing.[104] In antiquity, inanimate objects were regularly invested with a voice.[105] Even in the earliest examples of Greek epigraphy, those dating from about 700 B.C.E., the inscriptions were presented as the utterances of the objects upon which they appeared, a practice common to later inscriptions as well.[106] That first objects, and later texts, should be given a voice is apt because for the vast majority of the ancient and medieval population, the object's inscription or the text's words could be decoded only once they were orally transmitted by someone skilled in the art of reading. Only fairly recently has the eye begun to displace the ear as the chief organ of literary reception.[107] Throughout antiquity, and certainly through the Middle Ages and beyond, information was for the most part received and processed aurally, not visually.[108] Even as books came to be invested with more and more cultural authority and as that authority came to be widely recognized and accepted by the populace, the primary organs of transmission and reception remained, respectively, the mouth and ear. The heretical textual communities that Stock examines did not just offer competing *texts* that threatened to displace the Bible; they offered *readings* of the sacred text that clashed with the official and orthodox ones promulgated by the medieval Church. Theirs was chiefly a heresy of the mouth, not of the pen. John Wyclif's program of subverting ecclesiastical authority in the late fourteenth century was text centered, but to ensure the wide dissemination of his views, he wrote some of his works in English and sponsored the translation of the Bible into the vernacular. While the former strategy ensured that his books were read more widely (in the modern sense of a private reading as well as in the general medieval sense of being read aloud to a listening textual community), the latter strategy was truly radical, for it fundamentally challenged the strict control over scriptural interpretation that the church exercised by opening up sacred texts to private and communal readers (many of whom may have been women), who would then be able to draw from the text their own, potentially nonorthodox (and hence heretical) interpretations. The true danger of the Wyclif Bible and the other Wycliffite texts resided not in their misreadings or their textual changes and interpolations but in the possibility that those not trained in orthodox exegetical hermeneutics could for the first time gain direct access to sacred texts. These texts still required a reader to reach the majority of the population, but their availability in the vernacular effectively stripped clerics of their role as textual *interpretes*. Once translated into the vernacular, however, they stood invitingly open to both public and private negotiations.[109]

From Song to Text: Models of Poetic Composition

In considering the means and modes through which texts that evidence medieval English oral poetics were produced, we must not overlook the *vocalité* that is the chief legacy of the vital oral traditions from which our silent, textualized records descend.[110] Whether the oral poet is one who (re)composes in performance, recites verbatim from memory, or reads aloud from a written text, the poem and the tradition body forth upon his voice. Unlike written texts, which continue "frequently to speak without voice the words of the absent,"[111] oral texts exist only so long as they are embodied in a living voice.

In Anglo-Saxon England, there were at least three models of poetic composition, all of which, to varying degrees, shed light on the oral poetics of Old English texts; some of them may be the written products of literate poets, some may be the products of literate poets who dictated their texts to one or more scribes, and some may be the products of nonliterate poets who dictated their texts to one or more scribes. Because the last of these is the most familiar and in some circles the most favored model, let us proceed through this list backwards.

Bede's account of the cowherd Cædmon in the *Historia Ecclesiastica* provides intriguing evidence that some Anglo-Saxon oral poets may have dictated their texts to literate scribes. The many points of contact between Bede's account of Cædmon's composition of vernacular poetry and Lord's firsthand report of the compositional practices of South Slavic oral singers led many to accept Bede's story as a veritable case history of an Anglo-Saxon oral singer. In some quarters, Cædmon's *Hymn* is still considered to be the one unambiguous example of oral composition among our extant Old and Middle English poetry,[112] largely on the authority of Bede's narrative and the poem's generally agreed-upon status as the earliest extant vernacular verse to have been inscribed on a manuscript leaf. But several matters impinge upon Bede's story that should make us wary of accepting it uncritically and should similarly prevent us from labeling the *Hymn* an oral poem. Most obviously, outside the testimony of the narrative itself, the only evidence of the poem's putative orality derives from those written versions of it that have survived. Further, Bede himself does not provide the verse text of the *Hymn,* either in Latin or in the vernacular, even though there are indications that he was able to compose verse and prose in both tongues, but offers only a prose paraphrase of it.[113] Bede tells us that in response to the angel's prompting, "Thereupon Cædmon began to sing verses which he had never heard before in praise of God the Creator, of which this is the general sense" (417).[114] Bede even supplies his reasons for offering his Latin paraphrase rather than Cædmon's vernacular text in a statement that the Anglo-Saxon translator of the *Historia* leaves out of the Old English text:[115] "For it is not possible to translate verse, however well composed, literally from one language to another without some loss of beauty and dignity" (417).[116] Kiernan has recently raised once again the possibility that the extant Old English poem is a translation of Bede's Latin and is not, as has often been surmised, the original of Bede's Latin paraphrase.[117] This does not bear in any way upon Bede's story of Cædmon, but it does—as we will see in chapter 2—have important implications for how we ought to approach the poem generally attributed to the illiterate cowherd.

Finally, several other matters should cause us to hesitate before accepting Bede's story of Cædmon. The first is that Bede's story is unique: no similar account survives that chronicles the abilities and compositional practices of a preliterate singer of secular heroic material. We do have William of Malmesbury's description of Aldhelm's public performances of vernacular poetry, but this is far from a close parallel. Aldhelm was a diglossic, highly educated cleric who was a proficient composer of Latin prose and poetry. He may also have composed vernacular poems, but if he did, William's account strongly suggests that such poetry served chiefly as the means of luring the populace into church, where, presumably, they could be properly instructed and edified. Aldhelm's Latin poetry witnesses the depth of his engagement with the native verse-making tradition even when employing a very different poetic register, but he was, unlike Cædmon, highly literate and thus capable of writing down himself whatever vernacular poetry he may have composed.[118] This is not to rule out that Aldhelm was a dictating poet but merely to note that he, unlike the cowherd, need not have relied on dictation as the sole means of having his poetry preserved in writing.

The nature and subject matter of Cædmon's *Hymn* also throw a shadow on its originary status.[119] In explaining the genesis of Christian vernacular literature, Bede creates a text that "tells us how to think about its theme for the simple reason that [his] historical version was an attempt to explain and justify events, not foretell them."[120] Just as writing the *Historia* "offered Bede a unique opportunity to demonstrate how the organic nature of human society had both a structural coherence and a functional utility,"[121] so, too, did the story of Cædmon offer him the opportunity to appropriate the vernacular tradition for religious ends. If Cædmon did not exist, someone would have had to invent him.[122] And who would be better suited to this task than Bede, who presents through Cædmon his own readings of the beginnings of vernacular Christian poetry? The text of the *Hymn* that has come down to us is far from the unmediated product of an oral poet, but is, at best, the mediated and necessarily reshaped product of the collaboration between a preliterate performer and a literate scribe and it may even be a literate scribal translation of Bede's original Latin "paraphrase."

The second model of poetic production, the literate author who dictates his works to one or more scribes, is well attested in medieval literary history.[123] In the medieval mind, reading was more closely tied to hearing than it was to seeing, and "writing (in its modern sense of composition) was associated with dictating rather than manipulating a pen."[124] Textual composition often remained separate from the actual physical production of a manuscript, and, as a result, while some authors did physically inscribe their texts on the manuscript page, others did not. But as Mary Carruthers has demonstrated, there is a large gulf between an oral poet who (re)composes during performance and a poet—literate or preliterate—who dictates his poetry. In his ability to "dictate in his cell to three secretaries, and even occasionally to four, on different subjects at the same time,"[125] St. Thomas Aquinas clearly parallels the picture of Bede that Cuthbert provides in the *De Obitu*. But Bernardo's statement that in the course of dictating Thomas did not "seem to be searching for things as yet unknown to him; he seemed simply to let his memory pour out its treasures," when coupled with the other stories that Carruthers relates, points to Thomas's engaging in a rhetorical tradition dating back at least to ancient Rome in which orations were carefully worked out internally, perhaps going through several "versions," and were delivered orally before being committed to writing.[126]

John D. Niles has recently suggested that Old English poems such as Cædmon's *Hymn* and *Beowulf* may be the product of the collaboration between a dictating (perhaps preliterate) poet and a scribe skilled in the technology of writing.[127] However, we must, as does Niles, apply the theory of dictation cautiously because modeling poetic composition and inscription as discrete, unrelated, and perhaps even culturally distinct activities threatens to reinscribe orality and literacy as binary opposites. And if composing and inscribing poetry were separate endeavors in medieval England, one the provenance of preliterate (perhaps still pagan) poets and the other the provenance of literate Christian amanuenses, the question remains as to why a monastic (or later, other suitably literate) community would go to the considerable trouble of encoding on the page oral poems that derive from and in many ways celebrate the pagan culture that the church was eager to suppress.

The story of Cædmon provides an answer, but only a partial one. Although none of Cædmon's other poems are extant, Bede claims for him a repertory encompassing the breadth and depth of Christian doctrine:

> He sang about the creation of the world, the origin of the human race, and the whole history of Genesis, of the departure of Israel from Egypt and the entry into the promised land and of many other of the stories taken from the Scriptures: of the incarnation, passion, and resurrection of the Lord, of His ascension into heaven, of the coming of the Holy Spirit and the teaching of the apostles. He also made songs about the terrors of future judgement, the horrors of the pains of hell, and the joys of the heavenly kingdom. In addition, he composed many other songs about the divine mercies and judgements, in all of which he sought to turn his hearers away from delight in sin and to arouse in them the love and practice of good works. (419)[128]

By bringing vernacular oral poetics to bear on Christian material, Cædmon provided an effective means for disseminating Christian doctrine,[129] a point Bede makes most forcefully in his account of the cowherd-turned-singer's death. Cædmon, Bede tells us, "was a most religious man, humbly submitting himself to the discipline of the Rule; and he opposed all those who wished to act otherwise with a flaming and fervent zeal" (419).[130] No longer a simple cowherd who ruminates—in good monastic fashion—over the sacred material he is read before bringing it forth in the register of the secular tradition, Cædmon becomes, by the time of his death, an active, zealous defender of the faith. That Bede's story of Cædmon's life and death ultimately derives its contours from the hagiographic tradition subtly underscores its purpose in the *Historia*. Cædmon's "conversion" and his continued close collaboration with the community at Whitby both serve to further the glory and teachings of the God so dear to Bede.

The third model of poetic production, the literate poet who engages the specialized expressive economy of the oral tradition (consciously or unconsciously), has garnered the least critical attention and is the one that the following chapters will be devoted to exploring. When considered at all, this model has often been consigned to brief asides. Magoun, for example, did not see anything miraculous about Cædmon's ability to shape nontraditional subject matter—in the case of his one surviving poem, the origins of the Christian world—into highly traditional verse because "whatever he did hear would have been composed in the traditional manner out of the standing reservoir of formulas and themes and in conformity with the traditional metrical patterns according to which alone the singers could have sung."[131] Similarly, Jackson J. Campbell contends that "[a]lthough the conventions of the tradition were oral in origin, they could be, and were carried over into written literature. A poet who wrote his poem before it was performed in the refectory or the mead hall, still following all the conventions he associated with poetic composition, is well within the realm of possibility."[132] Despite these early speculations concerning the possibility that literate poets were able to employ traditional oral poetics, as well as some more recent ones,[133] these poets have continued to be seen as paradoxical, transitional, and marginal figures. When he reconsiders his flat opposition to such poets in some of his later writings,[134] Lord moves only slightly from his belief that a singer cannot "be *both* an oral and a written poet at any given time in his career."[135] The literate poet who deploys the expressive economy of oral poetics also does not receive many critical accolades; we need only think of the opprobrium usually heaped upon, among others, the authors of the late Chronicle poems (excepting *Brunanburh*), the author of the *Meters of Boethius,* and the author of the *Metrical Psalms.* To put the matter differently, it is often assumed that a poet's literacy significantly impedes his ability to negotiate the traditional oral idiom; that his use of this specialized idiom compromises his status as an accomplished, original artist; and that evidence of traditional oral poetics signals that he is an antiquarian, or worse, a hack.

The issue of the literate poet who employs the oral tradition becomes ever more vexed when we consider post-Conquest English literary history. Given the state of developing literacy in Anglo-Saxon England and the probable presence of an active oral tradition at some point, even if only very early, during the period, we cannot rule out that some written Old English poems are only slightly removed from their oral avatars, although, of course, barring the discovery of dramatic new evidence we will never be able to know for sure just how close any given written text is to its oral predecessors. When we move beyond the Conquest, however, speculation regarding the putative oral foundations of any given piece of vernacular poetry becomes even more problematic. The evidence of Aldhelm and Cædmon, as well as that provided in some poems themselves (notably *Beowulf, Widsith,* and *Deor*),[136] suggests that the oral tradition was active during the Anglo-Saxon period, but Middle English poetry, witnessing as it does the steady rise of the literate authorial consciousness that comes to dominate literary production in the West, is clearly situated much closer to the literate than the oral pole of the oral-literate continuum and hence stands at a greater remove from the world of oral composition than does Old English poetry.

The manner of poetic production changes as literacy gains ground, but the shift from producing poetry exclusively during public performance, with all its attendant pressures and demands, to producing it privately and in writing does not necessarily entail a concomitant and equally dramatic alteration in poetic articulation. New models of poetic composition develop following the rise of print culture, but the chirographic tradition that emerges and gains increasing cultural importance throughout the medieval period does not simply and immediately replace the older oral one. Rather, these traditions merge to form a partnership, one that is most readily apparent in a specialized expressive economy that enables oral poets to articulate traditional verbal art and literate poets to draw upon oral poetics as they write the oral tradition.

This expressive economy, which functions as a "fluent compromise among idiolect, dialect, and language as a larger entity,"[137] is deployed within the *performance arena* of living oral traditions,[138] but it is also a key constituent of nonperformative traditions, where it functions in what we might label the *compositional arena*. For many, if not most, of the medieval poets who are indisputably removed from any sort of performative compositional tradition,[139] poetic thought and poetic articulation nevertheless remain inextricably linked to oral poetics.[140] Traditional, dynamic, nonperformative oral poetics exerts a powerful influence on the composition of vernacular verse throughout the Anglo-Saxon period, and it continues to play a role, albeit a reduced one, in poetry composed as late as the late fourteenth century. The traditional expressive economy of oral poetics survives the transition from being used exclusively in the public, communal space of the performance arena to being employed in the far more private space of the compositional arena because just as poetic articulation depends heavily upon it, so, too, does poetic reception: oral poets speak the poetry that conforms to their intended audience's horizon of expectations. However radical, quick, and complete the shift from (re)composing orally in front of an audience to composing in the privacy of, say, a monastic cell may or may not have been, the horizon of expectations of those who received poetry shifted only very slowly, as the evidence of the earliest products of print culture—texts that look remarkably similar to the products of manuscript culture—bears out. There are many reasons why incunabulae replicate the design features of manuscripts,[141] but the desire to have the new typographic texts conform to the expectations that developed among readers (and patrons) in manuscript culture ranks among the most important. Even though the technology for producing books changed dramatically, the expectations of those who received the books did not. Further, "It would be surprising if the technology used in the making of the manuscript book had not been taken over into the printed one, since manuscripts were the only models printers had available and they were still being produced side by side with printed books."[142] The means of producing books may have undergone a sea change following the invention of movable type and the development of the printing press, but the aesthetics of the book, far from undergoing a similarly dramatic shift, remained constant because "the beginning of printing was seen only as a different way of writing, and although it affected the number of copies that could be produced, it did not at first influence the way one wrote or made [or received] books."[143]

For some critics, the arrival of literacy wrought a number of fundamental changes because "[w]ritten literature introduced the Anglo-Saxons to a new kind of artist, a different relation between artist and artifact, [and] an altered function of the artifact in society."[144] This view commands agreement, but only from our perspective do these changes appear to be so dramatic as some have found them to be. Throughout the medieval period, up through the early years of printing, neither poets nor audiences would have been aware of the far-reaching changes going on about them for the simple reason that the "new kind of artist" is not, strictly speaking, "new," and his appearance is anything but sudden. The literate poets who composed in the vernacular early in the period and who used the traditional oral register were not cut from whole cloth, the fabric of which had been hitherto unknown on the island. They represented a development of, rather than a departure from, the oral tradition that preceded them. Their poetic articulation recalls that postulated for oral poets not because they were consciously attempting to recreate oral poetry but because they were using the only idiom at their disposal for the articulation of poetry.

The determinative nature of the register is clearly apparent in Old English poetry, where the tradition's homeostatic expressive economy exerts considerable influence over matters of metrical form, verbal collocations, and narrative patterns to produce a corpus whose tectonics remains remarkably stable over the course of several centuries. However, the tradition's role in shaping how our extant Old English poetry means does not circumscribe what the poetry means or how poets can construct their poems. Oral poetics does not impinge upon the creativity of Anglo-Saxon poets any more than the syntax, metrics, and lexicon of the language(s) and register(s) deployed by contemporary poets hinder their articulation.[145]

Although compositional devices such as formulas and formulaic systems serve highly specialized functions within performative oral traditions, poets, both oral and literate, continue to use them because they are the very stuff of poetic articulation and of poetic thought: "Poets do not persist in employing traditional structures after the advent of literacy and texts out of a misplaced antiquarianism or by default, but because, even in an increasingly textual environment, the 'how' developed over the ages still holds the key to worlds of meaning that are otherwise inaccessible."[146] Contemporary inhabitants of literate societies have a particularly difficult time grasping this concept because for those of us who live in such societies, artistic achievement and integrity are ineluctably bound up with originality of expression and ideation. But as the following chapters will attempt to make clear, the central affective, metonymic character of oral poetics that helped ensure its survival before the advent of writing does not vanish when the ephemeral, unreadable texts of oral tradition come to be fixed in writing but continues to survive once the pen and written text replace the mouth and ear.

The notion of "ballad competence" that Vésteinn Ólason derives from Chomskyan linguistics, recalling as it does Lord's seminal comments on the "grammar" of oral tradition, is instructive here.[147] In considering how "Tristams kvæði" could so completely adhere to the contours of the Icelandic ballad tradition despite being based on a written French *roman*, Ólason suggests that "when it was composed by someone who had either read the saga or heard it read or faithfully retold, what might be called ballad competence must have been alive in the Icelandic community; either the original composer had mastered it, or it was sufficiently alive in the audience to result in the adaptation of the song to ballad norms."[148] The "ballad competence" that Ólason postulates is similar to oral poetics in that it signals the artist's and his or her intended audience's deep engagement with a traditional, shared mode of articulation,[149] but unlike oral poetics, ballad competence was one of several registers then (and still) available to ballad singers such as Mrs. Anna Brown, a highly literate eighteenth-century woman who "partook of two traditions which she kept apart in her mind; the literate culture and standard English of her day, and a lower-class culture transmitted in the local dialect."[150]

In other words, Mrs. Brown had at her command multiple distinct registers that she was able to engage as the situation demanded. Whereas she and others like her could choose between a variety of expressive economies and could so bring the appropriate registers to bear in their appropriate contexts, Anglo-Saxon poets could not. For them, vernacular poetry had to be articulated through medieval English oral poetics. Many Anglo-Saxon poets and scribes no doubt moved as easily between the separate registers of Latin and Old English as Mrs. Brown did between her registers, but their vernacular poetic register remains remarkably uniform whether they are translating a text from a Latin source or creating/copying one that exists only in the vernacular.

O'Brien O'Keeffe has recently shed a great deal of light on the admittedly thorny problem of how oral poetics may be preserved, transmitted, and developed through nonoral channels by arguing that the many "metrically, syntactically and semantically appropriate" variations contained in the manuscripts of Cædmon's *Hymn* bespeak "a . . . state between pure orality and pure literacy whose evidence is a reading process that applies oral techniques for the reception of a message to the decoding of a written text."[151] She continues and argues that these "oral techniques," far from being consciously cultivated as such, result from the scribes/poets' being "conditioned by formulaic conventions"—the tradition's originary and then still central oral poetics—as a consequence of having deeply internalized the idiom of the oral tradition through their experience with oral-derived (and perhaps even oral) texts, whether they read, copied, or took them down from dictation.[152] While we can never wholly discount the possibility that from the earliest times some poets writing in the vernacular were sufficiently far removed from the traditional oral idiom and possessed a sufficiently accurate sense of their position in English literary history (and of its diachrony) to have formulated a clear picture of past practices that they could then consciously invoke in the present moment,[153] we ought to proceed with great caution when attributing to medieval authors such a modern awareness of their tradition and their position within it.

As we will see in chapters 3, 4, and 5, the expressive economy of medieval English oral poetics underwent some dramatic changes as its position on the oral-literate continuum shifted ever more toward the literate terminus, but early in the Middle Ages and especially in the Anglo-Saxon period, the focus of chapter 2, oral poetics was so central that it was the only means by which poets, oral or literate, could produce poetry.

two

Anglo-Saxon Oral Poetics

The centuries following the Roman withdrawal from Britain in 410 C.E. rank among the most tumultuous in the island's history. The arrival of the Germanic tribes during the Age of Migration and the establishment of the Christian mission in Kent in the late sixth century were but two of the major upheavals that permanently reconfigured the island's racial, cultural, political, linguistic, and religious contours. Throughout the Anglo-Saxon period, the lineaments of what would become England slowly began to emerge: the scattered early kingdoms gave way to the Heptarchy, whose own dynamics were in continual flux as the seat of the island's political and cultural power shifted from its early base in Mercia to its later one in Wessex.[1] Although the Anglo-Saxon Chronicle bestows the title of *bretwalda* upon such early figures as Ceawlin of Wessex (560–91/2), Æthelbert of Kent (560–616), and Edwin of Northumbria (616–33), perhaps not until Alfred the Great's reign (871–99) did the title begin to reflect political reality.[2] But even though Alfred may be credited with helping to create English national solidarity, he and his successors ruled under the shadow of the Viking invasions that culminated in the establishment of Danish settlements in northern and eastern England and in the accession of Cnut in 1016 (who was followed on the throne by his son Harold in 1037), events that were again to reshape life on the island only a few decades before the most recent and most dramatic invasion, that of the Normans led by William the Conqueror. These invasions

33

were the most extraordinary and far-reaching of the many upheavals that marked the Anglo-Saxon period, but other changes were equally significant, if less dramatic: the growth of towns and the rise of cities; the spread and growing importance of commerce; the emergence of monasteries as the sites of learning and culture. In short, the Anglo-Saxon period was marked by the convergence of the complex, intertwined, and often competing forces out of which the English nation was forged.

The Uniformity of Old English Poetry

Despite the enormous and widespread changes occurring all around it, Old English verse, marked by its lexical, metrical, narrative, and perhaps even syntactic homogeneity,[3] was an island of stability in the sea of change that continually washed over the island. As long ago as the early nineteenth century, scholars called attention to the verse's characteristic redundant phrases, and later in the century practitioners of the German Higher Criticism were similarly focused on what by then had come to be labeled "epische Formeln," with one critic "postulating a common storehouse 'des grossen Phrazen-und Wortschatzes der Poesie,' available to all poets and used without the stigma of plagiarism"[4]—a view that was to be revived by oral-formulaic theory in the twentieth century. The lexical homogeneity of our extant Old English poetic remains has long been taken as evidence of a general Old English poetic *Kunstsprache,* one in which idiolectal and dialectal differences were so flattened or erased by the artificial, pan-traditional standard that "it is seldom possible to declare with confidence that a given poem was originally in a particular dialect."[5]

The meter of Old English poetry is also noteworthy for its remarkable uniformity. Metrical variation does exist—hypermetric and rhyming passages do occasionally occur[6]—but the dominance of the Germanic, stress-based, alliterative line strongly suggests that "to all intents and purposes there is only one meter"[7] within which Old English poetry could be articulated. Few other poetries have such a singular metrics. In the ancient Greek and South Slavic oral traditions, the traditions to which the Anglo-Saxon oral tradition has been most frequently and most profitably compared, metrical variety serves to distinguish different genres. Homeric prosody, like Old English prosody, is singular and has its own rules and tendencies, and it is essential to the expression of ancient Greek epic poetry, but it is only one of several meters available to poets within the larger ancient Greek poetic tradition. While the dactylic hexameter was used to articulate epic, the meter of satire, invective, and comedy was iambic, the usual meter of tragedy was the iambic trimeter, and the meter of the lyrics showed considerable variation.[8] South Slavic oral epic has two primary meters, the ten-syllable *deseterac* and the fifteen-syllable *bugarstica*,[9] but these are by no means the only meters available: the tradition's lyric (or women's) songs are usually in octosyllables, and rhyming dodecasyllabic and octosyllabic stanzas were common in South Slavic poems from the sixteenth to eighteenth centuries.[10]

Nowhere else in English literary history does such a heterogeneous poetic corpus—one that contains everything from a metrical charm against a sudden stitch, to a dream vision of the holy rood, to an account of the heroic pagan past brilliantly and seamlessly articulated within a decidedly anachronistic Christian framework—find expression in such a uniform poetics. That the surviving major codices of Old English poetry were all apparently produced in Wessex sometime in the century following the death of King Alfred the Great may explain some of the poetry's uniformity, especially given that Anglo-Saxon scribes modernized "the language of the texts they cop[ied] and put them into an orthographical shape consonant with a generalized poetic standard language, mainly late West Saxon."[11] But even Alfred's well-known desire to revive learning in England during his rule does not explain how this "generalized poetic standard language" developed at a time when the language itself was far from standardized. The optimist editorial practices adopted by several generations of textual critics serve to underscore the poetic language's "standardized" characteristics because editors habitually normalize manuscript evidence, regularize inconsistencies, add modern punctuation, and reconstruct problematic phrases in the course of producing standard, critical editions, but we should resist imputing a similar desire for uniformity either to the man generally credited with providing the impetus for collecting and inscribing much of the vernacular poetry extant from the Anglo-Saxon period or to the scribes/poets who copied or produced the texts.[12] Unlike those editors of *Elene* who relegate manuscript *rex* to their notes and replace it in its only two occurrences in the Old English poetic corpus with a native word at lines 610a and 1041b,[13] Anglo-Saxon scribes/poets do not appear to have made a similarly conscious effort to produce a uniform poetic corpus. The impulse to standardize Old English poetic texts is decidedly postmedieval.[14]

The evidence of the poetry itself further militates against viewing the uniformity of Old English verse as the manifestation of some sort of tenth-century West Saxon "house style." Although the language was in a constant state of development (as all languages always are), the versions of Cædmon's *Hymn* extant in a number of manuscripts dating from the eighth to the fifteenth centuries point to the remarkable stability of the poetic language over the course of several hundred years. The orthography of an early, Northumbrian version of Cædmon's *Hymn* preserved in the margins of an eighth-century Latin manuscript of Bede's *Historia Ecclesiastica* might give a literate West Saxon of Alfred's time momentary pause, but neither the dialect nor the lexicon would pose any special problem to comprehension. In the left column below is an edited version of the Northumbrian text that appears in Cambridge, University Library, Kk. 5. 16, the Moore Bede, on folio 128v; to its right is an edited version of the West Saxon poem that appears on folio 100r of the Old English translation of Bede's *Historia* contained in Oxford, Bodleian Library, Tanner 10, the Tanner Bede.[15] Despite the differences in orthography, dialect, and date,[16] the similarities between these two versions are readily apparent:[17]

1a	nu scylun hergan	nu sculon herigean
1b	heafaenricaes uard	heofonrices weard
2a	metudæs maecti	meotodes meahte
2b	end his modgidanc	and his modgeþanc
3a	uerc uuldurfadur	weorc wuldorfæder
3b	sue he uundra gihuaes	swa he wundra gehwæs
4a	eci dryctin	ece drihten
4b	or astelidæ	or onstealde
5a	he ærist scop	he ærest sceop
5b	ælda barnum	eorðan bearnum
6a	heben til hrofe	heofon to hrofe
6b	haleg scepen	halig scyppend
7a	tha middungeard	þa middangeard
7b	moncynnæs uard	moncynnes weard
8a	eci dryctin	ece drihten
8b	æfter tiadæ	æfter teode
9a	firum foldu	firum foldan
9b	frea allmectig	frea ælmihtig

Because it survives in multiple records that date from the eighth to the fifteenth centuries, Cædmon's *Hymn* stands as a singularly important witness to the diachrony of the Old English poetic tradition,[18] but we must cautiously assess the evidence it offers given its apparent cultural importance (while most Old English poetic texts survive in unique manuscript versions, seventeen versions of the *Hymn* are extant), its brevity (the poem's transmission may have been accomplished chiefly through memorization), and its vexed relationship to Bede's Latin text. Further, we must not forget that its stability, especially in those manuscripts written after the twelfth century, may well be attributable to its having been copied mechanically, not dynamically, by scribes unfamiliar with the language in which it was composed.

Another set of records, one not burdened in the ways that the *Hymn* is, sheds further light on the uniformity of Old English verse. The *Dream of the Rood* survives in a unique manuscript version contained in the Vercelli Book (Vercelli, Biblioteca Capitolare CXVII), a manuscript that N. R. Ker dates to s. x^2. Portions of the poem have also been inscribed in runes on the east and west faces of the Ruthwell Cross, a stone artifact dating to the late seventh or early eighth century.[19] Because there is no way of knowing, for example, whether the runes were carved into the cross when it was first erected in Dumfriesshire, Scotland, or whether they were added to it at a later date, perhaps by a runemaster familiar with (or working directly with or from a copy of) the Vercelli Book's version of the poem, the relationship between these poems remains far from clear. Despite the differences in date, dialect, probable place of composition, and method of inscription, there are many suggestive similarities between these poems.[20] As with Cædmon's *Hymn*, the dialectal differences would pose little trouble to a native speaker of either dialect who listened to the lines read aloud or who was able to able to decode the runes for him- or herself. Consider, for example, the following pairs of lines:[21]

Ongyrede hine . . . god ælmihtig (DrR 39),
[. . .] geredæ hinæ god almeʒttig (RCr I, 1)

Gestah he on gealgan heanne (DrR 40b),
on galgu gistiga (RCr I, 2)

Ahof ic ricne cyning (DrR 46b),
[. . .] ic riicnæ kyniʒc (RCr II, 1)

and finally,

Crist wæs on rode.
Hwæðere þær fuse feorran cwoman
(DrR 55b–56a)
Krist wæs on rodi.
Hweþræ þer fusæ fearran kwomu
(RCr III, 1–2)[22]

Accepting the widely held view that the runic inscription preserves an early, perhaps original, Anglian version of the poem helps us account for the poem's appearance on the cross and provides the basis for its early dating, but it does not shed much light on the stability of expression that the two texts witness or the mode(s) by which the poem was transmitted, as the distance between eighth-century Dumfriesshire and late-tenth-century southwestern England is great in many ways.

Examples of the largely inherited and widely shared lexicon that runs throughout the poetic corpus could be adduced almost at will.[23] The phrase "heofonrices weard" [guardian of heaven], for example, not only occurs at line 1b of Cædmon's *Hymn* but is repeated twenty-two other times in twelve other generically diverse poems.[24] Similarly, "ece drihten" [eternal Lord] appears twice in the *Hymn* (4a, 8a) and an additional ninety-three times in a total of fifty-nine poems.[25] The metrical principles from which this alliterative, stress-based prosody derives prevailed for several centuries prior to the Norman Conquest and may well be rooted in the prehistory of the West Germanic oral tradition from which Anglo-Saxon poetics descends.[26] We can gauge their centrality to medieval English oral poetic articulation by noting that they remain relatively intact from very early in the Anglo-Saxon period until after the Norman Conquest. Themes, type-scenes, and story patterns are as widely shared as lexemes.[27] Even the way Old English poetry is physically encoded in manuscripts remains stable throughout the Anglo-Saxon period. From the early, eighth-century copies of Cædmon's devout *Hymn* to the Creator to *Durham*, an *encomium urbis* generally accepted as the latest of the extant Old English poems composed in the regular alliterative meter, Old English poetry is written out in *scriptura continua* and evidences none of the specialized graphic conventions that we have come to associate with poetic inscription. Graphic cues that function as aids to the ocular reception of vernacular poetry do begin to develop during the Anglo-Saxon period and serve, toward the period's close, nearly the functions they continue to serve in the present day, but on the whole, the representation of poetry on the page—its physical encoding—remains constant until after the Anglo-Saxon period draws to a close. The version of the *Hule and Niȝtengale* contained in London, British Library, Cotton Caligula A. ix, a manuscript that dates from the late twelfth or early thirteenth century, marks a major change in the way English poetry is physically presented because, for what is perhaps the first time, English poetry is lineated as poetry:[28] the left margin is aligned and each line of poetry occupies a single line, is marked by final punctuation, and is followed by significant blank space.

Performance and Nonperformative Oral Poetics

In attempting to understand the broadly shared, inherited features of Anglo-Saxon poetics—its lexicon, metrics, thematics, and story patterns—we must, as oral theory has by and large been slow to do, acknowledge the important role literate, textual culture plays in its development because "*grammatica*, the discipline that governed literacy, the study of literary language, the interpretation of texts, and the writing of manuscripts,"[29] was a central component of Anglo-Saxon textual communities, both monastic and secular.[30] However, we need to bear in mind that just as the performance-based model of medieval English oral poetics fails to explain adequately the inherent (and inescapable) textuality of the Old English poetic corpus, so, too, does a source-based, intertextual model of Anglo-Saxon poetics provide only a partial explanation of its distinguishing structural and aesthetic characteristics. Working from the (often unexamined) principles that medieval compositional practices closely mirror more contemporary ones and that literary transmission and textual borrowing offer the only avenues through which the expressive economy of medieval English poetics circulates is as problematic as working from the (often unexamined) principles that medieval compositional practices find direct parallels in ancient Greek and twentieth-century South Slavic oral ones and that formulas, themes, and story patterns can only be transmitted orally by preliterate singers. Neither the exclusive product of oral nor of literate culture, Anglo-Saxon oral poetics rather results from the interplay of the two: rooted at some, perhaps very great, remove in an active, performative oral tradition, it nevertheless finds expression only in literate culture. To situate medieval English oral poetics more firmly within the broader compass of literate culture, we must first deemphasize its performative nature.

The belief in a vital, necessary, and sustaining link between performance and oral poetics is a fundamental tenet of oral theory, one grounded on the logical premise that poetry and performance were intertwined and inter-dependent in primary oral cultures.[31] The fieldwork conducted by Parry and Lord confirmed the link between preliterate poetic articulation and perform-ance because the traditional oral poetry that they encountered in their initial trips to then-Yugoslavia in the 1930s was articulated within a demonstrably performance-based oral poetics. As a result, Parry and Lord were able to observe the process by which nonliterate South Slavic *guslari* learned to enter the performance arena of the South Slavic oral tradition, a process Lord was later to detail in his seminal *Singer of Tales*.[32] But while Lord's observations on how South Slavic *guslari* acquire their skills are applicable to any number of oral traditions, they cannot be simply transposed to Anglo-Saxon England. Whether our aim is to explore one tradition or several, we must take into account not only such formal features of its expressive economy as its unique lexical, metrical, and narrative patterns but the cultural and oral-literate matri-ces from which individual traditions emerge. Thus Lord's model of how South Slavic *guslari* learn their craft and the model Jeff Opland has proposed for the South African *iimbongi* shed important light on the South Slavic and Xhosa oral traditions,[33] but they prove to be of only general value in understanding Anglo-Saxon oral poetics because on the crucial matter of performance these traditions diverge sharply.[34]

We have little native information regarding the actual processes involved in the production, transmission, and dissemination of poetry in Anglo-Saxon England, but what evidence exists helps establish the centrality of perform-ance to Anglo-Saxon poetics, as the productions of the scops reported by the *Beowulf*-poet and the narratives of *Widsith* and *Deor* all witness. In the prose records, Bede underscores how deeply performance and poetic articulation are intertwined in the vernacular tradition through his story of the poet Cædmon. In placing Cædmon and his poem squarely within the performative matrix of oral culture, Bede "seems to affirm those nineteenth-and twentieth-century cultural notions of the oral nature of archaic literature and the spontaneity of poetic performance."[35] But for Cædmon—and perhaps Bede—the performa-tive matrix is a locus of considerable anxiety. The cowherd's initial insecurity over performing (for reasons that neither he nor Bede ever makes explicit) drives him from the "gebeorscipe" [drinking party] in which all those present are apparently expected to enter the performance arena and produce poetry: they must "þurh endebyrdnesse be hearpan singan" (342) [in order sing to the harp].[36] But his departure provides only temporary respite for Cædmon, who, shortly after retreating from the gathering, is confronted in a dream by a figure (an angel?) who not only twice commands him to sing but also suggests what the cowherd's subject matter should be. Shortly thereafter, Cædmon produces his nine-line hymn to the Creator. Through this narrative, Bede effectively models the power and pervasiveness of the vernacular performative matrix.

In a significant addition to Bede's Latin text, the redactor of the Old English version of the *Historia Ecclesiastica* places Cædmon's subsequent (and unrecovered) poetic production in an even more complex cultural matrix and makes more explicit the division between his exclusively performative mode of producing verse and the literate technology by which the monks are able to preserve (and, presumably, transmit) it. Whereas the Latin text tells us that his verse was "so sweet" [carmen dulcissimum] "that his teachers became in turn his audience" [suauiusque resonando doctores suos uicissim auditores sui faciebat] (419/418),[37] the Old English version emphasizes the specific processes involved, relating that Cædmon's teachers in the monastic community "æt his muðe wreoton 7 leornodon" (346) [from his mouth wrote and learned]. Although the Old English text is not entirely clear on this point, it appears that Cædmon's teachers inscribed [wreoton] the vernacular words he uttered and perhaps even committed his poems to memory [leornodon], but, significantly, no mention is made of whether they attempted to appropriate his decidedly nonliterate mode of production.

The *Historia*'s account of Anglo-Saxon performative poetics and the other few extant contemporary accounts have proved to be both a blessing and a curse. Although they provide invaluable commentary on poetic production and have thus long been regarded as important touchstones in the mapping of Anglo-Saxon poetics, the model of poetic articulation they present—that of composition-in-performance—has been accepted by many oral theorists as *the* model of Anglo-Saxon poetic production.[38] As a result, not only have scholars ignored such evidence of literate nonperformative poetic composition as that witnessed, for example, in Cynewulf's runic "signatures," in his several references to "bec" [books], and in the poignant, first-person commentary that concludes several of the poems attributed to him, but they have unduly privileged the binarist model of poetic production and inscription that emerges explicitly in Bede's account and implicitly elsewhere. The depictions of poetic articulation preserved in Old English poetry and prose no doubt reflect what was *at some point* in Anglo-Saxon literary history the common and necessary mode of producing poetry. But instead of taking the accounts of the Latin and Old English versions of the *Historia*, the *Beowulf*-poet, Widsith, and Deor as evidence that Anglo-Saxon poets composed during performance, we should recall that in each of these instances, the authors invoke a temporally removed and hence romanticized and idealized performative matrix that may not represent contemporary praxis. The nature of the surviving evidence is such that we will never be able to determine with any degree of certainty just when the pen became the primary conduit for poetic articulation or when poets stopped composing vernacular verse during performance. But the poetic records reveal that evidence of written composition and of the literate habits of mind associated with such composition in no way precludes the continued presence of oral poetics, as the abundant evidence of the Cynewulfian canon witnesses. Sharing the same tectonics, the two modes of expression—oral and literate poetics—coexisted and informed each other throughout the period.

The close connection between performance and the transmission and continued survival of traditional oral art has been a central tenet of oral theory from Parry onward, and there is little doubt that the characteristic contours of verbal collocations, type-scenes, specialized syntax, larger narrative structuring—in short, all the constituents of the specialized registers evident in traditional oral poetries—developed as aids to the rapid composition of verse in performance. But while traditional oral registers were shaped in the crucible of performance, they do not exist solely in symbiosis with performance. In the South Slavic tradition, for example, performance plays a far more central role than it does in either the ancient Greek or the Anglo-Saxon tradition.[39] Of the three, only in the South Slavic tradition do we discover unambiguously oral texts (re)composed during performance; for the others, the most we can do is speak in terms of written texts that evidence oral poetics. Removing the performative component from oral poetics sounds the death knell of traditional *oral* poetry—that is, poetry that is both (re)composed and disseminated exclusively during performance in primary or largely oral cultures—but the effect of its removal on the traditional oral register is neither so dramatic nor so pronounced. The mode of presenting poetry shifts radically once it is severed from the performative matrix, but the channels through which it is articulated and received do not necessarily undergo a concomitant change because the traditional oral register remains a powerful and flexible significative idiom, whether it is produced by the mouth or the pen.[40] Because the register of oral poetics is much more than the sum of its formulaic verbal collocations, metrical conventions, typical scenes, and story patterns, *how* the poetry is articulated, *how* it means, and *how* it is received remain stable once writing becomes the primary avenue for poetic expression.[41]

But given the remarkable stability that results from the combination of its specialized structural constituents and highly metonymic idiom, how can we see the poet who engages oral poetics (either in performance or nonperformatively) as more than the prisoner of an extremely deterministic tradition? The answer lies in the dedicated register of oral poetics, a highly specialized and "idiomatic version of the language that qualifies as a more or less self-contained system of signification specifically because it is the designated and sole vehicle" for articulating poetry.[42] As such, it is no more limiting, restrictive, or deterministic than are the grammar and syntax of natural languages. If this were not so and the traditional oral register were truly the mechanistic, confining force it was for a long time surmised to be,[43] our manuscript records would show none of the flexibility of expression or suppleness of narrative patterning that they do. The formulaic tectonics of the register would not function metonymically but would rather be stripped of its significative powers in just the ways that formulas, clichés, and dead metaphors are in contemporary literate poetics.

If we compare the phrase "in geardagum" [in days of yore] that occurs at *Beowulf* 1b[44] with the formula "once upon a time" that recurs throughout children's literature, we discover that they both function as diectic temporal referents in setting the ensuing narrative in the distant, perhaps mythical or fictional past.[45] But this similarity aside, these formulas function in very different ways because a formula such as "once upon a time," like most formulas in a literate poetics, has "lost all evocative power."[46] Even though "once upon a time" continues to steer its readers/listeners towards a time other than the one they are currently in, it operates within an associative network that is so broad and undirected as to be unchartable. "In geardagum," by way of contrast, is firmly embedded in a highly metonymic referential system and is, especially when used at or near the beginnings of poems, demonstrably part of a larger traditional "I heard" narrative pattern that metonymically signals the beginning of a heroic narrative.[47]

In traditional oral poetics, fixed epithets regularly "reach outside of [their] individual instances to larger-than-textual realities and stand pars pro toto for complexes of ideas too evanescent for commitment to the single occurrence."[48] In contrast, the alliteration and chiastic structure of a fixed epithet such as "brave and bright, bright and brave" that is regularly attached to a character in Jane Yolen's children's story *Commander Toad in Space* serve an exclusively mnemonic rather than significative function. When we learn that Commander Toad is "brave and bright, bright and brave," an assessment consistently and simplistically confirmed throughout the series of tales devoted to his exploits, the epithet bears only minimal significative weight. In contrast, a fixed epithet such as "δῖος Ὀδυσσεύς" [godlike Odysseus] is a strand of a rich web of reference that is called forth indeterminately but powerfully with each occurrence of the epithet.

In a living or otherwise demonstrably oral tradition, linking performance and oral poetics is both necessary and logical, but doing so for a tradition that exists only on the written page requires arguing, circularly, that a poem evidencing oral poetics must be an *oral* poem because oral poetics is the hallmark of orally composed and transmitted poems. The nonperformative poetics advanced here does not require that we reject outright or in any way subvert the crucial and necessary interdependence of oral poetics and performance. Instead, it calls into question the practice of applying a performance-based model to the oral poetics that survives in *demonstrably written* Old English poetry.[49] Removing the necessity of performance from Anglo-Saxon oral poetics does not preclude the continued practice of producing poetry during performance. Rather it offers up another way of understanding those poetic records that have come down to us as indisputably written texts that nevertheless evidence oral poetics.

Oral Poetics and Written Texts

Composition-in-performance is a key component of some oral poetics, and it sheds important light upon a cognitive process radically removed from the literate experience. But if we wish "to spare ourselves the frustration of looking for things that are not there while overlooking those that are,"[50] we must develop a more flexible model of oral composition, one that will enable us to identify and explore the structure and aesthetics of Anglo-Saxon oral poetics without requiring that we ignore the physical evidence of Old English poetry's textuality as we listen in vain for the scop's (absent) voice. But because performance is the crucial event that both enables the expression of traditional verbal art and prescribes the mode of its reception, how are we to account for the preservation of entexted oral poetics in the voiceless, written records that survive? One way might be to ascribe to Anglo-Saxon poets both an awareness of their position on a poetic continuum stretching back to the distant past and the desire to reanimate an aspect of that past (i.e., traditional oral poetics) by consciously selecting it "from the fund of traditional knowledge in order to serve present needs."[51] But labeling the scops as self-conscious antiquarians requires imputing to them a deeply shared historical consciousness of and remarkable ability to manipulate the entity that modern scholars label the English poetic tradition. Anglo-Saxon poets employed traditional oral poetics not because they wanted to reanimate an antiquated style (for whatever reason) but because the register was a richly denotative, expressive medium that continued to provide channels for them to convey traditional and, as we will see below and in the following chapters, nontraditional meaning(s).

In a careful examination of the many metrically, syntactically, and semantically appropriate variants found among the versions of those few Old English poems for which there are multiple manuscript records, O'Brien O'Keeffe offers a convincing alternative model of how oral poetics is preserved and transmitted through a nonperformative, text-based process.[52] Seeing a direct connection between the variants in evidence among the fixed, textual records and those lexical (and narrative) variations that characterize oral poetry, she argues that they bespeak "a reading process which applies oral techniques for the reception of a message to the decoding of a written text."[53] To expand a point that runs implicitly through her argument, the poets/scribes who apply these "oral techniques" to the poems they are composing/copying employ these techniques because their direct experience with the register of traditional oral poetics has led them to internalize it, whether they have experienced it through their ears, their eyes, or some combination of the two. Douglas Moffatt rejects this view because he believes that it "requires our belief that Anglo-Saxon scribes, and presumably a great many others in their society, were not simply occasional, largely passive listeners to oral poetry of the sort that has survived to us but, on the contrary, were intimately knowledgeable of its technical features and finely attuned to its aesthetic nuances."[54] But the variants upon which O'Brien O'Keeffe focuses reveal neither that Anglo-Saxon "scribes understood in fairly precise terms the fundamental formulaic structure of Old English verse"[55] nor that those who received and transmitted Old English poetry did not have "much respect for the authorial *mot juste*."[56] Viewed from the strictly literate perspective Moffatt adopts, textual variants are derivations from a fixed, *author*ized text that offer competing readings (some "better" others "worse") that must be sifted through before one can finally arrive at the "correct" or "original" or "best" text. Those scribes who introduce nonauthorial readings or in other ways alter and hence trivialize their texts may be justly chastised.[57] But viewed from the perspective of oral poetics, the lexical variations in Old English poetry testify not to scribal indifference, incompetence, or insensitivity but to the degree to which multiformity, not fixity, is the tradition's norm. Because texts composed within the tradition are stamped with its impress, they are all equally authoritative, and the variants they witness (both those that are metrically, semantically, and syntactically appropriate and those that are not) do not bespeak the distance they have fallen from their *Ur*-forms—from, that is, their authors' ideals—but rather signal the continued presence of a vital, if not embodied, oral poetics. During the Anglo-Saxon period, "Whenever scribes who are part of the oral traditional culture write or copy traditional oral works, they do not merely mechanically hand them down; they rehear them, 'mouth' them, 'reperform' them in the act of writing in such a way that the text may change but remain authentic, just as a completely oral poet's text changes from performance to performance without losing authenticity."[58]

Finally, situating the poets and scribes responsible for producing the *written* corpus of Old English poetry within the ambience of oral poetics does not establish them as representatives of a "monolithic group whose members all shared the same habits, degree of competence, and predilection."[59] Anglo-Saxon oral poetics may be a cultural inheritance most easily perceived in the specialized, dedicated register of Old English poetry, but the skill with which poets/scribes engage and manipulate this register varies greatly. To argue that a poem evidences oral poetics and that its variants and physical encoding provide important keys to its residual orality is finally not to make an aesthetic judgment. As is true of poetry composed within a literate poetics, poetry founded upon oral poetics—performative or nonperformative—ranges from the insipid to the inspired.

Oral Tradition and Individual Talent

In just the way that orality and literacy are often held to be discrete cognitive states, so the notions of individuality and tradition are frequently cast as incompatible.[60] Donald K. Fry sums up the view of many oralists when he argues that "[t]he traditional poet performs with diction and structures borrowed from others, within inherited patterns. Isolating the traditional poet within his own corpus smacks of Romantic and post-Romantic notions of poetry and unique genius."[61] But whether we focus on syntax and argue, as Daniel Donoghue does, that syntactic patterns and preferences reveal a great deal about the individual styles of poems and presumably about the authors who stand behind them or whether we focus on aesthetics and examine the ways in which larger narrative patterns are deployed in various poems, the corpus of Old English poetry evidences everywhere both the poets' debt to and dependence upon oral poetics *and* their individual talents.[62] The four poems attributed to Cynewulf, one of the few Anglo-Saxon poets whose name we know, provide clear evidence of just how much freedom Anglo-Saxon poets had.[63] Although generally accepted as Cynewulf's, in some ways these poems differ so much from one another that if it were not for their runic "signatures," we might not have realized that they were composed by the same poet.[64]

Oral poetics provides poets with the tectonics of poetic articulation, but the works of verbal art that they produce will of necessity be idiosyncratic because poets do not negotiate the oral tradition with anything approaching the same degree of accomplishment.[65] In selecting narrative patterns, choosing (or creating) formulaic expressions, and otherwise engaging their craft, poets cannot help but leave a highly individual stamp upon their poems.[66] For Anglo-Saxon poets, the tradition was not a static, fixed entity that they strove to preserve but a dynamic, ever-evolving one that they modified and shaped according to their tastes and experiences. Within its elastic borders they exercised their individual genius as they were best able to or as they best saw fit, as poets always do, and like all poets—oral or literate—they also reshaped *and* preserved the tradition in the very act of engaging it.[67] But no matter how completely traditional a poem's diction or story pattern may be or how deeply steeped in oral poetics the poet is, what he creates cannot help but be "an original work of art, based on a variety of traditional materials brought together in a new way."[68] As a way of uncovering the individuality of traditional Anglo-Saxon verbal art, let us consider the very different ways in which several poets present, negotiate, and manipulate two commonly occurring narrative elements that are rooted firmly in oral poetics: the cultural institution of the comitatus and the theme of the beasts of battle.

Comitatus: Ideal and Praxis

The Germanic ideal of the comitatus is well known to students of early Germanic culture, and the reciprocal code of conduct underlying this important social institution has been noted from at least the time of Tacitus,[69] who in *Germania* observes that "furthermore, it is shocking and disgraceful for all of one's life to have survived one's lord and left the battle" (64) [Iam uero

infame in omnem uitam ac probrosum superstitem principi suo ex acie reces-
sisse].[70] The ideal does not figure prominently in Old English prose—the
Chronicle entry for 755 stands as the only noteworthy occurrence of it of which
I am aware—but its singular appearance is important for its paradigmatic
modeling of the ideal. In the so-called Cynewulf and Cyneheard episode, the
small troop of men with King Cynewulf when he is slain continue to fight after
his death "oþ heo alle lægon butan anum bryttiscum gisle, 7 se swiþe gewun-
dad wæs" (13) [until they all lay dead except for one British hostage, and he
was severely wounded].[71] Later in the narrative, Cynewulf's men, seeking to
avenge their king, corner Cyneheard and resoundingly refuse his offer of
money and lands, proclaiming that "hi næfre his banan folgian noldon" (13)
[they would never serve (Cynewulf's) slayer]. In the ensuing attack, Cyneheard's men choose to die at their lord's feet, as did the ill-fated troop that earlier accompanied Cynewulf.

Although not well attested in the prose corpus, the ideal of the comitatus is an integral concept in Old English poetry,[72] one that appears in texts as
diverse as *Beowulf, Genesis A, Andreas, The Dream of the Rood,* and Riddles 93
and 95. It finds perhaps its most eloquent and moving expression in the late
and fragmentary *Battle of Maldon,* one of the few Old English poems to which
we can confidently supply a *terminus post quem.*[73] In *Maldon,* the ideal is vocal-
ized by several of the outnumbered and doomed English warriors, including
Leofsunu, who declares, "Ic þæt gehate,   þæt ic heonon nelle / fleon fotes
trym,   ac wille furðor gan, / wrecan on gewinne   minne winedrihten"
(246–48) [I promise that I hence will not flee the space of a foot, but I will go
further on to avenge my lord in battle].[74] And shortly thereafter, Bryhtwold
memorably announces:

> Hige sceal þe heardra,   heorte þe cenre,
> mod sceal þe mare,   þe ure mægen lytlað.
> Her lið ure ealdor   eall forheawen,
> god on greote.   A mæg gnornian
> se ðe nu fram þis wigplegan   wendan þenceð.
> Ic eom frod feores;   fram ic ne wille,
> ac ic me be healfe   minum hlaforde,
> be swa leofan men,   licgan þence.
>
> (312–19)

———

[The mind must be the stronger, the heart the braver, the spirit the greater as our might diminishes. Here lies our lord all hewn into pieces, the good man on the earth. He who thinks now to go from this battle-play will ever regret it. I am advanced in years; I will not depart hence, but I think to lie by the side of my lord, by the very dear man.]

The ideal of the comitatus as it is presented in these two texts reinforces culturally sanctioned behavior and feeling and is an important element in the *paideia* through which Old English poets gave voice to oral culture's social and moral apparatus, but it is not intended to reflect an actual cultural praxis. The ideal serves a clear metonymic function in Anglo-Saxon oral poetics, whether it appears in a demonstrably late battle poem or Chronicle poem meant to recall the glorious spirit of past warriors (perhaps to serve some present political need) or in a powerful and moving meditation on the cross upon which Christ was crucified. Invoking it enabled poets to tap into a networked system of signification, the core element of which was the reciprocal nature of the bond: the lord offered protection and rewards, while the nobles offered their loyalty and service in battle.[75] But while this ideal finds perfectly fluent expression in texts seemingly far removed from the martial world it serves to call forth,[76] its appearance in *Beowulf,* that most traditional of all Old English poems, is problematic and provides a clear example of how individual talent merges and at times collides with traditional oral poetics.

As is evident from the stress laid upon it at the poem's inception, the ideal of the comitatus is woven deeply into the fabric of *Beowulf* and forms an important part of the larger background against which all the action in the poem takes place. In the poem's first seventy-three lines, we encounter Scyld Scefing, a paradigmatically "god cyning" [good king]; 'Beowulf Scyldinga,' another model of proper kingly behavior whose conduct young men should emulate;[77] and finally, Hrothgar, in whose court the ideal is fully realized. Following both Scyld and 'Beowulf Scyldinga,' Hrothgar earns the epithet "god cyning" (863b), and he and his men experience the expected mutual benefits upon which the comitatus relationship is founded: his generosity and renown earn him their loyalty and "seo geogoð geweox, / magodriht micel" (66b–67a) [the young warriors matured into a great troop of warriors]. Grendel's brutal attacks on Heorot immediately test this bond's strength, but while those members of Hrothgar's troop who succumb to the monster fail to deter his nightly visits to Heorot, they epitomize the ideal of the comitatus: they die defending their lord and the hall that is the very "heart" of their society.[78]

But after laying such a strong traditional foundation for and so stressing the ideal of the comitatus in his poem's first hundred lines, the *Beowulf*-poet begins to problematize it when, following Grendel's second attack, he informs us that

> Þa wæs eaðfynde   þe him elles hwær
> gerumlicor   ræste [sohte]
> gesægd soðlice   sweotolan tacne
> bed æfter burum,   ða him gebeacnod wæs,
> healðegnes hete;   heold hyne syðþan
> fyr ond fæstor   se þæm feonde ætwand.
>   (138–43)

[Then it was easy to find the one who sought a resting place elsewhere, a bed among the outlying buildings, when the hall-thane's hate was made clear; he held himself afterwards farther off and more secure, the one who escaped the fiend.]

The Danish warriors, or apparently at least a goodly number of them, break the comitatus bond and desert Hrothgar in his moment of greatest need, despite his having fulfilled extraordinarily well his part of the bond. Unlike Leofsunu, Beowulf, and other paradigmatically heroic members of a comitatus, whose ritual boasts include the vow not to retreat a single step from their foes, no matter how hopeless their predicament,[79] some of the Danish warriors fail to live up to the demands of the ideal.[80]

This partial breakdown of the ideal prefigures the more complete and narratively more important one that occurs later in the poem. When Beowulf approaches the dragon in the poem's second half, he does so armed with a special, metal shield and accompanied by a select group of young, untried warriors whom he "on herge geceas / to ðyssum siðfate   sylfes willum" (2638b–39) [chose among the host for this adventure of his own free will]. Mindful of the reciprocal nature of the comitatus bond, he has honored them by giving them treasure and "garwigend   gode tealde" (2641) [considered (them) good warriors], as a good king ought. For their part, these men have promised, in the words of one of them,

> ussum hlaforde
> in biorsele,   ðe us ðas beagas geaf,

þæt we him ða guðgetawa   gyldan woldon,
gif him ðyslicu   þearf gelumpe,
helmas ond heard sweord.

(2634b–38a)

———

[to our lord in the beer-hall, to the one who gave us these rings, helmets, and hard swords, that we would repay him for the war-gear if such need as this befell him.]

But far from presenting a paradigmatic working out of the comitatus ideal during the dragon fight, the *Beowulf*-poet again problematizes and ultimately subverts it. The failure of Beowulf's troop is dramatically represented—they flee to the woods at the dragon's first appearance and emerge from its shelter only after Beowulf and the dragon lie dead—but by telling his comitatus that engaging the dragon "Nis . . . eower sið" (2532b) [is not your undertaking] and so relegating them to the role of mere spectators, Beowulf himself fractures the ideal's foundation. In the lines cited above, Wiglaf forcefully invokes the ideal in his unsuccessful attempt to rouse his comrades to battle by recounting their king's generosity and the comitatus's publicly articulated pledge of loyalty, but his courageousness is not enough to offset the double failure that the poet presents: Beowulf's culturally sanctioned reliance on his own might leads him to dismiss his men, and they prove incapable of responding to him in his greatest distress. Whether we allow the failure of the comitatus ideal to resonate within the larger pattern of social destruction with which the poem concludes or take it as an isolated microstructural element, we are, at the end of *Beowulf*, clearly worlds away from Bryhtwold's and Leofsunu's resolute articulations—and enactments—of it.

The comitatus ideal figures integrally in *Beowulf*,[81] but unlike the *Maldon*-poet, whose narrative powerfully affirms the ideal, the *Beowulf*-poet significantly alters its contours and in doing so probes some of the fundamental tensions that arise when a heroic ideal collides with human nature.

The Theme of the Beasts of Battle: Tradition and Innovation

The theme of the beasts of battle that occurs more than a dozen times in a variety of poems including the *Battle of Maldon, Elene, Beowulf,* and *Andreas,* has as its basic pattern "the mention of the wolf, eagle, and/or raven as beasts attendant on a scene of carnage."[82] As with the comitatus ideal, *Maldon* offers what appears to be a wholly traditional instantiation of the beasts of battle theme. Just before the main fight begins, we learn that

> wæs seo tid cumen
> þæt þær fæge men   feallan sceoldon.
> Þær wearð hream ahafen;   hremmas wundon,
> earn æses georn;   wæs on eorþan cyrm.
>
>   (104b–7)

[the time was come that the fated men had to fall. There was a din raised, ravens circled, the eagle eager for carrion. On the earth there was an uproar.]

In *Elene,* the theme occurs three times, each time in its traditional martial context. But while the theme's narrative situation is entirely traditional,[83] Cynewulf's employment of it departs from the traditional paradigm. By associating the beasts initially with the Huns (27b–30a), Cynewulf strongly signals the impending defeat of the outnumbered Romans because the beasts "generally follow the winning side *before* the battle and prey on the losers afterward."[84] But in finally aligning the raven with the soon-to-be victorious Romans (52b–53a), Cynewulf dispels whatever tension may have attended the beasts' earlier association with the Huns. Foley warns against placing too much weight upon a theme's narrative situation because doing so "places the major responsibility for conveying meaning on the textual, situation-specific side of the ledger,"[85] but Cynewulf's treatment of this theme, far from depending upon the idiosyncratic, conferred meaning characteristic of post-traditional texts, relies as fully upon the theme's traditional inherent meaning as its other, more paradigmatic instantiations as the poet exploits the tension he creates by providing the theme with multiple (although closely related and highly traditional) contexts.

     In *Beowulf,* the theme is divorced from a martial context and so departs from its traditional template, the contours of which may well derive "from a striking and well-attested fact, namely, that the corpses of warriors fallen in battle were subsequently eaten by ravens and wolves, if left exposed on the *wælstow*."[86] But though it is severed from a scene of imminent combat and hence from its traditional (and logical) foundation, the theme retains its affective impact. In signaling the inevitable martial defeat and physical suffering in store for the Geats, the appearance of the carrion animals at the conclusion of *Beowulf* powerfully and economically betokens the awful and tragic destiny that awaits the Geats.[87]

In *Andreas,* the theme is even further removed from its traditional paradigm. The wolf, eagle, and raven who, in varying combinations, often signal the theme's presence are replaced by a "hornfisc" (370b) [pike] and a "græga mæw" (371b) [gray gull]. And instead of a martial context (even one as vaguely invoked as at the end of *Beowulf*), the theme is embedded within a sea-voyage type-scene.[88] But these differences in the theme's constitution and the different context within which it is employed do not diminish its traditional referentiality or its affective dynamics. Andreas's men are terrified by the stormy seas and do not expect to reach land alive, and the pike and gull fully expect to feast on the retainers' corpses: the "hornfisc plegode, / glad geond garsecg,   ond se græga mæw / wælgifre wand" (370b–72a) [the pike played, glided through the sea and the gray sea-gull wheeled, eager to prey on the slaughtered]. *Wælgifre* explicitly links this occurrence of the theme to several others[89] and connects it to all of the theme's other occurrences through the animals' expectation of feasting on carrion. Perhaps the strongest testimony to the coherence of the theme's affective dynamics is that the slaughter often considered to be both a logical and necessary component of the theme need not even be present for it to function. And, as *Andreas* makes clear, the usual beasts also need not appear because rather than serving as a model that permits no (or only minor) deviation, the theme provides a map for interpreting a specific narrative multiform whose details exist only as a "pool of variants . . . none of which is the norm from which the others represent departures."[90] As this brief excursus through some of the passages in which the beasts of battle appear reveals, Anglo-Saxon poets could freely manipulate the theme by providing it with shifting, multiple contexts, as Cynewulf does, or by removing it from its traditional martial context, as the *Beowulf*-poet does, or by reaching beyond the borders of their tradition to draw upon skaldic motifs, as the *Exodus*-poet does,[91] while metonymically summoning the theme's inherited meaning to very different narrative presents.

The Survival of the Traditional Oral Register

From the perspective of a traditional oral poetics, there is little to distinguish the phraseology of *Beowulf* from that of the late Chronicle poem the

Death of Edgar, despite the wide acclaim accorded the former and the opprobrium usually heaped upon the latter.[92] Consider, for example, the five lines
from the *Death of Edgar* that Stanley B. Greenfield and Daniel G. Calder
single out as illustrating the poet's ill-advised habit of piling up "older poetic
formulas with little regard for specificity of meaning":[93]

> And þa wearð eac adræfed   deormod hæleð,
> Oslac, of earde   ofer yða gewealc,
> ofer ganotes bæð,   gamolfeax hæleð,
> wis and wordsnotor,   ofer wætera geðring,
> ofer hwæles eðel,   hama bereafod.[94]
>
> (24–28)

[And then was the brave-minded warrior, Oslac, also driven out from his
native land, over the rolling of the waves, over the gannet's bath, the gray-
haired warrior, wise and clever with words, over the expanse of waters,
over the whale's home, deprived of his homes.][95]

Despite its obvious lack of poetic sophistication and what Greenfield and
Calder rightly label its "overaccumulation of formulas,"[96] this passage conforms
metrically to the generally accepted rules of Old English poetry[97] and prosodi-
cally to the phraseological rules for Old English poetic articulation.[98] Of the
passage's ten half-lines, eight find parallels in a total of four other Old English
poems: *Beowulf,* the *Fight at Finnsburh, Andreas,* and the *Seafarer:*[99]

> deormod hæleð (*Death of Edgar,* 24b)
> deormod hæleþ (*Fight at Finnsburh,* 23a)
>
> Oslac, of earde (*Death of Edgar,* 25a)
> aldor of earde (*Beowulf,* 56a)
>
> ofer yða gewealc (*Death of Edgar,* 25b)
> ofer yða gewealc (*Beowulf,* 464a)
> ofer yða gewealc (*Andreas,* 259a)
>
> ofer ganotes bæþ (*Death of Edgar,* 26a)
> ofer ganotes bæð (*Beowulf,* 1861b)

gamolfeax hæleð (*Death of Edgar,* 26b)
gamolfeax ond guðrof (*Beowulf,* 608a)
gomelfeax gnornað (*Seafarer,* 92a)[100]

ofer wætera geðring (*Death of Edgar,* 27b)
þæt ic on holma geþring (*Beowulf,* 2132b)

ofer hwæles eðel (*Death of Edgar,* 28a)
ofer hwæles eðel (*Andreas,* 274b)
ofer hwæles eþel (*Seafarer,* 60a)

hama bereafod (*Death of Edgar,* 28b)
sinca bereafod (*Beowulf,* 2746b)
ealdre bereafod (*Beowulf,* 2825b)
golde bereafod (*Beowulf,* 3018b)

If we are attentive to both the immediate context of the phrases and the traditional contexts they invoke, and if we recall the importance of variation in Anglo-Saxon poetics,[101] the passage's appositives for the sea, as much as they may grate upon the ears of modern scholars, are nevertheless completely acceptable, traditional collocations whose affective dynamics remain intact and whose reception by their intended listening or reading audience may have been far more favorable than it has been by modern scholars. Despite being more closely aligned to the uninspired versifier who composed the *Meters of Boethius* than to the gifted poet who gave us *Beowulf,* the *Edgar*-poet nevertheless effectively and fluently deploys the specialized expressive economy of Anglo-Saxon oral poetics.

Resituating the poem's half-lines within the larger traditional contexts they invoke helps bring their highly traditional nature into sharper focus. Whether or not Oslac was truly the brave warrior the *Edgar*-poet represents him as, he was a powerful noble and as such would certainly warrant being labeled a "deormod hæleð" along with the "niþa heard" Danish warrior Sigeferth of the *Fight at Finnsburh* (21a). Although the phrase "of earde" in the *Death of Edgar* has a chiefly literal meaning, it resonates with *Beowulf* 56a, where the phrase metaphorically alludes not just to the physical exile but to the death of another powerful and successful noble, Scyld Scefing. "Ofer yða gewealc" evokes images of a turbulent voyage, both literally and metaphorically, and it is so used in *Beowulf*, where the poet employs it to describe Ecgtheow's difficult journey to Denmark as he attempts to escape a feud he has stirred up. The *Andreas*-poet similarly uses the phrase "ofer ȳða gewealc" to describe the voyage that Christ and his men have just completed from Mermedonia and also to prefigure the stormy trip Andreas and his men will shortly undertake. The final shared phrases "ofer ganotes bæþ" and "ofer hwæles eðel" summon forth, in *Edgar* and all of their other poetic occurrences, almost exclusively negative images of the sea's expanse.[102]

The three remaining phrases in the passage, despite having no direct parallels in the extant poetic corpus, further illustrate the highly traditional tectonics of *Edgar*'s prosody through their close connection, syntactically and affectively, with half-lines in *Beowulf* and the *Seafarer*. "Ofer wætera geþring" and "þæt ic on holma geþring" invoke the watery travails that Oslac will experience and that Beowulf already has. The adjective *gamolfeax* occurs only in the three instances cited above and twice refers to honored rulers beset by severe troubles: it is used of Oslac following his expulsion and of Hrothgar after he has suffered through twelve years of Grendel's depredations. Its third occurrence refers not to a ruler but to the speaker of the *Seafarer*, whose sufferings are metonymically linked to those of Oslac and Hrothgar. "Hama bereafod" has three close analogues in *Beowulf*, all of which point to extreme deprivation. Twice referring to the dead dragon, "sinca bereafod" and "ealdre bereafod" effectively point to what it has lost through the feud. The context of the third analogous phrase, "golde bereafod," is closest to the one in which it appears in *Edgar:* following Beowulf's death, the Geats will, before their tribe becomes extinct, suffer a period of brutal deprivation that the phrase effectively articulates. Oslac, as well, stripped of his homes and all that they stand for and provide him, faces a similarly bleak fate.[103]

Approaching the *Death of Edgar* from the perspective of a culture in which texts are easily reproducible and readily available to all and in which composition has become a highly intertextual endeavor, we may be tempted to explain the lexical and contextual resonances of its sea-voyage passage by relying upon an intertextual model of poetic composition and by suggesting that the *Edgar*-poet may have had arrayed at his elbow copies of *Beowulf*, *Andreas,* or any of the many other poems that *Edgar* either directly or indirectly echoes.[104] Nor would invoking such an intertextual model be completely inappropriate: a good deal of our extant Old English poetry undoubtedly derives from written sources, and the trope of the talking book, which explicitly acknowledges written authority and hence signals the intertextual foundations of the poems in which it is deployed, appears in a number of poems.[105] And at the beginning of *Fates of the Apostles,* Cynewulf models modern, intertextual scholarly behavior by depicting "himself as a weary wanderer who has collected from afar the material used in his song, as if he himself had visited the lands where the apostles had preached the gospel":[106]

> Hwæt! Ic þysne sang   siðgeomor fand
> on seocum sefan,   samnode wide
> hu þa æðelingas   ellen cyðdon,
> torhte ond tireadige.
>
> (1–4a)

———

[So! Sad and weary with travel, sick at heart, I devised this song, gathered it from far and wide, how the nobles, bright and glorious, showed forth their courage.]

Books and scenes of reading also figure prominently in many Old English poetic narratives. To cite just a few prominent examples, Constantine peruses sacred books in his attempt to learn the location of the crucifixion (*Elene,* 198–211), Daniel reads the "worda gerynu, / baswe bocstafas" (722b–23a) [the mysteries of words, in crimson letters] that an angel writes on a wall, the cannibalistic Mermedonians in *Andreas* keep written records that help them keep track of when they can devour their captives (134–37), Matthew is credited with being the first "godspell . . . / wordum writan   wundorcræfte" (12b–13) [to write the gospel in words with wondrous skill], and Hrothgar's gazing upon the ancient, giant hilt that Beowulf presents him after the fight with Grendel's mother (1687 ff.) may be construed as a scene of reading.[107]

But while certainly an important constituent of poetic articulation in Anglo-Saxon England, the intertextuality evident in Old English poetry does not parallel the intertextuality that (in)forms contemporary literary composition. We know so little regarding the provenance and circulation of Anglo-Saxon manuscripts and about who their readers might have been that arguments concerning a given author's knowledge of another text can rarely be other than highly speculative. Even when a medieval text's relation to its source is direct and (seemingly) unambiguous, the intertextuality it evidences is unlike that which exists between contemporary texts and the sources upon which they draw.[108] As we will see in chapter 3 when we consider the case of a twelfth-century poet who appears to have worked directly from a known, extant source, the source provides only the narrative contours of his poem, while its metrics, lexicon, and affective dynamics derive from traditional English oral poetics and owe little to the very different poetics of its French exemplar.

But what most distinguishes medieval from modern intertextuality is the extraordinary degree to which contemporary authors are conscious of the processes in which they engage and the extent to which that consciousness reflects (and is perhaps demanded by) their audience's horizon of expectations. There is, for example, no doubt that T. S. Eliot consciously drew upon Petronius's *Satyricon* for the epigraph to *The Waste Land*[109] or that he similarly drew upon the Anglican burial service in titling the poem's first section "The Burial of the Dead." These and all the other learned, often cryptic, intertextual signals with which *The Waste Land* fairly bursts are carefully selected and manipulated by Eliot and serve as important constituents of his own unique poem. As such, they both resonate within the system of signification he creates for the poem and open it to worlds of intertextual meanings and hermeneutic free play (which he could not possibly have foreseen) as readers navigate the poem, a feat that they accomplish with varying degrees of reliance upon the authorial or editorial footnotes that lay bare the poem's intertextual infrastructure. In contrast, the intertextuality of a poem such as the *Death of Edgar* presents very different problems, requires that we ask of it a very different set of questions, and finally prevents us from viewing the poet who created it as an Anglo-Saxon Eliot because, simply, whereas Eliot could have and most certainly did have access to copies of Petronius, the Bible, Baudelaire, Dante's *Divine Comedy,* and all the other texts that he explicitly cites in his authorial footnotes (not to mention those that he passes over silently and that are revealed in the poem's editorial footnotes), chances are remote that the *Edgar*-poet had access to all, or perhaps any, of the texts whose diction he echoes.

To understand the intertextuality of *Edgar,* and of Old English poetry in general, we need not speculate about what texts an author may have directly borrowed from, as intriguing and profitable as such speculation often is, but should rather focus on the highly specialized, traditional oral register that the poets employed, a register that ably survives the transposition from spoken to written composition because of its continuing ability to convey traditional, inherited meaning. Poets do not persist in employing the traditional oral register "after the advent of literacy and texts out of a misplaced antiquarianism or by default, but because, even in an increasingly textual environment, the 'how' developed over the ages still holds the key to worlds of meaning that are otherwise inaccessible."[110] The register retains its utility for both the composition and reception of poetry even though the mode of composition has radically changed and even though new channels of reception are opening up and gaining increasing cultural centrality.

For the complex of meaning that inheres in the traditional oral register to be imparted successfully, the horizon of expectations of both poet and audience, producer and recipient, must be shared. And the interpretive strategies that we bring to bear on works of verbal art that evidence this register must be fully attuned to that register's system of signification. It is to this question of *how* Anglo-Saxon oral poetics means that we will devote the remainder of this chapter.

Oral Poetics and a Lexical Simplex: (x-)*belgan*(-*mod*)

Jess Bessinger and Philip H. Smith, Jr.'s, *Concordance to the Anglo-Saxon Poetic Records* lists some seventeen occurrences of the term *gebelgan* [to swell with anger; become angry; DOE s.v.], more than half of which are found in *Beowulf,* and additionally lists fifteen occurrences of several related terms, *abolgen* (6x), *bolgenmod* (6x), *abelgan* (1x), *abelge* (1x), and *belgan* (1x). As part of a detailed analysis of *Beowulf*'s traditional phraseology, Foley argues that the value of a phrase such as "bad bolgenmod" (709a) must be chiefly metrical because it is difficult "to see how it could have been a functional element in the poet's and tradition's working idiom" since it lacks "a clear essential idea ('[x] enraged in heart' is hardly a well-defined concept) as well as consistent alliteration and syntax."[111] But even though (x-)*belgan*(-*mod*) is not identifiably part of a formulaic collocation or of a larger formulaic system, we can discover its specialized affective dynamics by placing it against the background of the traditional register, a register that "leads the listener [or reader] to construe some formulaic utterances with a context that automatically brings to mind associations likely to influence interpretation; and students of the subject know that the presence of a given oral-formulaic element may likewise lead the same listener [or reader] to expect certain things to occur or at least to be mentioned."[112] This point holds equally well when applied to a complex narrative structure, such as a type-scene, with its interdependent and interlocking narrative constituents, or to a single lexeme, such as (x-)*belgan*(-*mod*).

Of the thirty-two times (x-)*belgan*(-*mod*) occurs in Old English poetry, it appears in a slaughterous context twenty-five times.[113] The remaining seven occurrences are not so situated, but of these, five are closely linked with extreme physical or mental suffering. For example, the dispossessed rulers of *Meters of Boethius* 25 "gebolgene weorðað, . . . mid ðæm swiðan welme / hatheortnesse" (45–47a) [become swollen with the strong surging of rage], and Solomon uses the lexeme negatively in *Solomon and Saturn* to connect Saturn with his "bittre cynnes" [bitter race]: "Ne sceall ic ðe hwæðre, broðor, abelgan" (330a) [nor will I, brother, make you swollen with anger].[114]

The ability of (x-)*belgan*(-*mod*) to signal impending slaughter is clearly evident in *Beowulf,* where all nine occurrences of the simplex are securely situated within slaughterous contexts. Given their narrative uniformity, it is tempting to view these occurrences paradigmatically, but the likelihood that our extant Old English poetry represents only a fraction of all the poetry produced in Anglo-Saxon England prevents us from knowing with any certainty whether the *Beowulf*-poet's handling of this simplex represents the most highly traditional usage of the term or whether it is yet another of his brilliant innovations.[115] But whether his use of (x-)*belgan*(-*mod*) is highly traditional or highly innovative or falls somewhere in between, the consistency with which he handles it and its clear affective dynamics provide a useful point of departure for a consideration of the simplex's traditional functions.

In *Beowulf,* the first occurrences of the simplex reveal a great deal about its affective dynamics and establish a standard for its employment from which the poet never deviates, forming as they do a crucial strand of the highly charged and affectively significant rhetoric of Grendel's approach to Heorot.[116] The simplex initially occurs at line 709a and describes the mental state of Beowulf, who "wæccende   wraþum on andan / bad bolgenmod   beadwa geþinges" (708–9) [lying awake in anger for the foe, with heart swollen in anger, awaited the result of the battle]. From a strictly literate poetics, this depiction of the hero may appear to be one of the poem's more notable narrative cruces because Beowulf has, simply, no reason to be so swollen with anger at this point: the Danes and not the Geats have suffered tremendously at Grendel's hands. Neither Beowulf's reception by nor treatment in the Danish court could have led him to such a state. Even Unferth, who in his role as "Everydane" voices the real, if unarticulated, collective doubts that have arisen in Heorot following Beowulf's brash announcement that he "Hroðgar mæg / þurh rumne sefan   ræd gelæran, / hu he frod ond god   feond oferswyðeþ / . . . ond þa cearwylmas colran wurðaþ" (277b–82) [may through magnanimity teach Hrothgar a remedy, how he, wise and good, may overpower the fiend . . . and how those surging cares may become cooler], casts little shadow over Beowulf's reception in Denmark.[117] In addition, the flyting that Beowulf and Unferth engage in concludes on an unambiguously positive note: Hrothgar is "on salum" (607a) [in joy], the hall resounds with "hæleþa hleahtor" (611a) [the laughter of warriors], and Unferth himself will shortly loan Beowulf Hrunting, the precious, battle-tried sword the Geat will carry with him when he ventures under the mere in search of Grendel's mother.

By shifting our perspective and viewing (x-)*belgan*(-*mod*) from the perspective of an oral poetics, we discover that the simplex does not solely describe Beowulf's state of mind in the moments preceding his fight with Grendel but imbues the narrative present with the accumulated associative weight of the simplex's traditional meaning. In informing us that Beowulf "bad bolgenmod," the surface of the narrative gives way as the poet signals (to an audience properly attuned to the idiom) that we have now entered a context in which slaughter is imminent. Attempts to discover the narrative logic (in the New Critical sense of the term) for Beowulf's being swollen with rage while awaiting Grendel's attack have largely been frustrated because they stem from a poetics alien to that of the text. The affective dynamics of Beowulf's rage, and not its narrative logic, is crucial to the scene. Beowulf need not become *gebolgen* in order to kill someone or something. On several occasions he dispatches monstrous and human foes without becoming enraged, but when (x-)*belgan*(-*mod*) does appear in the narrative, it clearly and metonymically signals the approach of an impending slaughter.

As happens elsewhere in the poem, (x-)*belgan*(-*mod*), while functioning in line 709a as a discrete element in the scene's and the poems affective dynamics, is also part of a doublet. Beowulf's anger is both recalled by and counterpointed to the rage that engulfs Grendel as he stands on the threshold of Heorot: "onbræd þa bealohydig,   ða (he ge)bolgen wæs, / recedes muþan" (723–24a) [swollen with anger, the hostile one then tore open the hall's door]. Even though the poet has just used the relatively rare (x-)*belgan*(-*mod*) some dozen lines earlier, both the simplex's narrative deployment and its crucial role in the scene's affective dynamics militate against seeing it as a simple repetition or the result of lexical clustering.

Grendel's physical journey toward Heorot culminates when he crashes open the "Duru . . . fyrbendum fæst" (721b–22a) [door . . . made fast with fireforged bands] and stands framed in the hall's mouth, but the tension of his approach does not reach its zenith in the moment when he physically sets foot in Heorot (725) or in the description of the "leoht unfæger" (727b) [unfair light] emanating from his eyes. Awful as these details are, the terror of Grendel's approach reaches its peak in the rare glimpse the poet allows us into Grendel's monstrous psyche. In informing us that Grendel, too, is *gebolgen,* the poet employs a narrative strategy that simultaneously reinforces those expectations of slaughter already activated by the simplex's earlier occurrence while also dramatically altering those expectations. Earlier, the monster had been the object of the man's slaughterous anger, but now humans become the object of his equally terrible rage. It is this latter expectation of human slaughter that the poem quickly fulfills in terrifying and graphic detail because immediately after Grendel crosses the hall's threshold he

> . . . gefeng hraðe   forman siðe
> slæpendne rinc,   slat unwearnum,
> bat banlocan,   blod edrum dranc,
> synsnædum swealh;   sona hæfde
> unlyfigendes   eal gefeormod,
> fet ond folma.
>
> (740–45a)

———

[seized suddenly a sleeping man at the earliest opportunity, tore him greedily, bit his joints, drank the blood in streams, swallowed huge morsels; soon he had entirely devoured the unliving one, the feet and hands.]

Although delayed until line 758 ff., the expected slaughter of the monster that figures prominently earlier in the scene begins on an equally graphic note: "Lic-sar gebad / atol æglæca;   him on eaxle wearð / syndolh sweotol,   seonowe onsprungon, / burston banlocan" (815b–18a) [He experienced bodily pain, the terrible awe-inspiring one; on his shoulder was manifest a very great wound, the sinews sprung apart, the joints burst asunder]. Grendel escapes the ignominy of dying in Heorot, but the nature of his wound and the traditional referentiality of (x-)*belgan*(-*mod*) signal the inevitability of his violent death.

The simplex figures prominently in the local affective dynamics of Grendel's arrival at Heorot and in the subsequent fight in the hall, but its function is not limited either to alerting the audience to the imminence of slaughter or to heightening the scene's tension. It also establishes an important and highly problematic link between Beowulf and Grendel (just at it will later serve to link Beowulf and the dragon), one that pointedly calls into question Beowulf's humanity by revealing a suggestive and troubling glimpse of his monstrosity.[118] Beowulf succeeds in his fight with Grendel only because he strips himself of society's trappings (his armor) and enters the brutal, bestial, and inarticulate world Grendel occupies. The romanticism of Rockwell Kent's well known pictorial depiction notwithstanding,[119] the Beowulf who, at the fight's conclusion, stands (in the door?), bruised, perhaps naked, covered in gore, mutely clutching the arm and shoulder that he has just wrenched off his foe, presents a disturbing picture of humanity's proximity to the monstrous.

In the dragon episode, (x-)*belgan*(-*mod*) appears four times, referring to Beowulf and the dragon twice each. The simplex initially occurs at the end of the scene in which the poet announces the dragon's presence and recounts the theft of a single cup from its hoard (2210b–20; at 2220b) and is repeated in the more detailed account of the theft and the dragon's reaction that follows at 2283b ff. After the dragon learns that a cup has been stolen, it waits "earfoðlice, oð ðæt æfen cwom; / wæs ða gebolgen   beorges hyrde / wolde se laða   lige forgyldan / drincfæt dyre" (2303–6) [wretchedly until evening came; then the barrow's guardian was swollen with anger and the hateful one would repay (the theft) of the precious cup with fire]. The (usually graphic) slaughter that is the expected corollary of (x-)*belgan*(-*mod*) seems absent in this instance, being perhaps at best implicit in the poet's comment that once the dragon emerged from its barrow, it was easy to see "hu se guðsceaða   Geata leode / hatode ond hynde" (2318–19a) [how the destroyer hated and harmed the Geatish people]. But while the people's horror is several times mentioned, there is no explicit account of slaughter associated with the dragon. What we encounter here is not a breakdown of the pattern in which (x-)*belgan*(-*mod*) signals an impending slaughter but a subtle refining of it. Rather than being completed by the expected graphic, visceral account of slaughter, the traditional paradigm is in this case filled out by the terrifying revelation that "no ðær aht cwices / lað lyftfloga   læfan wolde" (2314b–15b) [the hateful sky-flier would not leave anything at all alive there]. As this instance bears out, the simplex need not be embedded in an explicit account of slaughter for it to summon forth metonymically the affective dynamics its traditional context affords it. The final time (x-)*belgan*(-*mod*) occurs in *Beowulf,* it is once again explicitly linked with death. At line 2401b it follows the poet's assertion that Beowulf had survived many dangerous conflicts "oð ðone anne dæg, / þa he wið þam wyrme   gewegan sceolde" (2399b–2400) [until that one day when he had fight against the worm], and at line 2550b Beowulf initiates his gory and fatal encounter with the dragon by standing before its cave letting "ða of breostum,   ða he gebolgen wæs, / . . . word ut faran" (2550–51) [then from his breast, when he was swollen with anger / . . . words journey out].

In the Christian poems in which it appears, (x-)*belgan*(-*mod*) retains its traditional affective contours, even though the link between the simplex and slaughter is more elastic than it is in *Beowulf*. In *Juliana, gebelgan* is first used to describe Eleusius's fury at having his advances rejected by Juliana, and it occurs in a context that only faintly invokes slaughter. Both Eleusius and Affricanus are described as "hildeþremman" (64a) [warriors] who bear "garas" (63b) [spears] when they meet, and the specter of unspecified tortures that may arise from Eleusius's "hæstne nið" (56a) [violent enmity] hangs over Juliana. The second occurrence of the simplex is situated in a more explicit, but inverted and still unfulfilled, slaughterous context. Affricanus, after learning of Juliana's rejection of Eleusius, consigns her to destruction or death, and he returns to Juliana "yrre gebolgen" (90b) [enraged, swollen with anger]. Both men threaten her with torture before Eleusius decides that she is to be hung from a gallows by her hair, beaten for six hours, and then returned to her cell (227b–33a). Although this episode does not culminate in slaughter, the traditional affective dynamics of the simplex is invoked in the graphic physical punishment Juliana endures. The final occurrence of the simplex coincides with the onset of Juliana's final tortures and climaxes in the slaughter that the simplex has signaled throughout the poem: as she is thrust into a vat of boiling lead, the vat explodes and severely scorches, perhaps killing, seventy-five of the heathens who have gathered to watch her be tortured. Juliana emerges unscathed as a result of divine intervention, but the traditional pattern is explicitly fulfilled soon thereafter when her soul is separated from her body "þurh sweordslege" (671a) [through a sword-stroke].

In *Andreas*, the simplex occurs twice, and even though slaughter is absent both times, the simplex's affective dynamics emerges clearly in and is central to the scenes in which it appears. In its first occurrence, the mob of Mermedonians is described more as a troop of warriors preparing for battle than as a throng of cannibals going to select their dinner from a group of defenseless captives: "Duguð samnade, / hæðne heldfrecan,   heapum þrungon, / (guðsearo gullon,   garas hrysedon)" (125b–27) [The troop assembled, the heathen warriors thronged in great numbers (armor clanged, spears shook)]. The further observation that they were "bolgenmode,   under bordhreoðan" (128) [swollen with rage under the cover of shields] explicitly summons the traditional expectations of slaughter. No slaughter occurs, but the references to the Mermedonians being "wælgrædige" (135a) [greedy for the slain] and "wæl-wulfas" (149a) [slaughter wolves], when coupled with the graphic accounts of what they plan to do to their victims effectively substitute for it within the scene's affective dynamics:

> . . . hie banhringas   abrecan þohton,
> lungre tolysan   lic ond sawle,
> ond þonne todælan   duguðe and geoguðe,
> werum to wiste   ond to wilþege,
> fæges flæschoman.
>
> (150–54a)

———

[they thought to break his joints, quickly separate body and soul, and then divide among the experienced and inexperienced warriors, for the men as food and as a pleasant feast, the flesh of the one doomed to die.]

Such violent practices are the norm for the Mermedonians, who regularly "tobrugdon   blodigum ceaflum / fira flæschoman" (159–60a) [tore apart with bloody jaws the bodies of men].

The second occurrence of the simplex follows a similar pattern as Andrew is seized by a "werod unmæte" (1219b) [countless troop] of armed warriors who are "bolgenmode" (1221a). In this instance, the graphic account of the wounds he receives at the Mermedonians' hands substitutes for slaughter: "Wæs þæs halgan lic / sarbennum soden,   swate bestemed, / banhus abrocen. Blod yðum weoll, / haton heolfre" (1238b–41a) [The saint's body was tormented with wounds, soaked in blood, his bone-house shattered; blood welled in waves of hot gore]. The differences between the nonslaughterous account in *Andreas* and the slaughterous ones in *Beowulf* collapse in this instance because the final two half-lines find echoes (the former loosely and the latter precisely) in the lines that provide positive evidence of Grendel's destruction:[120] "Ðær wæs on blode   brim weal-lende, / atol yða geswing   eal gemenged, / haton heolfre,   heorodreore weol" (*Beowulf,* 847–49) [There the water was boiling with blood, the terrible surging of waves all mixed with hot gore, sword-blood]. Although a graphic account of slaughter is the traditional event usually signaled by the simplex (x-)*belgan(-mod)*, these examples from *Andreas* and the earlier one from *Beowulf* witness that the simplex admits other complements *that share the same*

affective dynamics, as we should expect in an expressive economy character-
ized not by fixity but by variation within limits.

Although the traditional referentiality of (x-)*belgan*(-*mod*) enables it to
resonate on an extratextual level with "an institutionalized, inherent meaning
of appreciable scope"[121] and metonymically to summon traditional, associative
meaning to the narrative present, not all simplices are similarly freighted with
traditional meaning. As Greenfield notes, adding the adverb *þa* [then, when] to
a verb of motion such as *gewat* [departed], *com* [came], or *hwearf* [turned]
does not render "the combination a formula"[122] any more than a collocation of
the type "X muþ," in which the syntactic and semantic values of the simplex
designated by X vary widely, constitutes a formulaic system.[123] The same holds
for the affective dynamics of simplices; not all will resonate within the traditional idiom to the same degree. Some, like (x-)*belgan*(-*mod*), *hwæt* (when
clustered with the other elements of the "hwæt paradigm"), and noun-epithet
phrases, will carry a great deal of significative and/or affective weight, while
others will not. For example, even though *irre* [anger, wrath] is related semantically to (x-)*belgan*(-*mod*), its metonymic contours are so broad as to resist
any but the loosest classification because it occurs so frequently and in widely
divergent contexts. In contrast, (x-)*belgan*(-*mod*) occurs with far less frequency
and functions almost exclusively within a sharply circumscribed context, one
in which explicit or implicit slaughter figures prominently.[124] From considering how oral poetics resonates within and beyond a single lexeme, we will now
explore how this expressive economy knits together into a narrative whole of
tremendous power the components of Beowulf's fight with the dragon.

Oral Poetics and a Narrative Complex: Beowulf's Fight with the Dragon

The dragon episode in *Beowulf* occupies fully the final third of the poem,
and its position within the canon of Old English poetry has been secure ever
since J. R. R. Tolkien delivered his 1936 Gollancz Memorial Lecture, "*Beowulf:
The Monsters, and the Critics.*" It continues to excite considerable interest
among both those newly acquainted with the poem and those who have long
read and reread it. But while serving as the locus for a great many critical studies,[125] the dragon episode's traditional dimension has gone, until recently,
largely unnoticed.[126] The lexical and prosodic tectonics of the dragon fight are
of a piece with the rest of the highly traditional poem it concludes, but the

episode's narrative singularity has tended to occlude the equally traditional nature of its story pattern.

From Parry's classic definition of a formula as "an expression regularly used, under the same metrical conditions, to express an essential idea"[127] to Lord's assertion that "we cannot call an action or situation or description in [traditional oral] poetry a theme unless we find it used at least twice,"[128] repetition, especially exact repetition, has been one of the chief criteria for identifying the small and large constituents of oral poetics. But since Anglo-Saxon oral poetics is not a limited, limiting, or mechanistic system of articulation and signification but a supple, responsive, and fluid one, the investigation of traditional structures need not be confined to those occasions when they exist in several closely related instantiations but may be profitably extended to a uniquely occurring element or pattern as well. Not all aspects of oral poetics will respond equally well to such an approach. When exploring the traditionality of lexemes, for example, having comparands is essential because a uniquely occurring word or compound can shed only limited light on its traditional referentiality and, in some cases, none at all. To take one example, we can determine little about the traditionality of the compound *swatswaðu* [bloody-track]. Even though it is formed of two fairly common elements, because it occurs only once in the entire corpus of Old English verse and prose at line 2946a of *Beowulf*, its status as a *hapax legomenon* effectively thwarts all efforts to reinvest it with whatever extratextual and extrasituational referentiality it may have possessed. We can recover the logic underlying the compound—wounded participants in battle may well leave behind them a readily apprehensible bloody track—and we can easily project the compound into more richly associative literal and metaphorical contexts, but we simply cannot resituate it with any degree of certainty within the framework of Anglo-Saxon oral poetics. In this instance, what evidence there is concerning *swatswaðu* suggests not its traditional nature, but its uniqueness. Because *swat* only rarely combines as the first element of a compound,[129] *swatswaðu* should perhaps best be seen as an element of the *Beowulf*-poet's idiolect rather than of the traditional idiom.

Even though exact repetition has never been so crucial to the identification of traditional thematics as it has been to the identification of formulaic diction,[130] the principle of multiple attestations has been, and, as a result, the traditional characteristics of narrative structures that have no comparands have remained largely unexplored. But while we may be unable to locate a uniquely occurring lexeme's place in the traditional idiom with any real confidence, such is not the case with uniquely occurring themes because the constellation of elements that constitute traditional thematics provides us with signals that help us situate even uniquely occurring themes and story patterns within the tradition's oral poetics and that, further, help direct their reception.

In considering the oral poetics that underlies and (in)forms the unique dragon episode in *Beowulf,* we will attempt to recover its traditional foundations by reading the episode from the inside out. Given the highly metonymic nature of traditional oral poetics, focusing on the microstructural affective dynamics of the situation- and text-specific narrative will enable us to glimpse the episode's traditional macrostructural dynamics, even though "of all the innumerable dragon-stories extant, there is probably not one that we can declare to be really identical with *Beowulf.*"[131] Attuning ourselves to the traditional dynamics of the dragon episode will not enable us to classify it absolutely as an example of a traditional multiform—to do so we would need to have at least one and perhaps several comparands[132]—and we must ever remain open to the possibility that it is a product of the *Beowulf*-poet's unique genius, but examining the episode's oral poetics may enable us to resituate it more fully within its ever-immanent tradition, something that would allow us to hear once again some of the traditional resonances of this singular, complex story pattern that brings the poem to such a powerful and, I would argue, traditional close.

In one of the first studies to probe the traditional contours of the dragon episode, Foley demonstrates that the three monstrous encounters that have long been seen as constituting the poem's narrative spine conform to what he labels the Battle with the Monster story pattern.[133] But while the dragon episode clearly follows this pattern, its more complex affective dynamics and greater narrative resonance distance it from the fights with Grendel and Grendel's mother and signal its related but discrete story pattern. Before examining the microstructural level of the dragon episode and its network of highly traditional narrative elements, we turn to the large narrative contexts within which each of the three monster fights occurs because it is on this level that evidence of the dragon fight's traditional story pattern begins to emerge.

Beowulf's Fight with the Dragon: The Contextual Macrostructure

Despite the monstrous presence of Grendel, his mother, and the other marvelous elements that attend Beowulf's two fights in Denmark, they are firmly grounded within the carefully circumscribed feud ethos so central to the poem and perhaps to early Germanic life.[134] From the outset, Grendel's actions against the Danes are viewed as violations of the Christian and social ethoi with which the poem's audience were familiar. His monstrous ancestry, unexplained hatred of the joyful human sounds emanating from the hall, and refusal to settle blood feuds in the socially prescribed manner by paying wergild all fix Grendel as an outcast from the society of God and man from the moment he first appears in the poem. As the poet stresses in laying bare Grendel's descent from Cain, Grendel is by birth opposed to the Christian God who orders the Anglo-Saxon world. And as a monster he is by definition exiled from and opposed to the world of *humanitas*.[135]

The feud ethos also contextualizes the actions of Grendel's mother. Her seizing of only one man, coupled with what may be her conscious and symbolic placing of his head on the "enge anpaðas" (1410a) [narrow paths] leading to her mere, strongly indicates that she attacks Heorot solely to avenge her son's death, a point the poet makes explicit: she "wolde hyre mæg wrecan / ge feor hafað fæhðe gestæled" (1339b–40) [would her kinsman avenge and moreover has carried forth the feud]. Her attack seems more a duty-bound and socially circumscribed attempt to redress the injury done her son than an instinctual and uncontrolled outburst. Through it she shifts the terms of the feud and further aligns them with human actions. What had before been broadly construed as a feud between humans and nonhumans suddenly takes on a wholly human character in her desire to exact vengeance and gain restitution for the death of her (monstrous) son. For both of Beowulf's fights in Denmark, the threats posed to Danish society and the course of the hero's response are mapped out and reaffirmed through contextual signals. For the poem's intended audience, the terms of the feuds are clear and familiar.

In sharp contrast to the two monster fights that precede it, the dragon episode, lacking as it does the Christian and social contexts that securely situate the fights in Denmark within a readily apprehensible context, thrusts the narrative onto decidedly difficult ground.[136] That some sort of feud is being invoked is clear, as are the roles and affiliations of those who participate in it. But this feud, predicated as it is upon a theft and involving a dragon and not some foe more closely associated with the human world, orients the audience neither sharply nor unproblematically. That someone enters the dragon's barrow and removes a cup is beyond dispute, but the significance of this theft remains clouded, and the text offers little clarification of the thief's shadowy nature or motivation.[137] The poor state of folio 182r (formerly 179r)[138] contributes mightily to the problem because all that can be read of the word variously emended to *þegn*, *þeow*, or as Theodore M. Andersson suggests, *þeof*, is its initial *þ*.[139] But even if this philological crux were to be indisputably settled, the larger issue of securely contextualizing this act of thievery would remain.[140]

Although the limited size of the extant poetic corpus and our inability to know what has been irrecoverably lost inevitably undermine any sort of statistical argument, the relative infrequency and demonstrable narrative marginality of thefts in Old English poetry suggest that the dragon fight is from its outset not securely contextualized for the audience. When Grendel and then his mother attack Heorot, their actions are situated in a well-known and familiar traditional context, one that helps determine how their actions will be received. In contrast, because the significance of the theft, the precise status of the one who takes the cup, and the nature of the theft remain notoriously opaque,[141] the dragon episode decenters the audience by evoking an unusual, perhaps nontraditional, context for receiving it.

Beowulf's Fight with the Dragon: The Oral Poetic Microstructure

Although the dragon episode's contextual macrostructure finds no parallel in Old English prose or verse, the episode's oral poetics provides clear signals that shape the narrative and direct the audience's response to it.[142] The dragon's deliberately vague description, Beowulf's decision to fight the monster alone, and the failure of Beowulf's sword, Nægling, constitute the story pattern's most salient affective elements. They are all highly traditional and have all been encountered earlier in the text, but only in the thematics of the dragon fight do they cohere into a tightly knit narrative whole.

The brief and cryptic description of the dragon—we learn only that it is "grimly terrible in its variegated colors" (3041a) [grimlic gry(refah)] and "spews flames" (2312b) [gledum spiwan]—recalls the earlier description (or to be more precise, nondescription) of Grendel and allows us to see that the affective principle underlying their presentations is the same. In each instance, the poet provides little concrete detail, and the audience must actively participate in the narrative process (filling in what in Iserian terms would be a significant gap of indeterminacy) by fleshing out the creatures in idiosyncratic and terrifying detail.[143] But the similarity between the two monsters ends here. Grendel undergoes a steady process of familiarization as the narrative progresses, one in which we learn not only his name but also his habits (and thus how to avoid death at his hands), his physical capacity (he seizes thirty men at a time), and his unvarying destination and time of arrival (Heorot, on a nightly basis).[144] Further, he lives within some sort of recognizable (if monstrous) society with his mother, who herself inhabits a fire-lit hall containing war gear that may serve a decorative function (1557a). The familiarization of Grendel that begins with the revelation of his name culminates when his body parts, first his arm and shoulder and then his head, are publicly displayed in the hall. These ritual displays of the monster's dismembered body reduce what was once an unknowable, indefinable terror to a trophy, a harmless curiosity that may continue indefinitely to elicit wonder and awe but that has nevertheless been stripped of its power to terrify.[145]

The dragon, in contrast, remains unknown and unknowable even in death. The Geats are able to take its measure once it lies dead on the headlands near its barrow, but they make no attempt to assert their community's collective power over the monstrous other by gathering to wonder at it. Rather, they hurriedly and unceremoniously dump its carcass into the sea, actions that contrast sharply with the ritualistic celebrations that attend the displaying of Grendel's arm and head. The failure to reduce the dragon to a trophy may ultimately stem from the truly unfathomable nature of the monster. It remains, even in death, so far outside the realm of human comprehension that the Geats do not even attempt to bring it—or any part of it—within their society's compass.

The dragon itself serves further to decenter the audience. Whereas the Grendelkin's attacks were highly focused (in Grendel's case predictably so), the dragon attacks widely and indiscriminately: "Ða se gæst ongan   gledum spiwan, / beorht hofu bærnan—   byrneleoma stod / eldum on andan" (2312–14a) [then the evil spirit began to spew flames, burn bright dwellings; the gleam of fire shone forth to the horror of men]. That its awful and immeasurable anger is not directed at any specific person or object but is to a large degree random adds greatly to the almost overwhelming air of indeterminacy associated with the dragon. Beowulf's hall is burnt, not because it has a special significance for the attacker, but simply because it happens to be in the dragon's path.[146] The dragon's power cannot easily be measured by human standards, and its aim is truly chilling in its scope. It does not just seek control of one hall during the night, but in the countryside surrounding its barrow it "no ðær aht cwices / . . . læfan wolde" (2314b–15b) [would not leave anything alive there]. Whereas Grendel mutely and perversely plays at being a "healðegn" (142a) [hall-retainer] and hence invokes an inverted and disturbing but recognizable and ultimately rectifiable paradigm of human power, the dragon remains "implacably dedicated to the obliteration of all history,"[147] of all that is human.

Within the dragon episode, Beowulf's comments at lines 2532b–35a serve to counterbalance the indeterminacy that marks the scene's beginning and to orient the audience by focusing on the figure of the solitary hero, the second major component of the dragon episode's traditional narrative pattern.[148] In telling his retainers, "Nis þæt eower sið, / ne gemet mannes,   nefn(e) min anes, / þæt he wið aglæcean   eofoðo dæle, / eorlscype efne" (2532b–35a) [This is not your venture, nor is it fitting for any man except me alone that he should spend his strength against the awe-inspiring one, perform a heroic deed], Beowulf offers for the third time a powerful articulation of the poem's familiar heroic ethos, one that stresses the importance of individual accomplishment within the collective martial endeavor. Earlier in the poem, he voiced a similar sentiment before facing Grendel (424b–26a). Although he does not explicitly make a comparable announcement before fighting Grendel's mother, stating only, "ic me mid Hruntinge / dom gewyrce" (1490b–91a) [I will achieve glory with Hrunting], he subtly and forcefully underscores that he, alone, will venture into the mere through the successive positioning of the first-person pronoun and the reflexive (perhaps pleonastic) dative pronoun.[149] In all three monster fights, Beowulf magnifies the danger of his undertaking and increases the terror and admiration that the episode elicits in the audience by engaging the foe alone.

But unlike his earlier boasting speeches, Beowulf's remarks in the dragon episode do not align themselves neatly along the poem's narrative axis.[150] Indeed, in its immediate narrative context, the announcement that he will fight the dragon alone is most disturbing. His approach to the battle indicates that he clearly perceives the dragon to be a foe unlike any he has ever faced. He fulfills the traditional motif of arming before a conflict and even carries a specially made iron shield instead of the more usual wooden one:

Heht him þa gewyrcean   wigendra hleo
eallirenne,   eorla dryhten,
wigbord wrætlic;   wisse he gearwe,
þæt him holtwudu   he(lpan) ne meahte,
lind wið lige.

(2337–41a)

———

[Then the protector of warriors, the lord of the earls, commanded a wonderful shield to be made for him; he knew well that forest-wood might not help him, linden wood against flame.]

Yet immediately following this display of prudence, he paradoxically refuses to allow his men to assist him in what he senses will be his most difficult battle. Were we to view this moment strictly from the situation-specific perspective of the poem's narrative, we might be tempted to cite it as an example of Beowulf's *ignorantia*,[151] especially in light of his subsequent fantastic statement that he wishes he could fight the dragon bare-handed as he did Grendel: "Nolde ic sweord beran, / wæpen to wyrme,   gif ic wiste hu / wið ðam aglæcan   elles meahte / gylpe wiðgripan,   swa ic gio wið Grendle dyde" (2518b–21) [I would not bear sword, a weapon, to the worm, if I knew how against the awe-inspiring one else I might fight according to my boast, as I formerly did against Grendel]. He immediately offers a reassuringly accurate assessment of the situation confronting him— "ic ðær heaðufyres   hates wene, / [o]reðes ond attres;   forðon ic me on hafu / bord ond byrnan" (2522–24a) [I expect there hot battle-fire, steam and poison; therefore I have on me shield and coat of mail]—but the inappropriateness of his former statement lingers. At the end of his long and storied life, Beowulf seems to grasp only imperfectly what may well be one of the basic lessons of martial life, namely that "[h]eroic existence is a series of increasingly difficult skirmishes in the one long battle."[152] Commissioning the metal shield is Beowulf's sole concession to the dragon's enormous power and his own advanced age and necessarily diminished physical capacity. In all other regards he behaves as if he were going to face Grendel, Grendel's mother, or some other foe whose power is more closely matched to his.

We can begin to align the episode's narrative and traditional axes by recognizing that Beowulf's decision to fight alone is central to the episode's affective dynamics. When the greatest hero alive, despite his advanced age and diminished physical capacities, publicly announces his resolve to face alone another severe, monstrous threat to a kingdom, as he had successfully done in his youth, the audience, privileged in their knowledge of the dragon's power and intentions and acutely aware of Beowulf's age and position within the kingdom, find themselves suspended between powerful and conflicting emotions. Beowulf's decision increases the audience's fear and admiration exponentially as their desire to have the dragon's threat eradicated clashes with their attachment to and perhaps even identification with Beowulf, especially since the hero's death in the approaching battle has been forecast from the scene's outset.[153]

In contrast to his speeches in the dragon episode, the public and more formally explicit *beot* [formal vow] that Beowulf makes in Denmark must be read in light of his youth and relative inexperience. He is a warrior in whom, early on at least, *fortitudo* far outweighs *sapientia*. Arriving at the Danish court eager to make a name for himself, he valiantly (if perhaps foolishly) vows publicly to engage single-handedly and unarmed the monster that has been ravaging Heorot for the last twelve years, a decision that derives unproblematically from the poem's traditional heroic ethos. Ridding Denmark of Grendel would certainly enhance the reputation of the fledgling monster-fighter, and destroying the awful "sceadugenga" (703a) [shadow-goer] unarmed and unassisted would bring him even greater glory. Beowulf responds swiftly—almost as a matter of reflex—to the challenge Hrothgar lays at his feet following the attack of Grendel's mother for very similar reasons.[154]

The final constituent of the dragon episode's narrative pattern is the failure of Beowulf's sword Nægling. Falling within the ambience of the "fallible sword motif" identified by Thomas Garbáty, Nægling's failure is often attributed to the hero's being too powerful for manmade weapons, a view that the *Beowulf*-poet himself endorses when he offers the unusually (for him) explanatory comment that it

> gifeðe ne wæs
> þæt him irenna   ecge mihton
> helpan æt hilde;   wæs sio hond to strong,
> se ðe meca gehwane   mine gefræge
> swenge ofersohte,   þonne he to sæcce bær
> wæpen wund[r]um heard; . . .
>
> (2682b–87a)

[was not given that iron edges might help him in battle; the hand was too strong, as I have heard, the one that overtaxed every sword with stroke, when he bore the wondrously hard weapon to battle.]

We witness him performing several deeds requiring almost superhuman physical ability, performances supplemented by both his own and other reports of his prowess, and he is by all accounts a remarkable physical specimen,[155] but Beowulf's power does not account solely for the troubles he has with weapons and we should, accordingly, not allow it or the poet's comments to bear too much weight.[156] In the fight against Grendel's mother, her tough hide causes Hrunting, Beowulf's manmade weapon, to fail,[157] and his strength plays, at best, an ancillary role in Nægling's destruction. Beowulf offers a tremendous and dramatic stroke, but the blade fails because he attacks what may well be the dragon's most heavily armored spot, its head. Wiglaf has much more success because he avoids the creature's head and strikes at a more vulnerable (and sword-saving) spot. Two swords do fail in Beowulf's hands, but in each case the extraordinary use to which the manmade weapons were put is the chief cause of their failure, not Beowulf's strength.

We can perhaps best gain perspective on Beowulf's strength by recalling that he may be related to Indo-European grip heroes who, like Heracles, will on occasion employ weapons, although they rely chiefly on their own main might when fighting.[158] What is often overlooked in discussions of Beowulf's strength is that it plays a crucial and positive role in all his battles with men and monsters. During his fight with Grendel's mother, Beowulf's strength, far from hindering him in any way, enables him to employ the "ealdsweord eotenisc" (1558a) [old sword made by giants] that he discovers in her dwelling: "þæt [wæs] wæpna cyst, — / buton hit wæs mare   ðonne ænig mon oðer / to beadulace   ætberan meahte" (1559b–61) [that was the best of weapons, except that it was more than any other man might bear to battle-sport]. And rather than seeing his crushing of Dæghrefn as another example of his inability to use weapons, we should align our reading of this event with Beowulf's. His dispatching of the Frankish warrior appears to be the second and final time over the course of his long martial career that he acts as a *handbona,* taking this compound, which occurs uniquely in *Beowulf,* in its most literal sense as "slayer with the hand," as Beowulf clearly does when he uses the term to describe himself. In explicitly linking his fights with Grendel and Dæghrefn in this manner, he demonstrates his conviction that they increased his reputation in precisely the same way.

That he singles out his killing of these two foes and offers no further examples or any statement that would indicate he habitually so destroyed foes suggests that these may have been isolated incidents. Indeed, Beowulf, in his assertion that his sword has served him well for many years (2499b–2502), and the poet, in labeling Nægling "iren ærgod" (2586a) [iron good from old times], allude to the sword's tried and successful past.[159] From both these comments we can infer that Nægling is not, like the sword Chaucer's Reeve carries, rusty from disuse.[160] Beowulf does state that he wishes he could fight the dragon unarmed (2518 ff., cited above), but we should see this comment as stemming from the exceptional honors that such battles bestowed on him in the past instead of casting it as a (rather oblique) comment on his (in)ability to employ weapons. Reading his remark as even a veiled admission of ineptitude creates at least one large interpretive problem: given the special status of swords in the poem's heroic society, an inability to wield weapons would, by definition, exclude the greatest hero of his day from participating in an essential aspect of that society.

We can best understand the failure of Nægling by reading it in its traditional, affective context and by recognizing that it forms the emotional, if not narrative, climax of both the dragon episode and the entire poem. As with Beowulf's decision to fight alone, recognizing the central role Nægling's failure plays in the episode's affective dynamics will permit us to disentangle it from other related moments and to perceive more clearly its traditional structure.

During the course of the dragon fight, Nægling fails not once but twice. Its initial failure occurs in the first of Beowulf's three encounters with the dragon and parallels, narratively and affectively, the failure of Hrunting, the sword that Unferth gives Beowulf before the fight with Grendel's mother. Under the mere and against the dragon, the failure of a manmade weapon forces Beowulf to confront the boundaries of human power and to step momentarily outside the realm of *humanitas* before undertaking actions that redefine it.[161] When Hrunting proves ineffectual against Grendel's mother, Beowulf uses his extraordinary power and employs the "eald sweord eotenisc" he discovers hanging on the wall, thereby transcending the human world and entering, however briefly, the mythological world of the *gigantas* [giants]. Although he tosses the manmade blade away during the battle, Beowulf appears to understand that the blade was overtaxed. He does not mention its failure but works to recuperate and reestablish its status by explicitly praising it as a "leoflic iren" (1809a) [precious iron] when he gives it back to Unferth after returning from the mere.

In the first encounter with the dragon, a manmade sword once again proves ineffective when turned against a nonhuman foe. However, when Nægling initially fails, no external alternative presents itself, and the hero seems to have arrived at the nadir of his existence. He cannot, as he earlier did, draw upon the technology of another world for the assistance that his own cannot provide; his hand-picked troop of warriors has deserted him; his specially made shield has proved unable to withstand the dragon's fierce onslaught; and the sword that has long served him well is not up to the challenge to which he puts it. Once Nægling fails to penetrate the dragon's hide, Beowulf is truly stripped of all but the most elemental resource: his courage. Rather than crossing the border into another, nonhuman realm as he does earlier, he turns inside himself and pushes human courageousness to new heights when he reengages the dragon with a weapon that has just failed. During the second of his three engagements with the dragon, Beowulf advances and strikes at its head with Nægling: "mægenstrengo sloh / hildebille,   þæt hyt on heafolan stod / niþe genyded" (2678b–80a) [(he) struck with great strength, with his battle-blade, so that it stuck in the head, driven by violence]. In a narrative strategy that greatly underscores the importance of the sword's failure, the poet explicitly states first that "Nægling forbærst" (2680b) [Nægling burst asunder] and then immediately that "geswac æt sæcce   sweord Biowulfes" (2681) [the sword of Beowulf failed in the battle], thus freezing the moment and prolonging its agony. At the very instant the sword fails, the tension and fear central to the episode reach their peak. All the references to Beowulf's doom that have punctuated the scene suddenly acquire an awful and inescapable reality.[162] In attacking the dragon head-on with a useless sword and then finally facing the monster armed only with Nægling's shattered hilt and a *wæll-seax* [dagger], Beowulf redefines human courage. The model for heroic behavior he offers is not suitable for everyone—Wiglaf, we should recall, chooses to strike the dragon's more vulnerable underbelly—but this in no way diminishes the gloriousness of Beowulf's gesture or the traditionality of the unique and uniquely powerful episode of which it is a part.[163]

Pre-Conquest Oral Poetics

One of the lessons to be learned from the history of scholarship on the Anglo-Saxon oral tradition, a history that proceeds in an almost unbroken line from the mid–nineteenth century to the present day, and from the continuing debates over the nature of the early medieval oral-literate nexus, is that establishing an oral poetics for Anglo-Saxon England is a complex and as yet very much incomplete task. Despite the concerted efforts of several generations of oralists and textualists, the field has yet to come to "terms with orality as a formative element in the texts it studies."[164] But as the polemics that marked and for many years threatened to stagnate the investigation of Anglo-Saxon oral poetics continue to diminish, the complex processes involved in the praxes of Anglo-Saxon poetic articulation have begun to emerge more clearly. O'Brien O'Keeffe's identification of the residual orality evidenced in the poetry's physical encoding, Doane's work on the Anglo-Saxon scribal "reperfomance" of texts, Renoir's focus on the context within which Old English poetry is produced and received, Stock's investigation of "textual communities," and Foley's theory of immanent art all stand as exemplars of the nuanced and responsive view of oral poetics that undergirds contemporary oral theory.[165]

As we turn in chapter 3 to consider oral poetics in the early Middle English period, a period that sees a continued acceleration in the spread of literacy and what may be reductively labeled the literate mentality, the need for such a nuanced theory becomes even more pronounced.

three

Post-Conquest Oral Poetics

During the late Anglo-Saxon and early Middle English periods, England's linguistic, political, and cultural geographies were all radically reshaped by internal and external forces. From the standpoint of English literary history, these years witnessed the decline of the uniform, autochthonous oral poetics that had dominated poetic articulation in England for more than four hundred years and the rise of diverse new systems of articulating, receiving, and physically encoding poetry, many of which continue to be important constituents of contemporary poetics. Unlike their Anglo-Saxon forebears, Middle English poets do not engage a stable, homeostatic expressive economy, one whose contours remain clearly identifiable across several centuries. Instead, they draw upon the idioms of a number of different expressive economies, some of which descend from and are deeply influenced by Anglo-Saxon oral poetics, some of which derive from continental traditions and hence owe no direct debt to medieval English oral poetics, and some of which can be best described as deriving from a mix of oral and literate poetics (both insular and continental). In contrast to Old English poetry, Middle English poetry is "amorphous" and "not the product of a coherent tradition with a systematic style and diction and a standardised language, but a series of fragmentary and imperfect responses to a multitude of European influences, in a language thrown open to the winds of change."[1]

The Erosion of Anglo-Saxon Oral Poetics

As the runic inscription on the golden horn of Gallehus witnesses,[2] the formal qualities of early Germanic verse remain remarkably stable from the middle of the fifth century up through the first decade of the twelfth, when the late, metrically regular *Durham* is generally believed to have been composed.[3] Within this relatively stable metrical system, Old English poetry does evidence some diversity, but those hypermetric, rhyming, and macaronic passages that occur occasionally in the poetic corpus conform more rather than less closely to the metrical principles that govern the production of Old English verse. To cite just a few examples, the Old English and Latin macaronic verses of the *Phoenix* and *A Summons to Prayer* are bound together by alliteration and are situated within the stress-based meter of Old English verse.[4] The same is true of the rhyming verses of the aptly named *Riming Poem*. So central are the metrical principles that underlie Old English verse that the determination of a poem's canonicity often hinges on the degree to which it conforms to the principles of Anglo-Saxon metrics that scholars have set forth. It is precisely because they are in the regular alliterative meter that Elliot Van Kirk Dobbie includes in his authoritative *Anglo-Saxon Minor Poems* six poems from the Anglo-Saxon Chronicle while he rejects ten other passages that Charles Plummer less than fifty years earlier printed as verse because he finds them metrically irregular.[5] *The Rime of King William*, contained in the Peterborough Chronicle entry for 108[7], is one of the poems Dobbie excludes from the canon of Old English poetry, apparently with good reason:[6]

> castelas he let wyrcean.
> 7 earme men swiðe swencean.
> Se cyng wæs swa swiðe stearc.
> 7 benam of his under þeoddan man . manig marc
> goldes. 7 ma hundred punda seolfres.
> Ðet he nam be wihte. 7 mid myclean un rihte
> of his land leode, for litte[l]re neode.
> he wæs on gitsunge be feallan.
> 7 grædinæsse he lufode mid ealle.
> he sætte mycel deor frið. 7 he lægde laga þær wið.
> þet swa hwa swa sloge heort oððe hinde.
> þet hine man sceolde blendian.
> he forbead þa heortas. swylce eac þa baras.

swa swi[ð]e he lufode þa hea deor·
swilce he wære heora fæder.
Eac he sætte be þam haran· þet hi mosten freo faran.
his rice men hit mændon. 7 þa earme men hit be ceorodan.
Ac he [wæs] swa stið· þet he ne rohte heora eallra nið.
ac hi moston mid ealle þes cynges wille folgian
gif hi woldon libban . oððe land habban .
land ððe eahta . oððe wel his sehta .
Wala wa . þet anig man sceolde modigan swa .
hine sylf upp ahebban . 7 ofer ealle men tellan.
Se ælmihtiga God cyþæ his saule mild heortnisse·
7 do him his synna for gifenesse.

———

[He ordered castles made and greatly oppressed wretched men. The king
was very fierce and took from his subjects many marks of gold and many
hundred pounds of silver. These things he took from his people, his subjects, with great wickedness and for little need. He was fallen into avarice
and greediness he loved above all else. He set up many royal game forests
and established laws so that whoever killed a hart or hind should be
blinded. He forbade that harts and likewise that boars should be hunted.
He loved the stags as if he were their father. Concerning the hares, he
ordered that they should run free. His powerful men complained and the
wretched men lamented it, but he was so cruel that he did not care about
all their enmity, but they above all had to follow the king's will if they
wished to live or have land or own property or stand favorably in his
sight. Alas that any man should be so proud as to raise himself up and
consider himself above all men. May Almighty God show mercy on his
soul and grant him forgiveness for his sins.]

There is so little in these lines that recalls the highly regular, stress-based alliterative metrics characteristic of Old English verse that we ought perhaps to
speak not in terms of the development of Anglo-Saxon metrics but in terms of
its collapse and replacement by non-native, continental systems.[7]

In addition to the evidence afforded by the fractured metrics of the *Rime
of King William*, the Peterborough Chronicle contains other, equally important, evidence of the erosion of Anglo-Saxon oral poetics. While the annal for
937 in the other four major manuscripts of the Chronicle presents the account
of the Battle of Brunanburh, one of the last great English triumphs over the

invading Danes, entirely in alliterative verse that adheres to the principles of Anglo-Saxon metrics,[8] the Peterborough Chronicle reports on this battle summarily and in prose: "Her Æðelstan cyning lædde fyrde to Brunan burig" [In this year King Athelstan led an army to Brunanburh].[9] A comparison of this line to those found in the Parker Chronicle reveals just how radically the expressive economy of the Peterborough Chronicle differs in this instance from the other, earlier versions of the Chronicle:[10]

> Her Æþelstan cyning,   eorla dryhten,
> beorna beahgifa,   7 his broþor eac,
> Eadmund æþeling,   ealdor langne tir
> geslogon æt sæcce   sweorda ecgum
> ymbe Bru`n´anburh.

> _____

> [At this time, King Athelstan, the lord of men, warriors' ring-giver, and also his brother, the noble Edmund, obtained by the edge of their swords lifelong glory in battle at Brunanburh.]

The abandonment of Anglo-Saxon poetics in the twelfth century evidenced in the Peterborough Chronicle is certainly not unique to that text, as the following few lines from *Fragment A* of the *Worcester Fragments* witness:

> [S]anctus Beda was iboren her on Breotene mid us,
> And he wisliche [bec] awende
> Þet þeo Englise leoden þurh weren ilerde.
> And he þeo c[not]ten unwreih, þe questiuns hoteþ,
> Þa derne diȝelnesse þe de[or]wurþe is.
>   (1–5) [11]

> _____

> [Saint Bede was born here in Britain among us and he wisely translated books so that through them the people were taught. And he freed those knots that are called the *Questiones,* whose mysterious secret is prized.]

The second Worcester fragment, *The Soul's Address to the Body,* is more regularly alliterative, but its rhyme and assonance are irregular, its line is longer and more prosaic, and neither its syntactic patterns nor its prosody recalls Anglo-Saxon poetics.[12] The same could be said of many other twelfth-century poems. Despite Olof Arngart's somewhat optimistic contention that the meter of the

Proverbs of Alfred is "a modification of the advanced type of O.E. alliterative line showing greater freedom of construction and alliteration,"[13] it, like the meter of Laȝamon's *Brut,* conforms only partially and imperfectly to Anglo-Saxon metrics: some lines alliterate without rhyme, some are in rhyming two- or three-stress couplets that frequently alliterate, and many neither alliterate nor rhyme.[14] Works such as the *Proverbs of Alfred,* the *Brut,* and the *Worcester Fragments* seem, despite their poetic foundations, to be more closely related to the rhythmical prose of Wulfstan and Ælfric than to classical Old English verse.[15]

Although many other texts from the transitional period are built upon metrical systems that similarly resist absolute classification,[16] many early Middle English poems are founded upon highly regular metrical systems. Significantly, metrically regular poems such as *Genesis and Exodus,* the *Hule and Niȝtengale, King Horn,* and the *Orrmulum* all derive their metrics from a variety of continental and classical models, not the insular one. As the four-stress line of Old English poetry gives way to a wide variety of metrical types and as rhyme displaces alliteration as a principal organizing device, medieval English verse of the transitional, early post-Conquest period comes to look and sound far different from the verse that preceded it. The octosyllabic couplets of *Genesis and Exodus* and the *Hule and Niȝtengale,* the rhyming three-stress couplets of *King Horn,* and the fifteen-syllable septenaries of the *Orrmulum* exemplify the formal diversity and metrical polyphony of early Middle English poetic expression.

Encoding the Oral Tradition

Despite the considerable differences between the metrics of Old English poems such as *Beowulf* and *Judith* and those of their early Middle English descendants such as the *Rime of King William,* the *Proverbs of Alfred,* and the *Brut,* Old and early Middle English texts remain linked in an especially vital way because from the Anglo-Saxon period until early in the thirteenth century, medieval English poetry continues to be written out exclusively in *scriptura continua,*[17] a fact obscured by the lineation, standardized separation of words, capitalization, and punctuation of modern editions of medieval English verse texts. In regularizing and normalizing these texts as they attempt to create a "best text," modern editors force upon them an inappropriate structural aesthetics, one that only imperfectly reflects the rather different aesthetics that was in effect at the time of the poems' physical encoding. We can highlight the dangers of such practices by recalling that while the stress-based alliterative half-line plays a central role in the contemporary reception of Old English poetry, the scops who produced the poetry and their intended audiences may have responded more directly to other metrical-rhythmical patterns that were apparent to them but that we at this great historical remove can no longer apprehend.

In her work on the development in Anglo-Saxon manuscripts of those graphic cues that from the late Anglo-Saxon period onward come to play an increasingly important role in the presentation and reception of written verse, O'Brien O'Keeffe demonstrates that the graphic conventions of these manuscripts, far from being simply a hash of modern practices, carry an important significative burden. Graphic cues for the presentation of verse such as punctuation, mise-en-page, spacing between words, and capitalization are all essential components of what M. B. Parkes labels the "grammar of legibility," that nexus of "rules governing the relationships between [a text's] graphic conventions and the message of a text conveyed in the written medium."[18] Such a grammar is crucial to the proper encoding and decoding of all written poetry, and it is especially important in the study of Anglo-Saxon texts because the way in which poetry is physically encoded provides "strong evidence of persisting residual orality in the reading and copying of poetry in Old English."[19] Even in the later Middle Ages, the presence or absence of such visual cues continues to reveal a great deal about a text's position along the oral-literate continuum because the further a text is from the oral pole, the greater the need there is for a more fully developed system of graphic conventions.

For example, the extremely low visual information contained in the eighth-century version of Cædmon's *Hymn* found in St. Petersburg, Russian National Library, Q. v. I. 18, suggests that it was copied into the margins of Bede's Latin text at a time when English poetry was only newly being committed to writing and when poetic reception was still chiefly, if not exclusively, aural rather than visual. Written out in three lines of *scriptura continua* across the bottom margin of folio 107r, the poem is marked only by a small initial capital *n* and a single mark of punctuation, a raised final *punctus*. The amount of visual information encoded in the early twelfth-century *Durham* is, in contrast, substantially higher. Filling twenty-one lines in column 2 of Cambridge, University Library, Ff. 1. 27, fol. 101v, *Durham* is marked by a large ornamental initial capital *i* as well as by several other capitals, and it is heavily pointed throughout. The poem's many points testify to the crucial role that graphic conventions for inscribing English come to play in the visual reception of verbal art, even though the precise nature of the information conveyed by the points, unlike those over which Peter Quince rides roughshod in *A Midsummer Night's Dream*,[20] is far from apparent.

However unclear the varied systems of pointing contained in the Anglo-Saxon poetic codices may seem from our perspective,[21] they may have been as apparent to contemporary Anglo-Saxon readers as our current system of full and partial stops is to us. While the development of a theory of Anglo-Saxon pointing that indisputably explains the varied systems encountered in Old English manuscripts would certainly be welcome, for our purpose we do not finally need to understand fully the logic and nuances of what may be varied, idiosyncratic practices but rather need chiefly to realize that pointing speaks directly to the ways in which the "growth of visual cues as interpretative supplements in the manuscripts charts the gradual alienation of the reader from vital formulaic tradition"[22]—from, that is, medieval English oral poetics.

The manuscript pointing of *Durham* well illustrates the difficulties involved in determining the logic underlying even highly pointed Anglo-Saxon manuscripts. Dobbie, in keeping with long-standing scholarly practice, arranges the text in half-lines marked by a caesura and adds modern punctuation, practices that serve to underscore and strengthen the poem's connection with "classical" Old English verse:

> Is ðeos burch breome   geond Breotenrice,
> steppa gestaðolad,   stanas ymbutan
> wundrum gewæxen.   Weor ymbeornad,
> ea yðum stronge,   and ðer inne wunað
> feola fisca kyn   on floda gemonge.
>
> (1–5)[23]

[This city is renowned throughout Britain, loftily established, the stones around it wondrously grown. The Wear runs around it, the river with strong waves, and therein dwell many types of fish in the mixture of the water.]

A very different picture emerges from a diplomatic transcription of these same lines:

Is ðeos burch. breome geond breoten
rice steppa ge staðolad stanas ymbu
tan pyndru. ge pæxen. peor. ymbeor
nad. eayðum. stronge. 7 ðer inne pu
na fola fisca.[24] kyn. onfloda ge mon
ge.

Some of the manuscript points seem to serve semantic purposes by marking phrasal or semantic boundaries as, for example, in "Is inðere byrieac bearnum ge | cyðed," which appears in Dobbie's version as "Is in ðere byri eac bearnum gecyðed" (9) [there is also in the city, as it is known to men]. That twenty-four manuscript *punctūs* thus occur at the end of what Dobbie has established as half-line clauses seems to offer further support for the semantic nature of the manuscript's pointing,[25] but in thirteen of these cases, the word that marks the end of the half-line is preceded by a point as well, a practice clearly illustrated in the poem's final lines but completely elided in Dobbie's edition. Compare the manuscript's presentation,

ðe monia pundrumge. purðað. ðes
ðe prit. seggeð. midd ðene drihnes.
perdomes. bideð.

with Dobbie's:

ðær monia wundrum gewurðað,   ðes ðe writ seggeð,
midd ðene drihnes wer   domes bideð.

(20–21)

———

[there many wonders occur, this the writing says, with the man of God awaiting judgment.]

Here and throughout the manuscript, pointing is highly reminiscent of the individual and expressive pointing evident in three of the major Anglo-Saxon poetic codices—the Exeter Book, the Vercelli Book, and the Nowell Codex—and is related to but distant from the much more regular system of metrical and semantic pointing that appears early in and continues to develop throughout the transitional period. Their real or perceived lack of poetic merit notwithstanding, the verses on the death of William I in the Peterborough Chronicle are systematically pointed to mark semantic units (and perhaps metrical ones as well) and suggest just how fully developed pointing practices had become by the middle of the twelfth century:

> niȝe teonan· Castelas he let pyrcean· 7 earme men spiðe
> spencean· Se cyng þæs spa spiðe stearc· 7 benā of his un
> der þeoddan man · manig marc ȝoldes· 7 ma hundred
> punda seolfres· Ðet he nā be pihte. 7 mid mycelan un

The step from this diplomatic transcription of lines 11 to 14 of folio 65r of MS E, Laud Misc. 636, to the presentation Cecily Clark adopts in her critical edition is small indeed because the manuscript's pointing clearly marks clausal boundaries:

> Castelas he let wyrcean,
> 7 earme men swiðe swencean.
> Se cyng wæs swa swiðe stearc,
> 7 benam of his underþeoddan manig marc
> godes 7 ma hundred punda seolfres.
> Ðet he nam be wihte
> 7 mid mycelan unrihte
>
> (108[7]; 106–12)[26]

Clark's layout of the poem enhances its grammar of legibility from our modern perspective, but the information gained by adopting her presentation over the manuscript's is not very great.

The Presentation of Early Middle English Verse

During the early Middle English period, those pointing practices that began to develop during the Anglo-Saxon and transitional periods become much more regular and consequently soon come to look much more familiar to the modern eye. By the time the *Orrmulum* is written down some fifty years after the date of the final entries of the Peterborough Chronicle,[27] the manuscript points mark semantic and metrical units and correspond closely to the modern system Robert M. White employs in his edition:

An enngell comm off heoffness ærd
Inn aness weress hewe
Till hirdess þær þær þeȝȝ þatt nihht
Biwokenn þeggre faldess,
Þatt enngell comm 7 stod hemm bi
Wiþþ heoffness lihht 7 leome .

(3336–41)[28]

———

[an angel came from heaven in the shape of a man to the shepherds who watched their folds that night. That angel came and stood by them, with heaven's light and brightness.]

In Oxford, Bodleian Library, Junius 1, the manuscript in which the *Orrmulum* survives, these lines appear on folio 33r as follows:

An en-[29]

gell com[30] off heoffness ærd⸗
Inn aness peress hepe. Till
hirdess þær þær þeȝ[31] þatt
nihht⸗ Bipoken[32] þeȝȝerefal-
dess. Þatt engell[33] com. 7 stod
hē[34] bi⸗ Wiþþ heoffness liht.
7 leome.

In addition to its punctuation, the manner in which words are consistently divided in Orrm's text reflects the degree to which it is oriented toward the eye. Not only does Orrm avoid the type of free morphemic division common to Old English poetic texts (and evident as well in many early Middle English texts) by dividing words syllabically, he is perhaps one of the first scribes regularly to employ hyphens at the end of a line to indicate that a word is continued on the following line.[35] But despite these forward-looking aspects of Orrm's extremely self-conscious and idiosyncratic text, it remains linked to contemporary texts such as the *Proverbs of Alfred* and Laȝamon's *Brut* because it is, significantly, still written in *scriptura continua*. Like the verse sections of the Peterborough Chronicle, Orrm's text exhibits a more fully developed grammar of legibility than most other transitional texts, but neither of the scribes who produced these texts saw the need to alter his practice of spatializing verse on the page to accommodate or facilitate its visual reception.

The early-thirteenth-century version of the *Proverbs of Alfred* preserved in Kent, Maidstone Museum, A. 13, and designated by Arngart as M provides important testimony to the continuing flux that attended the physical encoding of vernacular verse in the early Middle English period.[36] The poem's first section begins on folio 93r with two rhyming lines of text that are clearly spatialized as verse: the left margin of the text is aligned with the left edge of the first column, and there is significant blank space at the right end of each line. The manuscript lineation initially parallels that of Arngart's modern edited version:

þe erl and þe aþeling
þe ben under þe king.
                    (72–73)

_____

[the earl and the nobleman who are under the king.]

Arngart adheres to modern editorial principles and lineates the following two lines as verse, but in doing so he obscures the fact that in the manuscript's third line the scribe abandons the practice of writing only one short line of verse per manuscript line and attempts instead to fit two lines of text onto one manuscript line. As he does consistently, the scribe begins writing at the extreme left margin, but this third line runs into the right margin before he has finished inscribing it. Rather than cross the line indicating the column's right margin (as he does occasionally elsewhere), he writes the verse's final word, *deden*, in the blank space of the folio's second line, drawing a line around it to indicate clearly that it belongs to the third line:

deden
þat lond to leden · mid laweliche

[that land to lead with lawful deeds]

The scribe marks the division of these short verses with a raised *punctus*, the only punctuation mark in the entire section that is not final. In line 4, he immediately resumes the practice of writing one short line of poetry per manuscript line—whether they rhyme or not—a practice that Arngart's lineation reflects once again:

> boþe þe clerc an te cniht
> Demen euenliche riht.
> for after þat þe man soweth
> þar after he sal mowen[.]
>> (fol. 93r, col. 1, 4–7)

———

[both the clerk and the knight judge impartially what is right. For as a man sows, thereafter he shall mow.]

But in the final two lines of the section, the scribe adopts the procedure that he will follow without deviation in all the poem's subsequent sections and writes his verses out in *scriptura continua* that fills up the columns from their left to right margins (and occasionally beyond):

> and efrilches mannes dom to his ow|en
> dure chariweth·[37]

———

[and every man's judgment to his own door returns.]

Copied out as poetry, as in the first section, the poem would fill up many more folios than it would if copied out in *scriptura continua*, so economic factors may have caused him to forgo formatting the poem as verse. Whatever the scribe's reason for abandoning the practice of spatializing the poem as verse, he begins, from the second section onward, to point the poem heavily and regularly, with every point and raised *punctus* occurring at clausal and half-line boundaries.

In the first section of the *Proverbs of Alfred* we can see the scribe's several attempts to arrive at a suitable format for presenting his verse text by first writing one short line per manuscript line (a practice that quickly seems to have proved too space consuming) and then two short lines per manuscript line (a practice that immediately proves impracticable given the length of the poem's lines, the size of the scribe's hand, and the width of the manuscript's three ruled columns). However, he quickly abandons his experiment with different types of lineation and returns to the standard manner of physically presenting verse. But as he reverts to encoding his verse in *scriptura continua* he simultaneously adopts a system of punctuation that compensates for the lower visual information in these sections, one that will help readers (both those reading aloud to a group and those reading silently to themselves) visually to decode his poem.

While Kent, Maidstone Museum, A. 13, provides direct evidence of tension between two very different and competing ways of representing vernacular Middle English poetry on the manuscript page, London, British Library, Cotton Caligula A. ix, offers less direct but even more intriguing evidence about early Middle English conventions for encoding poetry, evidence that may help us determine approximately when the shift toward presenting poetry as verse took place. Among this codex's rich mixture of English and Anglo-Norman verse and prose and lay and religious texts is one long text, Laȝamon's *Brut*, whose encoding follows past practice and a series of texts—chief among which is the *Hule and Niȝtengale*—that may well be among the first poems in English to be spatialized as poetry.[38] The *Brut* is generally dated at least fifty years earlier than the rest of the codex,[39] and while it is tempting to see it as being anterior to the other texts in the manuscript, the vagaries of dating medieval texts consign any sort of evolutionary argument, no matter how appealing, to the realm of speculation.

Following general early Middle English practice, the *Brut* is written out entirely in *scriptura continua* from the left to the right margin of each of the manuscript's two columns.[40] The poem continues the practice of clausal pointing that developed early in the transitional period and, like the *Orrmulum,* uses the *punctus elevatus* for major medial pauses and the *punctus* for all other pauses.[41] While it appears that the *Brut*'s punctuation thus distinguishes between the caesura and end of a long line of verse, we must be cautious in assessing its system of punctuation because the two coeval scribes responsible for creating the Caligula version of the poem frequently reverse this practice and mark the final pause of a long line with the *punctus elevatus* and the medial pause with a *punctus* (that usually is placed in the low position, like a modern period, although on occasion it is raised to a medial height).

As they are in the *Orrmulum* and elsewhere, words in the *Brut* are divided chiefly between syllables or between double consonants, as in, for example, "sta þe" (4; fol. 3r, left column, 8–9), "bis ne" (15; fol. 3r, left column, 22–23), and "set te" (27; fol. 3r, right column 3–4). But while the *Brut* largely conforms to contemporary practice in this regard, free morphemic division is encountered on occasion as, for example, in "q ne"[42] (40; fol. 3r, right column 20–21). As in Old English texts, no punctuation links the morphemes of divided words. The poem's visual information, while higher than that of Anglo-Saxon codices, is low by late-twelfth-century standards, and its encoding recalls more the fluidity with which Old English verse was encoded than those conventions that developed to assist the visual decoding of written Middle English verse.

But while Cotton Caligula A. ix thus offers evidence that Anglo-Saxon practices for encoding poetry persist into the late twelfth century, in the English verse found alongside the *Brut* in the codex we can see clearly the lineaments of those conventions for encoding verse in writing that are still in effect. Occupying folios 233r–46r of the codex is the *Hule and Niȝtengale,* a learned, sophisticated poem that is technically and aesthetically unmatched by any other piece of vernacular poetry extant from the period. The *Hule* has highly regular metrics and treats its subject matter with a witty subtlety not to be encountered again in medieval English poetry until Chaucer. But the *Hule* is most important to the present discussion because it may well be one of the first poems in English to be spatialized as poetry on the manuscript page.[43] The left margins of the two ruled columns in which it is written are justified, the end of each line is regularly marked by a *punctus,*[44] lines in which the text stops short of the ruled right margin end with significant blank space, and those lines too long for the columns' boundaries are extended horizontally into the margin (but not to the line either above or below, even if they have blank space available). The presentation of several of the verses of the *Proverbs of Alfred* in the first section of Maidstone A. 13 recalls that of the *Hule,* but as we have seen above, the scribe who produced that text quickly abandoned what may have seemed to be a wasteful, unusual system in favor of one that perhaps had the virtues of being both more economical and more familiar.

Even though they generally witness a higher degree of incipient textuality than their Anglo-Saxon predecessors, manuscripts from the transitional and early Middle English periods continue to provide evidence crucial to the evaluation of a text's oral poetics because their visual array offers significant clues regarding the oral-literate matrix from which they emerge. In addition, the changes evident in the ways verse is physically encoded during the transitional and early Middle English periods are important for what they reveal about medieval culture's continuing movement toward the literate pole of the oral-literate continuum. As the processes for decoding written verse shift away from the oral and aural and become more and more fully oriented toward the visual, graphic cues such as spatialization, lineation, punctuation, and word division take on increasing importance.[45] But while the development of a grammar of legibility in the written records of the transitional period affords us the opportunity to chart with some certainty one aspect of medieval English culture's shift from orality to literacy, the course of this movement is not a uniform and unidirectional one toward social and cultural development but a dynamic and complicated process in which orality and literacy interact and intersect in a host of complex and "vital ways, sometimes cooperatively, sometimes conflictively."[46]

The Oral Tradition in Post-Conquest England

Although widely accepted as surviving into the post-Conquest period, the nature of the English oral tradition in this period and its continued influence on the production of vernacular verse have yet to be fully explored. The Parry-Lord theory of oral-formulaic composition has proved to be foundational to our general understanding of oral traditional poetry, but its emphasis on composition-in-performance, its reliance on the existence of pre- or nonliterate singers, and its insistence upon the mutual exclusivity of the so-called oral and literate minds severely limit its application to the source-based, written poetry produced in the early Middle English period.[47] And those who approach the post-Conquest oral tradition from the perspective of a strictly literate poetics have, beginning with Ruth Crosby's seminal studies of more than sixty years ago, largely confined their investigations to matters of presentation and transmission.[48] But while the focus on oral delivery in the Middle English period has unquestionably furthered our understanding of Middle English poetics, it has, paradoxically, hampered the investigation of post-Conquest oral poetics in much the same way that oral-formulaic theory's emphasis upon composition-in-performance inhibited the investigation of pre-Conquest oral poetics. While both provide important information regarding the primary oral/aural channel through which medieval English poetry was transmitted and received, the mode of transmission in itself reveals little about any given poem's mix of oral or literate poetics. A poet who reads his or her poem from a written text or recites a memorized version of a written text to an audience of listeners is engaging in an indisputably oral activity, but evidence of possible oral delivery *does not invariably signal* the poet's engagement of oral poetics, just as evidence of demonstrably written composition *does not preclude* the presence of nonperformative oral poetics.

As the Caligula A. ix versions of the *Brut* and the *Hule and Niȝtengale* well illustrate,[49] we cannot simply and automatically assume that evidence of oral transmission or written composition is indicative of, respectively, oral or literate poetics. The former, one of the first poems in English to appear after the Conquest, has no known English models. A verse chronicle of very uneven poetic merit, it traces the history of England from the time of its eponymous founder Brutus to that of Cadwalader, the last of the British kings. The latter is a much shorter poem in the tradition of Latin debate poetry whose artistry is universally praised. Judging from their length, subject matter, and relative levels of artistic achievement, the *Hule* stands out as the one far more likely to have been delivered orally. An engaging poem, produced by a well trained, imaginative poet writing "in a style of civilised, literary colloquialism,"[50] it seems well suited to the performative matrix through which much early Middle English poetry was disseminated. A talented reader (or memorizer) would encounter little difficulty bringing to life the poem's well-defined avian characters during a performance, a task made all the easier not only by the poem's highly regular metrics and high degree of visual information but also by the poet's habit of clearly marking the discourse of each bird through phrases such as "Þo quaþ þe Hule" (187) [then spoke the Owl] and "'Nay, nay,' sede þe Niȝtengale" (543) [No, no, said the Nightingale]. The *Brut*, in contrast, has little about it that suggests it was ever intended for oral delivery or that a performance of it would have had any but the most limited appeal to a listening audience. The poem is extremely long,[51] its rhythms and metrics are highly inconsistent, and some of its internal evidence (the lack of "addresses to the audience, real or invented, of the kind that characterize the genre of Middle English romance or Chaucer" and the fact that Laȝamon consistently uses the "singular pronoun of address") has led at least one scholar to claim recently that Laȝamon "appears to envisage a solitary reader."[52]

But while the *Hule* is certainly well suited to oral delivery and may have reached its intended audience principally through the mouths of readers or reciters, there can be no doubt that it is founded upon a highly literate poetics. Its meter may have developed from the native stress-based alliterative line,[53] but its debt to the French octosyllabic couplet cannot be ignored. A highly intertextual poem, it possesses clear generic affiliations, and throughout the poet "handles a wide range of source-materials with deceptive ease, introducing proverbs . . . and exemplary stories as if spontaneously, and lacing the debate with technical terms to give it the air of a lawsuit."[54] It also evidences little of the specialized expressive economy of medieval English oral poetics. And, as we will see below, when the *Hule*-poet does employ a component of medieval English oral poetics, he puts it to a nontraditional use.

In the entire canon of early Middle English poetry, there is probably no poem less well suited for oral delivery than the *Brut*,[55] whose subject matter and extraordinary length alone militate strongly against the possibility of its ever having been presented orally. Internal evidence stressing the poem's written genesis suggests further that the poet meant for it to be received through the eyes rather than the ears. In the poem's autobiographical prologue, the poet reveals himself to be a literate man who is at least bilingual and perhaps even trilingual.[56] His compositional process is highly intertextual and further reflects the literate poetics upon which his poem is founded. He announces that once the desire to compose his poem descended upon him, he "gon liðen: wide ȝond þas leode" (14) [began to journey widely throughout this land] in search of textual exemplars. He settled finally upon three, one written in English, one in Latin, and one in French.[57] Having presented this very clear model of literate—even scholarly—behavior, Laȝamon anchors his text yet more firmly to a literate poetics by briefly describing the mechanics underlying its physical production: "Feþeren he nom mid fingren: 7 fiede on boc-felle. / 7 þa soþere word: sette to-gadere. / 7 þa þre boc: þrumde to are" (26–28)[58] [He took feathers with his fingers and wrote on book-skins and those true words set together and compressed those three books into one]. The illumination representing a monk busily engaged in copying or perhaps composing a text contained in the ornamental *a* with which the *Brut*'s prologue begins in Caligula A. ix, Laȝamon's figuring of his text as a "boc" to be "rede" by his audience, the fundamentally intertextual nature of his own compositional process, and the demonstrable and far-reaching influence of his primary source, Wace's *Roman de Brut*, over the poem's narrative shape further situate the *Brut* within a highly self-conscious, literate poetics.

Elsewhere in his unusually autobiographical prologue, Laȝamon names himself, identifies his vocation, locates himself geographically, and asks for prayers for both himself and his father, all with a cultivated self-consciousness usually associated with the narrative voice of thirteenth- and fourteenth-century romances.[59] But despite the stress laid on the *Brut*'s literate poetics by both poet and illuminator, its lexicon, thematics, syntax, metrics, narrative patterning, and verbal collocations all witness the centrality of oral poetics to Laȝamon's compositional process.

As even this cursory comparison of the *Brut*'s and the *Hule*'s poetics and physical encoding reveals, when compared to the Anglo-Saxon oral-literate nexus, the one that develops in the post-Conquest period is positively labyrinthine because from it emerges, on the one hand, a poem heavily indebted to oral poetics that most likely was never performed and, on the other hand, a poem almost wholly dependent upon literate poetics that, even if it were not composed with a listening audience in mind, certainly lends itself easily to oral presentation. As we endeavor to trace the intricate weave of the post-Conquest oral-literate nexus, we must acknowledge the central role that oral delivery plays in the transmission and reception of Middle English poetry. But given the extraordinary range of texts that fall wholly or partially in the broad category of the Middle English oral tradition—texts as various as the early *Hule and Niȝtengale,* Chaucer's much later *Canterbury Tales,* and all those others that may have been orally delivered or that lay claim (even if only fictively) to oral delivery—we also need to distinguish carefully between oral delivery and oral poetics, for the former does not always signal the presence of the latter.

Performance and Performativity

Like so much else about the literary and cultural history of the post-Conquest period, the relationship between the vernacular poetic tradition and performance is complex and difficult to untangle. We know that from early in the period onwards poetic composition becomes a private, not a public, process, as poets need no longer enter the public space of the performance arena to articulate poetry but rather retire to their scriptorium or cell to do so. But despite being the product of literate authors whose compositional practices closely mirror our contemporary, private, nonperformative ones, performance continues to cast a large shadow over post-Conquest poetics, and the poetry everywhere evidences what appear to be signs of its fundamental performativity. Among the more important of these features are the poets' direct addresses to their listening audiences, the often overwhelming preponderance of highly iterative and largely meaningless tag phrases, and the loosely episodic and aesthetically inept structure of many narratives.

We still know frustratingly little about the performative matrix within which much early and later Middle English verse was disseminated. Many entertainers no doubt performed texts from memory, with varying degrees of adherence to their *Ur*-texts (written or oral) and with varying degrees of success. Many also may have read directly from a written text and may have deviated from it as little or as much as the occasion demanded and as their talent (or lack thereof) permitted. Some poets/entertainers may have entered the type of performance arena that oral poets do and may therefore have engaged a fully performative oral poetics. Many poets/entertainers may have worked partially within several or all of these categories as they performed, reciting from memory but not hesitating to improvise by importing blocks of memorized verse from elsewhere.[60] Many may even have composed new material in the midst of performing, either by tapping into the highly significant idiom of traditional oral poetics or by some other process of improvisation.

Although most of the population experienced texts only through performance, the performative features of post-Conquest poetry reveal far more about its general aurality than about the presence of an underlying, active oral tradition. The landscape of Middle English vernacular poetry is dotted with numerous subtly and overtly performative features that are generally taken as signs of the oral tradition's continued presence. However, because these features witness the poetry's aurality, they speak almost exclusively to its general mode of transmission, not to the poetics foundational to its composition. To cite just a few of the many possible examples, when the *King Horn*-poet declares that he "schal . . . singe" (3) to his audience ("ʒou" [you]) the tale of King Murray and his son Horn,[61] or when the *Kyng Alisaunder*-poet memorably if somewhat peevishly requests that his audience quiet down and behave so that he may begin his tale—"Now, pes! listneþ, and leteþ cheste— / ʒee shullen heren noble geste, / Of Alisaundre, þe rich[e k]yng" (29–31) [Now peace! Listen and stop wrangling—you will hear a fine story of Alexander the powerful king],[62] or finally when the *Gawain*-poet promises that "If ʒe wyl lysten þis lay bot on littel quile, / I schal telle hit as-tit, as I in toun herde, / with tonge" (30–32) [If you will listen to this tale but a little while, I shall tell it at once, as I in town heard with tongue],[63] they engage the rhetorical topos of performance, not the specialized idiom that is oral poetics. The same is true of the scenes of public reading captured memorably in Book II of Chaucer's *Troilus* and most famously in the frontispiece that accompanies the same poem in Cambridge, Corpus Christi College, 61.[64] But while narrative moments in which poets directly address their listening audiences or those that depict scenes of public reading testify to the vitality of oral delivery and the importance of aural reception in the English Middle Ages,[65] they do not necessarily reveal anything at all about the mix of oral and literate poetics contained in any given text but witness a text's "orality" only in the broadest sense of the term.[66] In this light, Albert C. Baugh's argument that the absence of a reading audience led fourteenth-century poets to compose "with oral presentation in mind, adopting a style, so far as they were capable of it, natural to live presentation"[67] is revealing because he locates orality in the poems' invocation of the discursive idiom of everyday speech, an idiom well removed from the special-ized, significative one fundamental to performative and nonperformative oral poetics.

Because performance was the most important conduit for literary dis-semination,[68] even the most highly literate poets in the post-Conquest period were crucially aware that their poems would reach the majority of their audi-ences through the ear, not the eye. While the presence of the topos of perform-ance has long been taken to signal the poets' engagement with oral tradition, the poets who employ it generally do so *without meaningfully engaging oral poetics.* Post-Conquest oral poetics is, as was the Anglo-Saxon oral poetics from which it descends, largely (if not exclusively) nonperformative, and the repre-sentations of oral performance within the extant corpus of Middle English poetry are therefore not reliable indices of oral poetics because they are the fic-tionalized and romanticized products of highly literate sensibilities.[69]

The key to the oral poetics that functions in the increasingly literate cultural milieu of the early Middle English period lies neither in actual per-formances, since these were generally text-based events,[70] nor in fictional rep-resentations of the performative matrix but in the presence of the specialized expressive economy of oral poetics. Instead of concentrating upon external and undependable representations of performance or upon fictional represen-tations of the performative matrix, we should focus on those features of early Middle English texts that point to their authors' engagement with oral poetics because as "[w]riting does not alienate a text from traditional meaning imme-diately[,] early written texts will still appeal to immanent meaning despite their written condition."[71]

Literate and Oral Poetics in Laȝamon's Early Middle English *Brut*

In his posthumously published *Middle English Literature,* J. A. W. Bennett argues that Laȝamon's "unique interest lies in the fact that though a literate poet, he continually shows signs and vestiges of an oral tradition that must have still operated in twelfth-century England in ways not distinctly different from those that Milman Parry has taught us to recognize in Homer."[72] In so foregrounding the role an active oral tradition plays in the text's production, Bennett articulates a view that must appear to oralists and nonoralists alike as paradoxical, if not simply untenable. The *Brut*'s status as a written text has, so far as I know, never been seriously questioned, in the way that, for example,

Beowulf's was beginning to be in the 1950s. As a result, even in the heyday of oral-formulaic criticism, a period in which scholars, in their exuberance to categorize texts as indisputably "oral" routinely overlooked (or elided) the written, textual nature of these same texts, Laȝamon's self-announced literacy and his self-acknowledged dependence upon written sources were apparently enough to deter the investigation of the *Brut*'s many features that seemed particularly indebted to either (or both) Anglo-Saxon poetics and the medieval English oral tradition.[73]

That the *Brut* should not have come under consideration by oral-formulaicists is not very surprising for a number of reasons: the poem's widely acknowledged aesthetic shortcomings, its sheer bulk (it remains one of the longest poems written in English), and the fact that it was (and still is) not available in a complete modern critical edition all may be credited with keeping its scholarly audience small.[74] Most importantly, the poem contains indisputable evidence both of the poet's literacy and of the poem's literate genesis and so, from the Parry-Lord perspective, was necessarily removed from the oral tradition. Laȝamon himself uses his prologue to establish the highly literate nature of his project and of his compositional practices. First of all, he carefully informs us that his text is not the product of his own imagination but rather rests securely upon several written texts. The "æðela boc" (15) [noble books] that provide the foundation of his text are, he tells us, "þa Englisca boc꞉ þa makede Seint Beda. / An-oþer . . . on Latin꞉ þe makede Seinte Albin. / ⁊ þe feire Austin" [the English book that Saint Bede made. Another . . . in Latin that Saint Albin and the fair Austin made], and one written by a "Frenchis clerc꞉ / Wace wes ihoten" (16–21) [French clerk named Wace]. This articulation of his debt to written sources—one of the earliest recorded in English—witnesses both his literacy and his project's literate poetics, but Laȝamon does not stop here: he further uses his prologue to lay bare his intertextual compositional practices. After "Hit com him on mode꞉ ⁊ on his mern þonke. / þet he wolde of Engle꞉ þa æðelæn tellen" (6–7) [It came into his mind and in his excellent thought that he would tell of England's noble men], he proceeded to journey "wide ȝond þas leode. / ⁊ bi-won þa æðela boc꞉ þa he to bisne nom" (14–15) [widely throughout this land and obtained those noble books that he took as his examples]. Once he had his three sources in his possession, he "heom leofliche bi-heold" (25) [gladly beheld them] and "þa soþere word꞉ sett togadere. / ⁊ þa þre boc꞉ þrumde to are" (27–28) [those true words set together and compressed those three books into one]. While the prologue is remarkable in itself for the way in which Laȝamon, perhaps as early as 1190, models what we can clearly recognize as literate practices, what makes it even more noteworthy is that he supplements his description of his project's intertextuality by signaling his close engagement with early Middle English material culture. Not only is Laȝamon responsible for composing the matter of his text, but he also claims responsibility for its material construction. By announcing that "Feþeren he nom mid fingren: 7 fiede on boc-felle" (26) [Feathers he took with his fingers and wrote on book-skins], Laȝamon situates himself squarely within the complex matrix of early medieval poetic composition *and* production.[75]

The sources Laȝamon names in his prologue simultaneously witness both his closeness to and his distance from the literate world. The first of the authorities he mentions is generally accepted to be a copy of Alfred's translation of Bede's *Historia,* but Madden notes that "far from making it form an integral portion of his own poem, or even occupy a prominent place in it, [Laȝamon] seems to have taken nothing from it except the story of Pope Gregory and the Anglo-Saxon captives at Rome."[76] The identity of Laȝamon's second source, the Latin text co-authored by St. Albin and St. Augustine, remains a mystery. Although no doubt fictional,[77] it serves precisely the same function in the poem's prologue that the very popular and widely known *Historia* does: Laȝamon uses its status as a written text to authorize and further validate the highly literate underpinnings of his own creation and does not draw upon it for specific narrative details. The third and final announced source, Wace's *Roman de Brut,* is itself a reworking of Geoffrey of Monmouth's *Historia Regum Britanniae* and is the only one of the named sources that plays a demonstrable role in shaping the narrative of the *Brut.* There is little evidence in the poem to suggest that Laȝamon had even a passing acquaintance with Geoffrey's Latin work, but because Laȝamon uses the French poem as a template for his own narrative we cannot discount the possibility that he worked closely with or perhaps even directly from a copy of the French text.

While we must credit Laȝamon with a highly literate foundation for his authorial making—he appears to have been at the very least bilingual and may have had command of Latin and perhaps even some limited knowledge of Welsh as well[78]—and while his compositional practices and writerly motivations clearly reflect our own modern practices, we ought not lean too heavily upon his seeming "modernity" when attempting to explain those characteristics of the *Brut,* such as its decidedly native lexicon and diction and its inconsistent versification, that set it apart from other early Middle English poems. For some, the poem's lexical and syntactical anomalies and idiosyncrasies witness the poet's antiquarian leanings, leading them to view Laȝamon as a poet who consciously clings to and desires to re-create the English past. As a result, the poem's numerous "odd" features are seen to reveal nothing more than the poet's rather limited and decidedly imperfect understanding of the poetics he seeks to evoke because even though he was "writing at a time when other English poets had switched to foreign ways of expression, [Laȝamon] advertises the English past by putting up *ye olde* signs."[79] Daniel Donoghue offers a more nuanced reading of the poem's peculiar blend of lexical, narrative, and metrical features and suggests that they ought to be read as the poet's response to the social and political complexities of life in late-twelfth- and early-thirteenth-century England. In Donoghue's view, Laȝamon "remains caught between the old and the new, the Anglo-Saxon and Anglo-Norman, in an age of competing allegiances, and from his middle position he balances the oppositions within the scheme of a historiographical tradition more complex than most of his modern admirers have allowed."[80] Laȝamon may well have felt the tug of conflicting cultural and social forces as emerging Anglo-Saxon nationalism collided with the newly imported culture and politics of the Anglo-Normans, but rather than seeing him as being forced ultimately to make a choice between his native language or Anglo-Norman, the "old" metrics, lexicon, and thematics or those imported by the Anglo-Norman invaders, fealty to "old" social systems and institutions or acceptance of those brought over from the Continent, we should see him rather as someone who negotiates as best he can between and among the disparate, unique, and often conflicting constellations of elements that constitute early Middle English culture. Laȝamon may have had the highly refined sense of his own position in the development of early Middle English literary culture and the sharp political awareness that generations of scholars have surmised for him, but he may also simply have relied upon the expressive economy that was his direct cultural inheritance.

Oral Poetics in the *Brut:* Lexical and Syntactic Evidence

Laȝamon's decidedly Anglo-Saxon lexicon,[81] his creation of compounds, and his seemingly odd syntax (to say nothing of his metrics and thematics) have led some scholars to conclude that the *Brut* reflects only the idiosyncrasies of a poet who has been labeled "a massive erratic in the history of English poetry."[82] Even J. P. Oakden, a scholar who gives Laȝamon more credit as a poet than many others do, contends that "it would be ridiculous to suggest that [he] created all" of the 217 compounds in the *Brut* that have native first and second elements but that are not found in the Old English poetic lexicon despite the fact that "Germanic parallels to these words can only be found in 17 cases."[83] E. G. Stanley acknowledges that "many of the compounds not found in ME outside the *Brut*, e.g. those with 'leod' as first element, clearly belong to the tradition of OE poetic compounds—some of them probably nonce-formations," but he cautions, "as used by Laȝamon, they seem to have been coined as tokens of a past re-created by re-animating fossils of an extinct art form."[84]

The nature of Laȝamon's poetic compounds can be brought more sharply into focus by considering the *leod-x* compounds Stanley singles out as belonging to the poetics that formed part of "the only language fit for poetry" in the Anglo-Saxon period, a language that the poet uses, further, in a way that is "differently self-conscious."[85] Madden's glossary contains the following *leod-x* compounds:[86] *leode-ælder* (I, 58) [leader; nobleman], *leod-cnihtes* (I, 318) [knight], *leode-ferde* (I, 36) [army], *leod-folc* (I, 86) [army; people of a country], *leod-kempen* (I, 257) [knight], *leod-king* (I, 22) [king of a nation], *leod-quide* (I, 123) [national language], *leod-ronen* (I, 389) [advice], *leod-scome* (III, 45) [national disgrace], *leod-scopes* (II, 542) [minstrel], *leod-swike* (I, 32) [traitor to his country], *leod-ðeauwe* (I, 87) [custom of a country], *leod-þeines* (I, 284) [leader; nobleman], and *leod-wisen* (I, 303) [custom of a country]. On the surface, it is difficult to discern what about these compounds or the way they are used sets them apart from their Anglo-Saxon forebears, especially as they clearly derive from Anglo-Saxon lexemes (e.g., *leodeælder* < OE *lēod* + *ieldra; leodquide* < OE *lēod* + *cwide*) and several of them are extant in Anglo-Saxon prose or poetic texts (*leodcyning* [*Beowulf*, 54a]; *leodrun* [*Bald's Leechbook*, II (1 Head) 64.1]).[87] Healey and Venezky's *Microfiche Concordance to Old English* reveals that in the extant corpus of Anglo-Saxon literature there are thirty-four compounds of the type *leod-x*, including such obvious parallels to Laȝamon's as *leodcyning* (*Beowulf*, 53a), *leodwearas* (*Genesis A*, 1833b) [men of a nation], *leodwerod* (*Exodus*, 77a) [host formed by a people], and *leodþeaw* (*Genesis A*, 1938a) as well as a number of others that easily could have appeared in the *Brut*: *leodrihte* (*Andreas*, 679a) [public law], *leodmægen* (*Elene*, 272b) [warriors], *leodfruma* (*Wife's Lament*, 8a) [prince; chieftain], and *leodbealewa* (*Beowulf*, 1946a) [harm that affects a people]. The argument put forth by Stanley (and less consistently by Oakden)[88] that the compounds in the *Brut* are simply the fossilized remains of a now defunct tradition takes into account neither the vibrancy of the compounds themselves nor the central role that compounding has played (and continues to play) in Indo-European lexicons.[89]

In *Beowulf*, compounds "occur more than fifteen hundred times, or at the rate of almost one every other line,"[90] and, more generally, in "Old English poetry there is one poetic compound in every three lines (though a few poems have an average of one compound per line."[91] Using the more conservative of these figures because the rate of compounding in *Beowulf* is generally accepted as being unusually high, we still arrive at a 33 percent frequency rate in Old English poetry, as opposed to the *Brut*, where the average of one compound per forty lines works out to a frequency rate of only 2.5 percent. While this dropoff is rather precipitous, the lower frequency of occurrence in the *Brut* points more to the currency of Laȝamon's poetic language than to his putative antiquarian sentiments. Where compounding had earlier enabled Anglo-Saxon poets to meet the demands alliteration placed upon them, by the time Laȝamon composes, compounds occur much less frequently because alliteration is no longer absolutely necessary to the articulation of English verse.

The first five hundred lines of the *Brut* contain some forty-five nominal compounds, a rate of one for every 11.1 lines of verse. These compounds fall into three categories: those that occur in Anglo-Saxon prose and poetry, such as *sea-streames* (165) [sea] (cf. *sæstreamas* [*Genesis A*, 1326a]), and *blod-gute* (317) [bloodshed] (cf. *blodgyte* [*Christ II*, 708b]); those that are not extant in Anglo-Saxon but are made up of two Anglo-Saxon elements such as *feie-sið* (154) [death] (cf. OE *fæge* [fated] + *sið* [journey] as well as the compounds *utsið* [a going out] and *forðsið* [departure; death]) and *wal-kempen* (391) [warrior] (cf. OE *wæl* [I. the slain; III. slaughter] + *cempa* [soldier] and the compounds *wæl-gæst* [*Beowulf*, 1331a] [deadly guest]) and *wælherigas* [*Genesis A*, 1983a]); and those not found in Anglo-Saxon that either contain one or two non-Anglo-Saxon elements, such as *wiðer-heppes* (204) (<OE *wiðer* [against] + ON *happ* [good luck]) and *wode-roten* (235) (<OE *wudu* [wood] + ON *rót* [root]) or that appear to be direct loanwords from Old Norse, such as *þrel-werkes* (229) [work fit for a slave] (<ON *þrælverk*). As we may expect given the evidence of the *leod-x* compounds, the ones Laȝamon builds on two Anglo-Saxon elements have close parallels in the extant corpus of Old English literature. Although *wæl-kempen* does not appear in the earlier prose or poetry, it easily could have: more than ninety compounds in the *wæl-x* system survive in Old English, among which are *wælgæst, wælherigas,* and *wæl-cræft* [deadly power].

Those compounds of Laȝamon's that fall into the third category—those not extant in the Anglo-Saxon corpus that combine Anglo-Saxon and Old Norse elements or that appear to be direct loans from Old Norse—not only observe the rules of Germanic compound formation but provide further evidence of the vitality and suppleness of Laȝamon's poetic idiom. Compounds such as *wiðer-heppes, wode-róten,* and *wil-tidende* (<OE *wil* [desirable] + ON *tíðindi* [tidings]) witness the ease with which Laȝamon was successfully able to incorporate new terms into his inherited poetic register. H. C. Wyld glosses the unique compound *wiðer-heppes* as "calamities, misfortune," while Oakden prefers the less precise "conflicts."[92] In context, both readings seem appropriate: "þar arose wale 7 win: 7 wiðer-heppes fela" (204) [there arose slaughter and strife and many *wiðer-heppes*]. In addition to fulfilling the semantic requirements established by the pair *wale* and *win, wiðer-heppes* fits seamlessly into the Anglo-Saxon syntactic pattern in which the indeclinable adverb *fela* is used following a partitive genitive. This same pattern appears numerous times in *Beowulf,* where we find, among others, the following phrases: "swa fela fyrena   feond mancynnes" (164) [so many of crimes the fiend of mankind], "þæt næfre Gre[n]del swa fela   gryra gefremede" (591) [that never Grendel so many of horrors would have performed], "uncuþes fela" (876b) [of unknown many], and "Fela ic laþes gebad" (929b) [much I of hateful endured].[93] Laȝamon was able not only to create new compounds that fit into an existing system but to coin new compound types that fit into established syntactic and lexical patterns: for example, the pattern genitive singular/plural–*fela* occurs regularly throughout the poem.[94]

The syntax of the *Brut* has generally been categorized—along with its lexicon and diction—as another of the poem's notably idiosyncratic features, and it is often invoked in support of the argument that Laȝamon was a conscious archaizer intent on reanimating a dead tradition.[95] Stanley notes that Laȝamon's "frequent use of inversions is reminiscent of Old English"[96] but goes on to argue that the poet's inversions, specifically, and his syntax, more generally, are decidedly "un-Anglo-Saxon." From Stanley's perspective, the poem's syntax is, unlike its lexicon, neither "conservative" nor "archaic" but rather clearly indicative of contemporary Middle English practice. Much of the poem's syntax does reflect general early Middle English usage, but a great deal in it also runs contrary to such usage. For example, even though he was writing at a time when word order was emerging as a crucial component of English syntax, Laȝamon inverts adjectives and articles so frequently that a modern reader's sense that the word order of a phrase such as "mid riche his folke" (268) [with powerful his people] is somewhat odd soon disappears as one reads on in the poem.[97] That the *Brut* should evidence such widespread syntactic inversions is even more surprising given that Laȝamon was not working with a language that was still solely dependent upon an inflectional system of grammar but rather with one in which the effects of leveling are dramatically apparent.

As we would expect of a text composed during a period when the English language was undergoing widespread changes, the *Brut* preserves some Anglo-Saxon inflections "like acc. sg. masc. *-ne* in *monine* [7878], *þisne* [7849], gen. and dat. sg. fem. in *-re* in *þissere* [7782], and *swulchere* [8277],"[98] but the leveled forms greatly outnumber those that are unambiguously marked with inflectional endings.[99] In addition to evidencing widespread leveling, the poem's accidence shows the effects of "nunnation," a process that results in "a final *n* [being added] to certain cases of nouns and adjectives, to some tenses of verbs, and to several other parts of speech."[100] Although what we discover in the *Brut* is not so much the leveling of the Anglo-Saxon inflectional system as its virtual collapse, the poem contains many instances in which the word order of a clause reflects that of Old English, instances that are, further, at odds with the analytic system within which Laȝamon composed poetry, one that provided the foundation for his language's nonpoetic syntax as well.

Like his adjective-article inversion, Laȝamon's constructions involving a superlative adjective and a genitive plural noun are often inverted. Alongside the expected word order of a phrase such as "Hail seo þu Arður: aðelest cnihten" (9913) [Hail to you, Arthur, noblest of knights] we frequently discover the inverted order of "Ded is Aurilie: kingene aðelest" (9049) [Dead is Aurelius, of kings the best]. Although this latter construction is characteristic of inflected languages and seems to be simply another of Laȝamon's idiosyncrasies, it derives from the highly specialized, dedicated poetic register that Anglo-Saxon poets employed. For example, in the first five hundred lines of *Beowulf*, the inflected genitive precedes its dependent noun ninety-eight times and follows it forty-five times. The *Beowulf*-poet moves easily between the word orders exemplified by "Grendles guþe" (483a) [Grendel's warfare] and "maga Healfdenes" (189b) [the kinsman of Half-Dane] in large part because in Old English prose and verse there "is no simple rule for the genitives of nouns, for they occur—both alone and in combination—in pre- and post-position."[101] Unlike modern speakers of English, Laȝamon was similarly able to pre- or postposition his genitive.[102] Laȝamon clearly saw phrases such as "aðelest Brutten" (10158) [noblest of the Britons] and "kingen alre kenest" (9511) [of kings of all the bravest] as formal and syntactical equivalents.[103] That these word orders frequently occur in close proximity to one another, as in "and Gorlois hire lauerd: mo[n]nenen alre laðest" (9439) [and Gorlois her lord of men of all the most hateful] and "for ich am on rade. rihchest alre monnen" (9445) [because I am in counsel richest of all men] and even occasionally in successive lines ("þer weoren Sæxisce men: folken alre ærmest. / 7 þa Alemainisce men: ʒeomerest alre leoden" [10605]) [then were Saxon men of people of all the most wretched / and those German men the most miserable of all people] further demonstrates the construction's fluidity within his idiopoetics.

If we take these syntactic features, along with others I have discussed elsewhere,[104] to be the products of Laʒamon's "archaistic" impulses, we put ourselves in the somewhat awkward position of imputing to a late-twelfth-century cleric of somewhat modest poetic talents a linguistic awareness rivaling that of twenty-first-century scholars who have access to worlds of texts and resources unknown to Laʒamon and who are further capable of undertaking sophisticated comparative syntactic analyses that he surely could not. Even though the library at Worcester some ten miles from his home in Areley Kings contained Old English texts, the availability of such texts does not speak to Laʒamon's ability or desire to read them. Further, we have no evidence that he was familiar with any of the Anglo-Saxon codices housed in the library at Worcester or that they played any demonstrable part in shaping his poem.[105]

When we place the *Brut* on the continuum that is the medieval English poetic tradition, the gap between it and the Old English verse that precedes it is not that much greater than the gap that separates the Chronicle poems, or a late classical poem such as *Durham,* from a more "typical" or "canonical" earlier poem such as *Beowulf.*[106] The early Middle English text's lexicon, diction, and syntax offer evidence not of the poet's idiosyncratic desire to invoke a dead tradition but rather of the natural changes that time (as well as social and cultural forces) wrought on Anglo-Saxon oral poetics. Dorothy Everett argues along these lines when she notes that early Middle English verse "could have been, and some of it must have been," descended from the Anglo-Saxon tradition. But because it was "more or less modernized in language and metre in the course of transmission—a process that would explain some of the characteristics of the verse and diction of Middle English alliterative poetry,"[107] the line of descent is blurred and often more fully obscured.[108]

Oral Poetics and Middle English *Abelʒen*

In the *Brut,* the affective dynamics of the simplex *abelʒen* [to anger or incense; to grow angry (MED s.v.)] and its variants *abolwen* and *abælh* is remarkably similar to that of the Anglo-Saxon simplex *gebelgan* [to swell with anger; become angry (DOE/s.v.)], from which it descends. As it does in Old English poetry, this lexeme functions in Laȝamon's poem as a traditional *sêma* by associatively and metonymically signaling the approach of an impending slaughterous encounter.[109] As do all *sêmata*, the simplex links what is "present and explicit to what is immanent and implied,"[110] and it thus serves as a conduit through which poets economically bring institutionalized meaning to bear on the narrative present and enable the interpretative channels through which their poems will be received.

Considering the way Laȝamon employs *abelȝen* during the episode in which Arthur accepts King Frolle of France's offer "to-dælen and to-dihten þis kine-lond mid fihte" (11791) [to divide and to rule this kingdom by fighting] "bi-twixen unke seoluen" (11790) [between ourselves] will allow us to see the extent of the simplex's traditionality. After a protracted narrative buildup in which Laȝamon reports several times that Frolle regrets having made this offer and in which the poet carefully chronicles the names of those who will witness the battle, the fight begins unremarkably: Arthur knocks Frolle from his horse, and Frolle succeeds in unhorsing Arthur by killing his steed. Because the two antagonists are unusually well matched, the fight promises to be a protracted affair—"beien heo weoren cnihtes kene: ohte men and wihte. / muchele men on mihte: and a maine swiðe stronge" (11935–36) [they were both brave knights, worthy and valiant men, great men in might and in strength very strong]— but during an assault by Frolle, one in which he succeeds in knocking Arthur's shield to the ground, Arthur sustains a "wunde . . . feouwer unchene long" (11961) [a wound . . . four inches long], the blood from which "orn a-dun: ouer al his breoste" (11963) [ran down all over his breast]. After receiving this wound, Arthur, who approached the fight gleefully anticipating that it would end with his adding France to his growing list of recent acquisitions and who perhaps did not expect much of a contest from Frolle, becomes "abolȝe: swiðe an his heorte" (11964) [very enraged in his heart]. The appearance of *abelȝen* is, in this instance, immediately followed by a graphic account of slaughter:

> . . . [Arthur] his sweord Caliburne: swipte mid maine:
> and smat Frolle uppen þæne hælm: þat he atwa helden.
> þurh-ut þere burne hod: þat hit at his breoste at-stod.
> Þa feol Frolle: folde to grunde.
> uppen þan gras-bedde: his gost he bi-læfde.
>
> (11965–69)

———————

[(Arthur) swung his sword Caliburn with might and struck Frolle upon the helmet so that it split in two right through the cuirass so that it stopped at his breast. Then Frolle fell to the earth of the field; upon that grass bed he relinquished his spirit.]

As is true in the Old English poems in which (x-)*belgan*(-*mod*) is situated within the thematics of slaughter, there is in the *Brut* considerable variation in the number of lines that elapse between the appearance of the simplex and the slaughter that it announces and thematizes, but *abelʒen* is directly linked to slaughter every time it occurs in the text.[111] I have elsewhere shown that the simplex points to narratively imminent slaughter and so functions as it does in Anglo-Saxon oral poetics,[112] and I will here focus on those instances in which Laʒamon's usage of it departs from its more traditional instantiations in Old English poetry and his own poem. These moments are of special interest because they demonstrate the continuing cohesion of this simplex's affective dynamics and illustrate the degree to which it serves as a useful and supple element of Laʒamon's poetics.

During the episode that details Uther Pendragon's unsuccessful attempts to build his castle (every night all the stones that were erected during the day are "iualled to þan grunde" [7898] [knocked to the ground]), Uther tells the young Merlin his counselors have revealed that if he "nime þi blod: ut of þire breoste: / 7 minne wal wurche: 7 do to mine l(i)me. / þenne mai he stonde: to þere worlde longe" (7900–902) [should take your blood out of your breast and make [his] wall with it and mix it with [his] lime then the wall may stand as long as the world]. Merlin finds this news justifiably alarming, but rather than quailing before the king, he responds by becoming "bælh on his mode" (7904) [enraged in his mind]. The simplex finds its expected complement at 7979–80, when Joram and the seven others who counseled Uther to mix Merlin's blood into the mortar for the castle are summarily beheaded, and here serves as the narrative equivalent of a squinting modifier. It not only signals an imminent death but also looks back to an implied (but ultimately realized) slaughter. We find precisely the same pattern at work when Constantine becomes "a-bolʒen" (14309) after learning that Modred's sons "þuhten to slan" (14308) [thought to slay] him. The slaughter thematized by "a-bolʒen" occurs both at 14332, when Constantine the "hefd . . . of-swipte" [the head . . . struck off] of Modred's unnamed son, and again at 14346, when he does the same thing to Meleus,

Modred's other son: "Constantin braid ut his sweorde: 7 þat hafde him of-swipte" [Constantine drew out his sword and struck his head off]. As he did earlier, Laȝamon once again expands the simplex's rhetorical horizon to include an implied but unrealized slaughter that, when coupled with the explicit slaughter that eventually occurs, effectively and affectively frames the simplex. Far from destroying the simplex's traditional referentiality or compromising the narrative integrity of the thematics of slaughter, Laȝamon's departures from the traditional pattern broaden and enrich it and so point to the elastic and accommodating framework of post-Conquest oral poetics. Although he composes in writing and not in the crucible of performance, Laȝ-amon engages an oral poetics that is as dynamic and as constantly evolving as those theorized for or witnessed in performance-based oral traditions.

Abelȝen is a verbal cue that preserves its (idiomatic) meaning in a synchronically divergent collection of Middle English poems and along a diachronic axis of considerable length. It survives in several other early Middle English texts (both prose and verse), among which are the *Orrmulum* and the *Hule and Niȝtengale*. Occurring some nine times in Orrm's long and truly quirky poem, *bollȝhen* is always either closely linked to an account of actual slaughter or, in one case, to a threatened, imminent slaughter. Orrm is a decidedly literate poet whose remarkably consistent, if highly idiosyncratic, system for representing his language in writing reveals that his chief orientation is ocular, and not aural or oral, but the simplex's traditional contours are still clearly visible and its affective dynamics is still intact in his poem because the dedicated register of oral poetics continues to allow authors to engage "the meaning-bearing potential of . . . tradition, even if at one expressive remove."[113]

In his account of Herod's last days, Orrm explicitly links the physical torment Herod suffers to the tyrant's lifetime of sinful behavior. For present purposes, what is most important about this episode is not that Herod suffers or that Orrm attempts to wring an obvious moral lesson from it. Rather, it is that even near death Herod continues to engage in the slaughterous behavior for which he is infamous. The doctors who are summoned to treat him are all put to death once they fail to alleviate his suffering and, in an insidious attempt to extend his control of earthly matters even beyond the grave, his men are instructed to kill a large number of recently imprisoned nobles immediately following his death so that his people will be too busy mourning their murdered husbands and fathers to rejoice over the tyrant's demise. In his desperation to end his suffering, Herod even attempts to take his own life with a knife he requests ostensibly to pare an apple. His (amazingly) still loyal servants thwart his suicide attempt, but news of it reaches one of his sons (whom the tyrant has imprisoned), who "warrþ swiþe bliþe þa, / 7 toc to lahhȝhenn lhude" (8141–42) [became so happy then and took to laughing loudly]. Upon learning of his son's reaction, Herod "warrþ wraþ 7 bollghenn, / 7 badd tatt mann himm sollde anan / Wiþþ swerdess egge cwellenn" (8144–46) [became angry and enraged and commanded that someone should at once kill him with a sword's edge], something that Orrm reports "wass þanne sone don / To forþenn himm hiss wille" (8147–48) [was then soon done to carry out his will].

Elsewhere in the poem, the simplex retains its word-power even when no slaughter occurs in its immediate narrative context. Herod's vows to murder the newborn Christ (7260–61, 7312–13) are preceded in each instance by the simplex (7145, 7159, 7197, 7201),[114] and the episode in which Christ prudently departs from Judea upon learning that the Pharisees are "bollȝhenn" with him contains a reference to Herod's slaughter of the innocents and concludes with a description of the crucifixion, two events that do not bear on the narrative moment being related but that serve as traditional and metanarrative complements to the simplex *bollȝhenn*. Used more restrictively in the *Orrmulum* (it applies chiefly to Herod, who is even invoked as a murderer in the one episode in which it refers to someone other than him) than it is in the *Brut* or in Old English poetry, the simplex nevertheless remains closely connected to the expressive economy of oral poetics even when it is used so narrowly by a poet of rather limited means.[115]

Abelȝen occurs as well in the *Hule and Niȝtengale*, a poem whose graceful execution, intelligence, wit, and overall artistry set it so far apart not only from the often plodding, uninspired work of Orrm, but from the rest of the extant verse contemporary with it that its appearance in the twelfth century has been viewed, with good reason, as a miracle. Because the simplex occurs only once in the poem, we cannot place too heavy an interpretive burden upon it, but it nevertheless sheds considerable light upon medieval English oral poetics because it further demonstrates that traces of the traditional expressive economy persist even within a radically different poetics.

The narrative context in which the simplex occurs is wholly traditional. Following the first extended and deeply insulting speech the Nightingale makes, one in which she adds a moral dimension to an argument that has to this point been solely based on aesthetics by dwelling upon the proverbial tendency of owls to foul their own nests, the Owl "sat tosvolle & ibolwe" (145) [sat puffed up with rage and swollen with anger]. The poet has laid a recognizably traditional groundwork for the simplex's appearance by having the Nightingale twice label the Owl an "vnwiȝt" (33, 90) [monster] and by having both the Nightingale and the Owl comment explicitly on the Owl's "cliures" (84) [talons] and the violence the Owl would like to perform on the Nightingale's body with them and her beak. Not only is the Owl capable of and prone to acting violently, the Nightingale does all she can to deserve being on the receiving end of the Owl's malevolence. After completing the "longe tale" (140) in which she voices the Platonic argument that their ugliness, lack of virtue, and low place in the great chain of being ensure the degraded habits of owls, "He song so lude & so scharpe, / Riȝt so me grulde schille harpe" (141–42) [She sang so loud and so sharp just as if one were strumming a shrill harp]. And in a move that underscores the scene's potential for fatal violence and heightens our sense of the Owl's outrage over the Nightingale's extended speech, the poet describes the Owl as being "tosvolle" (145) [puffed up with rage].

Once we learn that the Owl is also "ibolwe" (145) [swollen with anger], the final key to the scene's reception appears to be in place: all that is missing is the slaughter itself. But as readers of the poem know, no slaughter occurs here or elsewhere in the poem's 1794 lines. In fact, the poem ends without a single feather being more than metaphorically ruffled. Rather than resorting to violence to settle their quarrel, the two disputants civilly agree to fly off together to Portesham so that the very capable and learned "Maistre Nichole" (1778) can adjudicate matters. Not only does the simplex's traditional narrative complement never occur, but the simplex itself is put to a very different, posttraditional purpose. The *Hule*-poet builds up the expectation of slaughter before, during, and after the Nightingale's speech at lines 56 to 138, an expectation that culminates in the appearance of the traditionally freighted simplex *abelȝen*. But having done so, he immediately shifts the ground under the simplex and disconnects it from its traditional expressive economy by deploying it as the pivotal element in a nontraditional narrative moment. What follows the appearance of the simplex is not slaughter but the poet's comic revelation that the Owl is so swollen with anger that she looks "Also . . . hadde one frogge isuolȝe" (146) [as if (she) had swallowed a frog]. The figurative distension so important to the simplex's affective dynamics, a distension made explicit in the Old English (x-)*belgan*(-*mod*), is here literalized, and the violence that it thematizes is comically defused. Far from signaling the imminence of a violent outburst, as it does when Heremod is described as *bolgenmod* in *Beowulf*, when Arthur becomes *abolȝe* in the *Brut*, or when Herod becomes *bollȝhenn* in the *Orrmulum*, the simplex here signifies the literal, and somewhat ridiculous, physical distension that occurs when an owl swallows a frog whole.

The Nightingale remains wary of the Owl's potential for violence, mentioning her "scharpe clawe" (153) and her "cliuers suþe stronge" (155) [very strong talons], and the promise of violence surely underlies the Owl's restrained response to the Nightingale's initial *ad avem* attack—

Whi neltu flon into þe bare
& sewi ware unker bo
Of briȝter howe, of uairur blo?
(150–52)

———

[Why will you not fly into the open and show which of the two of us is of brighter hue, of fairer color?]

but the Nightingale, being far too smart to fall for such a transparent ruse, remains safely hidden among the branches of a hedge throughout the poem. In using *ibolwe*, the *Hule*-poet clearly taps into the traditional, dedicated register of oral poetics and exploits the traditional channels of reception it affords him, but he reveals his distance from the tradition by thwarting the audience's expectations and using the simplex in a narrowly denotative (and post-traditional) rather than richly connotative (and traditional) manner. He skillfully draws upon the simplex's traditional, inherent meaning in this episode by gesturing toward the violence (actual or implied) that the simplex signals in medieval English oral poetics, but he finally confers an idiosyncratic meaning upon it. The Owl looks less like a dangerously distended monster who will momentarily tear her opponent to shreds than like an indignantly puffed-up society matron of the type Margaret Dumont portrayed so ably on stage and screen.

The doublet *tosvolle,* a variant of *toswellen,* that precedes *ibolwe* further evidences the scene's dependence on a literate, not oral, poetics. In itself, the appearance of a doublet constitutes a departure from earlier practice because even though variation is an extremely important component of Anglo-Saxon poetics,[116] (x-)*belgan(-mod)* is only twice found in an appositive construction.[117] Every other time the simplex appears, it stands on its own. If we adopt J. A. Burrow and Thorlac Turville-Petre's reading and take *ibolwe* to mean "puffed up" we can see that the poet might have included *tosvolle* for emphasis so his audience would be sure to get the joke that follows, but there is finally little reason for accepting their reading over Stanley's "swollen with anger" or Bennett and Smithers's "swollen, distended (with rage)" both of which echo more closely the meaning assigned it by the MED: "puffed up with rage" (s.v.

toswellen, 3. Fig. a).[118] The appearance of the doublet does suggest the degree to which the affective dynamics of *ibolwe* has diminished for the *Hule*-poet (and/or his intended audience): because its traditional referentiality has become occluded, it can no longer instantiate the thematics of slaughter on its own but needs additional help. Not as securely linked metonymically to worlds of established, shared meaning as it earlier was, it needs direction and clarification (as do all *sêmata* in post-traditional poetics, whether or not they descend from oral poetics), in this instance by a term that comes to bear, and still does bear, the traditional significative burden that *ibolwe* bore in medieval English oral poetics.

In tapping into the traditional affective dynamics of this lexeme and then putting it to a decidedly post-traditional usage, the *Hule*-poet seems to stand apart from his Anglo-Saxon predecessors, but his actions differ only in degree, not in kind, from theirs. Just as the Anglo-Saxon poets who composed and physically encoded Old English poetry necessarily altered the tradition in the course of engaging and disseminating it, so, too, did Middle English poets constantly effect changes in their evolving tradition by, among other things, putting traditional metonyms to new, not wholly traditional uses and by incorporating into their poems non-native poetics metrics and thematics. As we trace the trajectory of oral poetics from its logical, if theoretical, genesis in a primary or wholly oral culture, to its commingling with a nascent literate poetics, to its continued survival (albeit in a diminished and diminishing capacity) in a culture increasingly dominated by a literate poetics, what stands out most strikingly is its flexibility and resilience. Oral poetics survives for so long and has such a great impact upon the literary history of medieval England because its channels of meaning remain open to poets who are entirely free to employ them (either wittingly or unwittingly) in traditional or nontraditional ways.

Oral Poetics and the *Brut*'s Thematics

One of the *Brut*'s most striking features is that it contains many narrative patterns, among which are scenes of feasts, voyages, arrivals, and combat, whose thematics are remarkably similar from one occurrence to the next. The consistent manner in which the narrative details of these scenes are presented and the high degree of verbal correspondences among the various occurrences of each theme or typical scene have been taken as unambiguous indicators of their fundamentally formulaic character. Most notably, Håkon Ringbom and

Dennis Donahue demonstrate that identifiable (and predictable) constellations of events and phraseology undergird many of the poem's frequently recurring scenes.[119] But Laȝamon's reliance upon an apparently fixed set of details each time he presents any of a number of typical scenes reveals little about his connection to medieval oral poetics because repetition, in and of itself, does *not* signal the presence of oral poetics. For example, the formulaic character of the many scenes of feasting in the narrative is readily apparent,[120] but their consistency derives more from Laȝamon's idiosyncratic and literate poetics than from traditional medieval English oral poetics. Laȝamon does almost invariably assign the same narrative pattern to his many scenes of feasting, but this is a pattern of his own devising. Some isolated elements of Laȝamon's feasting scenes, such as the joyous noise and the music and song that attend the occasion, clearly descend from Anglo-Saxon tradition, but their overall contours deviate so greatly from those found in Old English poetry that a structuralist reading of them yields only general insights. The narrative templates that Laȝamon creates tell us a great deal about the tectonics of his own poem and the importance of reiterative patterning to his local, literate idiopoetics but little, if anything, about its (and his) relationship to oral poetics. To calibrate accurately the ways in which oral poetics shapes Laȝamon's thematic structures, we must focus instead upon those narrative patterns that correspond closely to the thematics and affective dynamics of their Old English avatars. We must also supplement any structuralist inquiry we undertake with a careful consideration of the poem's aesthetics.

To illustrate the degree to which oral poetics informs Laȝamon's narrative, we will focus upon two scenes: a uniquely occurring one in which a lone hero battles a monstrous foe and a multiply attested one in which a woman greets and offers a cup to a man. Both of these are securely grounded in traditional Anglo-Saxon oral poetics, and because they are both found in Laȝamon's primary source, Wace, and in Wace's primary source, Geoffrey of Monmouth, they afford us the further opportunity of tracking these thematic structures as they pass through the hands of poets working in three very different traditions.

Oral Poetics and a Uniquely Occurring Narrative Pattern:
Morpidus and the Beast from the Sea

During the reign of King Morpidus, a terrible beast emerges from the sea one day and sets about harrying the countryside, indiscriminately devouring those men and beasts unfortunate enough to stumble into its path. Although his mother is a "chiuese" (3168) [concubine], Morpidus's heroic credentials are of the first order. He is, Laʒamon informs us, "monnene strengest. / of maine and of þeauwe: of all þissere þeode" (3170–71) [strongest of men of might and thews of all this people], who "of alle þingen heo weore god: ʒi[f] he neore to-wamed" (3174) [in all things would have been good if he were not given to violence]. He is also a fierce warrior who in the course of a single battle "mid his honden: þurh hæhʒere strengðe. / seouen hundred of-sloh: and swende mid wepnen" (3201–2) [with his hands through his great strength slew seven hundred and struck them down with weapons]. The beast possesses similarly impressive, but monstrous, credentials. Because it is described only elliptically as a "deor swiðe sellich" (3209) [a very strange beast], we are left to infer its size from its killing power: "oft an one dæie. hit makede an hundred fæie" (3212) [often in a day it killed a hundred people]. In its subsequent visits, "þat folc hit agaste: tunes it aweste" (3216) [it terrified the people and laid waste to the towns], so that Morpidus's people "a-w[a]i hold" (3217) [fled away]. When he learns about the monster's attacks, Morpidus immediately sets out "þiðerward . . . him-seolue to wæine. / to-ward þon deore: þer he dæð fæhte" (3219–20) [thither . . . to his own harm toward the beast, where he met his death]. Arriving upon the scene, he first commands "al his hird-folc: faren to are burʒe. / and hæhte heom þer abiden" (3222–23) [all his people to go to a town and ordered them to wait there] before he sets out to confront the beast. Although he possesses great strength, Morpidus prudently faces the beast bearing a veritable arsenal. His weapons include "a kene sweord: and enne koker fulne flan. / enne boʒe swiðe strong: and a spere swiðe long" (3225–26) [a sharp sword and a quiver full of arrows, a very strong bow and a very long spear]. Additionally, he has on one side of "his sadele an æx: and æt þe oðer halue an hond-sæx" (3227) [his saddle an axe and on the other side a dagger].

Their battle begins with Morpidus shooting his arrows at the beast. When these prove ineffective, he rides at it with his spear and strikes it in the throat, a blow that causes the beast to fall back and the spear's shaft to shatter (3227) [to-brac]. The beast suffers no real harm from this blow and soon rushes upon Morpidus, eviscerating his horse. Morpidus drives his sword into the beast's "hæued-bæn" (3242) [head-bone], but "þa hilt on his hand bræc" (3243) [the hilt broke in his hand]. The beast suffers a terrible wound but is still able to seize Morpidus in its jaws and "for-bat hine amidden a twa" (3245) [bit him in the middle in two]. The wounds they inflict on each other prove fatal, and at the battle's conclusion, both Morpidus and the beast lie dead.

As even this brief summary reveals, there are numerous points of contact between this thematic structure and the one that informs Beowulf's fight with the dragon.[121] In both, a hero of prodigious physical strength dies defending his kingdom in single combat against a terrible, alien creature that visits widespread destruction upon the countryside. In addition to their narrative similarities, they also share very similar affective dynamics. Both poets announce that the battles will be fatal to their respective heroes well before the battles begin, and both poets increase the tension surrounding an already truly dangerous undertaking by stressing that the heroes will fight the monsters single-handedly. As does Beowulf (2532–34), Morpidus ensures that he will face the monster in single combat by ordering his people to remain safely out of the way during the battle. There is an important difference between ordering one's handpicked band of warriors to remove themselves from the very danger it is their sworn duty to encounter and ordering one's subjects to protect themselves by staying out of harm's way, but the underlying affective principle is the same in each case: the hero's decision greatly increases his risk. When Laȝamon further tells us that Morpidus "ane . . . gon riden" (3223) [alone . . . began to ride], he heightens the scene's tension by tapping into the same pool of traditional meaning that the *Beowulf*-poet does when he tells us that on the night before Beowulf's fight with Grendel, "Sceotend swæfon, / þa þæt hornreced healdan scoldon" (703b–4) [the warriors slept who should hold the gabled house] and then tellingly adds "ealle buton anum" (705a) [all but one]. Beowulf himself does the same thing when he announces to his comitatus in the moments preceding the dragon fight that it is "ne gemet mannes,   nefn(e) min anes, / þæt he wið aglæcean   eofoðo dæle" (2533–34) [not fitting for any man except me alone that he should spend his strength against the awe-inspiring one]. In these and related instances,[122] Old English *an* [one, alone] focuses our attention upon the hero's solitary state and so emphasizes his increased vulnerability (there will be no one to assist him should he need help) at the same time that it establishes an ominous distance between the hero and what Edward B. Irving Jr. has labeled the "world of *humanitas*."[123]

Central to both episodes is the failure of each hero's weapon(s). As we saw in chapter 2, the failure of Beowulf's sword Nægling is the crucial affective moment in the dragon fight; once Nægling fails, Beowulf's death is assured. In the *Brut*, Morpidus's weapons similarly fail him. His arrows cannot penetrate the dragon's tough hide; his spear's shaft "al to-brac" (3237) [completely broke into pieces]; and his sword shatters in his hand following his frontal assault on the beast's head. The failure of his bow, the first weapon he uses against the beast and, accordingly, the first one to fail, exemplifies the scene's debt to oral poetics. The arrows he shoots at it have no discernable effect on the beast partly because he shoots them from some distance and partly because monsters have notoriously thick hides. But once "his flæn weoren iscoten: þæ iwærd his boʒe to-broken" (3234) [his arrows were shot, then his bow broke into pieces]. The impersonal force of iwærd (<Old English weorþan [become]) makes it clear that Morpidus does not break his bow in frustration or anger when the arrows fail to penetrate the beast's hide. Rather, the bow simply shatters into bits. Were we to approach this moment from the perspective of a literate poetics, we would be justified in chalking it up as yet another of the poem's artistic failings because bows are not in the habit of spontaneously self-destructing. But when we plug this moment back into the episode's larger, traditional context, it reveals itself to be not so much a narrative anomaly as an extension of the oral poetics that informs the episode and that elsewhere in the scene meshes more smoothly with its literate poetics. From the perspective of oral poetics, the affective dynamics that attends the bow's self-destruction is of a piece with the affective dynamics of the other weapons that soon fail Morpidus. Individually and collectively these failures metonymically point to the hero's imminent demise, even though they momentarily disrupt the poem's narrative surface.

Comparing this scene with the versions found in Laʒamon's chief source, Wace, and in Wace's chief source, Geoffrey of Monmouth,[124] throws its traditional foundations into sharper relief and reveals just how thoroughly oral poetics imbues Laʒamon's handling of it. In his typically economical fashion, Geoffrey states that

> in the midst of these his [Morpidus's] cruel outrages a calamity befell him that put an end to his wickedness. For a beast, more fell than any monster ever heard of before, came up from the Irish sea and preyed continually upon the seafaring folk that dwelt in those parts. And when Morvid heard tidings thereof he came unto the beast and fought with her single-handed. But when he had used up all his weapons against her in vain, the monster ran upon him with open jaws and swallowed him up as he had been a little fish. (60)[125]

Wace offers a similarly compressed treatment of the scene. In the *Roman de Brut,* a "Monstre marin, orible beste" (3421) [a sea monster, a terrible beast], similarly comes "de la mer devers Irlande" (3419) [from the Irish sea] to attack the countryside: "Par les viles, lez les rivages, / Feseit granz duels e granz

damages, / Homes e femes devurout, / E les bestes es champs mangout"
(3425–28) [Throughout the towns, along the shores it caused great suffering
and great harm—it devoured men and women and ate the animals in the
fields].[126] Morpidus learns of the beast's ravagings and journeys to meet it
alone (3436), only to have his weapons fail him before the beast devours
him (3441–51). Wace departs from Geoffrey by having the monster as well as
the king die as a result of the battle—"la beste si tost morut" (3461) [the beast
had died quickly]—but he otherwise adheres closely to Geoffrey's narrative, as
is his habit throughout the *Roman*.

Tradition and Innovation in the Brut's Thematics I: Rowena and the Ritual of Communal Drinking

The second component of the *Brut*'s thematics that we will examine
offers further evidence of the persistence of oral poetics in the early Middle
English period. It also illuminates the ways in which a poet drawing from both
oral and literate poetics is able to tap into a narrative pattern's inherent meaning in one instantiation and then in a succeeding instantiation is able to continue exploiting its traditional affective dynamics before altering its tectonics
and conferring wholly post-traditional meaning upon it.

In Old English verse, the scene in question, in which a well-born woman
publicly offers a drinking cup to the important men attending a feast, is embedded within the larger constellation of narrative patterns Anglo-Saxon poets call
upon to depict scenes of joy and feasting in the hall.[127] *Beowulf* offers a number of paradigmatic instantiations of this scene: during one feast Wealhtheow
circulates throughout Heorot before bringing the "medoful" (624b) [mead
cup] to Beowulf; during another, she serves Hrothgar, and perhaps Beowulf;
and at still another feast, the Geatish queen Hygd carries the mead cup "geond
þæt healreced" (1981a) [throughout the hall]. All the feasts depicted in the poem
share the same narrative contours in that they are invariably joyous, noisy occasions, but when the queens ritualistically act as cupbearers, the quotidian act
of serving takes on much greater significative weight: "In Hrothgar's hall
[Wealhtheow] is the instrument which sanctifies his status by naming him lord,
by serving him before all others and by causing each of the retainers to drink
after him."[128]

There is, for example, nothing about the feast held shortly after Beowulf's
arrival in Denmark that distinguishes it from any of the many other typical
feasts we encounter in the poem and elsewhere in Old English poetry: a joyous

noise rises from the assembled troop of hosts and guests, there is music, a scop sings (perhaps along with the music), and a "Þegn nytte beheold, / se þe on handa bær   hroden ealowæge, / scencte scir wered" (494b–96a) [thane performed his duty, the one who bore in his hands a decorated ale-cup, poured the bright drink]. This feast is thus marked as a typically joyous occasion, but once Unferth pointedly begins to question Beowulf about both his past accomplishments and his ability to withstand Grendel's attack, things threaten to unravel. Even though flytings do not usually end in violence,[129] Wealhtheow immediately takes steps to diffuse the potentially explosive tension that arises as a result of this one by enacting the socially constitutive rite of communal drinking. In proceeding throughout the hall, greeting individuals and offering them a drink, she acts as a *freoðuwebbe* [peaceweaver].[130] As she carries the cup from man to man, beginning with Hrothgar and ending with Beowulf, she reinforces the bond of *communitas* between the Danes and the Geats that the flyting threatens to dissolve.[131]

In the *Brut,* the scene occurs twice, and in each instance its thematic structure parallels those of its Old English instantiations. When she meets him, Rowena, the beautiful daughter of the Saxon Hengest, offers the cup to the British king Vortiger. After a space of several years, she has occasion to enact the ritual with Vortiger's son Vortimer, who comes into power following his father's forced abdication. At the ceremony in which the Saxon Hengest introduces his daughter to Vortiger, "Heo bar an hire honde: ane guldene bolle. / i-uulled mid wine: þe wes wunder ane god" (7135–36) [she bore in her hand a golden bowl filled with wine that was wondrously good]. Rowena, who is dressed almost regally in garments "ibrusted mid golde" (7134) [decorated with gold], proceeds to offer the cup to the king, saying for the first time, "in Ænglene londe. / Lauerd king wæs hæil" (7140–41) [in the land of the English, Lord king, be well]. Because the king only speaks "Bruttisc" and Rowena only "Ænglisc" and because he is further unacquainted with the customs of her continental homeland, he needs to have both the phrase "wæs hæil" (<OE *wes hal* [be well]) and the ritual's larger cultural context explained to him. Once he understands what the ritual entails, Vortiger embraces it (and Rowena) with gusto. After fulfilling his part in the ritual by offering her in return a drink from the same cup, he proceeds to seat her next to him at the feast, where he "ofte he heo custe: ofte he heo clupte" (7167) [often kissed her, often he embraced her]. He shortly thereafter marries her and so consolidates the bond between Hengest and himself that has been developing since the latter arrived in England accompanied by his brother Horsa and "þreo hundred [Saxon]

cnihten: alse hit weoren kinges" (6883) [three hundred [Saxon] knights who seemed like kings]. Although the ritual is presented in more detail in the *Brut* than it is in its Old English avatars, Laȝamon's additions build upon and expand the scene's traditional affective dynamics by highlighting its importance to both the culture depicted in the poem and the culture of Laȝamon's day. They also serve to focus our attention more sharply upon Rowena's pivotal role as a *freoðuwebbe* whose ritual actions serve to strengthen the recently established and politically and culturally important bond between the British king and the Saxons.

Laȝamon's treatment of this scene follows that of Wace's and Geoffrey's versions so closely that we should perhaps credit their point-for-point correspondences to an intertextuality of the type so central to literate poetics. In the *Roman de Brut,* the scene begins when Rowena comes out of her chamber looking "mult bele" (6948) [very beautiful] and carrying a "Pleine cupe de vin" (6949) [cup full of wine] that she offers to the king, saying "Laverd King, Wesheil" (6953). As in Laȝamon's poem, an interpreter translates what she says for Vortiger, who then happily enters into the ritual by returning the greeting to Rowena, saying (as he has been instructed in turn), "Drincheheil" (6972).[132] In Geoffrey's account, Rowena similarly enters the hall "aurem ciphum plenum uino ferens" (370) [bearing a golden cup full of wine] and speaks in her native language when she ritually presents the cup to Vortiger, saying, "Lauerd King: wassheil" (370). Vortiger's interpreter then steps forth to translate her language for and explain the ritual to the king: "She hath called thee 'Lord King' and hath greeted thee by wishing thee health. But the answer that thou shouldst make unto her is 'Drinc heil!'" (125).[133] Geoffrey's metacommentary on this cultural practice follows, during which he repeats the English words *washeil* and *drincheil* as he explains that the ritual continues to be an important part of the English cultural landscape: "and from that day unto this hath the custom held in Britain that he who drinketh at a feast saith unto another 'Wassail!' and he that receiveth the drink after him maketh answer, 'Drink hale!'" (125).[134] Wace follows suit by similarly repeating the English words *wesheil* (6977) and *drincheheil* (6978) and notes as well that Rowena thus introduces the ritual into English culture where, he asserts, it continues to play an important role (6975–86). Uncharacteristically, Laȝamon compresses, rather than dilates, the material he finds in Wace. Rather than offering the details about the ritual's Saxon origins and commenting upon its continuing cultural currency as Wace and Geoffrey do, Laȝamon says simply that "þurh þa ilke leoden: þa laȝen comen to þissen londe. / wæs-hail 7 drinc-hæil. moni mon þer-of is fain"

(7163–64) [through that same people that custom came into this land: wassail and drink hail. Many a man is pleased with that.][135]

The uniformity of this episode in three very different texts that descend from three very different traditions offers some tantalizing evidence regarding the cohesiveness of traditional thematics when they circulate between and among traditions, but we cannot finally place too much weight upon the parallelism of these scenes because it is the exception and not the norm. For some reason, Wace and Geoffrey directly imported a scene founded on medieval English oral poetics into their texts.[136] Whether they did so because the scene resonated affectively for them, because it struck them as a handy set piece through which to present and explain a curious and perhaps amusing English cultural practice, or for some other reason, we have no way of knowing. What we can determine, though, is that the scene retains its traditional contours, its traditional affective dynamics, and even elements of its native diction when it appears in two literate and entirely alien traditions.

The second time the scene appears in the *Brut* initially appears to be as paradigmatic as its first occurrence. Rowena once again approaches a British king, in this instance Vortiger's son and her stepson, Vortimer, and engages in the ritual in an avowed attempt to reestablish the political and social harmony that her marriage to Vortiger several years earlier has paradoxically ruptured. Outraged at the alliance Vortiger has entered into with the powerful and, more importantly, pagan Saxons, and worried that the pagans will convince the king to "bilæue . . . hæhȝe Godd: 7 luuie heore Mahimet" (7279) [leave . . . high God and love their Mohammed], the British renounce Vortiger shortly after his marriage, saying,

> Nulle we nauere-mare: þine iboden here.
> ne to þine hirede cumen: ne þe uor king halden
> ah hatien we wulleð: mid hæhȝere strengðe.
> all þine hæðene wines: 7 hærme igreten.
>
> (7292–95)

[We will nevermore obey your commands, nor come to your court, nor consider you king, but we will hate mightily all your heathen friends and greet them with harm.]

At the hustings held in London following the rejection of Vortiger, Vortimer, his eldest son, is chosen as king "mid muchele loft-songe" (7308) [with a great song of praise]. He immediately informs Hengest and Horsa that if they and their troops do not leave England at once, "he heom walde ufel don: baðe ablenden and anhon" (7314) [he will do evil to them, both blind and hang them]. Although they decide to fight Vortimer, the British prove too powerful, and the Saxons suffer heavy losses before being ignominiously driven from the island. Vortimer, despite threatening to "for-uaren" [destroy] his "aȝene fader" (7315) [own father], does not kill Vortiger but rather leaves him to wander the countryside, abandoned by the Saxons (who trick him into staying behind when they flee to their boats) and scorned by even the lowest of the people he recently ruled: "nes hit nan swa wac mon: þat him ne hokerede on" (7383) [there was not a poor man who did not scorn him]. Some five years after the removal of Vortiger and the subsequent forced departure of the Saxons, Rowena announces that she wishes to convert to Christianity and so initiates a process of reconciliation that will culminate in and be confirmed by the publicly enacted ritual of communal drinking. At the feast Vortimer holds in her honor, she initiates the ritual by going first to "are tunne. / þer wes idon in: þes kinges deoreste win" (7462–63) [a tun containing the king's dearest wine]. After filling "hir scale of wine. / 7 at-foren al þan dringe: heo eode to þan kinge" (7466–67) [her cup with wine, and before all the company, she went to the king]. The ritual moves toward its traditional and expected close when she again offers the toast she introduced into England, "Lauerd king wæs hail" (7469), and then proceeds to drink deeply from the cup before offering it to him. Like his father before him, Vortimer is charmed by Rowena's speech in a language ("Saxisc" [7473]) that he does not comprehend: "þan king þuhte gomen inoh: for hire spæche he loh" (7474) [the king thought it pleasant enough; he laughed at her speech].

It is at this point, however, that the scene's thematics deviates from its usual pattern as Laȝamon confers upon it a narrative complement that is wholly post-traditional. Rather than moving the scene toward its expected, traditionally determined conclusion, Rowena engages in a bit of legerdemain "while þe þa king loh" (7480) [while the king laughed] and draws forth from where she has it hidden "bi-neoðen hire titten. / ane guldene ampulle: of attere i-fulled" (7476–77) [beneath her breasts, a golden vial filled with poison]. When she then raises the cup once more "to hire chine" (7481) [to her chin] she calls attention to and reinforces the importance of the ritual's central gesture, the drinking of wine from a shared cup, but she does not complete the gesture by once again drinking from the cup. This time she only pretends to drink and instead surreptitiously empties the vial of poison into the cup. Once she has succeeded in poisoning the drink, "heo þa cuppe: bitahte þan kinge" (7482) [she gave that cup to the king] so that he may fulfill his part of the ritual by drinking "al þat win" (7483) [all that wine], something he unhesitatingly does. Her use of a poison that does not take effect immediately ensures the ritual's successful enactment. The festivities proceed apace and as "Þe dæi forð eode: blisse wes on hirede" (7484) [the day went forth, the company was blissful]. Having accomplished her goal, Rowena slips away unnoticed in the dead of night, and it is not until the next morning that Vortimer realizes "þat he hefde atter inomen" (7498) [that he had taken poison] and that he is beyond medical help: "ne mihte na lechecraft: helpen him næ wiht" (7499) [nor might any medical art help him at all].

The fluency with which Laȝamon introduces these changes into the scene's traditional thematic structure and the ways in which they play off of and do not simply disrupt the scene's traditional affective dynamics reveal just how pliable and flexible traditional thematics remains for him. He begins the scene by clearly announcing that Rowena's decision to convert is not born of any desire to reconcile with the British king but is rather part of a larger plan she has to avenge her father's having been driven from England by Vortimer, whom she further holds responsible for "hire freondene deað" (7435) [her friends' deaths]. As the scene develops and she begins to carry out her plan to kill Vortimer while pretending to perform the (in this case) conciliatory ritual of communal drinking, Laȝamon takes every opportunity to condemn her actions and to execrate her, labeling her, among other things, "þeo scaðe" (7456) [a wretch], "swicfulle" (7462) [treacherous], "luðere" (7470) [wicked], and "ufele" (7489) [evil]. Laȝamon's virulent comments (few characters in the *Brut*, including the traitorous Modred, suffer such abuse at the poet's hands) serve several purposes: they highlight the chief way in which this scene diverges from its paradigmatic instantiations (where the ritual always and only reaffirms communal and intertribal bonds[137]) as they simultaneously witness its newly conferred meaning and the post-traditional purpose to which it is put.

Laȝamon's changes also, and perhaps somewhat unexpectedly, reinforce the scene's traditional affective dynamics even as they alter it. The scene's tension arises from the interplay between its inherent meaning and the meaning Laȝamon confers upon it because its affective dynamics no longer depends on Rowena's successfully reaffirming an important social and political bond but rather on the disparity between her traditional words ("Lauerd king wæs hail: Uor þe ich am swiðe uæin" [7469] [Lord King, be well. On your account I am very glad]), her equally traditional actions (the circulation of a shared cup

[7478 ff.]), and the scene's wholly post-traditional narrative complement (Vortimer's death). Laȝamon is able to deploy this traditional structure both traditionally and post-traditionally because he is *not* a poet imprisoned by his tradition and because the narrative patterns of medieval English oral poetics are *not* prefabricated building blocks whose details and meanings are somehow fixed but are rather responsive verbal instruments that he is free to employ as he sees fit, as is every other poet who engages oral poetics. Even though Laȝamon confers a new, idiosyncratic, and post-traditional meaning upon the narrative pattern of the ritual of communal drinking the second time he uses it, the episode's traditional thematic structure continues to serve as a template for Rowena's poisoning of Vortimer. Here, as elsewhere, Laȝamon does not so much depart from the traditional expressive economy as incorporate it into and refract it through the diffuse lens of his own idiopoetics.

Vortimer's death affords us an especially good opportunity to see the ways in which oral poetics informs the *Brut*'s thematics because its narrative contours in both Geoffrey and Wace differ radically from those that Laȝamon gives it. On the broadest level, the narratives all share the same outline: in each text, Rowena brings about Vortimer's death, but only in Laȝamon does she take a direct hand in the act, and only in Laȝamon does she cloak her deceitful behavior behind the culturally acceptable practice of the ritual of communal drinking. In Geoffrey, Rowena does not directly participate in poisoning the king, but "gave him by a certain familiar of his own, whom she had corrupted with bribes innumerable, a draught of poison" (128).[138] The poison, Geoffrey continues, has an immediate effect: "No sooner had the noble warrior drunk thereof than he was smitten with a sudden malady so grievous that hope of his life was none" (128).[139] Wace's treatment is even less detailed: "Ronwen, cume male marastre, / Fist envenimer sun fillastre / Vortimer, que ele haeit, / Pur Henguist, que chacié aveit" (7157–60) [Rowena, that evil stepmother, caused Vortimer, her husband's son, to be poisoned because she hated him because he chased Hengest from the kingdom]. Laȝamon, in contrast, not only draws upon the episode's traditional thematics by presenting the ritual in great detail but also, from the outset, securely embeds his (post-traditional) presentation of it within its traditional affective dynamics. Rowena's announced desire to reconcile with Vortimer by converting to Christianity and her offering a variation of the ritual's initiatory greeting—"Hal wrð þu lauerd king: Bruttene deorling" (7452) [Hail to you lord king, the Britons' darling]—when she first arrives at his court clearly point this episode toward its traditional, positive conclusion. By tapping into the expressive economy of medieval English oral poetics and then departing from it, Laȝamon creates a scene whose power and complexity far outstrip those of the corresponding scenes in Geoffrey and Wace. While in the Latin and French texts, the poisoning of Vortimer is just another in a long list of regicides, in the English text it takes on added weight and signification because it is woven into a traditional narrative pattern that usually establishes, rather than destroys, the *communitas* that groups depend on for their survival. As clever as it is insidious, Rowena's poisoning of Vortimer shakes the very cultural and political institutions that the ritual of communal drinking elsewhere reinforces.

In his structuralist investigation of the themes in the *Brut*, Ringbom notes another episode in the poem that, like the Rowena and Vortimer episode, has no counterpart in Wace but may be related to Anglo-Saxon thematics because it "bring[s] to mind Queen Wealhtheow and Queen Hygd in *Beowulf*."[140] This scene involves a meeting between Brian, a cousin of the exiled king Cadwathlan, and his sister Galarne, who is abducted and raped by Edwin shortly after he takes possession of the kingdom from Cadwathlan. As part of a plan to kill Pelluz, a Spanish cleric attached to Edwin's court who can determine by reading the stars just when and where Cadwathlan will attempt to strike back at Edwin, Brian agrees to journey to Edwin's court. After landing in England disguised as a wine merchant, he changes disguises and journeys to Edwin's court dressed as a beggar. On a morning when Edwin "lette feden alleː þa neode hafden. / all þe blæðeː þe wuneden on þe burȝe" (15357–58) [commanded that all those who had need, all the destitute who dwelt in the town, should be fed], Brian gains entrance to the castle. During this meal, attended "bi þusend and bi þusende" (15360) [by thousands and thousands], the "quene bar to drinkenː 7 alle hire bur-lutlen" (15368) [queen and her serving women bore the wine], as does Galarne, who appears bearing in hand a "bolle . . . þer-mide heo bar to dringen" (15371) [a bowl . . . in which she bore drink]. Viewed from a structuralist perspective, the link between the Galarne–Brian episode and the other instances of serving emerges clearly the moment the women appear and begin to serve drink at the feast. When we move beyond the indisputable, but also indisputably minor, structural parallels between the Galarne–Brian episode and the scenes involving Wealhtheow, Hygd, and Rowena to which Ringbom links it (namely that a well-born woman serves drink in each episode) and interrogate instead its thematics and affective dynamics, we can see that in fact it is not grounded in oral poetics.

Although Edwin's queen does serve drink at the meal he organizes for his poor subjects, she is so unimportant a figure that the poet does not even name her the one time he mentions her. Her actions serve no local political purpose and only the broadest social and cultural ones. Her willingness to lower herself to serve the needy is certainly a touching gesture, but it points solely to her commendable generosity. Moreover, whatever limited signification her actions may carry is diluted not only because they are relegated to the scene's periphery but also because she herself is never distinguished, either by word or deed, from her attendants, a group of women who also serve drinks to those in attendance. Further reducing the importance of the women's actions is the fact that they are not the only high-born members of the court who serve the destitute guests at the meal: in a surprisingly forward-looking gesture, the king himself "gon to þeinen: mid alle his here-cnihten" (15367) [began to serve, with all his warriors]. In short, aside from the minor parallel of the queen's serving drink at the meal, the narrative contours and the thematics of the Galarne–Brian episode derive from a different poetics than does the thematics that informs traditional scenes of ritual drinking.

Tradition and Innovation in the Brut's Thematics II: Galarne, Brian, and the Thematics of Recognition

In noting the ways the Galarne–Brian episode is "especially" closely linked to "*King Horn* 1107 ff., where the motif of disguise and recognition at a banquet also appears,"[141] Ringbom apparently identifies yet another of the *Brut*'s traditional elements, the thematics of recognition. Even though he has shaved off his beard and is dressed as a beggar, Brian is immediately recognized by Galarne, who signals that she recognizes him by bestowing a gold ring upon him. Following her gift of the ring, which she presents to him under the guise of being generous to a randomly selected beggar, she hides herself "Ymong þan wrecche uolke" (15384) [among the wretched folk] so that she can tell him "tiðende: al of þas kinges hirede. / and heo him tahte Pelluz" (15387–88) [news of the king's court and she pointed out Pelluz to him].

In *Horn*,[142] the thematics of recognition is equally central to the scene in which Horn returns to his beloved Rymenhild after a protracted separation, but it is here that the similarity with the Galarne–Brian episode begins and ends. When Horn returns in disguise, Rymenhild fails to recognize him and thinks him nothing but a rude beggar and a "glotoun" (1124), despite his riddling but transparent reference to a dream she had that they had discussed ("ihc am a fissere, / Wel feor icome bi este / For fissen at þi feste" [1134–36] [I am a fisherman come from far in the east to fish at your feast]), his explicit allusion to the length of his separation from her (seue ȝere" [1140] [seven years]), and his offering of a punning toast to his own self ("Drink to me of disse, / Drink to horn of horne" [1144–45] [drink to me from the bowl; drink to horn from the drinking-horn). His overt hints, in fact, succeed only in puzzling Rymenhild:

> Rymenhild him gan bihelde,
> Hire heorte bigan to chelde.
> Ne kneu heo noȝt his fissing,
> Ne horn hym selue noþing:
> Ac wunder hire gan þinke
> Whi he bad to horn drinke.
>   (1147–52)

> ———

> [Rymenhild began to look at him, her heart began to grow cold; she knew nothing about his fishing nor anything of Horn himself. But she began to wonder why he bid her drink to Horn.]

After he finishes drinking the prodigious amount of beer she pours for him, Horn throws into the empty cup what should be a sure token of his identity, the very "ring igrauen of golde / Þat horn of hure hadde" (1164–65) [the very ring engraven of gold that Horn had from her] when he set out to prove himself worthy of her. But rather than suspecting a connection between the ring and the "Beggere . . . so kene" (1128) [beggar . . . so bold] who just gave it to her, Rymenhild reads the ring as proof "Þat horn isterue were, / For þe ring was þere" (1167–68) [that Horn was dead, for the ring was there] and Horn is not. Rymenhild returns to the "Palmere" (1171) to discover how the ring came into his possession, whereupon Horn maintains his deception by telling her that he accompanied Horn on a sea voyage, during which

> Horn was sik & deide,
> & faire me preide:
> 'Go wiþ þe ringe
> To Rymenhild þe ȝonge.'
>   (1185–88)

> ———

> [Horn was sick and died, and courteously he asked me: "Go with the ring to Rymenhild the young."]

Upon having her worst fears confirmed, Rymenhild commands her "Herte nu þu berste" (1192) [heart, now you ought to burst], and in her grief she attempts suicide by pulling forth a concealed knife that "To herte . . . heo sette" (1201) [to her heart . . . she set]. Horn intervenes before she can harm herself, and he finally reveals himself to her (1204–8).

Virtually the only thing that connects these two scenes of feasting is that the thematics of recognition, broadly construed, is narratively important to both. Aside from this, the scenes differ from each other in all their salient details. For example, Horn and Rymenhild are joined by an erotic, romantic bond, not the familial one that links Galarne and Brian; Rymenhild fails to see through Horn's disguise, while Galarne immediately picks Brian out in the throng of beggars; and Rymenhild and her plight are central to the entire poem, whereas Galarne disappears from the *Brut* as abruptly as she enters it. This list of differences could be easily expanded, but the ones cited are sufficient to reveal that the two scenes do not share the same narrative tectonics. Brian's disguise and his subsequent recognition by his sister are elements of Laȝamon's local, literate poetics, and as such they speak only to the immediate narrative context within which he employs them and bear only the meaning that he confers upon them. As we will see in chapter 5, the narrative contours of Horn's return to Rymenhild, in contrast, have a great deal in common with the Return Song, a widely attested and well-documented narrative pattern discovered in ancient Greek, South Slavic, and other oral poetics. Joined seamlessly to the *Horn*-poet's literate poetics, the return narrative draws upon the meaning that inheres in the oral traditional story pattern. In contrast, the thematics of recognition that Laȝamon employs derives, ultimately, from his idiosyncratic literate poetics.

When early Middle English poets composing with pen in hand engage oral poetics, they necessarily introduce into it changes as small as extending the affective dynamics of a lexeme into a new but traditionally sanctioned context and as large as putting a traditional thematic structure to a decidedly posttraditional use. The oral poetics that they draw upon as they articulate poetry is not a static, deterministic idiom which they strive to maintain in some sort of pristine state, but rather an expressive economy whose protean character and ability to transmit meaning ensure its continued vitality and hence its continued persistence as a component of medieval English poetics. Its imperfect and fractured survival is the topic of the following chapter.

four

The Tradition in Flux

Fragmentation and Survival

— As we might expect given the changes that were afoot in the English poetic tradition as early as the eleventh century—changes that were slowly and subtly but nevertheless steadily shifting the ground upon which the tradition was situated—oral poetics figures much less centrally, and often not at all, in the vernacular poetry composed in the Conquest's aftermath. Unlike their Anglo-Saxon predecessors, who could compose vernacular verse only within the deterministic system that is Anglo-Saxon oral poetics, post-Conquest vernacular poets had at their disposal an array of systems for articulating verse unmatched, before or since, in English literary history. As a result, those vernacular texts extant from the early Middle English period onward evidence a broad spectrum of oral and literate poetics. While oral poetics can figure prominently on virtually every level of a given early Middle English poem (as in the *Brut*), it may also be, at best, a peripheral component of another (the *Orrmulum*). Whether it is thoroughly interwoven into the very warp and woof of a poem (the rhetoric of flyting and the centrally agonistic narrative context of the *Hule and Niȝtengale*)[1] or appears as a localized and isolated component of a poem's surface structure (the lexeme *ibolwe* in the same poem), post-Conquest oral poetics continues to be closely linked to and dependent upon the specialized lexical and narrative idioms that for so long were fundamental to English poetic articulation.

Those post-Conquest poets who deploy oral poetics do not do so because they wish to preserve an antiquated and archaic mode of composing verse— one, moreover, that is very likely to be at least partially if not wholly inaccessible to their target audience. Rather, these poets employ oral poetics because its dedicated register continues to offer them an affectively powerful and economical way to express meaning, just as it provides those who receive their poems—whether visually as private, perhaps silent, readers or aurally as members of textual communities—with long-established and, more importantly, still functional channels of reception. Because oral poetics remains so freighted with traditional meaning(s) and because it continues to be compositionally useful (on both the lexical and narrative levels), post-Conquest poets are able to use it to express traditional, inherent meaning. And as we saw in chapter 3, this register neither impedes the written, nonperformative composition of vernacular poetry nor confines the poetic imagination. All the poets who engage oral poetics are also able to and frequently do use the traditional idiom to confer idiosyncratic, post-traditional meaning(s) upon their narratives, something that witnesses not just the flexibility of oral poetics but the degree to which it is able to combine seamlessly with literate poetics to create a powerful expressive economy. For Laȝamon most extremely, but for many other early Middle English poets as well, the articulation of vernacular verse and the production of meaning (as well as the creation of channels for its reception) depends upon a complex mixture of oral and literate poetics.

In using oral poetics in ways that stretch from the strongly traditional to the wholly post-traditional, these poets alter the tradition, but in so doing they are following the path of their Anglo-Saxon predecessors. Even though the tradition within which Anglo-Saxon poets composed was inextricably bound to oral poetics, they similarly (and inevitably) introduced changes, both large and small, every time they engaged what was for them a fluid, malleable, living tradition. The small size of the extant corpus of Old English verse, its remarkable metrical, lexical, and, to a lesser extent, narrative consistency, and the once widely held belief that the oral tradition somehow limited artistic expression (and accomplishment) and therefore flattened all poetic expression have combined to ensure that we have been able to see, until fairly recently, only as "through a glasse, darkely,"[2] the ways in which individual Anglo-Saxon poets altered, expanded, and redirected their deterministic (but not limiting) tradition. The constellation of poetic systems and practices available to poets composing in the vernacular and the varied and rapidly shifting natures of the expressive economies that comprise the stemmata of the post-Conquest oral-literate matrix make it easier for us to spot the changes introduced by early Middle English poets who, when they departed from oral poetics, often did so dramatically. But the tradition within which they worked, while admittedly offering them a greater range of metrical systems and an expanded lexical system for articulating poetry,[3] remained as fluid and flexible as it had been from the early days of the Anglo-Saxon period in the fifth century c.e. through its close in the eleventh.

Even though the Norman Conquest stands as a watershed in the development of English literary history, its effects on the vernacular verse produced in England were not fully apparent for several generations. Indeed, with a few notable exceptions—the *Hule and Niȝtengale* being perhaps the most important—the look and sound of virtually all the vernacular verse extant from the early Middle English period reveal its close, if imperfect, ties to the native English tradition. The metrics, lexicons, and general "vernacular tonalities"[4] of the poems found in the late entries of the Peterborough Chronicle, as well as works as varied as the *Poema Morale,* the *Worcester Fragments,* the *Orrmulum,* the *Proverbs of Alfred,* and the *Brut,* all witness their connection to native English poetics.[5]

To a poet situated at the far end of the period, the few poems extant from the transitional, early Middle English period would have sounded and looked strange indeed, since the formal and metrical bases of English vernacular poetry underwent a virtually complete transformation between the twelfth and the fourteenth centuries. Geoffrey Chaucer, the towering figure of late medieval English literature, no doubt speaks for many of his contemporaries when he summarily dismisses in a single line the whole tradition of alliterative composition by having the Parson announce to the Canterbury pilgrims that he is "a Southren man" who "kan nat geeste 'rum, ram, ruf,' by letter."[6] Although Chaucer, whose many poetic innovations and status in the court of London suggest that he was conscious of writing "al of the newe jet"[7] may here simply be criticizing his Northern and West-Midlands contemporaries for producing what to his urbane ears and eyes was surely unfashionable verse, the Parson's confessed inability to compose alliterative poetry nonetheless constitutes a pointed and only thinly veiled rejection of a poetics that may well have struck Chaucer and his Ricardian and Lancastrian patrons as being at best hopelessly outmoded and at worst reactionary.[8]

The opinion the Parson so succinctly voices was not unique to the four-teenth century: the process that would culminate in the native English poetic tradition's relegation to the margins of English literary culture began long before Chaucer put pen to parchment, perhaps within the first generation after the Conquest. Owing in large part to William's systematic decimation of the Anglo-Saxon nobility in the decade following the Norman invasion, secular and religious power on the island quickly became concentrated almost entirely within Anglo-Norman hands, ensuring that whatever audience native poetry might have would not likely be among the politically powerful. As the small number of vernacular English poetic texts extant from the period 1066–1275 suggests,[9] the newly installed Norman ruling classes and their Anglo-Norman descendants, like Chaucer and his Parson centuries later, apparently had little appreciation of or interest in the native English poetic tradition. Although it may be tempting to read a large political motive into this situation, we need not do so, for the Normans who invaded England and then settled there may simply and understandably have preferred (and hence supported and fostered through their patronage) verse founded upon their inherited, familiar tradi-tion, verse that celebrated their own cultural heritage and that was, moreover, composed not in the foreign tongue and alien metrics of a conquered people but in the language they themselves spoke and in metrical forms with which they were long acquainted.[10]

In the aftermath of the Conquest, English poetics underwent a number of radical changes. What had been for hundreds of years a univocal and met-rically uniform system for articulating verse became a polyphonous (if not cacophonous) one marked by a hitherto unknown metrical diversity. Most importantly, English poetics became far more international than it had been, and it developed the extraordinary "capacity to accommodate, in a wide but unified cultural setting, so many different 'norms' of subject-matter, method, and form."[11] Were we to place the *Worcester Fragments* or virtually any other early Middle English poem alongside the *Canterbury Tales*, the gulf between them would be so great as to appear virtually unbridgeable. We must, however, bear in mind that we are able to view English literary history from a perspec-tive unavailable to those who lived during the period: we can take in at a glance the diachronic developments of English poetics and so note the changes that it underwent but these changes, which were neither universal nor systematically implemented, may well have been virtually imperceptible to the people who lived at the time they were taking place. Unlike the world George Orwell created in *1984*, one in which cultural memories are subject to constant manipulation and in which policies (as well as people) that no longer serve their desired purposes can be completely and efficiently eradicated, in the cultural world of the Middle Ages, change, whether in the literary or the social world, occurred slowly and was always far from absolute. The literate poetics and practices that the Norman poets and scribes imported following the Conquest did not so much shove Anglo-Saxon oral poetics aside as enter into partnership with it. The merger was not finally a balanced one, as the history of the English poetic tradition bears out, but the process by which Anglo-Saxon oral poetics and its web of implication got crowded out was protracted.

The Fragmentation of Medieval English Oral Poetics I: Lexical Evidence

The history of the specialized register of oral poetics after the close of the Anglo-Saxon period was largely one of steady loss and continued fragmentation. While some traditional lexemes retained both their traditional affective dynamics and traditional referentiality, others retained only traces of them. In addition, many simply disappeared as the poetic and nonpoetic lexicons evolved and changed. Over the course of any language's history, the meanings of many native terms will shift, obsolete words will disappear, and, as is especially true of English, the native word stock will be freely and extensively expanded by the addition of foreign words so that many native words either acquire doublets (OE *ēam* [uncle] / Fr *oncle*) or are replaced by foreign ones (OE *eagþyrl* [eye-hole] replaced by ON *vindauga* [wind's eye], from which NE *window* derives).[12]

In considering what happens to lexemes that are demonstrably part of Anglo-Saxon oral poetics in the post-Conquest period, we will focus first on *helm* and *aglæca* because their histories respectively illustrate the way in which a lexeme (*helm*) that is stripped of its traditional referentiality and affective dynamics and hence no longer functions as a traditional meaning-bearing metonym nevertheless remains a common constituent of the post-Conquest poetic and prosaic registers. Next we will turn our attention to *aglæca*, a lexeme that lapses into obsolescence after the Conquest but that nevertheless retains its traditional referential and affective contours when it resurfaces in the poetic record some three hundred years later. We will close our discussion of the role oral poetics plays in the Middle English poetic lexicon by tracing the fate of *beot,* one of the many lexical elements of Anglo-Saxon oral poetics that is not attested in the post-Conquest written record.[13]

Helm *and the Loss of Traditional Referentiality*

In Old English prose, the primary meanings of *helm* are "helmet; the top, overshadowing foliage of trees; a covering."[14] Within the specialized expressive economy of Anglo-Saxon oral poetics, it bears an additional meaning, one that it does not have in the prose. Referring to what is perhaps the most important piece of armor a medieval warrior possesses—his helmet—in the poetry it acquires the additional metonymic meaning 'protector, guardian.' Of its eighty-seven poetic occurrences, *helm* means 'protector' forty-four times. When it occurs in the nominative and accusative singular, the percentage is even higher. Of the sixty-nine times the simplex occurs in these cases, it carries its metonymic meaning forty-three times. Although *helm* is far from the most res-onant of Anglo-Saxon lexemes, when deployed within the tradition's expressive economy, it consistently indexes the special nature of a vitally important rela-tionship, that between a ruler (human or divine) and his people, as it does in the phrase "helm Scyldinga" (3716) [protector of the Scyldings], which eco-nomically summons to the narrative present both Hrothgar's position in and his continued importance to Danish society.[15]

Helm occurs with great frequency in Middle English poetry, appearing in poems as diverse and chronologically distinct as Laȝamon's late-twelfth- or early-thirteenth-century *Brut* and John Lydgate's late-fifteenth-century *Pil-grimage of the Life of Man.*[16] But where a web of literal and abstract associ-ations once attended every occurrence of the simplex, its traditional metonymic sense largely disappears and only its concrete, prosaic one survives in Middle English, where it, like its Modern English descendant, *helmet,* means chiefly "[a] piece of (usu. metal) armour for the head."[17] *Helm* does retain the sense of "protection" in Middle English, but only in a very limited number of infre-quently occurring phrases, chief of which are "hope to helme" and "Helme of helþe."[18] When it does bear this sense, it refers only to the protection offered by abstract nouns, not people. Owing perhaps to its being a component of both the poetic and prosaic registers, *helm* remains a part of English poetics until the late fifteenth century, and while *helmet,* which derives most probably from the combination of OE *helm* and OF *heaumet,*[19] begins to supplant it beginning in the mid–fifteenth century, *helm* is attested as bearing the sense "armour for the head, helmet" as late as the middle of the sixteenth century.[20] But even though *helm* survives in Middle English poetry, it does so stripped of its traditional, associative meaning "guardian, protector." Various terms step in to fill the gap created once *helm* loses its traditional meaning, among the more important of which are *king* and *lord,* but none of them carry the sharply directed metonymic meaning that *helm* possesses in medieval English oral poetics. By the end of the fourteenth century, its sense comes to be replaced by a term that carries with it something akin to the sense *helm* has in medieval English oral poetics—*protectour* (<OF *protector* <Latin *protector*)[21]—but because its referentiality is post-traditional and conferred, the French-derived lexeme does not tap into the web of associative meanings that *helm* so frequently does.

Aglæca *and the Persistence of Oral Poetics*

In Old English poetry, the traditional referentiality and affective dynamics of *aglæca,* which the DOE translates as "awesome opponent, ferocious fighter," are clear and unproblematic.[22] Occurring slightly more than forty times in fourteen different poems, *aglæca* refers to characters such as Satan (*Christ and Satan,* 446a), assorted demons (*Juliana,* 268b; *Andreas,* 1312a), the cannibalistic inhabitants of Mermedonia (*Andreas,* 1131b), Grendel (*Beowulf,* 159a), Grendel's mother (*Beowulf,* 1259a), sea monsters (*Beowulf,* 556a), the dragon (*Beowulf,* 2520a), Beowulf (*Beowulf,* 2592a), and Sigemund (*Beowulf,* 893a),[23] characters who are all extraordinarily powerful and (in one way or another) threatening.[24] Additionally, they all tend primarily to be evil figures, or, in the case of Beowulf and Sigemund (and maybe even Grendel and his mother), darkly liminal and perhaps problematic ones.[25] In a very few instances the simplex refers not to characters but rather to the awful terror that descends upon warriors before a battle (*Elene,* 1187a) or to the unimaginable torment of being burned alive (*Daniel,* 237b), but such uses clearly fit into its traditional affective dynamics, which we may state programmatically as follows: *aglæca* allows poets to imbue a character (or more rarely a situation) with a host of unsettling and often deeply terrifying associations. Although not nested within any particular phraseological or thematic pattern found in Old English poetry, it is sometimes loosely connected to slaughter (either by or of the *aglæca*).

Because *aglæca* is unique to the poetic register, the term soon becomes obsolete once that system begins to fray in the post-Conquest period. In the entire corpus of Middle English literature, it appears only some nine times, in two versions of the late-twelfth- or early-thirteenth-century *Poema Morale,* those contained respectively in Oxford, Bodleian Library, Digby A. 4, and Cambridge, Trinity College, B. 14. 52; in the mid-thirteenth-century *Proverbs of Alfred;* in the late-thirteenth-century *South-English Legendary* (St. Mary Magdalene); in two poems, *Sir Gawain and the Green Knight* and the *Parlement of the Thre Ages,* both of which date from the mid– to late fourteenth century;[26] and in the early-fifteenth-century *Metrical Chronicle of Robert of Gloucester.* Curiously enough, however, while it is in the process of disappearing from the poetic register, it migrates briefly into the prose register and appears in a few prose works that are all roughly contemporary to the *Poema Morale,* among which are the Peterborough Chronicle, the *Lambeth Homilies,* the *Trinity Homilies,* and the *Ancrene Wisse.* These instances are instructive because even though it is being deployed outside the expressive economy of oral poetics and even though its referential base has shifted from the demonic and monstrous to the divine, the Middle English descendants of *aglæca* retain the term's traditional affective dynamics and continue to bear the sense of awful dread that the term always bears in oral Anglo-Saxon poetics.

We can see this clearly in the Cambridge, Trinity College B. 14. 52 homily *De Aduentu,* where the homilist uses the lexeme to refer not to a monstrous or demonic figure but rather to Christ's second coming and judgment on Domesday, "and þat tocume is swiðe ei[s]liche" (5) [and that coming is very awful].[27] And in another Trinity B. 14. 52 homily, *In Quadragesima,* the homilist describes as "eiseliche" the shame that the prophet Daniel warns "alle synfulle men shule þolen on domes dai" (67) [all sinful men must suffer on judgment day]. In the version of *Poema Morale* contained in London, Lambeth Palace Library, 487, it similarly describes the dread that will be visited upon the sinful as human history draws to a close.[28] Although primarily used to describe divinely inspired terror, *aglæca* is also used of extraordinarily powerful natural events as well, as the Chronicle entry for 1109 reveals: "Ðises geares gewurdon swiðe fela þunra, 7 þa swiðe ægeslice" (5–6)[29] [In this year there were very many thunderstorms, and they were very terrible].

Although *aglæca* is used traditionally in the homilies and the Chronicle, in the *Ancrene Wisse,* probably the latest of the prose texts in which the simplex occurs, it is put to a decidedly nontraditional usage. Rather than describing as it does elsewhere in Old and early Middle English literature, the awful power of a ravenous monster, the incomprehensible desire of a group of cannibals, the terrible power of a creature, or the terror that awaits the sinful on the day of the last judgment, in the *Ancrene Wisse* it describes the sad posturings of a "feble mon" (33:6) [feeble man] driven by nothing more terrible than the shameful desire to look upon a "ȝunge ancres" (33:8) [a young anchoress], a man who pathetically "halt him þah ahelich ȝef he haueð a wid hod 7 a loke cape" (33: 7–8) [held himself to be awe-inspiring if he had an ample hood and a closed cape].[30] But even when it is thus being used nontraditionally, the simplex continues to retain some of its metonymic associations. If it did not, readers of the *Ancrene Wisse* would be unable fully to grasp the passage's biting irony because the context within which the simplex occurs is devoid of any sort of physical or moral threat (real or perceived) and the author makes it abundantly clear that the only one to whom the "feble mon" appears in the least bit "ahelich" is himself.

Modern translations offer us a way of gauging the importance of the simplex's traditional metonymic meaning in the passage. In translating it as "formidable,"[31] M. B. Salu preserves an echo of its traditional word-power and enables its traditional channels of reception. In contrast, James Morton and Hugh White, who translate it, respectively, as "highly" (in the sense of "proudly") and "venerable," move the lexeme progressively further away from its traditional associations and channels of reception.[32] Although it would not be surprising to find the term used in similarly nontraditional ways in the Middle English poetic record, three of *aglæca*'s appearances in Middle English poetry are wholly traditional. It is applied to a nontraditional object the fourth time it appears, but it retains, indeed relies upon, a set of its traditional associations in this instance as well. As we noted above, *aglæca* first appears in the poetic register at the very end of the twelfth or the very beginning of the thirteenth century. When it appears in two of the seven extant versions of the *Poema Morale*—Trinity 14. 52 and Lambeth 487[33]—it once again refers, as it often does in Old English poetry, to demons, in both cases specifically to the "Eiseliche wihten" (Trinity, 285) [awe-inspiring creatures] who through their disobedience have been thrown out of heaven and condemned to dwell for all eternity in the fires of hell. The horrible spectacle of the fallen angels constitutes part of the punishment reserved for those "wreche sowle . . . þe sinegeden þurh sihte" (Trinity, 286) [wretched souls . . . who sinned through sight] and who will for all eternity fittingly be forced to gaze upon "þe loðe sathanas and belzebub se ealde" (Trinity, 287) [the hateful Satan and old Beelzebub] and the rest of their damned followers. In addition to the *Poema Morale*, *aglæca* also appears in the version of the life of St. Mary Magdalene found in the thirteenth-century Laud manuscript of the *South-English Legendary*,[34] in two thirteenth-century versions of the *Proverbs of Alfred*,[35] and then again in the mid–fourteenth century, when it resurfaces in *Sir Gawain* and in the *Parlement of the Thre Ages*.[36]

In the version of the compilation of some sixty saints' lives preserved in the *South-English Legendary*, the lexeme appears only in the life of St. Mary Magdalene, where it occurs three times in the poem's 643 lines. It is initially used to describe the poem's target audience, men who are, the poet tells us, "wise and vnwise, ʒongue and olde" (2) [wise and unwise, young and old].[37] It is next used to describe Mary Magdalene herself, after Christ forgives her her sinful past, drives out of her "seue deuelene" (138) [seven devils], and then sends her "a-boute . . . to sarmoni and to preche" (158) [about . . . to give sermons and to preach]. The third and final time it appears, in line 281, it describes the words spoken to Mary Magdalene by the Saracen prince of Marseilles, the land to which she and the other Christians come following their expulsion from Judea. In all three of these occurrences, the lexeme continues to carry with it some trace of its traditional meaning, although it does not resonate as powerfully in the *South-English Legendary* as it does elsewhere in Old and Middle English texts, something the lexeme's initial occurrence in the poem makes evident:

> Sleiʒe Men and egleche : and of redes wise and bolde,
> Lustniez nouþe to mi speche : wise and vnwise, ʒongue and olde :
> No-þing ich eov nelle rede ne teche : of none wichche ne of none scolde,
> Bote of a lif þat may beo lech^e : to sunfule men of herte colde.
>
> (1–4)

> [*Sleiʒe* and *egleche* men of counsels wise and bold, listen now to my speech, wise and unwise, young and old. I will not advise you about nor teach you anything concerning a witch or a scold, but of a life that may be beneficial to sinful, cold-hearted men.]

Far from being used of liminal, inhuman, semihuman, or otherwise problematic characters, *egleche* in this instance refers to the poem's intended audience. Perhaps because of this, the MED glosses it as "brave, fearless." Attaching these meanings to the term casts the poem's audience in a positive light, but it does so at the expense of severing the lexeme from its traditional associations. When we plug it back into its traditional expressive economy, the audience for this tale of sin, absolution, and dedication to God's word appears in a somewhat different, less wholly positive, light.

The first word of the poem, *sleiȝe,* provides a key to the matter. The MED, citing this occurrence, glosses it as "wise, prudent, clever, ingenious" (s.v. 1a). But like its modern descendent *sly,* ME *sleiȝe* also carries with it the meanings "crafty, cunning, deceitful" (s.v. 1d, 1e), meanings that resonate more harmoniously with the context of line 1 of this poem. Coupling *sleiȝe* (1e) with the traditional, associative meaning of *egleche* situates the poem's audience in somewhat murkier territory and leaves open the possibility that they may be more problematic figures than the MED allows, men noteworthy for their cunning and crafty ways who are yet neither beyond redemption nor among the redeemed. That the poem should be addressed to such men may be perfectly in keeping with its genre's aims: in chronicling the lives of saints, lives that frequently begin in sin and end in blissful holiness, hagiographers strive to reach both those who have already been redeemed (and who will thence find their faith renewed and reinforced by the narrative) and those who have yet to be redeemed (and who are, by definition, in dire need of salvation). The men whom the poet addresses, while not as clearly liminal and threatening as the few other *aglæcan* who populate Middle English poetry, are, nevertheless, perhaps not so clearly and unambiguously wise and bold as the glosses in the MED would lead us to think.

In its second occurrence—"Marie wax egleche" (157) [Mary became *egleche*]—the lexeme appears firmly placed within its traditional rhetorical context. As Mary Magdalene prepares to begin her mission preaching Christ's word "To sunfole men" (159), it is entirely fitting that she should "wax egleche."[38] While there is nothing in the narrative to suggest that she is going to be at risk while she travels about preaching, the threat of violent death is ever present in the genre of saints' lives, narratives that often modulate directly into martyrologies. By noting that she becomes "egleche," the poet reinforces the liminality of Mary Magdalene, the recently shrived and now reformed sinner who devotes herself to saving those who have fallen prey to precisely the sins to which she had been enslaved: "Mani on to cristinedom : heo brouȝte, and out of sunne, / Fram lecherie and hore-dom : þoru schrift, to Ioye and alle wunne" (161–62) [she brought many to Christianity out of sin, from lechery and whoredom, through confession, to joy and all bliss]. From the perspective of those she will seek to convert, the lexeme may resonate more fully with its traditional meanings because ministers of God are often terrifying figures to those still outside the fold (as well as to those within it).

The third and final time it occurs in the text, *egleche* once again resonates traditionally as the Saracen prince who has the lives of Mary and her followers in his hands challenges her "with egleche wordes and bolde" (281) to back up the claims she is making on Christ's behalf with concrete proof: "Miȝt þou proui with treuþe : þat þou prechest may beo wel i-holde?" (282) [Might you prove truly that what you preach may be true?].[39] The MED's glossing *egleche* as "brave, fearless," seems not wholly satisfactory in this instance because the Saracen prince is, after all, a ruler and has no reason whatsoever to fear Mary Magdalene, who never develops into an overtly threatening character but remains throughout a patient and gentle disseminator of God's word. Once again, a term that serves as a doublet in the line, *bolde,* provides a clue to how we ought to read *egleche. Bold* means not only "brave, courageous, daring, fearless" (s.v.1a), but also "overconfident, forward, rash; brazen, presumptuous, shameless, impudent" (s.v. 4a).[40] Given that Mary has expounded upon the virtues of a belief system that is in direct conflict with that of the prince and his people, it is understandable that the prince should respond with *egleche* words—with words, that is, that carry with them an unexpressed threat backed by the very real power the prince possesses. In this light, we can see that *bolde* more accurately describes the prince's rashness and overconfidence in questioning God's efficacy by so challenging his messenger than it does his fearlessness and courageousness in responding to Mary's gentle preaching.

Although *egleche* continues to carry with it some of its traditional associations when it appears in the *South-English Legendary,* these associations never come fully to the surface of the narrative. The poem's intended audience may well be unproblematically brave men, Mary Magdalene's status as a morally liminal character does not figure in this account of her life, she remains a model of nonthreatening behavior throughout the narrative, and, finally, the Saracen prince never so much as raises his voice to Mary and the other Christian exiles but instead offers them the sustenance they have failed to find elsewhere.

In the *Proverbs of Alfred,* the term appears once in the phrase "cnites egleche" (Trinity, 6). Embedded within a roster of the important and powerful men dwelling at "siforde" (Trinity, 1), whose numbers include "kinhis monie. / fele biscopis. / 7 fele booc-lerede. / herles prude" (2–5) [many nobles, and many bishops, learned men, and proud earls], and, of course, "erl Alfred" (7) [the noble Alfred], *egleche* apparently carries none of its traditional resonances. Their adeptness at arms may be what sets the knights to whom it applies apart from the others in this list, but we cannot be entirely sure of this: are the knights *egleche* because they are powerful, perhaps somewhat threatening figures with the capacity for violence, or has the term become detached from its traditional associations and been put to a post-traditional use in this instance, as it will be in a later text? Given the power of the lexeme's traditional referentiality in Anglo-Saxon oral poetics, it would not be surprising if some of its associative meaning attended its appearance in the *Proverbs,* but as neither the lexeme nor the narrative context offers us much guidance in this instance, we finally cannot get a firm grasp on its function here. What we may be sure of, though, is that it posed no problems to either of the redactors responsible for producing the Trinity and Jesus manuscripts, both of whom include it in their versions, to Sir John Spelman and Richard James, who made separate transcriptions of the Galba manuscript in the seventeenth century, or to Humfrey Wanley who transcribed Galba's opening lines in the early eighteenth century. Arngart, in *The Proverbs of Alfred,* notes the lexeme's connection to Old English *aglæca* and follows long-standing practice by defining this term as "*monster, warrior, hero.*" But in glossing *egleche* only as "*warlike, valiant,*" he severs it from its traditional roots and significantly narrows its semantic range. This maneuver places the knights in the *Proverbs* in a category that is post-traditional and hence separate from that inhabited by other *aglæcan*—something that may help explain why the term never acquires the meaning that Arngart attaches to it here but instead soon disappears from the written record. But before *aglæca* vanishes from the poetic and prosaic lexicons, it appears in several fourteenth-century texts, *Sir Gawain and the Green Knight* and the *Parlement of the Thre Ages,* as well as in the late-fourteenth-, early-fifteenth-century *Metrical Chronicle* of Robert of Gloucester.

Despite being a relatively rare term in the corpus of Middle English poetry, *aglæca*'s appearance in *Sir Gawain* has attracted little attention among the legions of the poem's editors. Sir Frederic Madden, producer of the poem's *editio princeps,* takes the lexeme quite accurately to mean "fearful, dreadful" but offers no comment on its etymology or role in the poem. Richard Morris, who in 1864 revises Madden's 1839 edition, offers the same translation and under the entry for the related adverb *aȝleȝ* gives its etymology as "Dan. *ave,* fear. Engl. *awe.* O.Eng. *agh.* Cf. A.S. *aglac,* misery, grief." In their 1925 edition, Tolkien and Gordon offer a different etymology for the lexeme, one that connects it to Old Norse *agi* [awe, terror] and the Old English suffix *-lic,* a reading subsequently adopted in all of the poem's principal editions.[41]

The lexeme has also not figured very prominently in the voluminous scholarly writings devoted to *Sir Gawain.* For example, Larry D. Benson, in his *Art and Tradition in Sir Gawain and the Green Knight,* devotes several pages to the description of the Green Knight and focuses explicitly upon lines 136–86, the passage in which the Knight's physique is discussed in considerable detail and in which he is described as an "aghlich mayster" (136) [*aghlich* knight]. Benson may have the phrase in mind when he comments that the poet's initial portrait of the Green Knight establishes the character as "nearly a monster, fearful and gigantic,"[42] but he neither comments directly on nor considers how *aghlich* shapes our perception of the character. In her extended consideration of the poem's stylistics, Marie Borroff turns her attention directly to *aghlich*. Acknowledging first that the adjective is "comparatively rare as a derivative of *awe*," she contends that because the poet's "choice of this derivative in prefer- ence to *awful*, which is cited from the thirteenth century on by the OED, is not motivated by meter or rhyme, . . . it seems reasonable to assume that *aghlich* was in general use in his locality."[43] But far from being metrically otiose— *aghlich* is the only alliterating lift in the line's second half—it unites the line's two parts.[44] While the infrequency with which this lexeme is attested in the extant written records prevents us finally from ascertaining whether it was in common usage in the poet's dialect area (or any other area for that matter), there is little doubt that it was a constituent of his idiopoetics. In addition to its singular appearance in its adjectival form, its adverbial form occurs once in *Sir Gawain* (2335) as well as twice in *Cleanness* (874, 937).

Elsewhere in her discussion of the poem's stylistics, Borroff returns to *aghlich* and argues that it "does not belong to the traditional diction of alliter- ative poetry" and that it also "does not have an established elevated meaning like that of, for example, *kyd*."[45] But the lexeme is in fact firmly rooted in tra- ditional oral poetics. In Old English poetry it always bears alliterative stress and it is as securely nestled within a web of traditional, associative meanings as any other traditional metonym. Even in the very different alliterative system that informs the metrics of the so-called Alliterative Revival,[46] *aghlich* con- tinues to be a central, not peripheral, metrical element. It appears rarely in the later Middle Ages, but when it does it continues to bear primary alliterative stress.[47] It also serves as a conduit through which poets can economically tap into the traditional associative meaning that attends the term.

Just as it often does in Old English poetry, *aglæca* occurs in *Sir Gawain* in a purely secular context and refers not to a hellish demon or inhuman mon- ster but to an unusually powerful, threatening, liminal human figure. Like Beowulf, the one other human *aglæca* whose physical traits are described in some detail, the Green Knight is immediately set apart from most men by his physicality. The poet introduces the Knight by cataloguing his numerous terrifying characteristics and emphasizing his threatening physical presence. Not only is the Green Knight "On þe most on þe molde on mesure hyghe" (137) [one of the largest on earth], but he is furthermore "Fro þe swyre to þe swange" [from the neck to the waist] very "sware and . . . þik" (138) [squarely built and . . . thick], and he possesses "lyndes and . . . lymes" [loins and . . . limbs] that are both "longe" and "grete" (139). Indeed, the Green Knight is so imposing a specimen that the poet surmises he is not entirely human but is in fact "Half etayn" (140) [half giant].[48]

While not all *aglæcan* are liminal figures—witness the dragon in *Beowulf*—most of them, including the demons who began their careers among the angels in heaven and the rapacious Grendelkin, straddle the boundary that separates good from evil and the human from the other-than-human world. The astonishing detail of the Green Knight's complexion—he is "oueral enker-grene" (150) [overall bright green]—his ability to survive an axe stroke that severs his head from his shoulders (421–29), and his generally rude behavior[49] reinforce the Green Knight's liminality and link him ever more securely to the *aglæcan* who precede him.[50] The physical threat the Green Knight poses is much more sharply focused upon first one and then another man (Arthur and Gawain, respectively) and so differs from the much more diffuse nature of Grendel's physical threat, but the Green Knight is every bit as terrifying to the inhabitants of Camelot as Grendel is to the inhabitants of Heorot, and, perhaps more importantly, the threat he poses to the stability of *Sir Gawain's* social order is just as terrible and as far-reaching as the threat Grendel poses to the social order of *Beowulf*.[51]

Aglæca appears at least two other times in the Middle English poetic record before lapsing permanently into obsolescence. In the Thornton version of the late-fourteenth-century alliterative poem the *Parlement of the Thre Ages,* it appears in the phrase "egheliche longe" (28), which the poet uses to describe not the terrible teeth or talons of a ravenous monster but the "auntlers" possessed by a buck that the poet encounters while out hunting one day.[52] And in the version of the *Metrical Chronicle* of Robert of Gloucester contained in Cambridge, Trinity College, R. 4. 26, dated to about 1400 by William Wright,[53] it describes Maud, daughter of Henry I, empress of Germany, and, following the emperor's death, wife of the earl of Anjou, a formidable woman who plays an important role in thwarting King Stephen's plans to annex Normandy.

The eleven-point buck that the narrator kills and dresses in the prologue to the *Parlement* is a large and wily specimen that has long succeeded in escaping the ranks of hunters who have attempted to bag it (thanks in large part to the efforts of the *sowre* that warns it of approaching danger),[54] but there is nothing very liminal about it. Although an unusually fine representative of its species, the buck is quickly revealed to be nothing more than the forest creature he appears to be. Furthermore, despite its impressive physicality and equally impressive rack, it poses no real threat either locally to those who hunt him or more globally to the human social world.[55] Within forty lines of first being mentioned in the poem, the buck lies "Ded als a dore-nayle" (65) [dead as a door-nail], and it is in short order graphically gutted and field dressed. While other *aglæcan* frequently wind up dead, none suffers the ignominious fate of this particular buck: after death, it is unceremoniously "hent by þe hede and heryett . . . vttire" (66) [seized by the head and dragged . . . out into the open] by the hunter, who informs us that he then

> Turned his troches & tachede thaym in-to the erthe,
> Kest vp that keuduart and kutt of his tonge,
> Brayde [owte] his bewells my bereselet to fede;
> And I s[lit]te hym at þe assaye to see how me semyde,
> And he was floreschede full faire of two fyngere brede.
>
> (67–71)

———

[turned his troches and fixed them in the earth, turned over that stag and cut out his tongue, pulled out his intestines to feed my hunting dog; and I slit him at the assay to see how it seemed to me and he was lined with fat fully the breadth of two fingers.]

In having the hunter treat the body of the buck so casually—as he guts it, he methodically and almost disdainfully disposes of those body parts that are of no use to him—the *Parlement*-poet reveals the degree to which *aglæca*'s traditional referentiality and affective dynamics have eroded for him because elsewhere in Old and Middle English vernacular poetry the bodies of *aglæcan* tend to remain mysterious and unsettling, even in death.[56] Any wonder that the buck's body might have elicited in the hunter (and by extension the poem's audience) while it was alive immediately dissipates once it is dead. After bringing it down, the hunter does not marvel over his catch's physicality but concerns himself solely with cleaning and then skinning its carcass. Unlike the other *aglæcan*, who are often the focal points of the narratives in which they appear, the buck is, at best, a peripheral figure in the *Parlement*. It does not figure in the dream vision that dominates the poem's narrative, and upon awakening from his slumber, the hunter returns to town apparently having forgotten all about the creature he had killed a few hours earlier.

The *Parlement*-poet's deployment of *aglæca* reveals that its traditional referentiality and affective dynamics are not so coherent for him as they are for the other Old and Middle English poets who use it. But even though the *Parlement*-poet applies the simplex to a creature far different from the ones to whom it elsewhere refers, and even though the creature to whom it applies is not central to the poem's narrative, *aglæca* nevertheless remains connected to its traditional foundations, and traces of its traditional meaning still attend it. The buck may not be an aggressive predator, a wily and dangerous (physically and morally) demon, a *handbona* who kills his enemies by tearing off their limbs or crushing them to death, or a shape-changer, but its physical characteristics do set it apart from the others of its species just as Beowulf's physicality distinguishes him from the Geatish warriors who accompany him to Denmark.

Even though its traditional resonance is muted in the *Parlement*, and even though it is deployed within a poetics that is chiefly post-traditional and literate, *egheliche* metonymically links the buck that is so graphically disemboweled in the *Parlement* to such figures as Grendel and the dragon, at whatever remove. Since neither the *Parlement* nor *Sir Gawain* can be dated with any real precision—they both are generally agreed to have been composed in the latter half of the fourteenth century—and since we cannot then confidently determine which of them was composed first,[57] we cannot argue that the simplex is less resonant in the *Parlement* because it is the more temporally removed of the two from Anglo-Saxon oral poetics. In fact, as tidy (and seemingly logical) as it would be to argue that the word-power of traditional lexemes diminishes in direct proportion to their temporal distance from the expressive economy in which their inherent, traditional meanings are rooted, we cannot make such an assertion, for if such were the case, the written poetic records of the later Middle English period would contain *only* fragmented, peripheral, and perhaps wholly vestigial remnants of oral poetics (as in the *Parlement*) and not the coherent, narratively vital elements we discover elsewhere.

In Robert of Gloucester's *Metrical Chronicle*, the lexeme occurs in only one of the nearly one dozen versions of this text that survive. The Empress Maud, to whom it refers, is a powerful opponent of King Stephen's who has at her command a sizable army. She succeeds in defending Normandy from Stephen and gaining a foothold in England, and her forces even manage to capture Stephen in their one martial engagement, although she immediately exchanges him for her brother who was captured in the same battle. But as was the case in the *South-English Legendary,* the redactor responsible for the version of the *Chronicle* in which it occurs does not allow the lexeme to stand alone but clarifies it by means of a doublet: "Þe lefdi," the poet tells us, "was egleche · & quointe of fale wrenche" (125) [The lady was *egleche* and skilled in many wiles].[58] The poem's editor, William Wright, follows Francis Stratmann in glossing the lexeme as "Bold, daring," but Wright silently removes the question mark that precedes Stratmann's definition ("? bold, valiant"). Maud is certainly both bold and daring, but there is nothing about her that links her to the more physically threatening, liminal *aglæcan* we have encountered elsewhere, although we must admit the possibility that in transgressing the accepted code of behavior for women she may have been a rather threatening figure to many men. While *egleche* carried with it some sort of resonance for the redactor of the version in Cambridge, Trinity College, R. 4. 26, it does not carry any for the redactor of the version in Oxford, Bodleian Library, Digby 205, who employs *qwent* [cunning] instead of Trinity's *egleche* and *sley* [sly] instead of its *quointe.*

As is true of the other Middle English descendents of Anglo-Saxon *aglæca,* the appearance of *egleche* in the Chronicle does not signal the continued survival of oral poetics but rather the degree to which this expressive economy has fractured because the term's associative resonances are clearly muted for Robert and for the multiple scribes who copied his poem.

Lexical Loss and Oral Poetics: Beot's Last Stand

We began our consideration of the ways in which oral poetics continues to shape the semantic fields of individual lexemes by examining the path *helm* follows in the post-Conquest period and saw that even though at some point between the late Anglo-Saxon and early Middle English periods it loses the specialized meaning it often has in oral poetics ("protector of a people"), its more general meaning ("piece of armor worn upon and designed to protect the head") remains intact and that it occurs in both the poetic and prose registers with this sense exclusively. We then turned our attention to *aglæca,* a lexeme almost completely restricted to the specialized register of oral poetics, and considered the ways in which and the degrees to which its traditional meaning persists even when it is used in texts written some four centuries after the Conquest. In turning now to *beot,* we encounter a lexeme that, like *helm,* occurs frequently in both Anglo-Saxon poetry and prose.[59] It evidences a spectrum of (related) meanings when deployed in the prose, but its field of meaning narrows considerably and becomes much more highly specialized when it appears in the poetic register. But unlike *helm*, which continues to be a constituent of both the post-Conquest poetic and prosaic registers, albeit stripped of its traditional resonances and associative meaning, *beot* does not survive much beyond the Conquest, making only a brief appearance in the early Middle English written records before completely and permanently disappearing. What distinguishes *beot* from these other lexemes is not only the suddenness and completeness of its disappearance but the degree to which its traditional contours remain consistent with those it possesses in Anglo-Saxon oral poetics. Whereas *aglæca* affords us the opportunity to witness the ways in which parts of the specialized lexis of oral poetics were able to merge seamlessly, if impermanently, into the very different system(s) of poetics that develop in the post-Conquest period, *beot*'s history reveals that other lexemes simply vanish from the written records once their expressive economy fractures.

In the Anglo-Saxon prose records, *beot* and its related nominal forms chiefly have the sense of "vow," "boast," "threat," and "peril, affliction" (DOE s.v. 2, 3, 4, 4a; *gebeot* 1, 2, 3, 4), senses that its verbal forms share as well: "to vow, promise something," "to utter threats, threaten, menace" (DOE s.v. *beotian* 1, 2, 2.c.ii; *gebeotian* 1, 2). Anglo-Saxon poets had at their disposal any number of lexemes to express "promise," "boast," or "threat," including, most prominently, *gilp* and *að* (and their compounds), words that Bosworth and Toller gloss, respectively, as "glory, ostentation, pride, boasting, arrogance, vain-glory, haughtiness" and "an oath, a swearing."[60] But when *beot* appears in the poetry, where it is attested twenty-three times,[61] its sense narrows almost exclusively to "vow (to perform a deed), especially formal vow of a warrior before battle" (DOE s.v. 1a). Thus, when the speaker in the *Wanderer* informs us that

> Beorn sceal gebidan,   þonne he beot spriceð,
> oþþæt collenferð   cunne gearwe
> hwider hreþra gehygd   hweorfan wille
> (70–72)[62]

———

[a man must wait, when he speaks a vow, until the brave-hearted one readily knows which way the thought of his heart will turn],

or when Hrothgar reveals to Beowulf that

Ful oft gebeotedon   beore druncne
ofer ealowæge   oretmecgas,
þæt hie in beorsele   bidan woldon
Grendles guþe   mid gryrum ecga
(480–83)

[very often men drunk on beer vowed, warriors over their ale-cups, that they would await in the beer-hall the warfare of Grendel with their terrible swords],

they allude to vows that are much more formal and more extremely binding than are the quotidian promises, threats, and the like that *gilp* and *að* signify.[63] Whether the lexeme is used to characterize Beowulf's resolve before the dragon fight ("beotwordum spræc" [2510b] [he spoke boasting words]) or to underscore the utter devastation of the fallen angels who along with Satan are driven from Heaven ("beot forborsten" [*Genesis A,* 70a] [their boasting was destroyed]), it signals a specialized, highly significative type of speech act, one that carries with it a set of expectations for the one who utters it and for characters in the poem and the poem's listening or reading audience.[64]

Although a commonly occurring element in both Anglo-Saxon poetry and prose, *beot* is rare in the written records of the post-Conquest period, where it apparently survives only in three texts dating from the end of the twelfth to the middle of the thirteenth century: the two versions of Laȝamon's *Brut* (where it occurs by my count a total of twenty times[65]) and the twelfth-century prose *History of the Holy Rood* (where it occurs once). It occurs eighteen times in the Caligula version of the *Brut,* where it consistently fulfills narrative and affective functions that closely parallel those it always has in Old English poetry, as is true of its singular occurrence in the *History of the Holy Rood.*[66] The scene in which troops gather in response to Arthur's call to Howel for help (10200 ff.) clearly models the ways in which Laȝamon habitually deploys this component of traditional oral poetics.[67] As he is mustering his troops for an all-out assault on York and the Saxon chief Colgrim, who is sheltering inside the city's walls, Arthur learns that the "wode 7 þan richen" (10160) [fierce and powerful] Emperor Childric has landed in Scotland and has efficiently and brutally begun taking control of the kingdom. Once he subdues the Scots, Childric plans to march to Colgrim's aid, something that leads Arthur to fret over how he, with his greatly outnumbered force, might best "mid his mon-weorede: his monscipe halden. / 7 fehten wið Childriche: þan stronge 7 þan richen" (10175–76) [with his troop maintain his dignity and fight with Childric the strong and powerful]. Arthur decides that the best course is to march to London, where he will be able to gather sufficient men to ensure that Colgrim "he seolf and his ferde⁏ fæie scal iwurðen" (10181) [himself and his troop shall be fated to die]. In response to Arthur's call for men, a huge and well-equipped army of "wode scalkkes" (10235) [fierce warriors] lands at "Hamtone." The warriors "beren to londe⁏ halmes 7 burnen" (10236) [bear to land helmets and coats of mail] and "mid spæres 7 mid sceldes heo wriȝen al þa feldes" (10237) [with spears and with shields they cover all the fields]. As the warriors continue to muster, Laȝamon reports "þat beot wes aræred" (10238) [that the *beot* was raised] as the men go about the business of preparing themselves for what promises to be a bloody, and for many no doubt fatal, martial engagement. The poet follows this general mention of warriors engaging in ritual boasting with a far more detailed and explicit account of what fate awaits Childric and his men should they dare to march upon London:

> heo beoteden swiðe⁏ bi heore quiken liue.
> þat heo wolden igræten⁏ Cheldric þene richen.
> þene [balde] kæisere mid muchele harme þere.
> And ȝif he nolde awæi fleon⁏ 7 touward Alemaine teon.
> and he wolde on londe⁏ mid fehte atstonden.
> mid balde his beornen⁏ beorkes abiden⁏
> here heo sculde bilauen⁏ þat heom weore alre l[eof]est.
> hafden and heore honden⁏ 7 heore white halmes.
> 7 swa heo scullen on londen⁏ losien heore freonden.
> hælden into hælle. hæðen hundes.
>
> (10239–48)

[they boasted strongly by their lives that they would greet the powerful Childric, the bold emperor, with much harm there. And if he would not flee and go toward Germany, and if he would here resist and fight with his bold men and endure loud boasts, here they would have to leave what they loved the most, their heads and hands and their shining helmets. And so here they would have to lose their friends and fall into hell, the heathen hounds.]

In this passage, the verb *beotian*, which the MED cites in only this occurrence, summons to a narrative present several important components of the heroic ethos, among which are the promise to fight to the death (the warriors swear "bi heore quiken liue") and an explicit account of what they will do to their enemies in the battle.

Later in the poem, *beot* appears at the end of the speech Arthur makes upon learning of Modred's treachery. During this speech, Arthur articulates what he will very shortly explicitly identify as his *beot* when he proclaims that he "Moddred . . . wulle s[l]an: 7 þa quen for-berne. / and alle ich wulle for-don: þa biluueden þen swike-dom" (14065–66) [will slay Modred and burn the queen and (he) will kill those who approved of their treachery]. He further announces that "þenne þas þing. beoð alle idone" (14071) [when this thing is all done], he will return to England briefly to install his kinsman Gawain as regent before returning to Rome, where he plans to live out his days as emperor. He concludes this speech with the following public proclamation, one that effectively underscores the depth of his commitment to the heroic course of action he has just laid out: "and iuorþ‹e› m‹i› beot seo[ð]ðe: bi mine bare life. / Scullen all mine feond: wæi-sið makeʒe" (14073–74) [and afterwards I will complete my *beot*; by my life I shall make all my enemies doomed to die].

Elsewhere in the Caligula version of the *Brut, beot* is similarly used, as it is in Anglo-Saxon oral poetics, to characterize directly reported speech,[68] but it is also used more generally of speech acts that are only indirectly related in the narrative. Following the death of Luces (13982–84) and Arthur's subsequent conquest of Burgundy, Arthur publicly declares his intentions to "faren into Rome: 7 ahnien al þa riche. / and beon him-seolf kaisere: þe Luces wuneden ære" (13953–54) [journey to Rome and conquer all the kingdom and become emperor himself where Luces earlier dwelt]. What sets this heroic proclamation apart from the ones we considered above is that Laʒamon first reports that Arthur "his beot makede" (13952) [made his *beot*] before summarizing—rather than directly reporting—its substance in lines 13953–54. Even though Arthur's speech is not directly reported, Laʒamon's use of the highly significative *beot* as well as the summary's rhetorical contours and affective dynamics clearly situates his discourse within the specialized, associative field of meaning that the lexeme occupies in medieval English oral poetics. In several other instances, characters in the poem use it to characterize speeches that their opponents have earlier made, speeches that neither the speaker nor the poet marks as a formal *beot* but that nevertheless are clearly so.[69] Cador, for example, uses *beot* (12441) to describe the speeches the Romans have been making in which they detail their plans to "cumen to ure burhʒes. / ure king binden: and to Rome hine bringen" (12441–42) [come to our towns and bind our king and bring him to

Rome], and Arthur earlier uses it to characterize Childric's speeches as he promises his men that he will "to nohte ibringen" [bring to naught] Childric's "balde ibeot" (10651) [bold *beot*]. Even in the few instances when *beot* is used of speech that is neither directly reported nor summarized by Laȝamon, it continues to serve as a conduit for traditional, institutionalized meaning, as when Aurelius's troop of thirty thousand riders "heore beot makeden" (8153) [made their *beot*] as they prepare to battle the Saxon Hengest or when Arthur's men respond to his rallying cry, "Nu we heom to alle: mine cnihtes ohte. / 7 Godd seolf us fulste: ure feond to afallene" (13880–81) [Now let us all go at them, my brave knights, and may God himself help us to kill our enemies] by offering a "mucle ibeote" (13885) [great *beot*] that, along with the noise of fifteen thousand trumpets, causes both "þa eorðe . . . beouien" (13884) [the earth . . . to tremble] and the "Romleoden wenden: rug to þan feohten" (13886) [Romans to turn their backs on the fighting].

While its numerous and varied appearances in Caligula demonstrate that *beot* remains clearly linked to the expressive economy of medieval English oral poetics, the evidence of the Otho version reveals that not all post-Conquest poets engage medieval English oral poetics to the same degree because the Otho-redactor usually either substitutes a different lexeme for it or simply excises it from his narrative. In three places, the extensive damage that the Otho manuscript sustained during the Cottonian fire prevents us from ascertaining with absolute surety just how the Otho-redactor dealt with occurrences of *beot* in Caligula,[70] but the weight of the evidence suggests that in the passages destroyed or otherwise rendered unreadable in the fire he may well have followed his usual practices by either substituting another term or, as he often does, by simply omitting the whole or half-line in which it occurs.[71]

If the Otho-redactor simply excised *beot* every time he encountered it in his exemplar (most probably Caligula), we could safely argue that he must have been unsure of the term's meaning and so avoided copying it into his text, a practice that would be in keeping with his putative desire to remove from his exemplar all of its unusual or archaic poeticisms.[72] His substitutions, however, offer a rather different picture. That the terms the Otho-redactor substitutes for *beot* often occupy semantic fields closely related to it suggests that he was not entirely puzzled by the term or completely deaf to its traditional resonances. Of the five lexemes—*eke* (3830) [also], *broc* (10493) [?threat], *þret* (12441) [threat], *balnesse* (12526) [?boldness], and *dred* (13885) [dread]—and two phrases— "mid worde seide" (10238) [said with words] and "mid hire bolde wordes" (10814) [with their bold words]—only two, *eke* and *drede,* may be the result of the redactor's not understanding *beot*. In Caligula, the poet tells us that the French "speken of þrætte. / 7 of prute ibeote" (3830) [spoke with threats and proud *beots*], while in Otho we learn "þat hii speke of þrete: and of prude eke" [that they spoke with threats and with pride also]. This line raises *prude* to nominal status (it functions adjectivally in Caligula) and stresses it instead of *ibeote* and all its attendant metonymic resonances. In Otho, the French do not contextualize their threats within a traditionally freighted *beot* but rather voice less resonant threats and evince their general pride. The Otho-redactor's substitution of *drede* for *ibeote* in line 13885 similarly alters the meaning of the line in which it occurs. As we saw above, Arthur's men let out a tremendous *beot* that causes the earth to shake and their Roman foes to turn their backs and flee the field. In the hands of the Otho-redactor, Caligula's "for þan mucle ibeote" becomes "for þan grete drede" [because of their great terror] an alteration that shifts our attention away from the Britons' aggressiveness and focuses it instead solely upon the Romans' fearful reaction to the noise that bursts from Arthur's men. In Caligula, the noise and the affective dynamics of *beot* combine to induce great fear in the Romans, while in Otho the noise of the trumpets alone suffices to bring about the same reaction. Caligula's treatments consistently resonate more fully with the expressive economy of oral poetics, but in these instances Otho's departures do not significantly alter the episode's narrative contours.

Of Otho's other substitutions, three—the phrases "mid worde seide" (10238) and "mid hire bolde wordes" (10814) and the lexeme *þret* (12441)—stand as unproblematically identifiable equivalents of *beot*. In each instance, not only does the phrase or word that is substituted occupy a semantic field recognizably close to the one that *beot* occupies in medieval English oral poetics, but each phrase or word dips into the broader semantic pools of the lexeme's nonpoetic meanings (c.f. DOE s.v. 3, 4, 4.a; *gebeot* 3; *beotian* 2, 2.a, 2.b, 2.c.ii). The substitutions dilute the affective dynamics of the scenes in which they occur, but in these cases we can still detect in the conferred meanings of Otho's substitutions traces, however muted, of *beot*'s traditional resonances.

The final two substitutions the Otho-redactor makes, *broc* and *balnesse*, fit the pattern of his other substitutions, but rather more problematically, since both are attested only once in the extant written records and so pose a different set of interpretive challenges. In its entry for *broc*, the MED supplies as a comparand OE *gebræc* [noise] and suggests that the Middle English term means "A loud boast or threat" (s.v.). Given the narrative context in which *broc* occurs as well as the fact that it directly replaces *ibeot* in a line otherwise identical in the two texts, there is little reason to question the meaning the MED assigns it.[73] It is entirely possible that the Otho-redactor employed the *hapax legomenon broc* because it contained for him resonances that we at this great remove can no longer hear, but the MED's conjecture confirms our sense that *broc* is the result of the Otho-redactor's attempts to employ a lexeme that is— to him, at least—a semantic equivalent of *beot*, something that allows us tentatively to place *broc* in the same category as his other substitutions.

Balnesse also occurs only once in Otho, but we must approach it somewhat differently, since, unlike *broc*, it has no entry in the MED. In his glossary to the poem, Madden confidently asserts that *balnesse*, itself another *hapax*, is a mistake for *baldnesse*, a lexeme that does not appear elsewhere in either text of the *Brut* and that is first attested in John of Trevisa's late-fourteenth-century translation of Higden's *Polychronicon*. Adopting Madden's view and taking it as a scribal error for *boldness* links the unique occurrence of *balnesse* with the phrase "bolde wordes," which, as we saw above, the Otho-redactor elsewhere uses as a substitute for *beot* (10814). However, *balnesse* may instead owe its presence in the text not to a scribal or authorial error but to its connection to the verb *bolnen*, "to swell, become distended" (MED s.v.). Although the nominal derivative of this word in *-nesse* is unattested, its senses of "puffed up (with vanity or pride); arrogant" (MED s.v. 3b) accords well with the poem's narrative context at this point as Arthur simultaneously reports and disparages the threats the Roman Emperor Luces has made against him. Pride and boastfulness, are, of course, necessary (and perhaps even foundational) elements of a *beot*, and in so coining *balnesse* the Otho-redactor may be demonstrating a more finely attuned artistic sensibility than he is usually credited with possessing. *Balnesse* allows Arthur to allude to the nature of Luces's threatening message without acknowledging it as the formal, traditional, and weighty speech act that it is.

As we noted above, if the Otho-redactor uniformly omitted or replaced *beot* every single time he encountered it in the text from which he worked, we could argue that the omissions would both indicate the degree to which the lexeme puzzled him and signal that he was unwilling to employ a term whose meaning was not clear to him. We could similarly explain his appropriate substitutions as being contextually determined. If he were, for example, unsure of what *beot* meant in Caligula line 12441, "7 heore beot makieð" [and make their *beot*], he could have been cued into it by its context. Just some forty-five lines earlier, the Roman messengers inform the Britons that Luces plans to invade Britain if Arthur will not submit to him, adding that after they defeat the

Britons they will take Arthur to Rome in chains (12355–91). But while we should not discount either the role authorial puzzlement plays in his omissions or the degree to which narrative context helped determine the Otho-redactor's substitutions, we cannot overlook that *beot* appears twice in Otho and that in each of these instances the lexeme draws directly upon its traditional pool of meanings.

Beot makes the first of its two appearances in Otho at line 11813, "þat his beot (ha)ueþ imaked: and his cniht-scipe for-sake" [that his *beot* has made and his knightly courage forsaken] a line that in Caligula reads, "þe his beot haueð imaked: and his cniht-scipe for-saken." The close correspondences between these two lines might lead us to think that perhaps the Otho-redactor decided to copy a word he did not understand in this instance, either by mistake or by design. While we cannot fully rule this out, we cannot place too much weight on the possibility that *beot* is here a mistake, and we cannot place too much weight on the redactor's desire to adhere to his exemplar because he elsewhere departs freely from the text of Caligula. There are numerous other lines in Otho that closely echo those of Caligula but in which the redactor plays an active, authorial, recompositional (as opposed to scribal, copying) role in creating his version by substituting another appropriate lexeme for Caligula's *beot,* as he does in line 12441, where Otho reads "and hire þret makieð: to come to vre borewes" [and their threat made to come to our towns] while Caligula reads "7 heore beot makieð to comen to ure burhȝes." Rather, we ought to see *beot* in Otho line 11813 as a word that the Otho-redactor chose to preserve at this point in his text because his artistic sensibilities dictated that he do so.

The second, and final, appearance of *beot* in Otho sheds further light upon its place in the redactor's poetics and upon his general poetic praxis. Coming just four lines after its first appearance, *beot* once again is used in an Otho line—"and his beot hadde imaked bi-vore al his cnihtes" [and made his *beot* before all his knights]—that closely resembles the corresponding line in Caligula, "and his beot imaked hafde: bi-foren al his duȝeðe." We may attribute its appearance in line 11817 to precisely the same factors that resulted in its occurrence in line 11813: that is, while we cannot rule out the chance that the redactor may have here copied from his exemplar a word he only partially comprehended or perhaps did not understand at all, *beot* may simply have struck him as an apt choice for this spot in his narrative.[74] We will never be able to determine precisely why the redactor elected to preserve Caligula's *beot* in these lines, but line 11816 contains an additional piece of evidence that sheds further light on the redactor's idiopoetics. While he chooses to retain the word *beot* in this instance, he replaces another term in Caligula that descends from Anglo-Saxon oral poetics, *duȝeðe* (<OE *duguþ* [tried warriors, DOE, s.v., 4.a]), with the less specialized and less highly significative term *cnihtes* [knights], something he does frequently but not absolutely throughout his text.[75] When the Otho-redactor chooses not to employ *doȝeþe*, which invariably appears in his text precisely in this form, he uses instead terms that are broad semantic equivalents for it,[76] a practice very much akin to the one he habitually, but not universally, engages in when he encounters *beot*.[77]

The final piece of evidence concerning *beot* that we will consider is, once again, small but telling: after employing the lexeme twice in the space of four lines, and so invoking and linking his narrative present directly to a larger, associative world of traditional meaning, the Otho-redactor chooses not to employ a substitute for the lexeme when it occurs again in Caligula line 11819, opting instead, as he often does, to omit the entire line, and so renders Caligula 11818–20,

and [h]e ne mihte: for scome muchelen: scenden hine seoluen.
bi-læuen his balde ibeot: þat he i burh hafde iseid.
Sæide þat he sæide: to soðe he hit wende,

———

[and he might not for great shame disgrace himself, go back upon the bold *beot* that he had said in the town. When he said what he said, he truly believed it]

as "he ne miht for scame synde him-seolue. / Ac saide wat he saide: to soþe he hit wen[de]" [he might not for shame disgrace himself, but when he said what he said, he truly believed it]. The Caligula lines are certainly not among Laȝamon's best, and here the Otho-redactor's paring and reshaping decidedly improve them. Since *beot* does not resonate very powerfully within the redactor's idiopoetics, we can easily understand why he would decide in this instance to cut it and so remove the third reference to the traditionally freighted speech act that Frolle somewhat rashly and unhappily (for him, at least) made regarding his desire to fight Arthur "him-seolf buten cnihte" (11815) [himself without any knights]. Even if the lexeme were one with greater currency and one whose meaning(s) would be more readily available to his intended audience, the Otho-redactor's own poetic sensibilities may have dictated omitting *beot* the third time it occurs in seven lines because the stacking of this, or virtually any other lexeme, might well have seemed aesthetically displeasing to both poet and audience. If *beot* is an exotic or archaistic term that owes its very appearance in Caligula not to the continued vitality and persistence of oral poetics but rather to Laȝamon's supposed "antiquarian sentiments," there is little doubt that it strikes the Otho-redactor, who creates his text anywhere from fifty to a hundred years after Caligula, as an even more unusual and rare term.[78] Viewed in this light, the Otho-redactor's decision to forego using the lexeme in line 11819 not only accords with his established practice (he omits it nearly as often as he inserts a substitute for it) but once again points to his artistic sensibility and sheds further light upon the way he actively recomposes his exemplar as he filters it through his own poetic abilities and sensibilities.

As the Otho-redactor demonstrates through the semantically appropriate substitutions he employs, he clearly remains able to comprehend *beot*. But because it is part of an expressive economy that does not figure very prominently in his idiopoetics, he does not employ the lexeme very often, preferring ones that may be more familiar, ones that are perhaps more current, and, most important, ones that may carry more readily accessible meaning(s) both for him and for his intended audience. Where *beot* was once a *sêma* that summoned to any given narrative present in which it occurred a whole network of interlaced and interdependent meaning(s), for the Otho-redactor its traditional resonances have become largely muted.

The Fragmentation of Medieval English Oral Poetics II: The Evidence of Thematics

Medieval English oral poetics depends not solely on a specialized lexical register but on a specialized thematic register that is also richly associative and freighted with inherent meaning. In this register, constellations of narrative events are knit into larger units of expression that are then "regularly used" by singers "telling a tale in the formulaic [i.e. oral] style of traditional song."[79] These traditional thematic units are "words" that provide poets with a ready means of framing the macro-structural contours of their narratives. But whereas formulas are always linguistically and culturally specific and thus are necessarily aligned only with each tradition's unique prosody, traditional themes are able to cross linguistic (and cultural) boundaries because they are not solely elements of the local expressive economy of any given tradition but are rooted in a far more global one.[80] We can perhaps best understand the ease with which traditional themes circulate among different traditions by seeing them as narrative deep structures, to borrow a concept from the world of Chomskyan linguistics, that maintain their ideational integrity even when they are articulated via the idiosyncratic linguistic and metrical surface structures of various different expressive economies because "even though [traditional themes] be verbal, [they are] not any fixed set of words, but a grouping of ideas."[81] The same theme will be constituted somewhat differently in different traditions (just as each instantiation of a theme within a given tradition will necessarily differ from every other instantiation of it within that same tradition), but it will retain its characteristic and defining contours. In contrast, because the word-power of traditional verbal formulas (and their larger, phraseological equivalents)—their ability to summon institutionalized meaning(s) to a narrative present—is located within the tradition's unique lexical register and bound inextricably to its metrical and phraseological rules, they resonate only within the confines of their individual traditions.

In an important study of the medieval West Germanic poetic tradition, Alain Renoir demonstrates that traditional themes are able to circulate among and between traditions to the extent that they do because they are expressed through a surprisingly wide spectrum of affective and ideational links and do not depend on a fixed set of narrative details that are always presented in the same order.[82] To draw upon one of his examples, in its paradigmatic occurrences, the well-attested theme of the hero on the beach centers on a hero who journeys from afar and stands poised on the threshold between two worlds in the company of an armed troop and in the presence of a shining object or objects. The hero's position at the physical border of two worlds and the presence of the shining objects are elements of a very cohesive and highly traditional narrative structure that metonymically cues the audience to an imminent slaughterous encounter. When this theme occurs early in *Beowulf*, a gap of some five hundred lines separates its initial presentation from the slaughter that is its necessary and expected narrative complement, but the theme retains its integrity and continues to play an important role in the poem's poetics throughout the intervening narrative because it "is sustained in our mind by strategically located mentions of flashing lights."[83] Because these objects continue to be freighted with the associative meaning that they have accrued as deeply embedded constituents of the narrative framework of the hero on the beach, they echoically present us with an "unmistakable instance of a familiar narrative device which signals carnage."[84]

Traditional themes and story patterns are able to circulate among linguistically and chronologically discrete traditions because they "have great vitality and function as organizing elements in the composition and transmission of oral story texts" no matter "how much the stories built around them seem to vary."[85] There are, to my knowledge, no instances in which a formulaic verbal collocation retains any of its traditional referentiality when the collocation is translated from one poetic tradition into another,[86] but we do find scattered widely across a variety of Indo-European cultures distinctly realized yet nevertheless closely related narrative patterns (on both the thematic level and the larger one of the story pattern), among which are physical journey (by sea or over land), single combat (between human or nonhuman antagonists), battle, exile, marriage, return, and feasting, to name but a few of those that have so far been identified as being common to ancient Greek, medieval English, and contemporary South Slavic oral poetics.[87] The prosodic differences between ancient Greek and Old English explain why feasting scenes in the *Iliad* and *Beowulf* share no verbal resemblance to one another. Their structural similarities are also limited and general. But if we trace the narrative and affective contours of these scenes back to their respective deep structures, we discover that the cultural work they perform and their traditional, inherent meaning(s) are in fact rather closely aligned despite the many surface differences separating them. The establishment or reestablishment of communal ties is a central component of both poems, and by extension of both traditions, and scenes of feasting provide poets in both traditions with a ready way to celebrate and even on occasion to interrogate this crucially important cultural praxis.[88]

Within the diachrony of the medieval English poetic tradition, precisely the same situation obtains: the traditional themes and story patterns that continue to appear in post-Conquest vernacular verse remain linked to their Old English predecessors through other than verbal means. As we saw in chapter 3, Morpidus's fight with the beast rests upon the same thematics as Beowulf's fight with the dragon. Verbal links between the episodes exist, as they may well be expected to, but they are more echoic than exact. For example, the ways in which Beowulf's sword Nægling "forbærst" (2680b) [burst asunder] and "geswac" (2681a) [failed] during the fight are echoed when Morpidus's bow becomes "to-broken" (3234), when his spear "al to-brac" (3237) [broke into pieces], and finally when his "hilt on his hand bræc" (3243) [hilt broke in his hand]. Similarly, forms of the highly significative lexeme *gebelgan* occur four times during the course of Beowulf's fight with the dragon.[89] *Abolwe*, an early Middle English descendant of *gebelgan*, occurs in the Morpidus episode as well, at line 3188, where it is used to describe Morpidus's mental state in the moments before he suppresses the Duke of Moraine's threat to his kingdom by single-

handedly killing more than "seouen hundred" (3202) [seven hundred] warriors during the clash between his forces and the Duke's. While *abolwe* occurs
only this one time in the Morpidus episode, the semantically related *wrað*
[anger] and *wemed* [angry] appear a total of four (and perhaps five) times in
the episode's first ten lines.[90] They are not so securely anchored to the traditional expressive economy of oral poetics as *abolwe* is and hence do not have
that lexeme's power or resonance, but *wrað* and *wamed* help shape the narrative's traditional affective contours by foregrounding Morpidus's defining
and at times deadly anger.

The appearance of *abolwe* serves to link Morpidus to characters such as
Beowulf and Grendel, who possess strength that sets them apart from everyone else and who are further particularly dangerous when enraged. But while
gebelgan plays a pivotal role in the affective dynamics of all the monster fights
in *Beowulf*, it is entirely absent from Morpidus's battle with the beast. In fact,
Morpidus's anger surfaces only once during the fight, and when it does it is a
peripheral component of the scene. After arriving at the seashore and shooting all his arrows at the beast, Morpidus proceeds to ride toward it "on his
stede sulc he walde awede" (3233) [on his steed as if he had become enraged].
His anger, however, gets pushed into the background by the dramatic actions—
the physical destruction of his bow and the splintering of his spear—that
immediately follow. As Morpidus prepares to deliver a blow to the beast's head,
one that will splinter the blade and result in the death of both hero and beast,
Laȝamon does not tap into the affective dynamics inherent in *abolwe* (and to
a much lesser degree in the semantically related *wrað*, *wemed*, *wandliche*
[?quick to anger; cf. MED, s.v.], and *awede* [become enraged]) but offers
instead an affectively flat description of the hero's actions at this tense and cli-
mactic moment: the king, we are simply told, "droh his sweord þe him wes
itase" (3241) [drew his sword that was readily to hand].

Unlike *gebelgan*, which taps directly into a rich network of inherent, traditional meanings, the affective dynamics of *awede* is conferred and derives
solely from its immediate narrative context. In fact, there is no precedent in
Anglo-Saxon literature for the use to which *awede* is habitually put from Laȝamon onwards. OE *awedan*, from which *awede* descends, occurs only some
thirty-five times in the entire corpus of Old English literature (mostly in Ælfric)
and usually means "to be or become mad or insane; to rage, rave . . . specifically as a result of possession by evil spirits or devils" (DOE, s.v., 1, 1a.). Some
characters who are described as being *awedde* are also murderers (and are usually enemies of the church, to boot) but others are simply characters who are

insane or who are cured of insanity.[91] The lexeme is not used in martial contexts (either human vs. human or human vs. monster), and, most importantly,
it occurs almost exclusively in the prose. In using *awede* for *gebelgan*, Laȝamon
injects a new element into the tradition that accords with the episode's thematic and affective contours and that continues to gesture toward the nexus
of associative meaning(s) that *gebelgan* always indexes.[92]

Far from reflecting his imperfect or incomplete understanding of the
scene's traditional contours, the changes he makes open a window onto his
authorial making and allow us to see, once again, that oral poetics does not
imprison him, or any other post-Conquest poet who engages it. Even devoid
of one of its fundamental elements (*abolwe*), the thematics of Morpidus's fight
with the beast nevertheless maintains its integrity and functions just as coher-
ently as *Beowulf*'s more fully traditional instantiation of it.

Oral Thematics in the Early Fourteenth Century: Bevis and the Beasts

Because they depend upon an often loose constellation of ideationally
and affectively connected narrative events rather than upon a fixed set of explicitly repeated ones that must be expressed through an equally fixed set of
formulaic collocations, traditional themes have considerable staying power.
But while the idioms of scene and story pattern are more global than those of
lexeme and phrase, the looseness and extreme malleability of the former also
leave them far more exposed to the vicissitudes of change (that affect them
both when they are deployed within their developing/changing native tradition and when they transfer between and among different traditions) than the
latter, which are ineluctably anchored to the specific languages and cultures in
which they occur. We know that many lexical metonyms fall quickly and permanently into obsolescence once they are no longer firmly situated within the
traditional register within which they developed and upon which they de-
pended for their traditional referentiality. Some continue to resonate, faintly
and imperfectly, with traditional meanings, but they are largely stripped of
their inherited meanings.

The fate that befalls traditional themes and story patterns once they are
no longer embedded within their traditional expressive economy and are deployed by poets who are not greatly influenced by oral poetics is somewhat
different, but many of them also simply disappear. Those that do find their
way into post-traditional texts display varying degrees of narrative and affective coherence. To return to the example from the *Brut* that we considered

briefly above and at greater length in chapter 3, even though Morpidus's fight with the beast differs from Beowulf's fight with the dragon in a number of minor as well as a few major ways, its traditional contours are still visible. Morpidus's fight may not approach Beowulf's in terms of artistic achievement or narrative significance, but the two episodes clearly are rooted in the same traditional oral poetics.

As a way of illustrating how traditional themes and story patterns continue to pulse, however faintly, with traditional meaning even when they are fractured almost beyond recognition, we turn now to *Sir Beues of Hamtoun,* a long metrical romance dating from the early- to mid-fourteenth century. Unlike Laȝamon, the *Beues*-poet appears to have been little influenced by medieval English oral poetics and, for the most part, adheres so closely to his written source, the twelfth-century Anglo-Norman *Boeve de Haumtone,* that there is little doubt that he worked directly from a written text. The two episodes upon which we will focus in the long, uneven but frequently quite entertaining *Beues* are Bevis's fights with a wild boar and his subsequent encounter with a venomous dragon. Because the former is based upon an episode in the Anglo-Norman *Boeve* while the latter is one of the *Beues*-poet's numerous additions to his source text, these two episodes afford us the opportunity to see how oral poetics figures both in what the *Beues*-poet incorporates directly from his source text and in what he either creates or imports into his text from other, traditional or post-traditional, sources.

In the Anglo-Norman *Boeve* a terrible boar that does not spare either the great or the small ("k'a nul ne esparnie, a granz ne a petiz" [421]) one day appears in the country ("Estevus un sengler venu en pais" [420]).[93] Boefs often hears talk about the boar ("Boefs oi parler sovent de ceo sengler" [425]) and decides to go hunt it. He eschews his hauberk ("il ne vout hauberk endoser" [427]), but he does carry with him on his good, fast charger both a steel sword ("une espeie de ascer" [428]) and a spear with an apple-wood shaft ("une launce de pomer" [429]). His beloved Josian weeps many a tear ("fist meinte lerme plurer" [432]) over his departure, and Boefs himself is greatly troubled ("Boefs fist meint mal desturber" [433]), but he nonetheless goes off to look for the boar, which he finds very quickly ("il le trova mult tost" [438]). Neither antagonist fears the other, and as soon as the boar sees Boefs, it begins to scratch the ground and open its great throat ("grant gule" [440]) wide as if it wanted completely to devour Boefs ("com c'il vosist tretut Boefs devorer" [441]). Boefs urges on his mount and bravely charges the boar. When he meets it, he manages to thrust his spear in its open mouth so deeply that it touches the beast's heart ("quer tocher" [445]), a stroke that results in the boar dying without further delay ("lui sengler tost murt saunz nul demurer" [446]). Boefs decapitates the boar and puts its head on the "tronsoun" (448) [stump] of his sword, which has somehow or other shattered ("ke il out fet debruser" [448]).[94] Josian witnesses Boefs's fight with the boar, and the episode ends with the comment that seeing him in action filled her with pleasure ("quant que ele li vit fere, le vient a pleiser" [452]).

The Middle English poem's version of the boar fight is three times longer than that of the Anglo-Norman poem (ninety-seven as opposed to thirty-two lines), but despite this considerable difference in their lengths, the episodes share the same narrative contours. As in *Boeve,* the sudden appearance of an extremely dangerous wild boar marks the episode's inception in *Beues.* Bevis decides to ride out after it and does so after prudently arming himself with a "gode brond" (759) [good sword], a "spere" (760), and a "scheld" (761) [shield].[95] Josian witnesses his departure, thinking all the while about how much she loves him (763–70). Bevis enters the woods and soon thereafter encounters the boar, just as he does in the Anglo-Norman text, killing it with a sword thrust to its mouth that strikes its heart (822–24). Bevis decapitates the carcass, fixes the boar's head on the "tronsoun" (827) of a shattered weapon, and returns to court. The episode concludes with Josian witnessing Bevis in action, something that brings joy to her heart (although significantly in the Middle English poem she sees him fight against a band of men, not the terrible boar).

While remaining true to his source's narrative contours, the *Beues*-poet freely departs from it.[96] Some of the changes he introduces are the result of the idiosyncratic poetic strategies that his poem, like all other traditional and post-traditional poems, everywhere evidences. The episode's conclusion offers a clear example of this sort of change. Whereas Boefs fights the boar in Josian's sight and returns directly afterwards to the court, Bevis fights away from the castle (from the safety of which Josian presumably witnesses the fight in the Anglo-Norman text), and his return is interrupted when he is set upon by a jealous steward who had hoped to win honor for himself by slaying the boar. From her vantage point in the castle, Josian witnesses their conflict, during which Bevis kills the steward and ten of the thirty-four men who accompany him. In addition to these changes, which are best understood as falling well within an author/translator's purview (for some reason he wanted to insert another battle scene into his poem), the episode in *Beues* contains a number of significant additions that point to the continued presence of traditional thematics in the poet's idiopoetics. When we complement the brief outline we offered above of the Middle English scene's similarities to its Anglo-Norman original with a consideration of those of its elements that derive from medieval English oral poetics, its connection to Beowulf's fight with the dragon and Morpidus's fight with the beast emerges clearly.

Let us return to the episode's beginning. The physical threat the boar presents is crucial to both the Anglo-Norman and Middle English version but surfaces in the texts in markedly different ways. In the Anglo-Norman episode, we are told simply that the boar is so fierce that it spares no man and that it would fear the approach of twenty hunters/chevaliers no more than it would a partridge (420–24). The boar in the Middle English text is similarly dismissive of those who would hunt it ("Þar of ne ʒef nouʒt a bene" [744] [thereof it did not give a bean]), but its violence is explicitly and graphically foregrounded—"Man and houndes, þat he tok, / Wiþ his toskes he al to-schok" (741–42) [the men and hounds that he took he shook furiously with his tusks]—and not consigned to the background as in the Anglo-Norman poem. Boefs rides out after the boar with little hesitation and absolutely no reflection, while Bevis not only "lay in is bedde a niʒt / And þouʒte, a wolde keþen is miʒt / Vpon þat swin" (751–53) [lay in his bed at night and thought he would exercise his power upon that boar] but decides he will do so "him self one" (753) [all by himself], a point that receives further stress when he determines "Þat noman scholde wiþ him gone" (754) [that no man should go with him]. The boar's physical danger is made dramatically clear because the entrance to its den is littered with the "bones of dede men, / Þe bor hadde slawe in þe wode, / Ieten here flesch & dronke her blode" (778–80) [bones of dead men the boar had slain in the wood. It had eaten their flesh and drunk their blood]. Bevis cries out to the "corsede gast" (781) [cursed creature] and challenges it to "ʒem me bataile wel in hast" (782) [quickly give me battle]. As soon as the boar sees him, "A rerde is brosetles wel an hiʒ / And starede on Beues wiþ eien holwe, / Also a wolde him haue a-swalowe" (784–86) [it reared its bristles high and stared at Bevis with hungry eyes as if it would swallow him]. When the boar then opens his maw "so wide" (787), Bevis attacks him by letting a "spere . . . to him glide" (788). Because the boar's "hyde was harde ase eni flent" (792) [hide was hard as flint], the spear not only fails to inflict any harm but also "barst to pises þore" (790) [burst to pieces there]. After calling attention once again to the spear's failure by repeating that it is "Now al to-borste" (793) [now completely shattered], the poet informs us that Bevis "drouʒ is swerd, him self to were, / And fauʒt aʒen þe bor so grim" (794–95) [drew his sword to protect himself and fought against the very grim boar].

In contrast to Boefs's brief engagement, Bevis's boar fight is quite protracted. The two antagonists fight for so long "Þat Beues was so weri of fouȝte, / Þat of is lif he ne rouȝte" (799–800) [that Bevis was so weary of fighting that he did not care about his life], a sentiment that the boar shares. The boar retreats ("Awai fro Beues he gan go" [802]), and in the brief respite that follows, Bevis prays "To god and Mari, is moder dere" (804) [to God and his dear mother Mary] before the boar attacks him for a second time. Bevis closes with the boar and strikes a blow that succeeds in slicing off two of its tusks as well as a portion of its snout (813–16). The boar responds to this by loosing a "loþeli cri" (821) [horrible cry] that carries all the way back to the castle. After killing the boar in the same manner as does his Anglo-Norman counterpart—with a sword thrust to the heart (through its open mouth)—Bevis mounts its head on the "trounsoun of is spere" (827) and celebrates his victory by sounding his hunting horn.

Stripped to its essentials, the episode in *Beues* may be schematized thus:

A savage beast arrives from unknown parts and kills and devours many men.

A great hero learns of the beast's depredations and carefully arms himself with sword, shield, and spear preparatory to facing the beast.

The hero consciously decides to fight the beast single-handedly and sets out in search of it.

Arriving at the beast's den, the hero stands in front of it and shouts out a challenge to the beast.

The beast responds to the hero's presence by charging him.

The hero throws his spear at the beast, but the spear fails to injure it and instead shatters after striking its tough hide.

The poet reiterates that the spear has shattered as the hero draws his sword and prepares to engage the beast.

What proves to be the first of two engagements between the combatants is protracted but ultimately indecisive, as neither causes much harm to the other.

After a short respite, they meet for a second time and this time the hero wounds the beast, causing it to utter a terrible cry.

During their second engagement, the hero delivers a fatal sword stroke to the beast, following which he decapitates its carcass.

The fight scene ends with the hero setting off to return to court with the beast's head fixed securely upon the shaft of his shattered spear.

We can observe here a number of minor as well as some major diver-
gences between this episode in *Beues* and its parallels in *Beowulf* and the *Brut,*
but despite their surface differences, the episodes' tectonics are rooted in the
traditional expressive economy of medieval English oral poetics. Because we
have explored this scene at some length above,[97] I will confine myself here to
some general comments about the differences in the English scene's traditional
affective dynamics and that of the Anglo-Norman version, a scene grounded
in a very different tradition. In each of the English texts, the damage to life
and/or property that the beast causes is made explicit, usually graphically so,
while the Anglo-Norman version contains only a brief and general allusion to
it. In every instance, the hero fights the beast single-handedly, but little narrative or affective weight attends this detail in the Anglo-Norman poem. Because
it is not important to the Anglo-Norman episode's tectonics or its surface real-
ization, it accordingly receives none of the stress that it does in the English
texts, where the hero's desire/decision/need to fight alone is a crucial component of the episode's affective dynamics.

Much the same is true of another narrative element, the failure of the
hero's weapon, that is found in all four episodes. In the English texts the dramatic failure of the hero's weapon (or in Morpidus's case, weapons) is one of
the episode's most important constituents, whereas it plays only a peripheral
part in the Anglo-Norman text. We can judge the relative unimportance of
Boefs's sword's failure by noting that he does not use it during the battle and
that it fails him only *after* the boar's death. In fact, his sword breaks not in the
heat of battle but apparently as a result of the stroke that he delivers to the
boar's carcass. He does not use the sword against the boar but kills the beast
using only his "launce." We cannot even locate precisely when his sword breaks,
since this event is so unimportant that the poet never actually mentions it: one
minute the sword is intact, the next broken. The "tronsoun," unlike Nægling's
shattered hilt, is not the pivot upon which the whole episode turns; rather, it
simply provides Boefs with a convenient way of transporting the boar's severed head.[98]

In terms of its aesthetics, execution, and narrative importance, the boar
fight in *Beues* reaches neither the heights of Beowulf's fight with the dragon
nor even the more modest level that Morpidus's battle with the sea beast occupies, but it does testify to the way in which traditional thematics remains available to authors whose idiopoetics are somewhat (or even, as in this case, very)
little influenced by the traditional expressive economy of oral poetics. We can
only surmise as to how the boar fight may have resonated for the poem's

intended audience, but its presence in the narrative and its surprising coherence suggest that its traditional channels of reception remained at least partially available to them.

The second, and final, episode we will consider from *Beues*, Bevis's fight with a dragon, has no precedent in the Anglo-Norman *Boeve*, and has generally been identified as one of the *Beues*-poet's three major interpolations.[99] As is true of the boar fight,[100] Bevis's dragon fight has not attracted much scholarly attention. Following Judith Weiss, who argues that the *Beues*-poet "glorifies [Bevis] as a Christian hero by endowing him with a fight against a dragon with devilish traits,"[101] Susan Crane notes in passing that the dragon fight is "[t]old in the manner of a saint's legend."[102] Pearsall, with his characteristic economy, summarily judges the episode to be "wholly gratuitous"[103] and lets matters rest there. But instead of viewing the dragon fight as a bit of interpolated hagiography or as an extended piece of uninspired narrative filler, we will bring its largely overlooked traditional thematics into focus by reading it against the background of medieval English oral poetics.

We must preface our discussion of Bevis's fight with the dragon of Cologne by acknowledging that our interpretive yield may be relatively modest because the episode's narrative contours are far less indebted to oral poetics than are those of the boar fight. Whereas the boar fight's traditional thematics is relatively complete and affectively functional (if splintered and diluted), the dragon fight's traditional elements are all but subsumed by the post-traditional matter that the *Beues*-poet injects into it. While it contains only scattered bits and pieces of traditional thematics that never achieve any sort of narrative or affective critical mass, Bevis's dragon fight nevertheless affords us the opportunity to see that the way of speaking that is medieval English oral poetics survives, faintly and imperfectly, even when its constituent elements are as isolated as they are in *Beues* from the network of interdependent and intersecting meanings that allows them to function so effectively in other, more fully traditional, contexts. After looking at Bevis's extended fight with the dragon of Cologne, we will conclude this chapter by briefly turning our attention to the dragon fight contained in *Guy of Warwick*, a verse romance roughly contemporary with *Beues*.

As we might expect, Bevis's fight with the dragon of Cologne contains a number of features that are clearly post-traditional. Among the more intriguing of these are the well, sanctified by a virgin's having bathed in it, that protects Bevis from the dragon (it cannot come within forty feet of its "so holi" [2807] water) and heals his wounds when a vicious blow of the dragon's sends him into it; the hero's explicit invocation (and reception?) of divine assistance (2860–68) (the dragon flees upon hearing Bevis call "To god . . . / And to Marie, his moder dere" [2867–68] [to God . . . and to his dear mother Mary]); the dragon's having at one time been a human king (2611); the dream Bevis has of his encounter with a "wod" king and the assistance a virgin offers Bevis in that conflict (2681–2700); Bevis's reaction upon first seeing the dragon (the sight of it fills Bevis with such dread that he would gladly "in han gon" (2768) [have gone in] "Hadde þerþe opnede anon" (2767) [had the earth immediately opened up]; the long and detailed description that the poet gives the dragon (2661–78); and, finally, the exaggerated (and perhaps comical) number of blows Bevis must deliver before he is able to behead his defeated adversary (2877).

Despite these and its other post-traditional characteristics, the dragon fight in *Beues* nevertheless evidences signs—fragments, really—of traditional oral poetics. While these features never coalesce as they do elsewhere and so do not play a significant role in the episode's structure or reception, they continue to index traditional meaning(s). Bevis's battle has a number of features in common with the other dragon fights we have examined:[104] the "vile dragoun" (2710) is so powerful that "Þar nis neiþer emperur ne king, / Þat come þar þe dragoun wore (2716–17) [there was neither an emperor or king who would approach the dragon] because it can slay "An hondred þosend men & more" (2718) [a hundred thousand men, and more]. The hero arms himself carefully and well before heading off to face the monster, and when he battles the beast, he does so alone. One of his weapons fails dramatically during the battle, and the battle itself begins inconclusively and is rather protracted. The hero's mount is slaughtered by the beast during the encounter, and Bevis is forced to continue his attack on foot. Bevis is gravely wounded during the battle, and the beast lies dead at the episode's conclusion. When thus laid out *in brevis*, Bevis's dragon fight appears to be at its core as highly traditional a construct as Beowulf's or Morpidus's. But while it undoubtedly shares some structural similarities with the other two episodes, its affective dynamics—and hence its ability to cue and direct its reception—is largely post-traditional.

The hero's decision to face his monstrous foe alone is a key structural and affective component of the dragon fight in *Beowulf*, and it plays a similarly central role in Morpidus's battle with the beast. Bevis also faces the dragon alone, but he does not set out intending—or even desiring—to do so. Rather, he sets out to face the dragon accompanied by the giant Ascopard, and he fully expects that Ascopard will play an active role in helping him kill the dragon. After getting his first glimpse of the dragon, however, the giant becomes paralyzed with fear, so Bevis must go on alone. Bevis denounces Ascopard's cowardice and pricks his horse forward, but the poet lays no special stress on these actions. Instead of emphasizing Bevis's greatly increased physical vulnerability following the formidable Ascopard's refusal to enter the fray, the poet immediately focuses upon the very understandable terror that descends upon Bevis when he gets his first good look at his foe (2765 ff.). In not painting a picture of a lone hero bravely approaching a deadly foe, the *Beues*-poet not only deflects our attention from Bevis's courageousness in continuing on alone but also subverts the scene's inherently heroic dynamics by foregrounding Bevis's cowardly (and rather comic) reaction upon first seeing the dragon. Even after Bevis recovers his wits and continues on, the scene never fully recovers its heroic footing and continually hovers on the border of burlesque. Absent from the episode are any comments by Bevis echoing any of Beowulf's memorably powerful statements, such as those beginning with "Nolde ic sweord beran" (2528b ff.) [I would not bear a sword]) or "Nis þæt eower sið" (2532b ff.) [This is not your undertaking] and there are no authorial comments such as the one Laʒamon offers: "þa hahte he [Morpidus] al his hird-folc: fare to are burʒe. / and hæhte heom þer abiden: and ane he gon riden" (3222–23) [then Morpidus commanded all his people to go to a town and ordered them to wait there and he began to ride alone].

The *Beues*-poet does not even exploit the sharp contrast between Bevis's actions and those of the suddenly cowardly Ascopard, who "Forþer dorste . . . go namore" (2740) [dared not to go further]. Bevis only weakly and somewhat indirectly castigates Ascopard, saying, "Schame hit is, to terne aʒe" (2757) [it is a shame to turn back] as he continues to ride toward the dragon. Contrast this to Wiglaf's address to Beowulf's comitatus (2633 ff.), a pointed, highly charged speech that sharpens our sense of the comitatus's irredeemable failure and spotlights Wiglaf's own considerable courage. Unlike his fellows, who all retreat hastily to the relative safety of some nearby woods, Wiglaf charges into the fray because, as the poet approvingly notes, "Ne gemealt him se modsefa" (2628a) [his courage did not melt]. After Beowulf's (and the dragon's) death, Wiglaf again addresses the comitatus, this time excoriating them for their cowardice and predicting that the future will be bleak for them and their close kin once their cowardice becomes widely known (2864 ff.). In the *Brut,* the people whom Morpidus orders to stay safely removed from the battle cannot be faulted for their cowardice, and in fact their distance from danger affectively counterpoints Morpidus's increasing proximity to it, something the poet reinforces by noting that after issuing his directive to the people (not warriors),

Morpidus "ane . . . gan riden" (3223). Bevis similarly rides on alone, but he does so by default, not heroic volition. His going on alone is dramatic—after all, he is a hero heading toward great physical danger—but his initial cowardly response to the dragon and the *Beues*-poet's failure to exploit (or even mention) his uniquely charged status as a solitary hero combine to strip this moment of virtually all its traditional power and tension.

We can see much the same pattern underlying the failure of Bevis's spear, another narrative component that the fourteenth-century episode has in common with its Old and early Middle English predecessors, but once again the parallels between its failure and those in the earlier poems are almost entirely superficial. Nægling's failure is perhaps the single most crucial affective element of *Beowulf*'s dragon fight, and in the *Brut,* the successive failures of Morpidus's arrows and spear are also important components of the scene's affective dynamics. In contrast, the failure of Bevis's spear carries little narrative or affective weight. Like Morpidus, Bevis initially (and wisely) attempts to kill the dragon from a safe distance, but the spear that he throws at it proves no more effective than the arrows Morpidus shoots. Not only does the spear fail to penetrate the dragon's tough hide, but it "to-barst on pices fiue" (2773) [burst into five pieces] like "þe hail vpon þe ston" (2772) [hail upon a stone]. The failure of these weapons forces the heroes to close quarters with their respective monstrous foes, but it is at this juncture that the episodes diverge. Laȝamon uses the arrows' failure to heighten the scene's tension and so continues to exploit the episode's traditional thematics, while the *Beues*-poet follows a far different, post-traditional path. Morpidus grips his spear and attempts to run it through the beast while on horseback, but the spear shatters, and his mount suffers a gory death at the beast's claws (and mouth). The moment when Bevis's spear shatters has the potential to be affectively powerful, as the hero has no other weapons at his disposal that he can deploy from afar and has no choice from this point on but to rely on his sword, which he "drouȝ alse bliue" (2774) [drew quickly] once the spear shatters. But the *Beues*-poet does not use the weapon's failure to amplify our sense of the hero's vulnerability, as the *Beowulf*-poet masterfully does, or to increase our anxiety over the hero's predicament, as Laȝamon does by detailing in rapid succession the failure of another weapon and a gruesome equine death. He simply reports that "Þo þai fouȝte, alse I ȝow sai, / Til it was hiȝ noun of þai dai" (2775–76) [then they fought, as I say to you, until it was high noon]. In so moving us away from his narrative's action, the *Beues*-poet undercuts the scene's traditional oral poetics by removing the sense of heightened and immediate danger that accompanies the failure of the weapons in the scene's other instantiations. He further undercuts it by shifting our attention from his narrative's events to *his* narrative presence. Instead of intensifying the narrative moment in the ways the *Beowulf*-poet and Laʒamon do—the former by returning to the failure a few lines after initially describing it[105] and the latter by depicting the failure of multiple weapons—the *Beues*-poet first breaks into his narrative by interjecting an authorial aside, "alse I ʒow sai," a comment that he then follows with a general observation on the protracted battle that ensues. The fourteenth-century poet thus reduces what elsewhere carries great narrative and affective import to just another inconsequential narrative detail, one that may well have struck the poem's intended audience as meaningless and perhaps even, to echo Pearsall, gratuitous.

The final aspect of Bevis's dragon fight that will concern us—the role anger plays in the episode—reveals most clearly the manner in which the poet incorporates (consciously or unconsciously) and departs from traditional thematics. During the dragon fight, *wod* [maddened, frenzied; MED s.v. 3 a, b, c] appears twice in the space of twenty-six lines, at, respectively, lines 2844 and 2870.[106] The first time he uses it, the *Beues*-poet draws upon its traditional resonances, but he deploys *wod* only after stripping Bevis, literally and figuratively, of everything but his helmet and sword. Bevis has had his spear shatter and his mount killed by a single blow of his foe's tail; he has suffered some serious wounds—his left shoulder is "cleuede heuene ato" (2799) [split evenly in two] and his "flesch gan ranclen & tebelle" (2832) [flesh began to fester and swell extremely] from the dragon's venom; and his armor has "al to-brast" (2834) [entirely fallen apart] after the venom falls on it. Standing with his flesh horribly distended and perhaps on the verge of bursting as his armor just has, Bevis surveys his destroyed hauberk, plaintively cries out to God, and then proceeds to attack "ase he wer wod" (2844) [as if he were enraged]. The *Beowulf*-poet systematically removes Beowulf's protection (the comitatus, his specially made shield, and, most importantly, his sword, Nægling), and at this point in *Beues*, it seems as if the *Beues*-poet is poised to follow suit. But rather than building upon the scene's traditional affective dynamics, he once again takes a post-traditional path. As much as we may appreciate Bevis's frustration and admire his courage in attacking the dragon despite being severely wounded and lacking the protection of his armor, his anger proves to be far from pivotal to the scene.[107] The dragon does not quail at Bevis's ferocious charge but rather responds in kind and "hard him gan asaile" (2845) [violently began to assail him]. It delivers a blow that splits apart Bevis's remaining piece of armor, his helmet, and knocks Bevis to the ground twice, before finally knocking him into the sanctified well, where he lies senseless. Bevis recovers his wits, is (again) healed by the well's waters, and once again faces the dragon, but this time, instead of becoming *wod* and courageously rushing upon his *attorsceaðan* [venomous foe], he falls to his "knes" and "To Iesu Crist he gan to calle" (2860). He not only "To god . . . made his praiere" (2867) but prays as well explicitly "to Marie, his moder dere" (2868). What he could not accomplish through main might, even after entering what was perhaps an altered state of consciousness similar to that entered on the battlefield by *berserkir*,[108] he achieves indirectly through his prayer. The dragon overhears Bevis's prayers and at once "fleȝ awei" (2870) [flew away], but Bevis successfully overtakes and soon thereafter kills him.

When *wod* next appears in the dragon fight, it does not bear even the limited traditional associations that it does in line 2844 but signals the extremity of the dragon's desire to escape, not a character's mental state prior to or during a deadly martial encounter. Whereas Bevis's *wodness* propels him toward extreme danger, the dragon's impels its flight from it. Apparently not wanting to tangle with a knight who has just sought God's help, the dragon "fleȝ awei, ase he wer wod" (2870). When the dragon is slain shortly after the second occurrence of the lexeme, the narrative fulfills the traditional paradigm by having slaughter follow a metonym that signals a special type of very intense anger, but the parallels here are limited to the surface. The *Beues*-poet appears to be on the verge of tapping into the metonymic power of *wod* the first time it appears, but he never fully does. The second time he uses it, he draws upon its primary meaning ("Of persons or other sentient beings: insane, mentally deranged, of unsound mind, out of one's mind" [MED s.v. 1.a]), one that is largely outside the ambience of traditional oral poetics.

A brief consideration of two other narrative instantiations of anger in the dragon episode further illuminates the place oral poetics occupies in the *Beues*-poet's idiopoetics. Before he decides to set out in search of the dragon, Bevis dreams that "a king, þat was wod, / Hadde wonded him þer a stod" (2685–86) [a king who was angry had wounded him where he stood]. Once again, the *Beues*-poet appears poised to draw upon the associative meanings that attend *wod* in medieval English oral poetics, especially since we learn that Bevis's wounds are so "biter & sore, / A wende, a miȝt leue namore" (2687–88) [bitter and so sore he thought he might not live any longer]. But even though the surface narrative of Bevis's dream conforms to the traditional pattern of intense anger–martial engagement–slaughter, the poet once again does not tap into the limited, but still considerable, significative power of *wod,* either because his idiopoetics and aesthetic sensibility lead him in a different direction or because he can no longer fully hear the lexeme's traditional resonances and so cannot draw upon its word-power. In this instance, the traditional pattern is neither fully articulated nor fully developed because the episode ends as Bevis awakes immediately after dreaming that "a virgine / Him brouʒte out of al is pine" (2689–90) [a virgin (earthly?) brought him out of his pain]. The very conscious foreshadowing of several of the dragon fight's most salient post-traditional features further evidences its distance from oral poetics. Before its metamorphosis, the dragon of Cologne was as fierce a king as the one who harms Bevis in his dream, and not one, but two, virgins—the unknown one who imbues the well with its protective powers by having bathed in it and the Virgin Mary—figure prominently in the dragon fight's narrative.

There is one other point in the dragon fight where anger comes into play. During their initial encounter, the dragon becomes "atened stronge, / Þat o man him scholde stonde so longe" (2777–78) [strongly annoyed that one man should stand against him so long] and subsequently launches the attack that results in the death of Bevis's mount. Narratively, this portion of the dragon fight conforms closely to the episode's traditional thematics: within a martial context, mention of a character's becoming enraged is followed shortly by slaughter. Its affective dynamics is similarly traditional. The horse's death increases Bevis's physical vulnerability and heightens the severity of the risk he is facing, points that the poet chooses to underscore by interjecting, "Helpe him god, þat all þing wrouʒt!" (2784) [Help him God, who made all things]. Once again, however, the *Beues*-poet alters the traditional paradigm through lexical substitution. Rather than using *wod,* a lexeme that from early in the post-Conquest period onward comes to take on some of the specialized meaning that *gebelgan* had, he employs *atened,* which the MED glosses as "annoyed, incensed."[109] The distance between *gebelgan* [swollen with rage] and *atened* [angry, vexed, annoyed] is enormous, and it only increases once we recall the larger, associative context within which *gebelgan* is always embedded. Because it is not a component of oral poetics, *atened* draws its meaning from the contextual superstructure within which the poet situates it. As a result, it can only bring to the narrative present the limited meanings available to all post-traditional lexemes. While an angry or irritated or vexed dragon remains a formidable foe, one that is *gebolgen* is exponentially more so.

When placed against the background of Beowulf's fight with the dragon, the one in *Sir Beues of Hamtoun* does not appear to be very traditional. Unlike

Bevis, Beowulf plans from the start to fight his dragon alone and does everything he can, including explicitly forbidding his comitatus to accompany him in the battle, to ensure that he does meet it alone. Beowulf does not use a horse but fights the dragon on foot, carrying with him only a shield, a sword, and a *wæll-seax*. Further, the episode in *Beowulf* contains no wells that are invested with protective and restorative powers because a virgin has bathed in them, Beowulf does not look for any divine assistance, and, last but not least, "ða aglæcean" (2592a)—Beowulf and the dragon—succeed in mortally wounding each other. But when read against the dragon fights contained in *Guy of Warwick,* a Middle English romance roughly contemporary to *Beues,* the episode in *Beues* stands as a surprisingly traditional narrative structure.

Post-Traditional Thematics: Beasts in Guy of Warwick

Judging from the number of extant Anglo-Norman and Middle English manuscripts devoted to his exploits, Guy of Warwick was an extremely popular hero on both sides of the Channel. His romance is preserved in some twelve Anglo-Norman manuscripts,[110] and it survives in two independent Middle English versions: Edinburgh, National Library of Scotland, Advocates' MS 19. 2. 1 (the Auchinleck Manuscript), and Cambridge, Caius College, 107. Although his romance has not enjoyed much favor among modern critics, its appeal lasted well into the late medieval and early modern periods, as two fifteenth-century versions attest.[111] *Guy of Warwick* stands as an important comparand to *Beues* because its eponymous hero battles several dangerous beasts—a boar and not one, but two, dragons. Additionally, because medieval English oral poetics plays a minor role in these battles and in the entire romance, considering these fights will throw the *Beues*-poet's oral poetics, diluted and fragmented as it is, into sharper relief.

Like the *Beues*-poet, the *Guy*-poet produces a very long, very popular romance so closely following its Anglo-Norman source that he, too, probably worked directly from a copy of a written exemplar. But beyond this, the two poets have rather different approaches. Most important, the *Beues*-poet departs from his source more frequently and more freely than does the *Guy*-poet. He adds several major episodes for which there are no parallels in his Anglo-Norman exemplar, and even when he imports material directly from his source, he filters it through an idiopoetics in which medieval English oral poetics continues to figure, if only to a limited degree. In contrast, because oral poetics does not play much of a role, if any, in the *Guy*-poet's idiopoetics, the signals his episodes send are post-traditional *even when* their surface details align themselves with more traditional patterns.

In an episode that appears in Auchinleck and CUL but not Caius, Guy and his companions one day come upon a "bore, a wilde best" (6720 / 6418),[112] while they are out hunting. They immediately release their hounds, but the boar is so savage that it not only escapes the hunters but manages to kill "An hundred . . . and mo" (6725 / 6423) [a hundred . . . and more] of the hounds that pursue it. Of "huntes ne of houndes adrad" (6729) [hunters nor of hounds afraid], the boar flees so swiftly and has such stamina that the knights run their horses into the ground chasing him, and "Alle þe houndes þat folwed him þere / Oȝain turned, oþer ded were" (6735–36 / 6431–34) [all the hounds that followed him there turned back, or were killed]. Only Guy and three of the hounds are strong enough and fast enough to track the boar, which leads them "out of þat cuntre" (6726 / 6427) [out of that country] before finally going to ground in some "þicke hegges" (6750 / 6448) [thick hedges]. Guy "lepe of his stede heye" (6754 / 6453) [leapt from his high steed], holding his sword in both hands, and "cam to þe bore as a kniȝt beld" (6756) [approached the boar as a bold knight]. The boar charges, but Guy calmly and "smertlich smot him anon, / Þat þe hert he clef euen atvo: / Alle ded he fel to grounde þo" (6758–60 / 6457–59) [smartly struck him at once so that he split the heart in two: then the boar fell dead to the ground]. The episode closes with Guy field-dressing the boar and sounding his horn because "Alon he was, him miȝt agriis: / Alto fer he was fram his kniȝt" (6762–63 / 6463–66) [he was alone and terrified, as he was far from his knights].[113]

The surface narrative of this boar hunt recalls that in *Beues* and perhaps, more distantly, that in *Sir Gawain*, but missing from it is any sense that the hero is at physical risk from the boar, which never acquires the status that the boars do in *Beues* and *Gawain*, where they are truly dangerous and formidable foes, ones that kills hounds, horses, and, in *Beues*, men. Guy's solo pursuit of the boar stresses his (and his mount's) superior strength, and it serves to increase our admiration for his physical abilities, not our concern for his safety. The fight itself is over in an instant as Guy dispatches the boar without breaking a sweat.[114] In a major departure from the more traditional affective dynamics of the other fights, the poet tellingly focuses upon the fact that Guy is alone only after the boar is slain, not before. Further, he does so not in response to the demands of the boar fight's thematics but to set up his narrative's next episode, one in which an earl sends his son to find who has poached "Hert oþer bore" (6772 / 6470) [hart or boar] in his forest. The dangerous situation that Guy finds himself in at this narrative juncture has nothing to do with his facing a deadly animal on his own but with local politics: he is vulnerable because he is alone in foreign territory.

Guy's first dragon fight is a similarly compact encounter that has little in common with the other dragon fights we have considered. One day Guy and his men see a "weri" (4117) [weary] lion, who has tangled with and is now being pursued by a dragon, "cominde þo" (4115 / 3853) [coming there]. The lion frightens all but Guy, who is so moved by the lion's plight that he cries "allas! / Whi, no haddestow help non?" (4118–19) [Alas! Why did you have no help?]. Guy asks for his mount, arms himself with a spear and a "gode swerde" [good sword], and rides toward the dragon (4129–32 / 3871–73). Once the dragon sees Guy, it ceases pursuing the lion and rushes at the hero "Wiþ open mouþe" (4135) [with open mouth]. Guy responds to its charge by bearing "his spere oʒaines him anon" (4136 / 3878) [his spear immediately against him]. When the dragon reaches Guy, the hero again overcomes his enemy with, predictably, the utmost ease: "In-to his þrote he it [the spear] þrest wiþ strengþe; / In his bodi was alle his schaft lengþe, / Þat ded to grounde he feld him þo" (4137–39 / 3881–84) [into his throat he strongly thrust his spear; the entire length of the shaft was in the dragon's body and he fell dead to the ground there]. So inconsequential is this brief dragon fight that the *Guy*-poet not only resists dilating it but believes that doing so would be a waste of his and his audience's time: "What schuld y make tales mo? / He smot of þe heued, & went oway" (4140–41) [Why should I make more tales? He struck off the head and went away]. The dragon is a minor player in the episode and is, indeed, far less important to the narrative than is the lion, who becomes Guy's faithful companion until a steward who is angry with Guy one day fatally wounds it when he comes across it napping in an orchard (4311 ff. / 4059 ff.).

As is their wont, Auchinleck and Caius closely follow the Anglo-Norman *Gui de Warewic*. Accordingly they neither offer a physical description of the dragon nor emphasize the dangers attendant upon Guy's solo engagement of it. Only in the fifteenth-century CUL version do we discover any sort of connection between this episode and oral poetics. The description of the dragon—

Hys hed was great and grennyng
And hys eyen, as fyre, brennyng.

Hys tethe scharpe, hys mowþe wyde:
Hys body was grett and vnryde.
He was grymme and he was felle
                    (3859–63)

———

[his head was large and his mouth gaping and his eyes were burning like
fire. His teeth were sharp, his mouth wide, and his body massive. He was
grim and deadly.]—

establishes it as a rather dangerous foe, and Guy calls attention, somewhat
obliquely, to his status as a lone hero when he announces, "I wyll go forth sek-
erlye. / Y wyll preue wyth all my myght, / Whedur y dare wyth þe ʒondur
dragon fyʒt" (3866–68) [I will go forth without fail. I will prove with all my
might whether I dare fight with that yonder dragon]. But in CUL, as well as in
the other versions, Guy is never in danger during this dragon fight, which he
sees as simply a way of proving his mettle and which ends when he quickly and
easily kills the dragon with his first and only spear thrust.

The episode in which Guy meets the second dragon shares some narrative details with the dragon fights in the *Brut, Beues,* and, to a lesser extent,
Beowulf.[115] It begins when an enormous dragon comes out of "Irlond" and ravages Northumberland, killing (and eating) the many men, women, and animals it happens upon. We learn that it is swifter than a steed, that it has claws
like a lion, as well as wings (7163–67 / 6833; 6827) and that its scaly hide protects it from harm (7161–62 / 6829–30). Guy happens to be present when the
dragon's distressing actions are first reported to the king, and without a
moment's hesitation he volunteers to seek it out and kill it. The king wishes to
send a hundred men with him, but Guy declines the offer and takes with him
only three knights (7181–200 / 6845–66). They soon find the dragon, and after
preparing himself for the battle, Guy explicitly prohibits the men accompany-
ing him from taking part in the fight (7204–6 / 6870–72). Guy strikes at the
dragon with his spear, which splinters without harming the beast (7213 / 6878).
In return, the dragon knocks down both Guy and his mount, stunning the hero
who "Neuer hadde . . . non swiche, y-wis" (7220 / 6884–85) [never had received
any such blow, indeed]. Guy quickly recovers, prays to God to "Saue [him]
from þis foule dragoun," draws his sword "anon riʒt" [at once], and "To him
he lepe wiþ gret miʒt, / & smot him in þe heued schod / A wel gret strok
wiþ-outen abod; / Ac no-þing sen þan was his dent" (722–31 / 6888–96) [leapt
at him with great might and struck him in the crown of the head with a great

stroke without delay; but that blow left no mark]. The dragon responds to this ineffective blow by neighing and attacking Guy so fiercely "Þat he a lappe rent out anon / Of his brini, þat alle his trust was on" (7241–42 / 6903–6) [that he immediately tore a piece out of the coat of mail in which he placed all his trust]. Fearing "Þat he no miȝt him deri nouȝt / Wiþ no wepen of stiel y-wrouȝt" (7233–34 / 6897–98) [that he might not injure him with any weapon made of steel], Guy seeks respite from the battle behind a nearby tree, but the tree offers little protection: the dragon is still able to strike Guy's shield so hard with its tail that it "euen ato . . . to-fleye" (7250 / 6913) [flew into two pieces], knocking Guy to the ground in the process. It then encircles Guy with its tail and squeezes him hard enough to break three of his ribs (7252–55 / 6917–20) before Guy "Atvo . . . him karf smartliche, / & deliuered him seluen manliche" (7257–58 / 6923–24) [in two . . . cut him quickly and delivered himself courageously] by severing its tail from its body. The dragon understandably lets out a tremendous roar when its tail is lopped off, one terrible enough that "Nis man in þe werld þat wer þer neye / Þat him no miȝt agrise" (7269–70 / 6934–36) [there is no man in the world who it would not frighten]. Despite having his hauberk "to-rent tofore" (7273 / 6939) [earlier torn], Guy continues to fight "Stalworþli" (7275) [courageously]. Having learned from his spear thrust and initial sword stroke that "it gained him nauȝt / To smite of the bodi bifore" (7276–77 / 6941–42) [it gained him nothing to strike the front of the body], Guy "Bineþen þe wenge . . . him smot" [struck him beneath the wing] with the result that this time, "Þurch þat bodi þat swerd bot. / Þurch þe bodi he him carf atvo: / Ded he fel to grounde þo" (7281–84 / 6944–46) [through that body the sword bit. Through the body he cut him in two; dead he fell to the ground then]. The episode ends with Guy withdrawing from the field "For stink þat of þe bodi come" (7288/6950) [on account of the stink that came from the body].

There are several noteworthy points of contact between Guy's second dragon fight and those that we have earlier examined, the two most notable being the hero's decision to fight the beast alone and the failure of his weapons during the battle. Although he fights the dragon alone, no tension attends Guy's decision. He initially declines the king's offer to have one hundred knights accompany him neither because he wishes to elevate his own heroic stock nor because he thinks that he alone has the strength and fortitude to tackle such a formidable foe. Rather, he does so because, as he says, "Nold neuer god ful of miȝt / Þat for a best onlepi / Schuld so miche folk traueli" (7192–94 / 6856–58) [Never would mighty God allow people to suffer so much hardship because of a single beast]. An unarticulated desire to protect others from harm may underlie this statement, but on the whole he seems far more concerned with not wasting anyone else's time on what he views as a chore that he is fully capable of handling alone. Even when he commands the three knights who accompany him not to join the dragon fight, the episode's affective dynamics remain flat, as he simply says "to his felawes hastiliche / Þat so hardi þer be non / O fot wiþ him for to gon" (7204–6 / 6870–72) [to his fellows quickly that there is no one so brave (?foolhardy) to go a foot further with him].[116] Guy's decision to fight alone underscores the intrinsic heroism of his endeavor, but because this episode is not embedded within the expressive economy of oral poetics, it lacks the associative resonances of those made by the other heroes.

Indeed, the *Guy*-poet never stresses, and barely even calls attention to, Guy's status as a lone hero. Just before he turns to face the dragon, Guy does not emphasize his own might or the dragon's deadliness as Beowulf does, he does not order his people to remove themselves to a safe haven until after the battle is over as does Morpidus, and he does not even obliquely accentuate his heroism as Bevis does when he points Ascopard's cowardice while galloping toward the dragon of Cologne. Rather, Guy only, and somewhat cryptically, urges his men not to be so foolhardy as to go "O fot wiþ him." Is he saying that they should not foolishly risk their lives facing an opponent whose power so greatly outmatches theirs? Is he saying rather that they should not waste their time and energy fighting the dragon, or is he saying something else entirely? Unlike the other heroes, whose actions and/or speeches accentuate and rein-force their status as solitary heroes, Guy simply makes his observation and then turns to fight the dragon.[117] Although his statement reveals both Guy's courage and his compassion, it also diminishes the nature of the challenge at hand because it suggests that fighting the dragon is, at some level, just a foolish en-deavor. In the hands of a poet situated more firmly within the tradition of medieval English oral poetics, Guy's declining the king's offer of assistance and the hero's separation from his companions would have served as narrative sign-posts highlighting both the riskiness of the venture and Guy's enormous courage.

The failure of the hero's weapons is another point at which the narrative surface of *Guy* aligns itself with those of the other narratives we have examined. But the failures of Guy's weapons, while important within the romance's nar-rative, have none of the affective weight nor thematic centrality that other such moments do. In the more traditionally grounded episodes, the failure of the heroes' weapons increases both their vulnerability and the audience's dread, and in every case the heroes suffer grave, and for Beowulf and Morpidus fatal, wounds. Guy gets knocked about somewhat by the dragon, first after his spear shatters and then after his sword stroke fails to have any effect, and he suffers three broken ribs when the dragon encircles him with its tail, but that is the extent of his injuries. The moments in which his weapons fail do not bring his courage into sharper focus and do not point to the fight's ineluctably fatal conclusion. In fact, the failure of Guy's spear and sword do not stand as especially significant narrative events but amount, finally, to little more than temporary inconveniences, ones that lead to his being ignobly buffeted by his enemy but not seriously harmed.

One of the aspects of Guy's fight with the dragon of Northumberland that distinguishes the poetics informing it most clearly from that of the other dragon fights is that in the Auchinleck and Caius versions, neither combatant is ever described as being the least bit annoyed,[118] let alone swollen with rage, before, during, or after the battle. Nowhere in the protracted narrative of their encounter—not when Guy first learns of the dragon's ravages, not after the dragon several times knocks Guy to the ground with blows more powerful than any he has before received, and not after Guy succeeds in slicing off the dragon's tail—is either combatant ever revealed to be angry. The *Guy*-poet is not averse to presenting glimpses of a character's psyche—Guy's fear is several times noted, and the dragon's physical pain is clearly registered through its awful outburst—but nowhere in the scene does their pain, fear, and/or frustration metamorphose into any type of anger, let alone the distorting and highly significative anger so important in medieval English oral poetics. The narrative surface of Guy's fight with the dragon of Northumberland parallels to a certain degree some of the other ones found in medieval English vernacular verse, but once we move beyond these parallels we discover that its thematics and affective dynamics are very different from those of episodes in which oral poetics plays a wholly determining role (*Beowulf,* the *Brut*) or even a partially determining one (*Beues*).

The dragon in *Beowulf,* the beast in the *Brut,* and even the dragon of Cologne in *Beues* are all extraordinarily formidable foes, and in presenting them the respective poets tap into, to varying degrees, the richly associative thematics and affective dynamics of medieval English oral poetics. Not surprisingly, given that he composed at a time when oral poetics was not *a* way to articulate vernacular verse in England, but *the* way, the *Beowulf*-poet's dragon episode stands as the fullest and most traditional of the treatments we have considered. Eschewing physical details as is his wont, he sketches in the dragon's past (it has been sleeping in the barrow it discovered some three hundred years earlier), presents the dragon's reactions upon learning that its hoard has been depleted, and, most importantly, offers us a glimpse into the terrifyingly opaque world of *draconitas* when he tells us of the dragon's desire to kill every living creature it encounters.[119] Embedded in this episode are any number of deeply associative thematic and affective threads whose effects build upon and resonate with one another to create a narrative that is extraordinarily powerful and terribly beautiful. As is true of all such texts rooted in traditional oral poetics,[120] the narrative surface of *Beowulf* both fulfills the demands of the narrative present and serves as an entrée to worlds of traditional meanings. Morpidus's anger, his insistence on fighting the beast alone, his headlong rush against the foe, and the failure of his weapons all resonate powerfully with medieval English oral poetics. Through this resonance, his fight acquires extratextual meaning and weight as its thematics and affective cues connect it to the tradition and enable the traditional, associative channels for its reception.

Something similar occurs in *Beues*, although to an admittedly (and expectedly) lesser extent. The traditional metonyms present in that text continue to function traditionally, but because they are deployed by a poet whose idiopoetics are far more post-traditional than traditional, they are no longer central components of the scene, and they bear only a portion of their once considerable significative power. Even though oral poetics plays a steadily diminished role as we move from the highly traditional *Beowulf* to the progressively less traditional *Brut* and *Beues*, its thematics and affective dynamics continue to link these three episodes together in important and informative ways. While the episode in *Guy* contains a formidable dragon and a solitary hero whose weapons fail him during his battle with the creature, because it is composed outside the compass of oral poetics, its thematics and affective dynamics prove to be of a different, post-traditional sort. The distance between the magnificent and terrible dragon of *Beowulf*, one that remains awful and unknowable even when it lies dead on the cliff, and the one in *Guy*, whose corpse gives off such a fetid odor that Guy "Neye þat bodi . . . no durste" (7289 / 6949–50) [dare not stay near that body], is attributable not only to the fact that the *Beowulf*-poet is an artist of the highest rank while the *Guy*-poet and his redactors are men of far more modest abilities, but also to the very different ways that the expressive economies within which each poem was composed generate meaning.

five

Continuations

Where oral poetics had once been central and necessary to the articulation and dissemination of vernacular verse in England, by the late medieval period its influence had so greatly diminished that it all but completely disappeared as a compositional mode as the English literary tradition came to be ever more completely dominated by literate poetics and by literate compositional practices and interpretive strategies. The form through which vernacular verse had to be articulated in Anglo-Saxon England enjoyed a surprising, if brief and still not satisfactorily explained, resurgence in the fourteenth century,[1] but the question of whether the metrics of the so-called Alliterative Revival was descended from Anglo-Saxon metrics or was the creation of the Revival poets remains unsettled. Among those for whom the line of descent is clear is R. W. Chambers, who argues that while the "old [i.e. Old English] verse appears in the *Proverbs of Alfred*, the *Brut* of Layamon, or the *Bestiary*," it does so only

> in a broken-down and apparently moribund form. Yet the alliterative school of poetry was far from moribund. There must have been some parts of the country where it maintained an energetic life, during Layamon's days and for generations after. For it reappears, and this time in full vigour and correctness, in the Fourteenth Century, contemporaneously with many other national triumphs.

It must have been very strong on the lips of men when it dived under, or it could never have emerged in this way. For the correct technique of the alliterative line must have been handed on from poet to poet: once lost, it could not have been recovered.[2]

Thomas Cable, in contrast, argues that "Middle English poetry does not show the continuity of [metrical] tradition that standard authorities . . . assert." Far from seeing the history of English metrics as one of steady progression and evolution, he contends that "[w]ith the Norman Conquest came a clear break, and what followed was a drastic misreading of what had preceded."[3] But even though the Revival poets were producing verse in the West Midlands and elsewhere in a variety of alliterative meters that to greater or lesser degree recall Anglo-Saxon metrics,[4] their poems were no more appreciably indebted to the expressive economy of oral poetics than were the nonalliterative works produced by their contemporaries in London and elsewhere. Earlier in English literary history alliterative metrics and oral poetics were necessarily intertwined, but by the fourteenth century they had become divorced. Composing poetry in the Anglo-Saxon period—whether in private and in writing or in public during a performance—meant engaging not just the alliterative, stress-based metrics foundational to Anglo-Saxon poetic articulation but the oral poetics that was ineluctably wedded to it. Utilizing the tradition's deterministic, four-beat, alliterative metrics was as much a sine qua non of Anglo-Saxon poetic production as was the employment of traditional lexical and thematic metonyms. But because post-Conquest poetic composition was no longer dependent upon any one type of metrics, those fourteenth-century poets who elected to compose in alliterative meter could just as easily, and perhaps more easily, have chosen any one of the many other verse systems then available to them. For some reason, the Revival poets decided that an alliterative metrics accorded best with their aesthetic, cultural, and political sensibilities, but had they wished to abandon it partially or entirely they had the option of doing so, unlike their Anglo-Saxon forebears.

No longer the extraordinarily homogenous and deterministic force it was throughout the Anglo-Saxon era, oral poetics came to be situated more and more on the periphery of the increasingly heterogeneous English poetic tradition, where it nonetheless continued to survive, sometimes as an active constituent of a given medieval poet's idiopoetics and sometimes as a more (or even completely) vestigial one. But what happened to oral poetics after the close of the Middle Ages? Did the specialized expressive economy that had shaped poetic articulation and guided poetic reception for nearly a thousand years sink with absolute finality, leaving nary a ripple when the medieval period ended and the early modern one began? For some time, the answer to this question appeared to be a simple "yes" because there was no doubt that by the beginning of the early modern period (and perhaps even somewhat earlier) oral poetics ceased to be a compositionally significant component of the medieval English literary tradition. But despite its steady marginalization, despite the virtually complete disappearance of its specialized lexical register, and despite the breakdown of the associative channels that enabled the circulation and reception of traditional meaning, widely scattered bits and pieces of medieval English oral poetics continued to surface into and well beyond the early modern period because its thematics and story patterns retained some of their word-power even when they were deployed by poets and received by audiences who were no longer fully able to hear or properly decode the traditional resonances of these narrative elements.

Those poets situated within a given oral tradition as well as those outside it whose idiopoetics were influenced by their tradition's oral poetics were best able to exploit the word-power of the lexemes, themes, and story patterns that constituted the tradition's expressive economy. But because the traditional meanings that attended these elements were independent of both their production and reception, they continued to be present, whether they were used traditionally or post-traditionally. As a result, a component of oral poetics would often carry with it some of its traditional resonance and would also often metonymically situate a given narrative present within a much larger, associative web of meanings even when it surfaced in a post-traditional context. In some instances, the traditional resonances it emitted might be too faint for a post-traditional producer or recipient to discern, so its traditional meanings would remain unrealized. And even if post-traditional poets and audiences were able to hear an element's traditional resonances, they were unlikely to be able to make much sense of them because their post-traditional interpretive channels were largely inadequate for understanding traditional verbal art.[5] The problem was less one of production than of reception. Traditional metonyms deployed outside the expressive economy of oral poetics did not lose their unique ability to discharge their traditional, inherent meanings, even though these meanings might be largely imperceptible to post-traditional poets and audiences.

An analogy from the natural world helps clarify matters. Our eyes are able to see a considerable range of light waves, and our ears allow us to hear sounds whose frequencies range from twenty to twenty thousand cycles per second, but we know that our visual and auditory senses are rather limited and that we accordingly see only a narrow band of the entire light spectrum and hear only a small range of the sounds produced in our world.[6] But our inability to detect ultraviolet rays or sounds above twenty thousand cycles per second without the aid of specialized instrumentation has no bearing whatsoever on the existence of these and other similar natural phenomena. In much the same way, the fact that traditional metonyms no longer regularly register on the radar screen of our post-traditional hermeneutics tells us more about the changes in our communal interpretative strategies than it does about the metonyms' functionality (or their lack thereof).

Oral Poetics and Post-Traditional Texts: Lexical Survival

Of the three types of *sêmata* that constitute the expressive economy of traditional oral poetics, the lexical ones are least likely to retain any of their traditional referentiality or metonymic functionality, for the simple reason that they remain so tightly tied to their idiosyncratic, traditional register that they cannot survive its fracturing. The lexemes that poets import, consciously or unconsciously, from a no longer current register are always clearly marked as such, and as a result they bear less, rather than more, meaning because they appear simply as archaic, fossilized, and often puzzling remnants of a former way of speaking, not as dynamic elements of it. The idiosyncrasies of Edmund Spenser's language well illustrate this. As J. C. Smith and E. de Selincourt note in their early-twentieth-century edition of Spenser's poetry, "To an archaism which is inimitable because it is purely capricious, [Spenser] was drawn at once by its reminiscent picturesqueness and by its musical possibilities." Continuing in this vein, they assert that the identifiably old words or "words that were rapidly passing out of fashion" at the time Spenser wrote, such as "'eftsoons,' 'ne,' 'als,' 'whilom,' 'uncouth,' 'wight,' 'eke,' 'sithens,' [and] 'ywis,'" along with such neologisms as the adjective *daint* and the verb *to cherry*, give his poetry its uniquely "Spenserian colour."[7] Amongst his contemporaries, this idiosyncratic "colouring" seems to have earned the poet more censure than praise: Samuel Daniel criticized Spenser's "'aged accents and untimely words,' and . . . Ben Jonson . . . charge[d] that 'in affecting the ancients he writ no language.'"[8] Sir Philip Sidney, in his *Defence of Poetry*, similarly found that while Spenser's "*Shepherds' Calendar* hath much poetry in his eclogues," "[t]hat same framing of his style to an old rustic language I dare not allow, since neither Theocritus in Greek, Virgil in Latin, nor Sannazzaro in Italian did affect it."[9] Spenser's archaic diction and linguistic idiosyncrasies have fared little better in modern times; most tellingly, they have excited little interest in modern critics, who for the most part quite understandably pass silently over these formal matters and devote their attention to larger narrative and thematic ones.[10] What is finally most important about Spenser's register is not that it is laden with (or choked by) archaisms and neologisms but rather that it relies as completely upon conferred meanings as all post-traditional registers do. Spenser's weaving of such terms as *eftsoons* and *ywis* into the fabric of his poetry is of a piece with all other such archaistic endeavors.[11] That is, it does little more than add a patina of alterity, of old-soundingness, to his work and neither taps into nor even gestures toward any traditional, associative meaning(s) the lexemes may have at one time possessed. They are for him, as they were for his intended audience, merely static elements of a register he can neither fully engage nor fully understand.[12]

Although the Nobel prize–winning contemporary Irish poet Seamus Heaney does not share Spenser's archaistic predilections or designs, he also frequently uses obsolete, nonstandard lexemes in his poetry. But despite being manipulated by a poet well aware of their complex cultural, political, and in some cases traditional resonances,[13] the obsolete and/or nonstandard lexemes that Heaney employs function in his verse in ways very similar to those of Spenser's archaic terms: while Heaney's specialized terms are clearly metonyms, their role in his verse is finally as circumscribed as is that of Spenser's non-metonymic archaisms and neologisms.

Throughout his poetry, and especially in his magnificent translation/reworking of *Beowulf*,[14] Heaney uses words from his childhood vernacular that he associates with "a familiar local voice, one that had belonged to relatives of [his] father's, people whom [Heaney] had once described (punning on their surname) as 'big-voiced scullions.'"[15] In his *Beowulf*, this voice sounds clearly forth through such terms as *thole, bawn,* and *keening* and in a startlingly beautiful line such as "He is hasped and hooped and hirpling with pain" (975). Heaney's comments on *thole* well illuminate what we might label his poetry's "scullion speech." When he encounters the Anglo-Saxon lexeme *þolian* while reading the poem in Old English, he at first finds it "completely strange with its *thorn* symbol [þ] instead of the familiar *th*," as would all readers who are unfamiliar with Anglo-Saxon orthographic practices. But what sets Heaney apart from other modern readers is that he "gradually realized that [*þolian*] was not strange at all, for it was the word that older and less educated people would have used in the country where [he] grew up."[16] Recognizing this leads him to realize that *thole,* a word he recalls hearing one of his aunts use, stands as "a little bleeper to remind me that my aunt's language was not just a self-enclosed family possession but an historical heritage, one that involved the journey *þolian* had made north into Scotland and then across into Ulster with the planters, and then across from the planters to the locals who had originally spoken Irish, and then farther across again when the Scots Irish emigrated to the American South in the eighteenth century."[17] Heaney is deeply apprecia-tive of *þolian*'s "far-flungness," and of the ways that it and the other "little bleeper[s]" that appear throughout his work metonymically connect him to the (oral/aural) world of his childhood. However, the lexemes he imports from his past have a rather different (and perhaps not undesired) effect upon his readers. For them, these terms cannot (re-)establish ties to the world of the "big-voiced scullions" Heaney so elegantly and warmly recalls because it is a highly localized one to which they have neither any connection nor any access. To put matters differently, *thole* resonates for Heaney in ways that it never can for those of us who do not share his experiences—either locally within his family or more generally within the Ulster in which he grew up during the 1940s and 1950s—and it is only by dint of his explanatory comments that we become aware of how powerfully the "scullion voices" continue to speak to and through him via this lexeme.

But for readers who have no experience of and so cannot hear these voices, and for those who do not share Heaney's cultural background (and perhaps even for many of those who do), such strange-looking and strange-sounding lexemes as *thole, bawn,* and *hirpling* are disorienting and maybe even discomfiting components of his translation. Puzzled readers can find them in the OED[18] but not in other less comprehensive or less historically focused dic-tionaries.[19] The editor of the seventh edition of the *Norton Anthology of English Literature,* vol. 1A, addresses the issue of the occasional lexical inaccessibility of Heaney's *Beowulf* by having the translator provide explanatory footnotes for some, but not all, of the old or unusual terms he employs.[20] The decision to include notes in this volume was clearly driven by the editors' sensitivity to the needs and expectations of its chief consumers, undergraduate students at American colleges and universities, but one can easily imagine that the trans-lator's notes would have been equally useful to those who encountered Heaney's translation in either the edition brought out by Faber and Faber in England or

Norton's single-volume, facing-page American edition. Beyond the thought-ful introduction in which Heaney discusses, among other things, the poem's "scullion voice," a brief note on Anglo-Saxon names by the scholar Alfred David, and a chart of family trees, neither of these editions contains any further explanatory notes. *Thole* presents little trouble to professional medieval-ists, attested as it is from the Anglo-Saxon period all the way through the later Middle Ages,[21] but for many of Heaney's readers, especially those without an OED to hand, the lexemes will remain inscrutable and the worlds of meaning to which they gesture so powerfully for Heaney will remain forever unknow-able and inaccessible.

Within his poem, Heaney's "scullion speech" serves several purposes: it allows him to acknowledge and to celebrate the alterity of the original poem without undermining his project or overwhelming his readers; it enables him to weave a political thread subtly and powerfully into the larger fabric of his translation by consciously inserting unusual, in some cases nearly impene-trable, northern Irish lexemes into what is often considered to be the most paradigmatic of Old English poems;[22] and it forces his readers to come to terms with (or at the very least to confront) the limitations that their distance from this "scullion speech" and their own idiolects place upon their reception of his translation. In many ways, Heaney's "scullion speech" functions as a highly focused, self-contained, and private poetic register. If we are fully to "get" his translation, we must attempt to enter the world of associative meaning that he puts before us. But even if we dutifully track down all the instances of "scul-lion speech" and then seek their meanings in the OED, we will still find the door to the idiosyncratic world of meaning Heaney creates, his "further lan-guage," only partially open. The metonyms he offers us and the nexus of asso-ciative meanings that permeate and power them will remain forever part and parcel of the idiosyncratic, and so limited, referential system he creates.

As a poetic register, Heaney's "scullion speech" is far more fluid, flexible, and alive than Spenser's archaic register, but what finally aligns it more with Spenser's than with that of, say, the *Beowulf*-poet, is that the meanings it gen-erates are conferred, not traditional. Heaney's lexical register may be grounded in what is for him the still richly resonant oral world of his Ulster childhood, but within his poetry and within his idiopoetics, it is simply another element in the complex nexus of intertwined meanings that he creates. He does not create the meaning of lexemes such as *thole* or *bawn* or any of the others that constitute his poetry's "scullion speech" but rather creates a space for them to function metonymically within the boundaries of the highly idiosyncratic, post-traditional world of his *opera*. Anyone who has access to his texts, whether through visual or aural (or both) channels, is invited to enter this world of Heaney's creating, but because it is rooted in the singular experiences of his past, we finally can only and always know it imperfectly and at a distance.[23]

Oral Poetics and Post-Traditional Texts: The Survival of Thematics

Unlike the specialized lexemes of oral poetics that become obsolete and disappear once their specialized register fractures, its thematics remains relatively intact throughout the Middle Ages. The theme of the hero on the beach that Renoir uncovers in *Sir Gawain* is not nearly so powerful or so cohesive as it is in the number of other earlier medieval Germanic poems in which it occurs,[24] among which are *Beowulf* and the *Hildebrandslied,* but the theme is indisputably present and its affective dynamics is still discernable in the fourteenth-century poem. For example, the first two of the three times the poet employs the verb *blykke* [to shine, gleam] in the poem fit securely into the thematics of the hero-on-the-beach type-scene. When the Green Knight first surveys the suddenly quieted group of Christmas revelers at Camelot, he "runischly his rede yʒen . . . reled aboute" [fiercely rolled his red eyes about] and "Bende his bresed broʒez, blycande grene" (304–5) [wrinkled his bristled brows, shining green].[25] That the brows of this frighteningly large, rude, aggressive, and unnaturally green figure not only bristle but gleam adds to the liminality of the "aghlich mayster" (136) who confronts Arthur and his courtiers. *Blycande* also cues the audience in to an approaching slaughterous encounter. The audience does not have to wait long for the bloodshed that is the (expected?)[26] narrative complement of this metonym because Gawain shortly thereafter strikes the Green Knight's head from his shoulders.

The second occurrence of *blykke* helps to link the Green Knight's unsettling entrance with the even more disturbing events that follow his beheading. In describing the immediate and grisly aftermath of Gawain's stroke, the poet informs us that the Green Knight's blood "brayd fro þe body, þat blykked on þe grene" (429) [spurted from the body, that shone on the green] just before adding the startling information that

> nawþer faltered ne fel þe freke neuer þe helder,
> Bot styþly he start forh vpon styf schonkes,

And runyschly he raȝt out, þere as renkkez stoden,
Laȝt to his lufly hed, and lyft hit vp sone;

(430–33)

———

[the man neither faltered nor fell at all for that, but stoutly he went forth upon unweakened legs and fiercely he reached out, where the men stood, seized his fair head, and lifted it up at once]

The shedding of the Green Knight's blood fulfills the theme's narrative demands, but this second occurrence of *blykke*, interwoven as it is into the fabric of a scene of slaughter that is its (expected?) complement points to the theme's narrative continuation, something that the Green Knight's failure to succumb to Gawain's blow and his chilling reminder that Gawain will, in a year's time, "fotte / Such a dunt as þou hatz dalt—disserued þou habbez / To be ȝederly ȝolden" (451–53) [get such a blow as you have dealt—you have deserved to be promptly repaid] powerfully underscore. The third and final time *blykke* appears in the text, it is removed from a slaughterous or martial context: as Gawain wends his way home after receiving the Green Knight's return blow, we discover that "þe blykkande belt he bere þereaboute / Abelef as a bauderyk bounden bi his syde, / Loken vnder his lyfte arme, þe lace, with a knot" (2485–87) [he wore the shining belt about (his neck), obliquely as a baldric bound by his side, fastened under the left arm, the lace, with a knot]. But even though in this case the shining object appears well after the last drop of blood has been spilled in the poem, it retains its metonymic function and remains inexorably linked with bloodshed because the poet couples it closely to the wound Gawain received at the Green Knight's hands. Before mentioning that Gawain has taken to wearing the green girdle "In tokenyng he watz tane in tech of a faute" (2488) [as a sign he was detected in the stain of a fault], the poet notes that "Þe hurt watz hole þat he hade hent in his nek" (2484) [the injury was healed that he had received in his neck]. The "blykkande belt" does not point to an imminent slaughterous encounter, but it does serve to keep the possibility of physical danger alive in our minds by pointing back to a recently concluded and dramatically transformative, if nonfatal, one. The gleaming green girdle transports us back to the encounter at the Green Chapel, a scene marked by the "schene blod" [bright blood] that "ouer [Gawain's] schulderes schot to þe erþe" (2314) [over (Gawain's) shoulders shot to the earth] and by the "bryȝt sworde" (2319) [bright sword] Gawain immediately draws in his defense.

I have focused on the narrative presence of a shining object or objects not only because it is present in a wide range of Old and Middle English verse texts[27] but because it is one of the elements of medieval English oral poetics that has survived from the Middle Ages to the present with its traditional affective dynamics relatively intact. The fires that dot the French landscape the night before the decisive battle at Agincourt in Shakespeare's *Henry V* (IV. Cho. 8–9) and the "Millions of flaming swords, drawn from the thighs / Of mighty Cherubim" whose "sudden blaze / Far round illumin'd hell" (664–66) in book I of Milton's *Paradise Lost* are but two of the very many instances in post-medieval literature in which shining objects are important constituents of a poetic text's thematics and affective dynamics. The connection between shining objects and slaughter may have been forged in the highly specialized expressive economy of medieval English oral poetics, but it retains its traditional meaning even when used in the very verbal expressive economies of post-medieval poetry, contemporary prose fiction, and even in the visual medium of film. Two examples out of the many instances in which the affective dynamics of shining objects in a prose work is much the same as it has been in poetic works from the Anglo-Saxon period onward will suffice to illustrate the point. I take the first from *The Two Towers*, the second book of Tolkien's *Lord of the Rings*, and the second from Roddy Doyle's recent novel *A Star Called Henry*.

Near the middle of *The Two Towers*, several members of Tolkien's fellowship—the human Aragorn, the elf Legolas, the dwarf Gimli, and the wizard Gandalf—meet with Theoden, king of Rohan, and request his aid in battling the dark forces that are threatening their world. The king is sympathetic to their request and musters more than a thousand riders, who once assembled, "Loudly and joyously . . . shouted" (152) when their king comes forth to lead them into battle against Saruman's forces. In preparation for the coming battle, Gandalf "threw back his grey cloak, and cast aside his hat, and leaped to horseback. . . . His snowy hair flew free in the wind, [and] his white robes shone dazzling in the sun" (153). As the troop of riders thunder off to battle, the "glitter of their spears" catches the eyes of the lady Eowyn "as she stood still, alone before the doors of the silent house" (153). Once the enemy is engaged, Tolkien continues to present us with a number of flashing objects, including the swords of Aragorn and Eomer that "flashed from the sheath as one" (163). The sword of the former, furthermore, "rose and fell, gleaming with white fire" (163) as its wielder hews down his enemies, many of whom are so dismayed at the sight of this shining, well-known blade that they shout, "The Blade that was Broken shines again" (163) before fleeing from it.

Given that Tolkien, who for twenty years was the Rawlinson and Bosworth Professor of Anglo-Saxon at Oxford, regularly drew extensively upon his knowledge of Old English for character and place names and a fiction writer whose novels everywhere witness his heavy reliance upon Anglo-Saxon thematics, rhythms, and perhaps even story patterns,[28] we should not be surprised when he foregrounds a shining object just before or during a battle scene.[29] However, while Tolkien's scholarly background may illuminate many facets of his work, it does not provide equally satisfactory explanations for all of them. This is especially so in the case of the thematics under consideration here. Even if we were to grant that he was aware that shining objects regularly appear in martial contexts in the Old English poetic records, this would not establish whether he was aware of their traditional, metonymic qualities. Tolkien may have seen them as surface elements he could use to heighten the decidedly medieval flavor of the fantastic world he created, in precisely the way that the lexemes he employs that are rooted in the Anglo-Saxon past, such as *frod* [wise], *helm,* and *wyrm* [reptile, dragon], to cite just a few, do. We will never be able finally to know just how he regarded these shining objects or whether he was aware that they were rooted in the thematics of medieval English oral poetics, but how these elements made their way into his novels is far less important than the simple facts that they are present and that they continue to function in much the way they did within the expressive economy of medieval English oral poetics.

At the opposite end of the spectrum from Tolkien, a specialist in Old and Middle English language and literature who also wrote several works of heroic fantasy, we find Roddy Doyle, a contemporary author whose realistic novels chronicle the lives of working- and lower-class Irish men and women. His most recent work, *A Star Called Henry,* is something of a departure for him in that it is a work of historicized fiction, but in its focus upon Henry Smart, a young man who is economically and socially marginalized, it is very much of a piece with the rest of his novels. Doyle sets the story of Henry's early life against the tumultuous background of early-twentieth-century Irish history as Henry, who is forced to make his own way in the world from age five onwards, becomes deeply embroiled in the Irish Rebellion as a member of the Volunteers and Citizen Army, the precursor of the present-day Irish Republican Army. On Monday, April 24, 1916, the troop to which Henry is attached storm and then barricade themselves in the Dublin General Post Office in one of the first military actions of the weeklong uprising known as the Easter Rebellion.[30] As the young, inexperienced, and rather ragtag army of the newly designated Irish Republic await their first martial encounter with the British forces that have been sent to suppress the uprising and restore the disrupted social order, Henry edgily mans his position behind the barricade, rifle at the ready, searching "for khaki, horses, the glint or clink of metal, hooves, engines—anything that would allow me to declare war" (101).

As he waits for the inevitable arrival of the British forces, physical and emotional tension mount steadily within him and the other members of his troop who, like Henry, "hadn't a hope" and "were waiting for the world to drop on [them]":

> My trigger finger was aching, my calves, the elbow that anchored the arm propping up my rifle; every muscle and sinew I owned was hardening, screaming. A hint, the slightest thing or sound would save them and release all the anger and rage I'd been storing for today. I wanted to demolish every bit of glass and brick in front of me. The creak of stretched leather, a boot on a kerb, the sun on a badge, any tiny thing would let me go. (101)

Despite the mention of the shining objects, the theme's traditional complement, bloodshed, does not follow but is deferred as the scene is in short order twice defused, first by the acknowledgment of a "gobshite" on the outside that he was "only havin' yis on!" when he shouted that the British military was approaching and second by the arrival, not of the military, but of a group of angry women who demand that they, revolution or no revolution, be given the government payments they are due while their men are off fighting in France. Despite the several comic touches that infuse the scene—as the "gobshite" beats a hasty retreat, he yells "There's worse than the military coming now!" (102)— the situation threatens to turn tragic as the women, or the "shawlies," as Henry dubs them, do not retreat but instead begin to climb the rebels' barricade. Michael Collins, one of the army's commanders, orders Henry to shoot "the first one that tries to get in" (104), but the standoff between the women and the rebels finally comes to a peaceful conclusion. However, when the British forces finally arrive two days later, the bloodshed that is the theme's traditional complement is fully realized. The ensuing fight is both extremely bloody and extremely one-sided as a large number of the greatly outgunned rebels are killed by sniper fire or bomb shells, and many of those who manage to escape the GPO alive are shortly captured and summarily executed.

The link between shining objects and slaughter is one that our post-traditional hermeneutics cannot easily or satisfactorily explain. That the post-traditional authors who insert shining objects into their narratives and the audiences who encounter them in the texts they receive may well be wholly unaware that they are deploying and receiving a richly associative metonym whose affective dynamics has remained stable from the Anglo-Saxon period onward offers further evidence of just how deeply anchored parts of oral poetics continue to be within our contemporary expressive economy, whether we are consciously aware of them or not.

Oral Poetics in a Post-Traditional World: The Evidence of Story Patterns

In this final section, we will examine one of the largest, most amorphous, and most widely shared (diachronically and synchronically) components of oral poetics, the story pattern. Why they survive is a question that we cannot at this point answer. Is there something about them that speaks to the deepest parts of our collective cultural beings and our collective anxieties and/or desires? Is the history of our cultural being and memory somehow encoded in them? The reasons story patterns survive may forever elude us, but when we turn to consider how they survive, we find ourselves on much firmer ground. One of the keys to their continued narrative presence is that story patterns are by far the most elastic component of traditional expressive economies. Lexical metonyms function properly only within the confines of the tradition within which they originated: once they are removed from the specialized linguistic register of their tradition, they are no longer able to serve as fully functioning pathways to the worlds of rich, associative meanings foundational to traditional oral poetics. The thematics of oral poetics has a better survival rate because it is not as completely dependent upon a given expressive economy as lexemes are and because traditional themes are composed of constellations of details that are less, rather than more, fixed. Story patterns are even less dependent than thematics upon any set of specific narrative details, and the tightness of their narrative weave accordingly varies considerably. As a result, their articulation may be much fuller and their narrative details more fixed in some instantiations than in others. But whether an author employs a more or less fully developed version of a story pattern, it will continue to emit its traditional signals to a correspondingly greater or lesser degree because it is "more than a narrative latticework; not only does it have considerable potential for variation, but it is also dynamic and process-directing and it lies at the foundation of more complex story-types."[31]

To illustrate this point about traditional story-patterns, let us turn now to one of the most widely occurring and well documented ones, the Return Song. This story pattern not only bridges the linguistic, cultural, and temporal boundaries that separate the various Indo-European traditions but also bridges generic boundaries and is found in a variety of narratives, where it is sometimes a well-developed and central structural element and sometimes a far more fractured and marginal one.[32] As Lord detailed them more than thirty years ago, the paradigmatic constituents of this story pattern are Absence, Devastation, Return, Retribution, and Wedding.[33] While all five often appear, many permutations of this traditional pattern also occur.

The return pattern is clearly discernable in the early Middle English romance *King Horn*, where it is in fact multiply attested. In one of the narrative's several cycles of absence and return, Horn is forced to leave Westernesse (Absence) after his lifelong companion Fikenhild falsely accuses him of sleeping with Rymenhild, the king's daughter, who swoons at Horn's departure and suffers acutely during his seven-year absence (Devastation). Several years later, Horn returns in disguise when he learns that Rymenhild has been promised to another king (Return) and promptly exacts revenge by killing his rival, King Modi, and all the men at the feast, "Biþute [Horn's] twelf ferin / & þe king Aylmare" (1242–43)[34] [except (Horn's) twelve companions and King Aylmare] (Retribution). Horn's decision to defer his marriage to Rymenhild until after he wins back his birthright from the "Payns" [pagans] who long ago killed his father and consigned him and his companions to a watery death (91 ff.) breaks the pattern but in so doing initiates it *in brevis* once again. Horn's departure (Absence) this time leads to Rymenhild being forced into marriage with Fikenhild. On the day of her wedding, Rymenhild is so distraught that "He wep teres of blode" (1406) [she wept tears of blood] (Devastation). When Horn returns again, he and his men, disguised as "harpurs, / . . . and gigours" (1471–72) [harpers . . . and fiddlers], gain entrance to Fikenhild's newly and cunningly constructed castle, where they dispatch the traitor and his men with alacrity (Retribution).

The traditional pattern's thematics also helps us to understand an episode that from the perspective of literate poetics is rather puzzling. When Horn returns to Westernesse after learning of Rymenhild's impending marriage to King Modi, he does so dressed as a beggar. He does not need this disguise to protect himself (he discards it before he goes over to the bridal feast to kill Modi) and his actions toward Rymenhild seem cruel and aimed at driving her to suicide. But when we place his actions against the background of the traditional story pattern, we can see them as the traditional elements that they are. Far from being gratuitous cruelties inflicted upon his faithful and *very* long-suffering beloved, they allow him to test her fealty and to plumb the depth of her love for him. It is only after he has satisfied himself on these accounts that he "wipede þat blake of his swere" (1203) [wiped the black from his neck] and unambiguously reveals himself to her, saying,

> quen so swete & dere,
> Ihc am horn þinoʒe,
> Ne canstu me noʒt knowe?
> Ihc am horn of westernesse.
> (1204–7)

[queen so sweet and dear, I am your own Horn. Do you not know me? I am Horn of Westernesse.]

Similarly, the second time he returns—also in disguise—he takes no action against Fikenhild when he first enters the traitor's castle but rather "sette him on þe benche / His harpe for to clenche" (1475–76) [seated himself on the bench, his harp to pluck]. The song he sings for Rymenhild so distresses her that "heo makede walaway" (1478) [she made a lament] and falls "yswoʒe" (1479) [in a swoon]. The poet is silent as to this song's content, but given Horn's predilection for self-referential stories and the importance of testing the beloved in the traditional pattern, it is tempting to surmise that its subject might be Horn and Rymenhild's relationship. Even without certain knowledge of the song's content, the scene still comfortably fits into the traditional story pattern. Whether he engineers the song as a test or not, Horn clearly reads Rymenhild's reaction to it as proof of her continuing attachment to him because it is only after she swoons that he leaps into action:

> He ʒede vp to borde
> Wiþ gode suerdes orde.
> ffikenhildes crune

Þer ifulde adune,
& Al his men a rowe
Hi dude adun þrowe.
        (1485–90)

———————

[He went up to the table (and) with the point of his good sword he there
cut off Fikenhild's head and threw down all his men in order.]

After having postponed his wedding to Rymenhild for seven years and after
twice having to rescue her from the attention of unwanted suitors, Horn finally
marries her, an action that brings the return story pattern to a conclusion that
is as expected and as fully traditional as that of the *Odyssey* or any number of
South Slavic epics in which it occurs.

There is no disputing that in the hands of a Homer or a talented *guslar*
the return story pattern proves to be a far more nuanced and powerful expressive instrument than it does in the hands of the *Horn*-poet. But once we make
allowances for the enormous differences between the ancient Greek and South
Slavic traditions and the early Middle English one and calibrate our response
to *Horn* accordingly, we can see that its story pattern is not an awkward, frequently puzzling, mechanical device whose purpose seems wholly to keep the
narrative clipping along at its near breakneck pace but rather a "word" that
both indexes the tradition from which it descends and helps key our response
to it.[35]

The return pattern is also foundational to the narrative of the fourteenth-
century romance *Sir Orfeo*, even though it is not so fully realized as it is in *King
Horn*.[36] Orfeo suffers the loss of his wife Heurodis (Absence) and is so distraught that he gives his throne to his steward and wanders alone in the woods
for ten years (Devastation). He is eventually reunited with Heurodis and comes
back to his kingdom (Return), where he and his queen rule happily until their
deaths. If we were to measure *Sir Orfeo*'s story pattern mechanically against the
schematic of the Return Song, we would come to the conclusion that it only
partially fulfills it, as neither the retribution nor the wedding element is in the
poem. But if we view the story pattern as the more supple component of
verbal art that it is, we can see that *Sir Orfeo* in fact offers a rather paradigmatic
instantiation of it. In lieu of the retribution that other heroes mete out upon
their return to those who have betrayed them, we have Orfeo's testing, in disguise, of his steward. Orfeo borrows a beggar's clothes and wanders into town,
where he soon meets the steward, from whom he seeks aid: "Icham an harpour

of heþenisse: / Help me now in þis destresse" (513–14) [I am a heathen harper; help me now in this distress].[37] The steward responds by telling him, "Of þat ichaue þou schalt haue some. / Euerich gode harpour is welcom me to / For mi lordes loue, Sir Orfeo" (516–18) [You shall have part of whatever I have. Every good harper is welcome to me, for the love of my lord, Sir Orfeo]. Because the steward graciously welcomes the disguised Orfeo and because the steward proves himself to have been unfailingly loyal to Orfeo throughout the king's ten-year absence, there is no need for the hero to enact the retribution that reestablishes the social order that had been disrupted by his absence. In lieu of the wedding that often closes the story pattern in other of its instantiations, we have instead have the reassertion and public resumption of Orfeo and Heurodis's marriage.

Such departures from the Return pattern's paradigm witness the vital, ever-shifting nature of oral poetics. If those poets who engage oral poetics were unable to calibrate traditional story patterns as they saw fit by, say, adding some elements and deleting others, the necessary and sustaining tension between traditional form and individual narrative moment would not have opened up narrative and aesthetic space that poets could then explore as they wished but would rather have stymied the production of traditional verbal art by forcing upon poets preformed structures from which they could not deviate.

Not all poets who deploy traditional story patterns do so in so accomplished and effective a manner as the *Orfeo*-poet. The dizzying cycles of loss and displacement that King Horn goes through before eventually visiting retribution upon all those who have harmed him, his family, and his long-suffering betrothed, and then reestablishing the social order of not one or two but three societies reveals the *Horn*-poet to have a very different relationship to this particular inherited story pattern, as well as a perhaps far more limited understanding of it. Where the *Orfeo*-poet's handling is finely nuanced and consonant with the texture of his poem, the *Horn*-poet's lacks subtlety and, frequently, logic.

For an example of a text in which the story pattern is a rather more peripheral and underdeveloped but nevertheless present and functioning compositional element, we need look only to *Sir Gawain*.[38] As is true of the other lexical and thematic traces of medieval English oral poetics contained in this finest of all Middle English romances, the Return pattern is incomplete and fractured. Absence, Devastation, and Return all figure in *Sir Gawain*'s narrative, and they all function traditionally. There is, notably, no Wedding at the poem's conclusion, but the work of social (re)constitution it usually performs is taken over by the court at Camelot, who immediately welcome Gawain back into their ranks and make him, via their adoption of the green girdle, a symbol of their entire society.[39] The one element that we have passed over, Retribution, is also the trickiest because while retribution is usually meted out by the returning hero to those who have threatened or disrupted his domestic social order, in *Sir Gawain* it is Gawain who suffers it at the hand of the Green Knight. In a deft inversion of the traditional story pattern, the *Gawain*-poet transforms Gawain from one who responds to the social threat the Green Knight poses to Camelot (and who will mete out retribution) into one who poses a threat to someone else's social order (and who will be the target of retribution). That this sort of category shifting disrupts without destroying the pattern testifies once again to the remarkable malleability and responsiveness of traditional oral poetics.[40]

We will close our discussion of traditional story patterns by moving considerably farther afield from the world of medieval English oral poetics so that we may consider a different story pattern, one that has become a staple not only of contemporary narrative fiction but of narrative films as well. As elsewhere in this chapter, the following discussion is meant to be illustrative rather than exhaustive.

Standing Alone: Affective Dynamics and the Lone Hero

In our discussion of Beowulf's fight with the dragon in chapter 3, we argued that the affective dynamics of his single-handed engagement with this terrible, monstrous foe was a key component of the narrative, one that enabled and guided the response of the poem's intended audience. Elsewhere in this study we have considered the affective dynamics of a number of similar moments, most of which culminated in the death of the lone hero, his foe, or both. When viewed collectively, these episodes can best be understood as instantiations of a traditional story pattern, one that may be fleshed out by a virtually limitless number of surface details but that has at its narrative and affective heart a lone hero's (usually) fatal engagement with a deadly foe.

While the corpus of prose fiction fairly bursts with texts that employ identifiable variations of this traditional story pattern, we will shift our focus and consider instead how it works in films because the unique register of film—its visual and aural ways of speaking, as it were—is as specialized as and in many ways reflects that of traditional oral poetics because both registers are closely dependent upon a variety of auditory or visual signals that cue the audience to an approaching narrative event and that further help determine the audience's response. Since the early days of the movies, filmmakers have created a number of now widely shared signals that economically trigger an associative network of meanings.[41] As is to be expected, these metonyms have a rather limited associative range given that the expressive economy within which they originated has neither the temporal span nor cultural centrality of oral poetics. But the visual expressive economy of movies also contains many metonyms that are descended from traditional oral poetics, and it is with a brief discussion of one of them that this study concludes.

The Lone Hero in the Wild West: High Noon

The corpus of western movies contains any number of narratives in which the story pattern of the lone hero plays an important role. For the present, very limited purposes, one example will suffice, that of Fred Zinnemann's 1952 *High Noon*, an especially compact and tightly focused articulation of the lone hero story pattern. Against the background of the western high country, the movie opens with the gathering of three not very reputable-looking riders. Scruffy, with a menacing air about them, they come together in purposeful silence and with only curt signs of recognition. The movie's title song, sung off camera by Tex Ritter, deftly establishes the narrative's background as well as the feverish affective pitch that the movie will maintain throughout its eighty-four minutes running time:[42]

> The noonday train will bring Frank Miller—
> If I'm a man I must be brave,
> And I must face that deadly killer
> Or lie a coward,
> A craven coward,
> Lie a coward in my grave.

The song continues and effectively maps out the difficult position in which the narrative places the marshal—his sense of duty demands that he face Miller, a recently pardoned murderer, even though his wife of a few hours is a Quaker who vows to leave him if he does—but it does so only partially because the film's considerable tension rests not just on the marshal's relationships to his foe and his spouse but on his relationship to the community he has so devotedly served. After contemplating fleeing with his wife and actually beginning to do so, the marshal's sense of duty compels him to return to the town that owes its social stability and burgeoning prosperity largely to him. He attempts to form a group of special deputies who will fight alongside him, but he fails to find a single person from among all of the town's constituencies who is willing to stand by him, including his former deputy. Their reasons range from the ruffians' friendship with Miller to the churchgoers' desire to keep the town free of gunplay for fear that northern investors will see their town not as a good place to build factories but simply as another lawless western outpost. Even the marshal's predecessor refuses his request for aid, partly because he is retired and crippled by arthritis but, more disturbingly, also because he has absolutely no illusions about the value of self-sacrifice. As he says, the reward for lawmen who risk their lives in the service of the community is that "[y]ou end up dying all alone on a dirty street. For what? For nothing." He mournfully repeats, "It's all for nothing. It's all for nothing" when the marshal, his hand-picked successor, leaves him for what both men expect to be the last time.

Throughout the movie, the marshal is filmed in solo shots that accentuate his isolation as powerfully as the phrase "al one" does in *Sir Gawain* or the phrase "oð ðæt an ongan" does in *Beowulf.* The only genuine offers of help he receives—both of which he refuses—come from an old, one-eyed alcoholic and a fourteen-year-old boy. As the clock ticks inexorably toward noon, the marshal's desperation turns to resignation. We see him at one point sealing a letter in an envelope upon which he puts the following instructions: "To be opened in the event of my death." Abandoned by his wife of two hours, scorned by his former deputy, urged to flee and so sacrifice his honor and his future peace of mind for the sake of the town's economic growth,[43] stripped of all hope, and perhaps aware that "[i]t's all for nothing," the marshal nevertheless strides resolutely down the center of the town's deserted main street to face head on what everyone believes to be his certain death.

A fuller treatment of the film than can be offered here would reveal further illuminating and intriguing points of contact between its instantiation of the story pattern and those found within the corpus of medieval English literature: for example, the camera focuses on a series of shining objects (the gun barrels of the marshal and the men awaiting Miller's return, the clock's pendulum, the marshal's badge) just prior to the fatal showdown; the marshal receives necessary and crucial help from a young, untried (and in this case unexpected and unorthodox) fighter—his wife—in just the way that Beowulf receives help from Wiglaf; the marshal at one point is afraid of what is facing him, as is Bevis; the marshal's former deputy urges him to jump on his horse and leave without fighting Miller and even attempts to saddle the horse for him in a scene that recalls the one between Gawain and his guide at the entrance to the Green Knight's valley; and finally, the deaths of Miller and his men restore the community's social order, as the deaths of the monstrous foes do. Unlike Beowulf and Morpidus, the marshal does not die, but as is the case with Gawain, the marshal's heroic actions do not lead to his social reintegration into the community. Following the death of Miller, a scene played out on a street empty except for the three participants, the marshal and his wife—the two survivors of the showdown—suddenly find themselves in the middle of an appreciative swarm of townspeople. But rather than glorying in the people's sudden outpouring of gratitude, the marshal silently removes his badge, drops it in the dirt at his feet, mounts a waiting buckboard with his wife, and rides out of town without glancing back. There is no longer a place for them among that community, just as at the conclusion of *Sir Gawain* there is no longer a place for Gawain in Camelot.

There are a great many ways in which the story pattern of *High Noon* differs from its more traditional instantiations, but its overall movement and especially its affective dynamics remain remarkably consistent with those of the other patterns we have considered even when it differs from them. For example, the marshal's weapons do not fail him but work quite well throughout the battle. He does, however, repeatedly fail to enlist any help against the four outlaws, and this failure, even though it is less tangible—and perhaps less overtly charged—than the weapon failures that the other heroes experience, nonetheless fulfills precisely the same role in the film's affective dynamics that those other failures do: they greatly heighten our sense of his vulnerability.

The broad scope and the plasticity of story patterns, as well as some perhaps undiscoverable organizing principles, account for their continued survival and for their continued ability to fulfill their traditional functions. Evidence of their survival is all around us, both in the narratives that contain them and in the responses of the audiences who receive them. I recently had this point brought home to me in a small but telling way while watching Clint Eastwood's *Space Cowboys* (2000) with a sophisticated and not overly sentimental eleven-year-old who was, further, initially not very interested in joining her father and younger brother to watch a film about a group of former test pilots who in their sixties are finally given the chance to go into space. Despite her resistance, however, my companion got sufficiently caught up in the movie's affective dynamics that she shed a few tears when one of the characters volunteered to strap himself upon a bomb that he would then pilot into deep space so it could be safely detonated, thus ensuring in this one act both his own death and the safety of those on the earth below him.

Arguing that this one moment in an admittedly modest film and the few tears quietly shed over it witness the survival of an entire tradition may seem reductive, but the ubiquity of the tradition's thematics and story patterns and their continued power to elicit responses in those who receive them neverthe-less place *Space Cowboys* and the response it engendered in my daughter upon a continuum that stretches back through the English Middle Ages and perhaps even much earlier. Oral poetics remains present because it continues to offer artists powerful channels through which they can speak to and move their audiences.

Notes

Preface

1. Although he approaches this issue from a more performative perspective, Foley, *Singer of Tales in Performance*, 62–63, similarly begins his consideration of "the rhetorical persistence of traditional forms" by "not only admitting but stipulating and setting a calibration for the documentary nature of the evidence," something, he notes, that "Oral Theory has frankly been loath to do."

ONE.   The Medieval English Oral-Literate Nexus

1. The criticism devoted to this matter is far too voluminous to list here. See Foley, *Oral-Formulaic Theory and Research*, and the electronic updates available at www.oraltradition.org.

2. Havelock, *Preface to Plato*, 27, succinctly explains some of the cultural functions poetry fulfills in an oral society, where it "provided a massive repository of useful knowledge, a sort of encyclopedia of ethics, politics, history and technology which the effective citizen was required to learn as the core of his educational equipment. Poetry represented not something we call by that name, but an indoctrination which today would be comprised in a shelf of text books and works of reference."

3. See Derrida's comments in *Of Grammatology*, esp. 3–93. For a critique of Derrida and of deconstruction's insistence on the primacy of textuality, see

Parks, "Textualization of Orality," 47–52. As Parks notes, for Derrida, writing, "far from merely representing oral speech, is its very precondition" (47). See further Ellis, *Against Deconstruction*, 18 ff.

4. Doane, "Introduction," xii.

5. On the roles of texts in ancient and medieval cultures, see esp. Havelock, *Literate Revolution;* Clanchy, *From Memory;* Eisenstein, *Printing Press;* Ong, "Writing"; and Rosalind Thomas, *Literacy and Orality.*

6. Fuller discussions and important critiques of the Great Divide model can be found in Finnegan, *Oral Poetry* and *Literacy and Orality,* 139–74; Stock, *Listening for the Text;* Foley, *Immanent Art, Singer of Tales in Performance,* and *How to Read,* esp. 22–57; and Renoir, *Key to Old Poems.* Joyce Coleman offers a spirited and wide-ranging but finally rather myopic critique of this theory in *Public Reading,* 1–33.

7. Stock, *Listening for the Text,* 7.

8. Cf. Ong, "Writing," 29.

9. Havelock, *Preface to Plato,* 201.

10. *Republic,* III, 387b, 64. I cite Bloom's edition.

11. As Patterson, "On the Margin," and Robinson, "*Medieval,* the *Middle Ages,*" note, the ways in which western European society from the so-called early modern period on has figured the Middle Ages, in both scholarly and popular venues, provide particularly sharp illustrations of this process at work. See also Aers, "Whisper," and Amodio, "Tradition, Modernity."

12. Ong, "Writing," 26. Ong cites Edmonson, *Lore,* 323, who contends that only about 106 languages have produced written literatures.

13. Stock, *Listening for the Text,* 6.

14. Havelock, "Alphabetization of Homer," 4.

15. See also Finnegan, *Oral Poetry,* 272, who suggests that "the oral/written distinction, so far as it exists, is more like a continuum (or perhaps a complex set of continuums)," and O'Brien O'Keeffe, *Visible Song,* 25.

16. Doane, "Introduction," xiii. Ong, "Orality, Literacy," 1, defines "primary orality" as "the pristine orality of cultures with no knowledge of writing."

17. Bäuml, "Unmaking," 89.

18. See further Harwood, "Alliterative *Morte Arthure,*" 253.

19. In "Homer as an Oral-Traditional Poet," a paper first read in 1984 but not published until shortly before his death in July 1991, Lord offered an important clarification between improvising and oral traditional poets, reminding us that "'[c]omposition in performance' or possibly 'recomposition in performance' are satisfactory terms as long as one does not equate them with improvisation, which, to [his] mind, means to make up a new nontraditional song from predominantly nontraditional elements" (76).

20. See further Foley, *How to Read,* 11–21, *et passim.*

21. On the important distinction between "inherent" and "conferred" meaning, see Foley, *Immanent Art,* 8–9.

22. Cf. Lord's discussion of this in "Homer as an Oral-Traditional Poet," 78–80.

23. On the role the audience of traditional oral poetry plays in shaping the poetic production, see Foley, "Traditional Oral Audience" and most recently, *How to Read,* 130–33; Finnegan, *Oral Poetry,* 214–35; and Niles, *Homo Narrans,* 49–61.

24. O'Brien O'Keeffe, *Visible Song,* 52.

25. Parry, "Epithet and the Formula I," 82–83.

26. Havelock, *Preface to Plato,* 88–89.

27. Benson's contention in *Art and Tradition,* 116, that "[p]robably the late four-teenth-century writers were not even aware that the line they used represented a changing tradition" is particularly apposite here. For a different view, see Stanley, "Linguistic Self-Awareness."

28. See Foley's discussion in *Immanent Art,* 12, of the Bhopa who perform episodes from Pabuji epic in front of "a *par,* a tapestry on which are depicted scenes from the larger epic."

29. Cf. Lord, *Singer of Tales,* 30–98.

30. Much of the humor of Monty Python's depiction of Thomas Hardy's attempts to compose what will come to be *The Return of the Native* derives from its transforming the private act of literate composition, with all its fits and false starts, into a public spectacle along the lines of a football match. In the skit "Novel Writing (Live from Wessex)" from the 1973 Arista recording *Matching Tie & Handkerchief,* Hardy sits at a desk in front of a large "bank holiday crowd" and begins his eleventh novel while expert announcers analyze every word or doodle he produces. I am grateful to Min Amodio for her assistance in locating a transcript of this sketch.

31. Fish, "Introduction," 13.

32. See further Amodio, "Affective Criticism, Oral Poetics," 54–62, and "Contemporary Critical Approaches."

33. A hypertext novel, and hypertext in general, can be seen as a logical extension of the subjective perspective in that readers must literally navigate their way through a "text" that has no fixed or absolutely determined path. In this way, hypertext authors are rather like modern versions of traditional poets in that they create texts with fluid narrative paths that are not easily (if at all) retraceable. See further, Foley, *How to Read,* 219–25. On hypertext's relation to orality, see Joyce, "No One Tells You This."

34. However, see Dagenais, "That Bothersome Residue," 256, who argues that the constitution of the "textual fields" used to distinguish orality and literacy "can be found in the physicality that is parchment and sound."

35. Fish, "Interpreting the *Variorum,*" 171.

36. Doane, "Oral Texts, Intertexts," 84–85.

37. Unless otherwise noted, all translations are mine.

38. Klaeber, *Beowulf;* Zupitza and Davis, *Beowulf;* Kiernan et al., *Electronic Beowulf.*

39. Cf. Lord, *Singer of Tales,* 99 ff., and more recently Foley, *How to Read,* 11–21.

40. "Chaucers Wordes unto Adam, His Owne Scriveyn," in Benson, *Riverside Chaucer,* 650. See also Chaucer's comments in *Troilus and Criseyde,* V, 1793–98. Orrm, writing near the end of the twelfth century, anticipates Chaucer's concern with accurate transmission in a passage of the *Orrmulum,* I, 95–110, that is unusual for the period in which it was written:

7 whase wilenn shall þiss boc
  Efft oþer siþe writenn,
Himm bidde icc þatt hét write rihht,
  Swa summ þiss boc himm tæcheþþ,
All þwerrt út affterr þatt itt iss
Uppo þiss firrste bisne,
Wiþþ all swillc ríme alls her iss sett,
  Wiþþ all se fele wordess;
7 tatt he loke wel þatt he
  An bocstaff write twiƷƷess,
EƷƷwhær þær itt uppo þiss boc
  Is writenn o þatt wise.
Loke he well þatt hét write swa,
  Forr he ne maƷƷ nohht elless
Onn Ennglissh wrítenn rihht te word,
  Þatt wite he wel to soþe.

———

[And whosoever wishes to write this book another time, I command him that he write it correctly, just as this book teaches him throughout afterwards just as it is in this first example, with all such rhymes as are set here, with all the many words; and let him be sure that he write a letter twice everyplace in this book where it is written in that manner. He should look that he carefully write it so, for he may not write anything else correctly in English, that in truth he knows well.]

All citations of the *Orrmulum* are to R. White's edition.

41. Lerer, *Chaucer and His Readers,* 143.

42. Because the poem "survives only in [John Shirley's] hand," Lerer, ibid., 121, suggests that while Shirley may have "responded to many familiar things in *Adam Scriveyn*[,] . . . he just might have created them, as well." See also A. Edwards and Pearsall, "Manuscripts," 259.

43. O'Brien O'Keeffe, *Visible Song,* 9.

44. An exception to this general trend is Hoffman, "Exploring the Literate Blindspot."

45. Clanchy, *From Memory*, 231. See further, G. Brown, "Dynamics of Literacy," 109, who stresses that "literacy is a complicated phenomenon both in past and present cultures . . . because its fundamental meaning, the ability to read and write, involves many degrees of performance, purpose, and efficacy among various groups and communities." See further Lerer, *Literacy and Power*, 22; the articles contained in Boyarin, *Ethnography of Reading;* and Rosalind Thomas, *Literacy and Orality*, 1–28.

46. As Clanchy in *From Memory*, 271, importantly notes in medieval England, "Reading and writing were not inseparably coupled with each other, as they are today. A person might be able to write, yet not be considered literate."

47. Lerer, *Literacy and Power*, 20.

48. Magoun, "Oral-Formulaic Character," 447.

49. Ibid.

50. This view was challenged almost immediately. Shortly after Magoun's initial foray into oral-formulaic theory, Schaar refuted Magoun's first principle by demonstrating, in "On a New Theory," 303, that "the proposition 'all formulaic poetry is oral' does not follow, either logically or psychologically, from the proposition 'all oral poetry is formulaic.'" Shortly thereafter, Benson, in "Literary Character," questioned formularity as an indicator of orality by detailing the formulaic character of what he took to be demonstrably written Old English poetry. Curschmann, too, addressed the false binarism that he saw underlying the work of many oral-formulaicists when he argued in "Prologue," 148, that "[a]s far as we can still see into the literature of the Middle Ages, the distinction between written and oral is never absolute." For a fuller discussion of the early responses to the early articulations of oral-formulaic theory, see Foley, *Theory of Oral Composition*, 67–70.

51. See esp. O'Brien O'Keeffe, *Visible Song*, 1–46.

52. Foley, *Immanent Art*, xii; emphasis in orginal. See also Lord, "Homer as an Oral-Traditional Poet."

53. Wordsworth, "Preface to Lyrical Ballads." I cite the 1800 preface to the second edition from Stillinger's edition (*William Wordsworth*), 460.

54. Consider, for example, the poet Elizabeth Bishop, who left unpublished a number of poems, many of which remained drafts even after she had worked on them for years.

55. Kristeva, "Word, Dialogue and Novel," 37.

56. Doane, "Oral Texts, Intertexts," 79.

57. Foley, *Immanent Art*, 17.

58. In some oral traditions, poets reflect in private upon the songs they know, and may even practice them beforehand. See Finnegan, *Oral Poetry*, esp. 52–88.

59. Stock, *Listening for the Text*, 146.

60. See further Bäuml, "Varieties."

61. Kelly, "Anglo-Saxon Lay Society," 36.

62. See, for example, the very different points raised by Opland, *Anglo-Saxon Oral Poetry*, 150–57, and Lerer, *Literacy and Power*, 61–96. Frank, "Search," 20, notes that "King Alfred's official biographer, Asser, had portrayed that ruler's fondness for vernacular poetry, but only as a reader and memorizer; never as an oral singer or frequenter of bards." Cf. also Keynes and Lapidge, *Alfred the Great*, 14.

63. Cf. Machan, "Editing, Orality."

64. On the literature produced in post-Roman Britain, see further Lapidge and Sharpe, *Bibliography of Celtic-Latin Literature,* and Howlett, *Celtic Latin Tradition.*

65. See further Lapidge, "Anglo-Latin Background."

66. To cite only two examples, the monks who wrote down Cædmon's poetry and Alcuin's famous letter to the bishop Speratus in which he chastises the monastic community for reading secular poetry both attest to the place of the vernacular within Anglo-Latin culture. See further, Olsen, "Old English Poetry" and *Speech, Song,* 10 ff. In the same vein, Calder argues, *Cynewulf,* 24, that "Cynewulf's works themselves bear witness to a vital connection between the Anglo-Saxon present and the world of ancient Latin letters." See, more recently, Orchard, "Both Style and Substance." Bullough, "What Has Ingeld," argues convincingly against identifying Abbot Hygbald of Lindisfarne with the addressee of Alcuin's letter, as generations of scholars have done.

67. G. Brown, "Dynamics of Literacy," 113.

68. Lapidge, "Aldhelm's Latin Poetry," 209. On Aldhelm's life and career, see Gwara, *Aldhelmi Malmesbiriensis,* 1–46.

69. All citations of William's *Gesta* are to Hamilton's edition (*De Gestis*).

70. As Opland is careful to note in *Anglo-Saxon Oral Poetry,* 124–27, what William means by the phrase "carmina nativae linguae" is not at all clear, although Whallon, in *Formula, Character, and Context,* 130, sees little reason to doubt that the poetry Aldhelm performs "was like *Beowulf* itself." See also Frank, "Search," 30–35.

71. Lapidge, "Aldhelm's Latin Poetry," 228.

72. Ibid., 211. For an insightful and thorough investigation of Aldhelm's Latin poetry, see Orchard, *Poetic Art of Aldhelm.*

73. Ziolkowski, "Cultural Diglossia," 198.

74. Cf. Bede's *Historia Ecclesiastica,* XXIV (XXII). Unless otherwise noted, all citations are to Colgrave and Mynors's facing-page edition and translation (*Bede's Ecclesiastical History*).

75. Ziolkowski, "Cultural Diglossia," 199.

76. Baugh and Cable, *History of the English Language,* 83. On Latin loanwords in Anglo-Saxon England, see Serjeantson, *History of Foreign Words,* 11–50 and 259–92, and Baugh and Cable, *History of the English Language,* 83–90.

77. Ziolkowski, "Cultural Diglossia," 195. For a contrasting view, see Sisam, "Notes on OE Poetry," 36, who argues that there is "ample evidence" that "confirms

that copyists of Old English texts were not expected to reproduce their originals letter for letter, as they were when copying Latin and especially Biblical texts." Similarly, Reames, "*Mouvance* and Interpretation," 160, suggests that "[o]n the basis of current theory, one would expect medieval compilers and scribes to have been much more restrained about changing Latin works than they were about tinkering with vernacular ones. For one thing, the languages themselves were sharply differentiated in medieval people's experience. Insofar as Latin was the domain of learned literacy, with well-established rules and fixed standards of correctness, it cannot have invited scribal revision and updating as the relative orality and fluidity of medieval vernaculars did. In addition, Latin texts may have been protected against scribal change by the special prestige of Latin as the language of antiquity and *auctoritas*." But see now Olsen, "Proteus in Latin," and Ziolkowski, "Oral-Formulaic Tradition."

78. Bäuml, "Unmaking," 89; emphasis in original.

79. Cf. Havelock, *Preface to Plato;* Harwood, "Alliterative *Morte Arthure.*"

80. Houston, *Literacy in Early Modern Europe,* 1.

81. See further Rosalind Thomas, *Literacy and Orality,* 52–73, 128–57.

82. James Campbell, *Anglo-Saxons,* 22.

83. Liestøl, "Correspondence," 27, argues that runes were important devices for communication in twelfth-century Scandinavia and notes that they "must have been generally known and used by members of all social classes," although he admits that "it is impossible to say" how long they were so used and what precise functions they served. We cannot draw a direct parallel between twelfth-century Scandinavia and early Anglo-Saxon England, but this evidence is suggestive and may well point to some of the uses to which runes were put in the developing Anglo-Saxon culture. On the development and uses of runes in the period, see further, Parsons, *Recasting the Runes,* 16–26.

84. Lerer, *Literacy and Power,* 16, argues that even though "runes as a living, working script died out early in the Anglo-Saxon period" they continued to serve as "one more system of scriptorial cryptography: a way of coding messages or numbering the pages of books written by the scribes of Christian doctrine." O'Brien O'Keeffe, *Visible Song,* 58, similarly argues that the Pater Noster's being written in paired runic and Roman letters "adds another stratum to the meaning of the poem" because the "Pater Noster is silently spelled out in what were esoteric, powerful characters." For a contrasting view, see Wormald, who contends in "Anglo-Saxon Society," 9, that in Anglo-Saxon England, "Substantial written composition must be the work of Christians, because the runes used by pagans were not (so far as is known) deployed at length." For a recent reconsideration of runic writing in England, see Parsons, *Recasting the Runes,* esp. 101–29, who argues that the newly established Anglo-Saxon Church influenced a conscious reform of the Anglo-Saxon runic alphabet.

85. Radio, television, and films, for example, provide nonliterates with ready access to the world of print. Similarly, many banks are equipped with special machines that check the thumbprints of those who cannot endorse their checks with a signature.

86. See further Fish, "Interpreting the *Variorum*," 171–73.

87. Stock, *Listening for the Text*, 37.

88. Drawing largely upon the Anglo-Saxon charters, Kelly, "Anglo-Saxon Lay Society," 62, demonstrates that "English had been used since the seventh century to record material of lay interest." Cf. McKitterick, "Introduction," and, on the vernacular's role in Anglo-Saxon schools, G. Brown, "Dynamics of Literacy."

89. Kelly, "Anglo-Saxon Lay Society," 52.

90. On the use of documents as an index for the growth of literacy, see Clanchy, *From Memory*, 2–80.

91. Arngart argues, in *Leningrad Bede*, 13, that the St. Petersburg manuscript "was executed within fifteen years of the completion by Bede of his History and by all accounts only nine years later" than the Moore MS which is generally dated to 737. But see Parkes, "Scriptorium of Wearmouth-Jarrow," who suggests that the St. Petersburg Bede may be the older of the two. See further Fulk, *History of Old English Meter*, 426–28.

92. O'Brien O'Keeffe notes, in *Visible Song*, 33, that of the four scribes whose work is visible in the St. Petersburg Bede, the "stints of the first two scribes, which supply the first eight quires, are clearly later than the work of scribes C and D." This point is especially important, for the work "of scribes C and D may, therefore, well be the oldest witness to the text of the *Historia ecclesiastica* in existence" (33). Scribe D is also, significantly, the one who copies the section of the *Historia* that contains Bede's "epanaleptic alphabetic acrostic distichs on St. Æthelthryth," a complex poem "which shows early development of [the] graphic conventions" of inscribing Latin verse (28). Robinson and Stanley, *Old English Verse Texts*, 2.1–2.21, reproduce facsimiles of all the manuscript pages containing vernacular versions of the poem.

93. The hands of four scribes, known as A, B, C, and D, can be detected in the manuscript. Although the *Hymn* is generally accepted as being in scribe D's hand, Kiernan has recently called this attribution into question. To Kiernan, "Reading," 172n16, the vernacular poem appears to have been added to the manuscript later (something that its situation in the margin of fol. 107r strongly suggests) "by a different scribe with similar but not identical handwriting."

94. There is much evidence of corrections by the four scribal hands, as well as by many later hands, but the chronological notices and dates found on fol. 159 are the only other noteworthy marginalia in the manuscript.

95. See O'Brien O'Keeffe, *Visible Song*, 43–61, and Kiernan, "Reading," for important discussions of the *Hymn*'s manuscript history.

96. Regarding his version, Bede tells us, in *Historia Ecclesiastica*, 416/417, that "Hic est sensus, non autem ordo ipse uerborum, quae dormiens ille canebat; neque enim possunt carmina, quamuis optime conposita, ex alia in aliam linguam ad uerbum sine detrimento sui decoris ac dignitatis transferri" [This is the sense but not the order of the words which he sang as he slept. For it is not possible to translate verse,

however well composed, literally from one language to another without some loss of beauty and dignity].

97. Irvine, "Medieval Textuality," 185. Too much ought not be made of the *Hymn*'s quite literal marginalization. Irvine, "Bede the Grammarian," 28n28, points to the great importance that attended glosses in the Middle Ages when he notes that the format of many ninth- to eleventh-century grammatical and literary manuscripts "shows that the gloss was an integral feature of the book." See also Irvine, *Making of Textual Culture*, 371–94, and Hasenohr, "Discours vernaculaire," 298–303.

98. As Wormald, "Anglo-Saxon Society," 17, notes, "[T]he Anglo-Saxons set out the awesome obligations of a holy society in vernacular literature and legislation which at this time has no European parallel." See Karen Quinn and Kenneth Quinn, *Manual,* 1–29, for a list of manuscripts containing Anglo-Saxon prose and Ker, "Supplement."

99. Foley, *Singer of Tales in Performance,* 75.

100. Zumthor, "Impossible Closure," 32, notes that the effects of printing on the Middle Ages, of colonization in Africa, and of the computer in the Western world are all "strong cultural trauma[s]," but he significantly does not include the effect of the technology of writing on the early medieval English manuscript culture as another example of such "trauma."

101. For an opposing view, see, among others, Jabbour, "Memorial Transmission," 181, who argues that there "can be no transitional stage moving from oral to written tradition. The introduction of writing comes, so to speak, at a stroke."

102. Rosalind Thomas, *Oral Tradition,* 34, makes a similar point with regard to the interaction of orality and literacy in ancient Greece when she argues that the "mere presence of writing [was] not enough to prompt its widespread use. Moreover, written and oral methods of communication or validation may exist side by side for a considerable time after the influx of writing. The old oral methods [were] not abandoned immediately, if indeed at all."

103. Ong, *Orality and Literacy,* 82.

104. Mendoza, *Talking Books,* 1–18, discusses this trope from the perspective of ethnopoetics.

105. Such is also the case in the medieval period. See, for example, the Old English riddles contained in the Exeter Book MS, 3501, Exeter, Cathedral Chapter Library.

106. Cf. Havelock, "Preliteracy of the Greeks."

107. Even for private readers during the Middle Ages, subvocalization was a standard practice. As Ziolkowski, "Cultural Diglossia," 195–96, suggests, "[T]he act of reading itself was both intensely oral and visual; a text was read not simply through being scanned with the eyes, but also through being mouthed or sounded aloud." On reading in the Middle Ages, see also Clanchy, *From Memory,* 253–93 (esp. 266–72); Illich, *In the Vineyard,* 35–39; Janet Coleman, *Medieval Readers;* and Saenger, "Silent Reading" and *Space between Words,* 1–17, 273–76.

108. The visual remained important throughout the period, however. Clanchy, *From Memory*, 253–60, notes that objects with significative force were often attached to documents.

109. This is perhaps the essence of the Lollards' threat: as Janet Coleman, *Medieval Readers*, 209, notes, "*De Hereticao Comburendo*, which brought in the death penalty for Lollard heretics, drew attention to lay literacy as a fundamental aspect of their sedition: 'They make unlawful conventicles and confederacies, they hold and exercise schools, they make and write books, they do wickedly instruct and inform people.'" See also Hudson, *Selections from English Wycliffite Writings*, 13, who argues that "the English texts [of Wyclif and his followers] are of crucial importance: they used, in a way that had not systematically been attempted since the days of Ælfric, the vernacular for the discussion of theological and political topics. To contemporary opponents, as the discussion of the biblical translation between 1390 and 1410 makes clear, this was a major charge against the Lollards: to those interested in the development of English as a medium for literature and education, on the other hand, it is their greatest achievement."

110. I follow Zumthor's use of this term as outlined in *La lettre et la voix*. See Schaefer's discussion in "Hearing from Books," 18, and "Alterities." Jager, "Speech and the Chest," has proposed the term "pectorality" as a supplement to "orality."

111. John of Salisbury, *Metalogicon*, I, chap. 13, Hall and Keats-Rohan's edition: frequenter absentium dicta sine voce loquuntur.

112. To cite just one example, Fry, "Cædmon as a Formulaic Poet," 41, contends that in the Old English poetic corpus "only *Cædmon's Hymn* can confidently be called oral." He discounts the orality of Bede's *Death Song* because it appears not to have been produced during a performance but rather "may have been written ahead of time and recited from memory." See below, note 126.

113. For Kiernan, "Reading," 158, this narrative strategy on Bede's part reveals that he "never had any intention of preserving the original Old English version. To put it bluntly, English literature did not for Bede fit into the grand scheme of things."

114. Quo accepto responso, statim ipse coepit cantare in laudem Dei Conditoris uersus quos numquam audierat, quorum iste est sensus (416).

115. For discussions of the three major changes that the late Old English translator makes in Bede's text, see Kiernan, "Reading," 165, and Dobbie, *Manuscripts of Cædmon's Hymn*, 22–23.

116. [N]eque enim possunt carmina, quamuis optime conposita, ex alia in aliam linguam ad uerbum sine detrimento sui decoris ac dignitatis transferri (416).

117. Arngart, *Leningrad Bede*, 30–31, summarily dismisses this view. Frantzen, *Desire for Origins*, 146, concludes that should the vernacular *Hymn* prove to be a translation from Bede's Latin, "Old English literary history will be in for a refreshing period of revision of some of its most cherished commonplaces about translation and Cædmon's contributions to the tradition." See further Fry, "Cædmon as a Formulaic Poet," 42n10.

118. As Benson, "Literary Character," 341n30, notes, "If William of Malmesbury can be trusted, then it is possible that Aldhelm was an oral singer. . . . If so, literacy and oral verse-making co-existed from very early times in England. It is equally possible that Aldhelm wrote his poems, since, again on William's authority, they survived in manuscript until at least the time of Alfred, who regarded Aldhelm as the best poet of his age." On Aldhelm writing out his own work, see the prose *De Virginitate*, LX, trans. Lapidge and Herren, in *Aldhelm: The Prose Works*, 130–32.

119. Cf. Frantzen's deconstructive reading of Bede's tale, in *Desire for Origins*, 130–67, as well as Frank, "Search" 29–30. Fry, "Cædmon as a Formulaic Poet," 46n21, cites some earlier criticism that is skeptical of Bede's account.

120. Frantzen, *Desire for Origins*, 144.

121. Rosenthal, "Bede's *Ecclesiastical History*," 3.

122. Bede further secures Cædmon's position as the font of vernacular poetry by claiming, "It is true that after him other Englishmen attempted to compose religious poems, but none could compare with him" [Et quidem et alii post illum in gente Anglorum religiosa poemata facere temtabant, sed nullus eum aequiperare potuit] (415/414).

123. See Clanchy, *From Memory*, 125–26, 270–72.

124. Ibid., 270–71.

125. Bernardo Gui, "Life of St. Thomas Aquinas," cited in Carruthers, *Book of Memory*, 3.

126. See Carruthers, *Book of Memory*, 4–7, 22–28. Finnegan, *Oral Poetry*, 134–69, has shown that a good deal of oral poetry is composed carefully beforehand, sometimes as the product of a group effort, and then presented orally in just the way literate authors of the Middle Ages would compose their thoughts internally and then dictate the finished product to their scribes. Although there is insufficient evidence to judge whether such was the case in the Middle Ages, Finnegan's point and its possible applicability to the medieval English oral tradition need to be borne in mind. Magoun's comments on the blind Milton's compositional practices in "Bede's Story of Cædmon," 53 and n12, are also instructive in this regard.

127. See Niles, *Homo Narrans*, 89–119, for a discussion of these types of collaborations, which he labels "oral poetry acts." As we move beyond the Anglo-Saxon period, the model of inscription through dictation becomes less and less viable because authors increasingly come to compose pen in hand, in private. For example, A. Edwards and Pearsall note in "Manuscripts," 259, that Chaucer appears to have had "the *Boece* and *Troilus* professionally copied, and that the copy (with exemplar) was then returned to him so that he could correct it, and that this procedure might be repeated with the same scribe," a procedure that reflects current practice in the world of publishing.

128. Canebat autem de creatione mundi et origine humani generis et tota Genesis historia, de egressu Israel ex Aegypto et ingressu in terram repromissionis, de aliis plurimis sacrae scripturae historiis, de incarnatione dominica, passione, resurrectione

et ascensione in cælum, de Spiritus Sancti aduentu et apostolorum doctrina; item de terrore futuri iudicii et horrore poenae gehennalis ac dulcedine regni caelestis multa carmina faciebat. Sed et alia perplura de beneficiis et iudiciis diuinis, in quibus cunctis homines ab amore scelerum abstrahere, ad dilectionem uero et sollertiam bonae actionis excitare curabat (418).

129. The strategy employed by Abbess Hild and the monks at Whitby appears to be much more sound than that which Aldhelm may have employed. Although the evidence is not beyond dispute, for Aldhelm the vernacular may have served only as the vehicle with which to catch his audience's attention. Having drawn his audience into the churches, Aldhelm may then have abandoned tales offered in "ludicra verbis" (in the vernacular?) in favor of more strictly doctrinal material. But see Fry, "Cædmon as a Formulaic Poet," 46, who comments that whether the story of Aldhelm's singing on the bridge "means Aldhelm used Christian diction in vernacular poetry or that he recited secular poems as bait and switched to Christian preaching separately remains uncertain." See the discussion of Aldhelm earlier in this chapter in the section "The Diglossic Medieval World."

130. Erat enim uir multum religiosus et regularibus disciplinis humiliter subditus; aduersum uero illos, qui aliter facere uolebant, zelo magni feruoris accensus (418).

131. Magoun, "Bede's Story of Cædmon," 57. But see Fritz, "Cædmon," 334, who argues that Cædmon's choice of subject matter "places him immediately within the tradition of Christian-Latin poets beginning with Commodian in the third century."

132. Jackson J. Campbell, "Oral Poetry," 88.

133. See, for example, Foley, "Formula and Theme," 220, 231, and Opland, "*Scop and Imbongi.*"

134. See esp. Lord, "Merging of Two Worlds" and "Homer as an Oral-Traditional Poet."

135. Lord, *Singer of Tales,* 129; emphasis in original. In "Homer as an Oral-Traditional Poet," 79, Lord contrasts oral poetics with the "written literary nontraditional poetics" that informs the works of authors such as Ezra Pound and T. S. Eliot and concludes that the "very self-conscious way [such literate poets construct their texts] . . . argues an attitude toward a text that is not part of the mentality, or 'mindset,' of oral-traditional poets."

136. We must, of course, approach the evidence these poems offer on this matter with caution. The *Beowulf*-poet's depiction of scops actively composing does not mean that such a mode of composition was still current but may simply reflect the poet's idealized and fictionalized version of past practices. See Amodio, "Res(is)ting the Singer."

137. Foley, "Orality, Textuality," 38.

138. On the performance arena, see Foley, *Singer of Tales in Performance,* 47–49.

139. This is not to imply that these poets did not disseminate their works orally, either by reading them or performing them from memory, a process in which we nec-

essarily encounter variation, but of a different sort from the type we discover when the poetry is (re)composed during performance because for these poets composition and performance were markedly discrete endeavors. On the types of variation associated with memorial presentations, see McGillivray, *Memorization.*

140. Magoun, "Bede's Story of Cædmon," 60, makes the similar point that "[a] lettered singer, say, Cynewulf," had to engage the oral tradition—and its specialized poetics—because it was "probably the only way an Anglo-Saxon could conceive of composing narrative verse," although he does not pursue the matter beyond this.

141. See the studies in Griffiths and Pearsall, *Book Production.*

142. Blake, "Manuscript to Print," 404.

143. Ibid., 403. The aesthetics of the book has been relatively stable since the first manuscripts were written, although hypertext is currently challenging it. For the first time, books no longer have the sort of physicality they have always possessed in print culture but can now exist completely outside it as constellations of electronic impulses.

144. Opland, "From Horseback," 30.

145. Lord's comparison in *Singer of Tales,* 35–36, of the specialized nature of the performance-based tradition he explored with natural grammar applies equally well to nonperformative poetics: "[I]n studying the patterns and systems of oral narrative verse we are in reality observing the 'grammar' of the poetry, a grammar superimposed, as it were, on the grammar of the language concerned. Or, to alter the image, we find a special grammar within the grammar of the language, necessitated by the versification. The formulas are the phrases and clauses and sentences of this specialized poetic grammar. The speaker of this language, once he has mastered it, does not move any more mechanically within it than we do in ordinary speech."

146. Foley, *Immanent Art,* 7.

147. See also Kellogg, "Oral Literature," and Andersen, *Commonplace and Creativity,* esp. 17–29.

148. Ólason, "Literary Backgrounds," 122.

149. In the case of the ballads, especially those that consciously draw upon the ballad tradition, the intended audience may not have a particularly close connection to the tradition. For example, as Würzbach notes in "Tradition and Innovation," 189, Bob Dylan's song "A Hard Rain's A Gonna Fall" derives its structure from the ballad tradition (being particularly close to "Lord Randall") but subtly transforms the "procedures typical of the traditional ballad" in large part so it can conform to the expectations of the contemporary audience at which it was aimed. On contemporary Scottish ballads, see Niles, *Homo Narrans;* Andersen, *Commonplace and Creativity;* and the essays collected in Harris, *Ballad and Oral Literature.*

150. Ólason, "Literary Backgrounds," 118.

151. O'Brien O'Keeffe, *Visible Song,* 41. Doane's theory of "reperformance" ("Oral Texts, Intertexts," 80–81) and Bradbury's theory of "resinging" ("Literacy, Orality" and *Writing Aloud,* 90–93) are complementary to O'Brien O'Keeffe's.

152. Fry anticipates this when he explains the miracle of Cædmon's gift of poetry in "Cædmon as a Formulaic Poet," 47, "in terms of unconscious absorption of formulaic diction." See also Magoun, "Bede's Story of Cædmon," 58.

153. As Frank, "Search," 28, reminds us, "Historical imagination, the ability to paint the past as if it were something other than the present, did not have to wait until modern times to be born. The poets of Anglo-Saxon England were just as free as those in the eighteenth century to stress the differences between ancient days and the present."

T W O . Anglo-Saxon Oral Poetics

1. As Howe, *Migration*, 5, notes, "[F]or the Anglo-Saxons, there was considerable evidence that they were a loose amalgam of shifting kingdoms and dialect groups rather than a cohesive people." See also Foote, "Making of *Angelcynn*," and Wormald, "*Engla lond*," on "Britain."

2. Although *bretwalda* is the widely used term, Bosworth and Toller, *Anglo-Saxon Dictionary,* s.v., argues that "its more correct form appears to be bryten-walda," a claim supported by the DOE's entry for *bryten-anwealda*. Of the five Chronicle occurrences of this term, *bretwalda* appears only in A 827.4. As the editors of the DOE note, s.v., "[T]he etymology of the first element is not clear; *brytenanwalda* (from *bryten* 'spacious, wide') suggests 'king over a spacious realm', but it may be derived from or influenced by *Bryten* 'Britain.'" See further James Campbell, *Anglo-Saxons*, 53–59, 99–100, and Fanning, "Bede, *Imperium*, and the Bretwaldas."

3. While there is evidence of some widely shared tendencies that set it apart from the prose, Mitchell, *Old English Syntax*, II, 989, notes that Old English poetic syntax retains many "ordinary prose patterns." See also F. Cassidy, "How Free?"

4. Watts, *Lyre and the Harp,* 47.

5. A. Campbell, *Old English Grammar*, 10. See also Sisam, "Dialect Origins," 138, and esp. Foley, *Traditional Oral Epic*, 9–12, 171–200. Like the Homeric *Kunstsprache*, the Anglo-Saxon poetic lexicon was a rich, flexible tool that was never a part of the language of daily discourse. Because Kirk's comments in *Homer*, 4, on the character of the highly specialized Homeric idiom bear directly upon the language of Old English poetry, they merit a full presentation: "It is an artificial, poetical construction containing elements both of vocabulary and of phraseology that originated at different dates over a [considerable] period. . . . Some parts of it are highly conventional and consist of fixed or formular phrases, each designed to express a particular idea within the limits of a particular rhythmical impulse. The famous fixed epithets—goodly Odysseus, king of men Agamemnon, black ship, well-built hall, windy Troy and so on—are merely the most prominent aspect of a highly developed *system* of formular language that allowed the unlettered singer to develop a poem of a length and complexity far beyond

the range of one who selects each word anew and for itself alone." But see Blake's objections, in "Dating of Old English Poetry," 16–17, to Sisam's "proposal that [Old English poetry] was written in a literary *koine* which did not represent any one dialect but included elements from them all."

6. Bliss, *Introduction to Old English Metre,* 23, notes, however, that "this single meter can take different forms, more or less strict." The hypermetric and rhyming passages constitute only a fraction of all surviving Old English poetic lines. Cf. Bliss, "Origin and Structure," and Hieatt, "Alliterative Patterns." On rhyme in Old English poetry, see Stanley, "Rhymes in English Medieval Verse," and Macrae-Gibson, *Old English Riming Poem.*

7. Bliss, *Introduction to Old English Metre,* 23.

8. The meter of the lyrics ranged from the simple repetition of a single measure to complex combinations such as the archilochean dicolon and dactylo-epitrites in which two diverse cola combine to create the line's rhythm. See further West, *Greek Metre,* 138–52, and Bowra, *Greek Lyric Poetry.* On phraseology found in different genres that employ hexametrical diction, see Foley, "How Genres Leak."

9. See Foley, *Traditional Oral Epic,* 85, and Stoltz, "Oral Epic Verses."

10. On the South Slavic lyric meter, see Foley, *Immanent Art,* 192n4. Lord discusses the diachrony of South Slavic meter in "Merging of Two Worlds," 24–30.

11. Stanley, "Unideal Principles," 273.

12. But see now the essays collected in Keefer and O'Brien O'Keeffe, *New Approaches,* and Robinson, *Editing of Old English.*

13. *Rex* occurs some twenty-three times in the prose.

14. See Kiernan, "Old English Manuscripts."

15. Following Dobbie, *Manuscripts of Cædmon's Hymn,* I print the poem in half-lines for comparison.

16. On the date of the Moore Bede, which is generally accepted as having been written in the first part of the eighth century, see Ker, *Catalogue;* Fulk, *History of Old English Meter,* 426–28; and Gneuss, *Handlist,* item 25. On the Tanner Bede, which is generally dated to the early tenth century, see Bately, *Tanner Bede,* 33.

17. In both cases I have silently removed all editorial capitalization and punctuation. See Dobbie, *Manuscripts of Cædmon's Hymn,* for a discussion of these and the other extant versions of the *Hymn.* For a list of the manuscripts, see 8–9.

18. For different approaches to Cædmon's poem, see O'Brien O'Keeffe, *Visible Song,* 23–46; Lerer, *Literacy and Power,* esp. 33–48; and Frantzen, *Desire for Origins,* 130–67.

19. For recent studies of the Ruthwell Cross, see the papers collected in B. Cassidy, *Ruthwell Cross.* The late-tenth-century Brussels Cross has inscribed upon it two lines that are reminiscent of the poem as well.

20. Cf. Stanley, however, who argues, in "Unideal Principles," 232, that the two rood poems, Riddle 35, and the Leiden Riddle constitute "peculiar cases and hardly

allow of the proper deployment of the procedures of textual scholarship, peculiar, that is, because the history of their transmission from pre-tenth century Northumbrian to late West Saxon, though considered by many to be typical for Old English verse in general, is not attested by more than one earlier Northumbrian and one later West-Saxon witness for each."

21. I cite the *Dream of the Rood* and the Ruthwell inscription from *ASPR*, II and VI, but have silently dropped the macrons from Dobbie's edition of the Ruthwell inscription.

22. This is an illustrative, not exhaustive, list of the parallels between the two texts.

23. For more detailed discussions of the Old English formula and formulaic systems, see, among others, Lord, *Singer of Tales,* 30–67; Fry, "Old English Formulas and Systems," "Some Aesthetic Implications," and "Old English Formulaic Statistics"; Niles, *Beowulf,* 121–37; Foley, *Traditional Oral Epic,* 52–239; Riedinger, "Old English Formula" and "Formulaic Relationship"; and the essays collected in Stoltz and Shannon, *Oral Literature.*

24. It appears in the a-verse seven times, but this difference does not bear on the point at hand. The other poems in which this phrase appears are *Genesis A* (4), the *Metrical Charms* (1), *Exodus* (1), *Daniel* (3), *Andreas* (2), *Dream of the Rood* (1), *Elene* (2), *Guthlac A* (2), *Juliana* (1), the *Metrical Psalms* (2), *Menologium* (1), and *Judgment Day II* (1). The parenthetical figures indicate the number of occurrences in each poem. All citations for *Cædmon's Hymn* and the other poems listed here are to the *ASPR* edition: *Daniel, Exodus,* and *Genesis A* are in vol. I; *Andreas, Elene,* and *Dream of the Rood* in vol II; *Juliana* and *Guthlac A* in vol. III; *Metrical Psalms* in vol. V; and *Cædmon's Hymn, Judgment Day II, Metrical Charms,* and *Manologium* in vol. VI.

25. The majority of these occurrences (41) are found in the *Metrical Psalms,* which perhaps ought to be counted as one poem. But even if we count the *Metrical Psalms* as only one poem, the phrase appears in some sixteen texts, among which are *Genesis A* (9), *Christ* and *Satan* (8), *Daniel* (6), and *Beowulf* (1). *Christ and Satan* is in *ASPR,* I; all citations to *Beowulf* are to Klaeber's edition unless otherwise noted.

26. Cable has called into question the stress-based, alliterative foundation of Anglo-Saxon meter and has posed an alliterative-syllabic model (in which the latter's importance far outweighs the former's), but his contention, in *English Alliterative Tradition,* 132, that "alliteration is superficial" and serves chiefly as a "useful classifying rubric" has not won widespread support. Hickes, cited in Conybeare, *Illustrations,* v–vi, was among the first to suggest that Anglo-Saxon poets "observed the legitimate rules of Latin prosody, and measured their feet by syllabic quantity."

27. Foley, *Traditional Oral Epic,* 331–32, lists the themes that have so far been identified in Old English poetry along with a selective bibliography.

28. Robinson and Stanley, *Old English Verse Texts,* suggest that two short Old English poems, the *Leiden Riddle* (found on folio 12v of Leiden, Rijksuniversiteit, Vos-

sianus Lat. 40 106 [Ker, *Catalogue,* app. No. 19]) and the *Gloria II* (found on folios 55v–56v of London, British Library, Cotton Titus D. xxvii [Ker, *Catalogue,* no. 202]) may be lineated as poetry, but the evidence is finally inconclusive. See further O'Brien O'Keeffe's discussion of the *Leiden Riddle* in *Visible Song,* 142n12. Robinson and Stanley reprint facsimiles of these folios as items 4 and 29.1–29.3, respectively. Even if we were to grant that these poems are lineated as poetry in their manuscripts, they would stand in sharp contrast to the remainder of the Old English poetic corpus as the only extant witnesses to this type of encoding and hence would have to be judged as highly idiosyncratic departures from usual practice.

29. Irvine, "Medieval Textuality," 184.

30. Irvine, "Bede the Grammarian," 16n6, defines *grammatica* as that "whole discipline devoted to literacy and the study of literary texts, including principles for exegesis." See also Irvine, *Making of Textual Culture,* 1–22 *et passim.*

31. A good example of the prominence accorded performance is offered by Knight who observes in "Oral Transmission," 170n7, that "although Lord is mostly talking about orally composed poetry, he shows that oral *performance* is the key to the larger structural idiosyncrasies of oral poetry (that is, idiosyncrasies larger than the so-called formula) and this we can assume in the case of *Sir Launfal*" (emphasis in original), a written, Middle English romance.

32. Lord, *Singer of Tales,* 13–29.

33. See Opland, *Xhosa Oral Poetry,* 57–89.

34. On performance in African traditions, see Opland, ibid., and the essays collected in Haring, *African Oral Traditions.*

35. Lerer, *Literacy and Power,* 33.

36. I cite the Old English version of Bede's *Historia Ecclesiastica* from T. Miller's edition (*Old English Version*).

37. I cite the Latin text and English translation of Bede's *Historia Ecclesiastica* from Colgrave and Mynors' edition (*Bede's Ecclesiastical History*).

38. "Oral composition" remains a slippery phrase that encompasses any number of different models of poetic production. Finnegan, *Oral Poetry,* 71, notes that some "oral composition" "is almost entirely oral, in the way that many Yugoslav singers composed/performed; but some may be based more or less directly on a written text (and this happens more often than is sometimes remembered with Yugoslav poetry) but is nevertheless recited orally. Other poems may be composed with oral performance as the aim, or composed without the initial use of writing for later written publication, or be specially dictated to a literate assistant—and so on." See Amodio, "Res(is)ting the Singer," for a discussion of the problematics that attend the representation of scopic activity in Old English poetry.

39. Finnegan, *Oral Poetry,* esp. 88–133, considers some of the many different ways performance figures in a wide variety of oral traditions.

40. And as Foley, "Word-Power," 293, argues, "The integers of expression and perception, the cognitive categories that function optimally only within the enabling event of performance, retain in their textual forms a rhetorical vestige of that performance that cannot be ignored." While agreeing with him, I would further stress that entexted oral elements play a dynamic and not vestigial role. See further Foley, *Singer of Tales*, 60–98.

41. The view that Anglo-Saxon oral poetics is a richly associative, highly significative idiom can be traced back at least as far as Creed, who, writing in 1961, argued in "On the Possibility," 101, that "every time a singer performs the same theme he and his audience hear and appreciate that performance against the music of all other performances of that theme." He further pointed to the associative dimension of traditional oral expression when he claimed that the "audience—singer included—*hears* each new performance of a theme *counterpointed* against all the old performances it has heard" (emphasis in original).

42. Foley, "Word-Power," 287. Although for Foley, this register remains closely linked to the act of traditional oral performance, his observations apply equally well to the register of a nonperformative oral poetics.

43. We can trace this view back to Parry's highly influential remarks in "Studies," 317, that the formulaic diction of the Homeric poems reflects "not only the desire for an easy way of making verses, but the complete need of it. . . . Without writing, the poet can make his verses only if he has a formulaic diction which will give him his phrases all made, and made in such a way that, at the slightest bidding of the poet, they will link themselves in an unbroken pattern that will fill his verses and make his sentences."

44. "In geardagum" finds close parallels in the phrase "on fyrndagum" [in ancient days] of *Andreas*, 1b and *Vainglory*, 1b. For *Vainglory*, see *ASPR*, III.

45. On deictic indicators, see Lyons, *Semantics*, 677–703.

46. Orwell, "Politics and the English Language," 159.

47. Parks discusses this pattern more fully in "Traditional Narrator."

48. Foley, *Immanent Art*, 23.

49. Finnegan, *Literacy and Orality*, 124–25, stresses the interdependence of oral poetics and performance in arguing that the "style of delivery (tempo, mood, dynamics or tone, to mention just some aspects), the drama and characterization conveyed by the performer, the audience's involvement through interjections, responses, verbal interplay or choral participation in response to the main performer's lead—all these are not extra, optional embellishments, as they might seem if we follow a written paradigm, but a central constituent of the literary act." In this, she follows Foley, Richard Bauman, Dell Hymes, Dennis Tedlock, and Dan Ben-Amos, among others, who increasingly are expanding the scope of oral theory by bringing to their studies insights derived from ethnopoetics and the ethnography of speaking.

50. Renoir, "Oral-Formulaic Rhetoric," 135.

51. Stock, *Listening for the Text*, 164.

52. Pasternack, *Textuality*, 8, takes a similar approach, arguing that "inscribed verse lays itself open to recomposition by subsequent poets" and that "in certain respects scribes and readers could function as poets themselves."

53. O'Brien O'Keeffe, *Visible Song*, 41.

54. Moffatt, "Anglo-Saxon Scribes," 812.

55. Ibid., 811.

56. Stanley, "Unideal Priniciples," 256.

57. See Moffat, "Anglo-Saxon Scribes," 808–14; Patterson, *Negotiating the Past*, 77–113; and Stanley, "Unideal Principles."

58. Doane, "Oral Texts, Intertexts," 80–81.

59. Moffat, "Anglo-Saxon Scribes," 827.

60. Noteworthy exceptions are Finnegan, *Literacy and Orality*, 59–85; Bäuml, "Varieties," 260 ff.; Andersson, "Tradition and Design"; and Creed, "Remaking of *Beowulf*." But even these studies depend to varying degrees upon a conception of the tradition as something static and monolithic. For example, while Creed argues, in "Remaking of *Beowulf*," 136, that the *Beowulf*-poet "radically reshaped the tradition," he asserts that the poet was motivated to do so "in order to preserve it."

61. Fry, "Old English Formulaic Statistics," 3.

62. Dronke, *Poetic Individuality*, 11, makes a closely related point when he argues that a "poetic tradition has no deterministic power over the poets of individual talent who take that tradition as their point of departure."

63. These poems are *Elene, Juliana, Christ II*, and the *Fates of the Apostles.*

64. Donoghue argues, in *Style in Old English Poetry*, 113, that "there is considerable evidence for distinguishing the style of *Christ II* from that of *Elene* and *Juliana*: the six tables for auxiliaries, Sharon Butler's corrected tables, and a number of observations from literary critics. The *Fates* is also distinct—unlike any of the other three signed poems in the six tables." Calder, *Cynewulf*, 143, detects a "marked variety" in the Cynewulfian canon, one that suggests that "for Cynewulf each poem was a conscious experiment, that within the limits of his inherited stylistic traditions and the restrictions of his own habitual manner of expression, Cynewulf attempted something quite different in each work and did so in a distinctly individual way." Among those who see more homogeneity in Cynewulf's verse, see Fulk, *History of Old English Meter*, 31–68, who questions "whether the incidence of auxiliaries and initial auxiliaries is an accurate gauge of authorial difference" (64n75), and "Cynewulf: Canon, Dialect, and Date," as well as Orchard, "Both Style and Substance," who sees in the poems' formulas, many of which he notes are unique to the Cynewulf canon, a uniformity of diction and stylistics that leads him to conclude that "the four signed poems are indeed what they appear to be: the finished products of a single poet." I am indebted to Andy Orchard for making a prepublication copy of this article available to me.

65. See Foley, *Traditional Oral Epic*, 158–200, who considers the idiolectal traditional language of a South Slavic oral singer against the dialectal idiom of the singer's region and the pan-traditional language of the larger, multiregional area.

66. As Donoghue, *Style in Old English Poetry*, demonstrates, syntactic patterns serve as important indicators of individual style. Similarly, Kendall, *Metrical Grammar*, 10, argues that "[n]o two scops' metrical grammars would have been exactly alike; in addition to individual differences, there must have been regional and dialectal variations, although the poetic tradition ensured remarkable uniformity over a wide area and a considerable period of time, and only at the end of the Old English period, with let us say, *The Battle of Maldon*, are significant changes manifest." See now Orchard, "Both Style and Substance," who offers compelling evidence concerning the evidence of Cynewulf's idiopoetics in all four poems attributed to him.

67. The place of the individual poet within oral theory has not attracted very much attention. Parry early on denied the possibility of individuality within the Homeric idiom in "Studies," 317, and Lord, "Composition by Theme," 73, relegated it to something of an afterthought: "[E]ven as [a singer's] knowledge of formulas . . . is sharpened to precision by the act of singing his first song, so his idea of themes is given shape as he learns new songs and perhaps ultimately creates songs of his own."

68. Benson, "Originality of *Beowulf*," 43.

69. See Lindow, *Comitatus, Individual and Honor*, 10–41. Woolf notes, in "Ideal," 63, that both Caesar and Sallust comment upon "the heroic duty of a warrior to die with his lord," but in her view, Tacitus's several short chapters "provide the fullest description of this institution and its operation in Gmc. times" (11).

70. I cite Tacitus from Furneaux's edition.

71. I cite the Anglo-Saxon Chronicle from Bately's edition of MS A. For a fuller treatment of the episode's historical and political dimensions, see S. White, "Kinship and Lordship."

72. Woolf, "Ideal," 81, argues to the contrary that the "ideal of a man dying with his lord . . . was not an ancient and traditional commonplace of Old English heroic poetry." But see Frank, "*Battle of Maldon*," 197, who points to the cross-cultural currency of this ideal when she notes that classical "ethnographies and histories in the century and a half between Caesar and Tacitus report that not only Germanic, but also Celtic, Persian and Macedonian warriors preferred to die rather than survive a slain lord; Old Testament narratives from the same period depict the loyalty and martyrdom of the seven Macabees and their mother, exhorting one another to die nobly and heroically for a transcendent law." See also Frank, "Germanic Legend" and "Ideal of Men," and Stephen Evans, *Lords of Battle*.

73. Although the poem can be dated with confidence to some time after the battle it commemorates, the evidence afforded by the poem itself must be approached with caution, as the manuscript that contained it (London, British Library, Cotton

Otho A. xii, art.3) was among those lost in the Cottonian fire of 1731. Because of this, we have had to rely since then exclusively on the transcript David Casley made several years before the fire. On dating the poem, see McKinnell, "On the Date," and Anderson, "*Battle of Maldon.*" Clark, "On Dating," and Scragg, *Battle of Maldon,* both disagree substantially with McKinnell's late dating. Clark argues that the meaning of Old English *eorl* in the "technical sense 'ealdormann'" does not arise in the post-Cnutian period as "a result of semantic borrowing from Scandinavian *jarl,*" as McKinnell suggests, but that the colloquial meaning of *eorl* as "'our own leader' had [been current] during the tenth century" (1). Similarly, Scragg, *Battle of Maldon,* 27, argues that the *Maldon*-poet's use of *ealdorman* "as a title, though technically improper by the standards of the south and west, may have been influenced by poetic needs and should not be seen as proof of composition long after the battle took place."

74. All citations of *Battle of Maldon* are from Scragg's edition (*Battle of Maldon A.D. 991*).

75. While noting that it is usual for a lord to distribute treasure to his comitatus, Lindow, *Comitatus, Individual and Honor,* 11, stresses the reciprocal nature of the bond when he cites Tacitus's claim that "it is quite common, and, indeed, expected that [retainers] will offer gifts of grain and cattle to the chieftain." Beowulf explicitly enacts this aspect of the comitatus bond when he turns over to Hygelac everything Hrothgar gave him for dispatching the Grendelkin.

76. See, for example, *Andreas,* 405–14.

77. However, we note that the existence of a 'Beowulf Scyldinga' is not universally accepted. See Orchard, *Critical Companion to Beowulf,* who argues, 100–105, esp. 103n35, in favor of emending manuscript *Beowulf* to *Beow* at lines 18a and 53b, as many editors and translators do.

78. The most important work on Heorot's centrality to the poem's metaphorics remains Irving, *Rereading Beowulf,* 133–67, but see also Earl, "Role of the Men's Hall," and Hume, "Concept of the Hall." Cramp, "Hall in *Beowulf,*" considers the hall from an archeological perspective.

79. Beowulf offers a particularly powerful articulation of this aspect of the comitatus bond—one that recalls Leofsunu's in *Maldon* (246–48)—during the dragon fight when he announces that he will not "oferfleon fotes trem" (2525a) [flee the space of a footstep] from the "atol inwitgæst" (2670a) [terrible foe] he will soon face.

80. However, we should note that the warriors who fail to sacrifice themselves in accordance with the comitatus's ideal of heroic conduct appear not to suffer much social opprobrium, as Unferth's retention of his position as Hrothgar's þyle despite his failure to engage Grendel suggests. Even Beowulf, it should be noted, outlives two of his lords, one of whom, Hygelac, dies in a battle that Beowulf survives.

81. In addition to the instances examined above, the ideal also figures prominently in the Finnsburh episode and in Beowulf's fights with Grendel and Grendel's mother.

82. Magoun, "Theme of the Beasts," 83. In the course of his formalist analysis of the theme, Griffith, "Convention and Originality," 184, refines Magoun's summary by suggesting that "a more detailed abstract of repeated motifs can be made: 'in the wake of an army, the dark raven, the dewy-plumaged eagle and the wolf of the forest, eager for slaughter and carrion/food, give voice to their joy.'" For a list of passages containing the beasts of battle theme, see Griffith, "Convention and Originality," 181–82, and his appendix, 197–99. Other noteworthy studies of the beasts of battle theme include Renoir, "Judith," "Crist Ihesu's Beasts of Battle," and Key to Old Poems, 162–64; and Metcalf, "Ten Natural Animals."

83. Fry, "Themes and Type-Scenes," 36, stresses the theme's traditionality by arguing that it constitutes an important element of a larger narrative pattern that he labels the "approach-to-battle type-scene."

84. Ibid., 41; emphasis in original. See also Olsen, Speech, Song, 45–50, and Bonjour, "Beowulf and the Beasts," 566. For Elene, see ASPR, II.

85. Foley, Immanent Art, 225.

86. Bonjour, "Beowulf and the Beasts," 565.

87. That the beasts speak to one another about their grisly (from a human perspective) plans, something unique to Beowulf, further points the poet's innovative handling of this theme.

88. Its close association with the sea-voyage type-scene in this instance has led Olsen, "Aesthetics of Andreas," 408–9, to suggest that it ought to be classified as a unique example of what she labels the "Sea-Beasts of Battle" theme.

89. Wælgifre appears in two other occurrences of the theme in Judith at lines 207a and 295b (ASPR, IV).

90. Fry, "Themes and Type-Scenes," 37.

91. See Frank, "Skaldic Tooth," who argues that the theme is given a northern accent by the Exodus-poet.

92. In earlier times, Edgar appears to have been more warmly received. Wanley and several others who attempted to compose Old English poetry in the seventeenth century drew upon the poem as a source of diction, or in Wanley's case, for actual half-lines. See Robinson, "Afterlife of Old English," 284–89. Pearsall's comment, in Old and Middle English Poetry, 65–66, that while the poem demonstrates that the Edgar-poet "still has some inkling of what poetry is supposed to be like," on the whole "his imitation is lame and repetitive" typifies the poem's modern reception.

93. Greenfield and Calder, New Critical History, 248.

94. ASPR, VI.

95. The ealdorman Oslac, whose expulsion from his seat of power in Northumbria by the supporters of the newly crowned (and shortly to be murdered) King Edward is commemorated in this passage, appears to have been one of several powerful earls who opposed the accession of Edward and supported instead the claim of Edward's

younger brother Æthelred. See further Stenton, *Anglo-Saxon England*, 372–73, and James Campbell, *Anglo-Saxons*, 192.

96. Greenfield and Calder, *New Critical History*, 248.

97. However, while noting that the entry for 975 "in 'A', 'B', 'C' is in alliterative metre," Whitelock, *English Historical Documents*, 228n2, hastens to add that it is "of a quality to make one glad that the chroniclers mainly used prose."

98. Foley, *Traditional Oral Epic*, 201–39.

99. I cite *Fight at Finnsburh* and *Seafarer* from *ASPR*, II and III, respectively.

100. Despite the differences in these phrases, I have included them here because these are the only three occurrences of *gamolfeax* in the poetic and prosodic corpora. *Gamel* and its derivatives are rare words, occurring only twenty times. As the first element of a compound, it occurs elsewhere only in *gamolferhþ* (*Genesis A*, 2868a).

101. For discussions of this aspect of Anglo-Saxon poetics, see Robinson, *Beowulf*; Brodeur, *Art of Beowulf*, 39–70, 272–83; and Niles, *Beowulf*, 139–43.

102. The lone exception to this is *Beowulf*, 1861b, where Hrothgar employs the phrase positively.

103. Although generally critical of *Edgar*'s poetic achievement, and although in *New Critical History*, 126, they describe its author as one of the period's "lesser poets," Greenfield and Calder acknowledge in passing that line 28 "is effective in its contrast of home with homelessness" (248).

104. The first three and a half lines of *Edgar* alone contain half-lines that are exactly or very closely repeated in *Daniel*, *Christ and Satan*, the *Phoenix*, the *Order of the World*, the *Panther*, *Genesis A*, *Andreas*, *Riddle 84*, and *Exodus*. The *Phoenix*, the *Order of the World*, the *Panther*, and *Riddle 84* are all in *ASPR*, III. For an important reconsideration of several other Chronicle poems, see O'Brien O'Keeffe, "Deaths and Transformations."

105. The trope appears in the following poems: *Genesis A*, 227b, 969b, 1239b, 1723b; *Fates of the Apostles*, 63b; *Elene*, 364b, 670b, 852b; *Christ II*, 785b; *Guthlac B*, 878b; *Meters of Boethius*, 25 54; *Battle of Brunanburh*, 68b; and the *Lord's Prayer II*, 20b. All are in the *ASPR*: *Fates of the Apostles* in vol. II, *Christ II* and *Guthlac B*, in vol. III, *Meters of Boethius* in vol. V, and *Battle of Brunanburh* and *Lord's Prayer II* in vol. VI. On the textuality of Old English poetry, see further Pasternack, *Textuality*.

106. Anderson, *Cynewulf*, 118.

107. See Lerer's discussion of writing's cultural situation in Anglo-Saxon England in *Literacy and Power*, 158–94.

108. Cf. Parks, "Song, Text, Cassette."

109. Nam Sibyllam quidem Cumis ego ipse oculis meis vidi in ampulla pendere, et cum illi pueri dicerent: Σίβυλλα τί θέλεις; respondebat illa: ἀποθανεῖν θέλω.

110. Foley, *Immanent Art*, 7.

111. Foley, *Traditional Oral Epic*, 216.

112. Renoir, "Oral-Formulaic Rhetoric," 104.

113. It occurs in direct connection with slaughter fourteen times, in connection with extreme physical suffering that fails to result in death only through divine intervention six times, and in looser connection with slaughter an additional four times.

114. *Solomon and Saturn* is in *ASPR*, VI. The other occurrences of *gebelgan* in this context can be found at *Genesis B*, 552a, and 558b; and *Resignation*, 79a and 110a, both in *ASPR*, I and III, respectively.

115. That *Beowulf* and *Riddle 40* are the only secular poems in which the simplex occurs may in fact argue strongly for its being another of the *Beowulf*-poet's innovations. The simplex's appearance in religious poems is paralleled in Old Norse, where the adjective *bolginn* [swollen] (usually with the emotion specified as in "bolginn af reiði" [swollen by anger]) tends to cluster in the religious literature. I am indebted to John Lindow for this observation.

116. Renoir, "Point of View," remains the *locus classicus* for this topic. See additionally Brodeur, *Art of Beowulf*, 88–95; Greenfield, "Grendel's Approach"; Irving, *Reading of Beowulf*, 22–28, 103–104; Storms, "Grendel the Terrible"; O'Brien O'Keeffe, "*Beowulf*"; and Lapidge, "*Beowulf*."

117. Irving, *Rereading Beowulf*, 38–47, puts forth the view of Unferth as "Everydane" and persuasively argues against the various received opinions of Hrothgar's *þyle*.

118. On Beowulf's monstrosity, see further Greenfield, "Touch of the Monstrous," and Robinson, "Elements of the Marvelous." The only other human character to whom the simplex refers is Heremod, a successful king who becomes monstrous to his people. As we will see in chapter 3, *aglæca* functions similarly in the poem by explicitly linking the heroes Sigemund and Beowulf with Grendel and the dragon and associatively with a host of other terribly powerful—and problematic—figures.

119. Kent illustrated Leonard's translation of the poem. The illustration to which I refer here can be found between pp. 38 and 39 of this edition.

120. Perhaps to erase any lingering doubts that the poem's audience might have as to Grendel's fate, the poet reveals that the monster "in fenfreoðo   feorh alegde, / haþene sawle;   þær him hel onfeng" (851–52) [had laid down his life in his fen-refuge, his heathen soul: there hell took him].

121. Foley, *Immanent Art*, 214.

122. Greenfield, *Interpretation*, 33.

123. But see Magoun, "Theme of the Beasts," and Creed, "Making of an Anglo-Saxon Poem." On the "X muþ" system, see Fry, "Old English Formulas," and for a critique of it, see Niles, *Beowulf*, 125–26.

124. *Irre* and its variants occur in Old English prose some 755 times and in the poetry some 101 times, while (x-)*belgan*(-*mod*) occurs only some 58 times in the prose and some 32 times in the poetry.

125. Because the literature devoted to the dragon fight either directly or indirectly is too voluminous to list comprehensively, I offer here only a partial and admit-

tedly highly selective list: in addition to Tolkien, "*Beowulf*," see Gang, "Approaches to *Beowulf*"; Bonjour, "Monsters Crouching"; DuBois, "Dragon in *Beowulf*"; Rogers, "Beowulf's Three Great Fights"; Sisam, "Beowulf's Fight with the Dragon"; Niles, "Ring Composition"; Irving, *Rereading Beowulf*, 99–132; Shilton, "Nature of Beowulf's Dragon Fight"; Sorrell, "Oral Poetry" and "Approach to the Dragon-Fight"; and Rauer, *Beowulf and the Dragon*. See also Orchard, *Critical Companion to Beowulf*, 227–37 and 227n83.

126. See Foley, *Immanent Art*, 231–42.

127. Parry, "Traditional Epithet," 13.

128. Lord, "Composition by Theme," 73.

129. *Swat* occurs as the first element in only four other compounds: *swatclaþe* [handkerchief] (4x); *swatfag* [blood-stained] (1x); *swatfah* [blood-stained] (1x); *swatline* [napkin] (1x); and *swatþyrlu* [bloody track] (1x). As a second element in a compound, *swat* occurs only in the compounds *hildeswat* [hostile vapor] and *heaþoswat* [war sweat; blood shed in battle] preserved in *Beowulf* at 2558a and at 1460a, 1606a, and 1668a.

130. See, for example, Magoun, "Theme of the Beasts," 82, who notes that "[w]hereas a formula to be a formula must involve exact or almost exact repetition, a theme, unrestricted in its totality by metrical considerations, is not limited to word for word repetition, though it must inevitably be built up out of formulas." On verbatim repetition in formulas, see Riedinger, "Formulaic Relationship." For a recent example of how important exact verbal repetition continues to be in studies of the formula, see Orchard, "Both Style and Substance."

131. Sisam, "Beowulf's Fight with the Dragon," 97.

132. In chapter 3, we will see that although there are no Old English parallels to the dragon episode in *Beowulf*, the early Middle English *Brut* contains an episode that closely parallels it and that affords us further evidence of its traditionality. On the dearth of analogues to this episode in early Germanic literature, see Rauer, *Beowulf and the Dragon*, 9–23.

133. The chief constituent motifs of this pattern, as identified by Foley, *Immanent Art*, 233, are "Arming, a *Beot* (or verbal contract), the monster's Approach, the Death of a Substitute, and the Engagement itself."

134. See Byock, *Feud;* W. Miller, "Choosing the Avenger"; and Kahrl, "Feuds in *Beowulf*."

135. See Irving, *Rereading Beowulf*, 100–101. On the theme of exile, see Greenfield, "Formulaic Expression." The Grendel episode is further grounded for the audience because it fits the narrative pattern of the traditional theme of the hero-on-the-beach. See Crowne, "Hero on the Beach"; Fry, "Hero on the Beach" and "Heroine on the Beach"; and Renoir, "Oral-Formulaic Theme Survival."

136. Various attempts to place the dragon episode within a Christian framework have been advanced (see esp. Goldsmith, *Mode and Meaning,* and Lee, *Guest-Hall of Eden*), but as Irving, "Nature of Christianity," 20, incisively notes, "[M]isguided insis-

tence on supplying some sort of Christian ending for the poem in the face of the facts has led to unlikely assumptions and distortions."

137. As Andersson, "Thief in *Beowulf*," 496, remarks, "There is not enough evidence in the *Beowulf* text to reveal the details of the thief's prehistory or his status."

138. Kiernan, *Beowulf and the Beowulf Manuscript*, 65–169, discusses in detail the foliation of the composite manuscript of which the Nowell Codex is a part. See also Orchard, *Critical Companion to Beowulf*, 12n5, 268–73.

139. But see Kiernan et al.'s discussion of fol. 179r in *Electronic Beowulf* and Stanley, "Unideal Principles," 258–59, esp. 258n5.

140. In "Thief in *Beowulf*," Andersson turns with duly noted caution to Old Norse analogues as a means of explicating the theft in *Beowulf*, in large part because theft plays a surprisingly small role in the extant Old English poetry. He observes that Old Norse poetry similarly contains few instances of theft and comments that "[t]he *Poetic Edda* provides only two occurrences of 'þjófr'" (496). Bessinger and Smith, *Concordance*, s.v., list only six occurrences of *þeof* (a count that does not include Andersson's proposed emendation, as the ASPR text that provides the basis for the concordance reads *þ[eow]*), and these occur in five poems: *Christ III* (2x), *Riddle 47*, *Riddle 73*, *Maxims II*, and *Beowulf* (1x each). None of the non-Beowulfian occurrences provide any significant contextual parallels to the dragon episode. In contrast, *þeof* and its variants occur more than 260 times in Old English prose works.

141. On this point see Anderson, "Treasure Trove," 153, who argues that "the intruder was blameless in regard to the manner in which he acquired the dragon's cup," and Andersson, "Thief in *Beowulf*," 494, who suggests that "the removal of a single item does not contravene the laws of treasure trove."

142. For a more detailed discussion of oral poetics and contemporary reader-based theory, see Amodio, "Affective Criticism," 54–62.

143. Cf. Niles, *Beowulf*, 7–9, and Lapidge, "*Beowulf*," 393.

144. However, the wealth of detail that the poet provides about Grendel does little to clarify the monster's incomprehensible nature. For example, Lapidge, "*Beowulf*," 378, notes that "if the poet wished to avoid communicating anything of the monster's nature, he chose an ideal name for it, for the etymology and meaning of the name *Grendel* are unknown."

145. Although we are not told what ultimately becomes of Grendel's head, it, too, may wind up on the wall of Heorot just as his arm and shoulder did.

146. In the course of arguing for the hall's centrality in the poem's metaphorics, Irving, *Rereading Beowulf*, 102, suggests that Beowulf's hall was, in fact, the target of the dragon's maliciousness: "Having been first deeply penetrated by the human invader, the death-world of the dragon now bulges out in its turn to invade and coil menacingly around the living world outside and to seek to destroy its heart, the most important symbol of social life, the king's hall." This argument has obvious appeal, but a random, widely destructive power seems perhaps more characteristic of what Irving labels the

"world of *draconitas*" (101). The opacity of a dragon's thinking and the indeterminacy of its attacks make it even more terrifying from the human perspective.

147. Ibid., 100.

148. The Geatish history that occupies such a large percentage of the poem's final section serves a similar function. In reporting the Swedish-Geatish feuds, the poet attempts—but fails—to make the dragon fight comprehensible to the audience by placing it against the backdrop of human feuds. For a contrasting view, cf. Kahrl, "Feuds in *Beowulf*," who argues for the structural and thematic equivalence of Beowulf's feud with the dragon and the Swedish-Geatish feuds.

149. See further Mitchell, *Old English Syntax*, I, §271–74, on the distinction between necessary and pleonastic datives. The "ic me" construction is relatively rare in the poetry, occurring only thirty-seven times in eleven different poems (of these more than half appear in the *Metrical Psalms* and the *Metrical Charms*). Of the four occurrences in *Beowulf*, three are voiced by Beowulf (677a, 1490b, 2523b), and Hrothgar employs it once (1772b) when he recalls the glory of his power in the period preceding Grendel's attacks.

150. On the role of formal, ritualized, public boasting within the battle with the monster story pattern, see Foley, *Immanent Art*, 234.

151. See Kaske, "*Beowulf*," for a different reading of this decision. To him, the dragon fight "is a brilliant device for presenting in a single action not only Beowulf's final display of his kingly *fortitudo*, but also his development and his ultimate preservation of personal and kingly *sapientia*" (24).

152. Irving, *Reading of Beowulf*, 217.

153. Such forecasts of Beowulf's death do not diminish the episode's tension because, as Brodeur, *Art of Beowulf*, 89, observes, "Suspense can be maintained without withholding all knowledge of an action's outcome until the final moment; it resides in the degree and quality of emotional tension imposed upon the listener in the effective prolongation of the conflict between fear and hope."

154. However, his decision to fight Grendel's mother occurs within a somewhat more complex narrative context. When, as Irving notes in *Rereading Beowulf*, 44, Hrothgar "adopt[s] or coopt[s] Beowulf into the new pseudo-Danish role of son and hall-guardian," the Danish king firmly situates the Geat within two of Germanic society's most important positions. In Beowulf's careful arming and acceptance of a famous, battle-tested sword we may see a tacit acknowledgment of his new position within and obligation to Danish society. But cf. Leyerle, "Beowulf the Hero," 92, who argues that Beowulf's unreflective answer is "the kind of *beot* warned against in *The Wanderer* (65–72)."

155. The Danish coastguard comments directly on Beowulf's impressive physical presence when he tells the newly arrived troop of Geats that he "Næfre . . . maran geseah / eorla ofer eorþan,   ðonne is eower sum" (247b–48) [never (has) seen a mightier warrior on earth than is a certain one of you].

156. For example, Sorrell, "Oral Poetry," 48, approvingly cites the *Beowulf*-poet's remarks on this matter and like Garbáty, "Fallible Sword," and others, does not look beyond the proffered explanation.

157. Although the text is silent on this point, a spell similar to that cast over Grendel (cf. 801b–5a) may help protect her as well. Cf. Chance, *Woman as Hero*, 103. However, see Rogers, "Beowulf's Three Great Fights," who argues against the existence of such a spell.

158. Irving, *Rereading Beowulf*, 92–94, emphasizes the narrative importance of Beowulf's hand grip. See Chambers, *Beowulf*, 62–68, 365–81; Glosecki, *Shamanism*, 197–210; and Stitt, *Beowulf and the Bear's Son*, for discussions of *Beowulf*'s connection to the "Bear's Son" folktale.

159. Beowulf himself reports on his past success with his sword at lines 555b–57a: "hwæþre me gyfeþe wearð, / þæt ic aglæcan   orde geræhte, / hildebille" [however, it was granted to me that I was able to hit the awe-inspiring one with the point of my sword].

160. *Canterbury Tales*, General Prologue, I [A], 618.

161. It can be argued that this pattern begins with his spurning of assistance—in any form—in the fight with Grendel. But he voluntarily and consciously rejects human society's assistance from the start of the Grendel episode, whereas in the later fights he initially seeks to exploit the apparent technological advantages that human culture has developed—swords, armor, shields—only to have them fail him.

162. See the comments at lines 2510–11a and 2423b–24.

163. In arguing, that "in the last part of the poem, [*Beowulf*'s] audience would probably have shifted their identification to Wiglaf, who comes to occupy the position of the faithful retainer," Earl, "*Beowulf*," 85, offers a contrasting reading of the dragon fight's affective dynamics. See also Foley, *Immanent Art*, 231–42, who argues that Wiglaf's emergence as Beowulf's heroic successor is central to the scene's structure and affective dynamics.

164. Doane, "Oral Texts, Intertexts," 75.

165. O'Brien O'Keeffe, *Visible Song*; Doane, "Ethnography"; Renoir, *Key to Old Poems*; Stock, *Implications of Literacy*; Foley, *Immanent Art*.

THREE.   Post-Conquest Oral Poetics

1. Pearsall, *Old and Middle English Poetry*, 85.

2. The inscription, transcribed into the Roman alphabet, reads, "Ek HlewagastiR HoltijaR horna tawido" [I Hlewagastir of Holt made the horn].

3. For a different opinion on the poem's metrics, see Cable, *English Alliterative Tradition*, 52, who argues that *Durham* "shows a clear break from the classical meter of Old English poetry."

4. The alliteration of *A Summons to Prayer* is defective in a small percentage of the poem's thirty-one lines. In several other poems, among them *Lord's Prayer II*,

Lord's Prayer III, and *Gloria I,* Latin verse is interspersed with Old English and hence does not come into the ambience of Anglo-Saxon metrics in the way the Latin verses do in *Phoenix* and *Prayer.* See further Wenzel, *Macaronic Sermons.*

5. The passages Dobbie rejects, in *ASPR,* VI, xxxiii, n1, are from the annals for 959 (MSS DE), 975 (DE), 975 (D), 979 (E), 1011 (E), 1057 (D), 1067 (D), 1075 (DE), 1086 (E), and 1104 (E). MS D of the Anglo-Saxon Chronicle is London, British Library, Cotton Tiberius B. iv, and MS E is the Peterborough Chronicle, Oxford, Bodleian Library, Laud Misc. 636.

6. But see Lerer's reappraisal of the poem in "Old English and Its Afterlife," 18–24. See also Judasinski, "Rime of King William," who sees the poem as belonging to a twelfth-century tradition of anti-forest polemics. For the sake of comparison and because it is not usually anthologized, I cite the poem in its entirety here, following Plummer's lineation in *Two of the Saxon Chronicles.* Plummer's pointing, reproduced here, follows that of the Laud MS that contains this unique passage. Following Clark, *Peterborough Chronicle,* I have silently expanded the manuscript contraction for *þet.*

7. Although it appears with some frequency in Old English poetry (especially in the four poems attributed to Cynewulf), end-rhyme plays an incidental if not merely ornamental role in Anglo-Saxon metrics, with the exception of the Old English *Riming Poem.* See further Stanley, "Rhymes in English Medieval Verse," and Macrae-Gibson, *Old English Riming Poem.*

8. The other major manuscripts of the Chronicle, followed by their most recent published editions are MS A (Cambridge, Corpus Christi College, 173), the Parker Chronicle, Bately's edition; MS B (London, British Library, Cotton Tiberius A. vi), Taylor's edition; MS C (London, British Library, Tiberius B. i), the Abingdon Chronicle, O'Brien O'Keeffe's edition; MS D (London, British Library, Cotton Tiberius B. iv), the Worcester Chronicle, Cubbin's edition; and MS F (London, British Library, Cotton Domitian A. viii), the Domitian Bilingual, Baker's edition.

9. Plummer, *Two of the Saxon Chronicles,* 107. MS F, the Domitian Bilingual, also offers a prose account in the annal for 938: "Her Æðestan cing 7 [Ead]mund his broðer lædde fyrde to Brun(an)byri. 7 þar gefeht wið Anelaf 7 Criste fultumegende sige hæfde 7 þar ofslogan .v. cingas 7 .vii. eor[las]" [In this year, King Athelstan and his brother Edmund led a troop to Brunanburh and there they fought with Anelaf and with Christ helping were victorious and there slew five kings and eight earls]. I cite MS F of the Anglo-Saxon Chronicle from Baker's edition.

10. I cite MS A of the Anglo-Saxon Chronicle from Bately's edition, 70. Bately dates MS A to "some time between the years 1001 . . . and *ca* 1012/13" (xiii). See further Gneuss, *Handlist,* item 52. Plummer, *Two of the Saxon Chronicles,* xii, suggests that the Peterborough Chronicle, MS E, was "written in the first instance about the year 1122, and continued in various hands to 1154."

11. I cite the poem here from Dickins and Wilson, *Early Middle English Texts.* The *Worcester Fragments* survive in a single, damaged, thirteenth-century manuscript,

Worcester Cathedral, F. 174. Brehe discusses *Fragment A*'s metrics and offers a new lineation of it in "Reassembling the *First Worcester Fragment.*"

12. For a more extensive discussion of the poem's prosody, see Moffat, *Soul's Address*, 25–39.

13. Arngart, *Proverbs of Alfred*, II, 225.

14. However, Le Saux contends, in *Laȝamon's Brut*, 193, that it is "undeniable" that "Laȝamon's free verse preserves the half-line structure of Old English verse," and she goes on to cite approvingly Loomis's contention in *Arthurian Literature*, 105, that the poem's "basic verse form is still the alliterative line with four accents and a slight pause in the middle." For Fulk, *History of Old English Meter*, 264, the metrics of early Middle English poems such as the *Brut*, the *Grave*, and the *Proverbs of Alfred* sets them apart from Old English poetry because the later verses are "longer, containing more unstressed words . . . the alliteration is inferior, and the language is decidedly prosaic." See further his comments on late developments of Anglo-Saxon metrics (251–68). Cable, *English Alliterative Tradition*, 61–62, admits that the relationship of Laȝamon's meter to "classical Old English meter is complex," and he further raises the possibility that Laȝamon "misunderstood" Anglo-Saxon metrics and should perhaps be seen as having "simply . . . gotten the meter wrong."

15. See Blake, "Rhythmical Alliteration"; Brehe, "'Rhythmical Alliteration'"; and Moffat, *Soul's Address*.

16. Madden's description of the *Brut*'s metrics in *Laȝamons Brut*, I, xxiv, one that would well serve to describe the metrics of the *Proverbs of Alfred*, has yet to be improved on since it appeared in 1847: "The structure of Laȝamons poem consists partly of lines in which the alliterative system of the Anglo-Saxons is preserved, and partly of couplets of unequal length rhiming together. Many couplets indeed occur that have both of these forms, whilst others are often met with which possess neither. . . . The relative proportion of each of these forms is not to be ascertained without extreme difficulty, since the author uses them everywhere intermixed, and slides from alliteration to rhime or from rhime to alliteration in a manner perfectly arbitrary."

17. But see O'Brien O'Keeffe, *Visible Song*, 23n1, who notes that there are "two insignificant exceptions" to this general practice. Both the *Metrical Epilogue* to the *Pastoral Care* and "the commendatory verses, 'Thureth,' in BL, Cotton Claudius A. iii, 31v" are written out as inverted triangles—an arrangement, she continues, that "actually works against the sense of the words." Robinson and Stanley, *Old English Verse Texts*, raise but do not press the possibility that these poems are lineated as poetry. See above, chapter 2, note 28.

18. O'Brien O'Keeffe, *Visible Song*; Parkes, "Contribution of Insular Scribes," 2. He expands on this definition in *Pause and Effect*, 23: "A scribe had no immediate respondent to interact with, therefore he had to observe a kind of decorum in his copy in order to ensure that the message of the text was easily understood. This decorum— the rules governing the relationships between this complex of graphic conventions and

the message of a text conveyed in the written medium—may be described as 'the grammar of legibility.'"

19. O'Brien O'Keeffe, *Visible Song*, 6.

20. See V.i. 108–17 in G. Evans, *Riverside Shakespeare*.

21. But see O'Brien O'Keeffe, *Visible Song*, 155–87, and Parkes, *Pause and Effect*, esp. 30–34, 41–49.

22. O'Brien O'Keeffe, *Visible Song*, 192.

23. Dobbie's edition is in *ASPR*, VI.

24. A *c* has been added directly above the *o* in the manuscript.

25. As Parkes in *Pause and Effect*, 102, notes, "Numerous scribes from the ninth to the fifteenth century placed a *punctus* after the end of each verse, even when the pause was already indicated by layout. Since in many instances the pointing does not coincide with either a sense or a syntactical break, the scribes seem to have been providing an extra signal of what they perceived as a prosodic unit."

26. Clark's edition cited here is *Peterborough Chronicle*. For a facsimile of Laud Misc. 636, see Whitelock's edition (*Peterborough Chronicle*).

27. For a discussion of the *Orrmulum*'s date and possible place of composition, see Parkes, "On the Presumed Date."

28. Throughout this chapter I cite the *Orrmulum* from R. White's edition.

29. A second *n* appears directly over this one in the manuscript.

30. A second *m* appears directly over this one in the manuscript.

31. A second *ᵹ* appears directly over this one in the manuscript.

32. A second *n* appears directly over this one in the manuscript.

33. A second *n* appears directly over the *n* in "engell."

34. This macron is doubled, as are many others in Junius 1.

35. Burchfield, "Line-End Hyphens," 182, notes that in "Junius 1 [the hyphen] is used almost invariably, and when it is not, it is nearly always because there was insufficient room at the edge of the manuscript."

36. See further C. Brown, "Thirteenth-Century Manuscript."

37. I indicate the manuscript's ruled right margin in the first line by the symbol '|.' In Arngart's edition (*Proverbs of Alfred*), these lines appear as follows:

and efrilches mannes dom
to his owen dure charieweth.

38. The *Brut* covers the first 192 leaves of Caligula A. ix (fols. 3r–194v) and is followed by two poems by Chadri, *La vie de Seint Josaphaz* (fols. 195r–216r) and *La vie des Set Dormanz* (fols. 216v–29v), a short French prose chronicle from the Saxon conquest to the reign of Henry III (fols. 229v–32v), the *Hule and Niᵹtengale* (fols. 233r–46r), the English poems *Death's Wither-Clench* (f. 246rv), *An Orison to Our Lady* (f. 246v), *Will and Wit* (f. 246v), *Doomsday* (f. 246v–47r), *The Last Day* (fols. 247–48v), *The Ten Abuses* (f. 248v), *A Lutel Sloth Sermun* (fols. 248v–49r), and *Le petit plet*, also by Chadri (fols. 249r–61v).

39. The *Brut* is dated anywhere from c. 1189 to c. 1250. See further Madden, *Laʒamons Brut*, I, iii–xi, xvii–xxi, Wyld, "Laʒamon as an English Poet," 3–5; Stanley, "Date of Laʒamon's 'Brut'"; Le Saux, *Laʒamon's Brut*, 1–13; Bryan, *Collaborative Meaning*, 183–90; and most recently Roberts, "Preliminary Note."

40. The somewhat later version of the *Brut* contained in London, British Library, Cotton Otho C. xiii, is similarly encoded.

41. See Parkes, *Pause and Effect*, 69, 73.

42. With a superscript *e* over the *q*.

43. The other English poems that follow in the Caligula A. ix codex are also encoded as poetry, as are the two French poems that precede it and the one that follows it.

44. Stanley, in *The Owl and the Nightingale*, his edition of the *Hule*, notes roughly one hundred exceptions to this practice in the poem's nearly eighteen hundred lines. He observes further that "Stops also occur, meaningfully, at times in the middle of lines" (13). For example, in the manuscript medial points occur in lines 367 ("þu liest. on me hit is isene." [You lie. In my case it is clear]) and 464 ("sholde ich bileue: nai warto." [Should I remain? No, what for.]) In Stanley's edition, these lines appear respectively as " Þu liest! On me hit is isene" and "Sholde ich bileue? Nai! Warto?" I cite the poem here and subsequently from Stanley's edition.

45. For an important discussion of the role word division played in reorienting the ways in which medieval texts were received, see Saenger, *Space between Words*.

46. Doane, "Introduction," xiii.

47. For example, in one of the first essays to approach Middle English poetry from the oral-formulaic perspective, Waldron admits, in "Oral-Formulaic Technique," 792, that the "categorical distinction" that the Parry-Lord theory draws between oral and literate composition inhibits the search for oral formulas in fourteenth-century alliterative verse because "we can be sure that most of these poets are literate—indeed, many of the poems are fairly close translations from Latin or French."

48. On the question of oral presentation in the Middle English period, see Crosby, "Oral Delivery" and "Chaucer"; Baugh, "Middle English Romance" and "Improvisation"; Waldron, "Oral-Formulaic Technique"; McGillivray, *Memorization*; W. Quinn and Hall, *Jongleur*; and Grudin, *Chaucer*.

49. Another version of the *Brut* survives in Cotton Otho C. xiii (fols. 1–145), and another version of the *Hule* exists in Oxford, Jesus College, 29 (fols. 156r–68v).

50. Stanley, *Owl and the Nightingale*, 22.

51. In Madden's edition, it runs to just over 32,000 short lines. Because Brook and Leslie opt to print it in long lines, it runs to only 16,095 lines in their edition.

52. Brewer, "Paradox," 205.

53. Cf. Stanley, *Owl and the Nightingale*, 30–36.

54. Pearsall, *Old and Middle English Poetry*, 94. For a detailed discussion of Middle English debate poetry, the genre to which the *Hule* belongs, see Conlee, *Middle English Debate Poetry*, xi–xxxvii.

55. The *Orrmulum* presents a stiff challenge to the *Brut* in this regard, but the former's doctrinal focus may have made it more attractive to a listening audience. On the possibility of the *Brut*'s having been read aloud, see Brewer, "Paradox," 204, who suggests that a poem such as the *Brut* "might well be read aloud in the thirteenth century, but it lacks obvious oral qualities."

56. In addition to English and French, Laȝamon may also have had some Latin. He employs the few Latin terms that appear in the poem in metrically and semantically appropriate ways that may witness his knowledge of the language, but it is impossible to determine from the available evidence how firm his grasp of Latin was.

57. The English book is generally agreed to be the Anglo-Saxon translation of Bede's *Historia Ecclesiastica,* and the French text is, as Laȝamon himself notes, the *Roman de Brut* of Robert Wace. The identity of the Latin book that Laȝamon tells us was made by "Seinte Albin / 7 þe feire Austin" (17–18) [Saint Albin and the fair Austin] has not been satisfactorily ascertained but there can be little doubt that it is spurious. See below, note 77.

58. Throughout this chapter I cite Brook and Leslie's edition of the Caligula A. ix text of *Brut (Lazamon)* unless otherwise noted.

59. Horvath, "Romance of Authorship," offers an insightful reading of the rise of this consciousness.

60. McGillivray, *Memorization,* 5, labels this phenomenon "memorial transfer," which he defines as "the movement of material from one part of a text to another part which is physically remote, but which is liable to confusion with it because of similarities of situation, content, or language."

61. All citations to *King Horn* are to Hall's edition of the version contained in Cambridge, University Library, Gg. 4. 27. 2

62. I cite Smithers's edition of the version of *Kyng Alisaunder* contained in Oxford, Bodleian Library, Laud Misc. 622.

63. I cite Tolkien and Gordon's revised second edition (*Sir Gawain*).

64. See further Pearsall, "*Troilus* Frontispiece."

65. For a full treatment of this matter, see Joyce Coleman, *Public Reading.*

66. *Pace* Crosby, "Oral Delivery," 102, an author's direct address to an audience of listeners does not prove to be "the surest evidence of the intention of oral delivery" because while the poet's address to his listeners is an integral part of medieval English oral poetics, it quickly becomes a fundamental trope of literate poetics as well. See Parks, "Traditional Narrator," and B. Rosenberg, *Folklore and Literature,* 140–61.

67. Baugh, "Middle English Romance," 9.

68. Cf. Stock's notion of "textual communities" in *Implications of Literacy,* 88–240. Although more concerned with the spread of non-orthodox thought, Stock's point that nonliterates were able to "participate in literate culture, although indirectly" (91) through public readings and sermons has important broader applicability as well.

69. See Renoir, *Key to Old Poems*, 169–74, and Amodio, "Tradition, Modernity," 47–55.

70. This holds whether a performer reads from a text before him or presents one he earlier memorized because in both cases the performance is grounded in a text.

71. O'Brien O'Keeffe, "Performing Body," 53.

72. Bennett, *Middle English Literature*, 68. The more commonly held view, voiced succinctly by Salter, *English and International*, 48, is that Laȝamon's poem witnesses his conscious and "strong concern for the adaptation of older literary forms for newer purposes."

73. For an important catalogue both of general studies of the oral traditional nature of Middle English poetry and especially of studies that specifically attempt to apply the Parry-Lord theory to post-Conquest vernacular verse texts, see Parks, "Oral-Formulaic Theory." For oral-formulaic approaches to the *Brut*, see Ringbom, *Studies in the Narrative Techniques*; Donahue, *Lawman's Brut*; and Noble, "Layamon's *Brut*."

74. Unflattering comments about the poem and the poet's ability are sprinkled widely throughout Middle English literary criticism. Lewis, "Genesis of a Medieval Book," 18, spoke (and continues to speak) for many of the poem's readers when he announces that "the poem is long [and] much of its matter is dull." Tatlock, *Legendary History*, 485, observes that "so few people have dwelt on its high merit and freshness that one fancies few have read it with absorption and a leisured mind," a comment as true today as when Tatlock wrote it more than fifty years ago. The first volume of the poem's still incomplete modern critical edition (EETS ns 250) appeared in 1963, and the second volume (EETS ns 277) appeared in 1978. Leslie was still at work upon the third and final volume (the textual and critical notes and glossary) at the time of his death.

75. Although Laȝamon's description of the physical aspects of his writing procedure may be, as Clanchy, *From Memory*, 125, argues, "idealized and simplified," it remains significant because in it the poet participates in two activities, composing and writing down, that, while virtually interchangeable to our modern sensibilities, were not usually paired in medieval England. As Clanchy points out, "'Reading and dictating' were ordinarily coupled together, not 'reading and writing.' . . . Writing was distinguished from composition because putting a pen to parchment was an art in itself" (125–26).

76. Madden, *Laȝamons Brut* I, xi–xii.

77. Madden, in ibid., xii, long ago noted that Laȝamon's second purported source "is more difficult to identify, nor is it easy to understand how St. Austin, who died in the year 604, and Albinus, Abbot of St. Austins at Canterbury, who died in 732, should be conjoined in the same work."

78. See above, note 56.

79. Stanley, "Laȝamon's Antiquarian Sentiments," 30.

80. Donoghue, "Laȝamon's Ambivalence," 563.

81. As Monroe, "French Words," and others have noted, the *Brut*'s lexicon contains a very small percentage of non-native words.

82. Pearsall, *Old and Middle English Poetry,* 112.

83. Oakden, *Alliterative Poetry,* II, 132.

84. Stanley, "Laȝamon's Antiquarian Sentiments," 30.

85. Ibid.

86. In the list that follows, I cite only the first occurrence of each compound and do not cite variant spellings or oblique cases. See Madden, *Laȝamons Brut,* III, 581, for a more exhaustive list of the poem's *leod-x* compounds.

87. See Oakden, *Alliterative Poetry,* II, 148–49, for a complete list of the Anglo-Saxon elements underlying each of Laȝamon's *leod-x* compounds.

88. Although his view of Laȝamon's language often parallels Stanley's, Oakden allows that some of Laȝamon's compounds come close to reaching the aesthetic heights that Anglo-Saxon ones regularly do. Oakden, *Alliterative Poetry,* II, 131, classifies as "beautiful" such Anglo-Saxon compounds as *æppelfealu* [reddish yellow], *beadoleoma* [war-gleam; sword], and *fætedhleor* [ornamented cheek] and identifies *dæisið* [death], *eorðhus* [cave], *fæisið* [death], *feðerhome* [wings], *forþfare* [perish], *goldfah* [gold-covered], *hokerleoð* [scornful song], *leirstow* [cemetery], *lifdæȝen* [term of life], *morð-spelle* [murder], *nailsax* [nail-knife], *qualesið* [mortality], *siȝcræft* [magic], *sorhsið* [mishap], *wadæi* [day of doom], and *writrune* [letters] as being of the same type.

89. In his exhaustive and still unsurpassed treatment of compounding in Germanic, Carr, *Nominal Compounds,* xvii, notes that this method of word formation is "not peculiar to the Germanic languages, for it is inherited from the parent Indo-Germanic language, together with the other type of word-formation by means of suffixes, but in none of the extant Indo-Germanic languages has it been so extensively developed as in the modern Germanic languages."

90. Niles, *Beowulf,* 138.

91. Oakden, *Alliterative Poetry,* II, 114.

92. Wyld, "Studies in the Diction," 187; Oakden, *Alliterative Poetry,* II, 163.

93. All citations to *Beowulf* are from Klaeber's edition. These and the following translations in this section intentionally reflect the original word order of the quotations cited.

94. For a complete listing of this pattern, see Berger, "Concordance," 405–8, s.v. *feole.*

95. Laȝamon's possible motives—political or otherwise—for engaging in "antiquarian" behavior have long been the focus of critical discussion. See esp. Tatlock, *Legendary History,* 483–531; Stanley, "Laȝamon's Antiquarian Sentiments"; Donoghue, "Laȝamon's Ambivalence"; and Noble, "Laȝamon's Ambivalence Reconsidered."

96. Stanley, "Laȝamon's Un-Anglo-Saxon Syntax," 51.

97. Although certainly unusual, this sort of inversion is not unique to Laȝamon; it survives until through the fourteenth century, appearing several times in *Sir*

Gawain—"bor alþer-grattest" (1441) and "Bi alder-truest token" (1486)—and at least once in Chaucer—"Up roos oure Hoost, and was oure aller cok" (*Canterbury Tales*, General Prologue, I [A], 823, Benson's edition [*Riverside Chaucer*])—but it is a decidedly rare construction by the fourteenth century.

98. Brook, *Selections*, xx.

99. For example, Madden, *Laȝamons Brut*, I, xlv, notes that "[f]eminine nouns both of the simple and complex order [i.e. weak and strong classes] are much alike in their terminations. All the cases in the singular end in *e*. . . . In the plural, the nom. acc. and dat. end in *en* or *e*, and the gen. in *ene*."

100. Ibid., xxx.

101. Mitchell, *Old English Syntax*, I, 550.

102. He also employs of-periphrasis, "Arður þa liðe word iherde: of þan leode-kinge" (11237) [Arthur those pleasing words heard of the people-king], although this construction is relatively rare and appears chiefly in the poem's later sections. The infrequency with which of-periphrasis appears in the *Brut* reflects the general state of the language: in the twelfth century, 93.7 percent of all genitives are inflectional, a percentage that drops to 68.8 percent by the first half of the thirteenth century. These figures are derived from Russell Thomas's charts in "Syntactical Processes," 64–72.

103. Of the 106 times he uses a synthetic genitive with a superlative adjective in a five thousand-line sample of the poem, the genitive is prepositioned forty-seven times and postpositioned fifty-nine times.

104. See Amodio, "Some Notes" and "Laȝamon's Anglo-Saxon Lexicon."

105. However, cf. Donoghue, "Laȝamon's Ambivalence," 542, who raises the possibility that Laȝamon and his near-contemporary, the so-called "tremulous" glossator of Worcester, might have been part of an early post-Conquest movement that promoted the study of Old English language and literature.

106. On the problems that attend the dating of Old English texts, and for two very different approaches to this issue, see Amos, *Linguistic Means*, and Fulk, *History of Old English Meter*, 348–428.

107. Everett, "Laȝamon" 26.

108. Madden makes a similar point in *Laȝamons Brut*, I, xxiv, when he comments about the *Brut* that "the colloquial character of much of the work renders it peculiarly valuable as a monument of language, since it serves to convey to us, in all probability, the current speech of the writer's time as it passed from mouth to mouth."

109. A *sêma*, Foley explains in *Homer's Traditional Art*, 13, "is a sign that points not so much to a specific situation, text, or performance as toward the ambient tradition, which serves as the key to an emergent reality."

110. Ibid., 26.

111. In addition to the Arthur/Frolle episode, *abelȝen* is linked to an explicit slaughterous encounter eighteen other times: 784/786; 850/861 ff.; 3188/3195; 3648, 3679/3720; 7532/7617; 7904/7979–80; 10594/10595–96; 10609/10607–8, 10615–16; 13065,

13156/13204; 13870/13889–90; 14174/14196; 14309/14332, 14346; 15123, 15132/15149–50; 15457/15464; 15790/15840. In two instances *abelᵹen* is closely linked to a threatened slaughter (12599/12607; 14076/14081–82) that then occurs somewhat later (13301 ff./ 14255), and in one it is used to describe the mental state of a cannibalistic monster (12944) who is disfigured in a battle with Arthur (13000–13012) before being beheaded by Bediver.

112. See further Amodio, "Old-English Oral-Formulaic Tradition," 7–16.

113. Foley, *Singer of Tales in Performance*, 94.

114. The description of Herod's slaughter of the innocents occurs at 7995 ff. and so seems too distant from the simplex to have any meaningful link to it.

115. As Pearsall, *Old and Middle English Poetry*, 102, aptly puts it, Orrm's "methods of filling out his verses, combined with a propensity to explain and repeat everything several times over, make for infinite tedium."

116. See Robinson, *Beowulf*, 88n99.

117. Of these two instances, only one is unambiguously an appositive construction. In *Guthlac A*, the devils besetting Guthlac are first described as being "bolgenmode" (557b) and then immediately as "wraðe wræcmæcgas" (558a) [angry outcasts]. In what is not strictly speaking an appositive construction, the evil men who are the subject of *Meters of Boethius*, 25, are similarly described as being "gebolgne" (45a) shortly before we learn that in their breast "swiðan welme / hatheortnesse" (46b–47a) [anger greatly welled]. Both poems are in *ASPR*, III and V, respectively.

118. See Burrow and Turville-Petre, *Book of Middle English*; Stanley, *Owl and the Nightingale*; Bennett and Smithers, *Early Middle English Verse*.

119. Ringbom, *Studies in the Narrative Technique*, 77–104; Donahue, *Lawman's Brut*, 68–162.

120. As Ringbom demonstrates, in *Studies in the Narrative Technique*, 85–90, the feast scenes in the *Brut* regularly follow the pattern:

1. The blowing of trumpets (horns)
2. The laying of the table
3. The sitting down to table
4. The bringing of water
5. The serving of drink and food
6. Drinking and eating
7. Music and singing
8. Gifts
9. Phrases denoting happiness.

121. Cf. McNelis, "Laᵹamon as Auctor," 254n3, who notes in passing some similarities between the dragon fights in *Beowulf* and the *Brut*.

122. See, for example, *Beowulf*, 2461a, where it signals the extraordinary distress of the old man who witnesses his son "ride / giong on galgan" (2445b–46a) [ride young

on the gallows] or lines 100–1 in the same poem, where it ominously signals the onset of Grendel's attacks. The heroes in the newly constructed Heorot live "eadiglice, oð ðæt an ongan / fyrene fre(m)an feond on helle" [blessedly until one began to do evil deeds, a fiend in hell]. But see Greenfield, *Interpretation*, 55, who argues that a phrase such as "oð ðæt an ongan" cannot bear any "implications of meaning" because its ideational structure is too general and its diction is "unimpressive."

123. Irving, *Rereading Beowulf*, 100.

124. Cf. Houck, *Sources*.

125. Inter hæc & alia seuicie suæ gesta contigit ei infortunium quoddam quod nequitiam suam deleuit. Aduenerat namque ex partibus hibernici maris inaudite feritatis belua. quæ incolas iuxta maritima sine intermissione deuorabat. Cumque fama aures eius attigisset accessit ipse ad illam & solus cum ea congressus est. At cum omnia tela sua in illa in uanum consumpsisset. accelerauit monstrum illud & apertis faucibus ipsum uelut pisciculum deuorauit. I cite Geoffrey's *Historia Regum Britanniae* in English translation here and subsequently, unless otherwise noted, from Sebastian Evans's edition (*History of the Kings*). I cite Geoffrey's Latin text from Griscom's edition (*Historia*), 295.

126. I cite the *Roman de Brut* from Arnold's edition. I am indebted to my colleague Christine Reno for her assistance with my translations of the Anglo-Norman text.

127. See further Enright, *Lady with a Mead Cup*, esp. 1–37. For readings of Laȝamon's treatment of this scene that differ from the one offered here, see Donahue, *Lawman's Brut*, 175–78, and, most recently, Bridges, "The King, the Foreigner."

128. Enright, *Lady with a Mead Cup*, 22.

129. See further Clover, "Germanic Context."

130. We should note, however, that Wealhtheow acts on a far more local level and with a more immediate goal (keeping the peace in Heorot following Beowulf's and Unferth's exchange) than the women in Old English poetry to whom this term is directly applied, women whose marriage into another tribe may help establish lasting ties between their and their husbands' tribes. However, this result does not always obtain, as the painful story of Hildeburh reveals. See further Enright, *Lady with a Mead Cup*, esp. 21–24; Kliman, "Women in Early English Literature"; and Sklute, "Freoðuwebbe."

131. The other two scenes of ritual drinking are similarly freighted. Wealhtheow engages in the ritual again during the feast held to celebrate Beowulf's defeat of Grendel and although there is no hint of discord at this feast, it is telling that she steps forward in the moments following the conclusion of the scop's account of Hengest's visit with Finn in which violence erupts with disastrous results for all. With the words of the scop still hanging in the air, Wealhtheow performs her ritual duties and so offers a sharply positive counterpoint to the actions of Hengest and Finn as she attempts to secure Beowulf's future loyalty to her sons. The scene involving Hygd is the least well

developed of the three instantiations of this thematic structure in the poem, but it is clear that she similarly functions as a peaceweaver during the feast held to celebrate Beowulf's safe return to his homeland when she participates in the ritual.

132. Laȝamon's Vortiger is similarly informed that the ritual response to "wæs hæil" is "Drinc hail" (7152), but he chooses instead to say in "Bruttisc" "Maiden Rouwenne꞉ drinc bluðeliche þenne" (7160) [Maid Rowene, drink blithely].

133. Uocauit te dominum regem. & uocabulo salutacionis honorauit. Quid autem respondere debes꞉ est. drincheil (370).

134. Ab illo die usque in hodiernum mansit consuetudo illa in britannia. quia in conuiuiis qui potat ad alium dicit washeil. Qui uero post illum recipit potum꞉ respondet drincheil (370–71).

135. Wace goes Laȝamon one better by explaining the mechanics of the ritual in more detail and by making explicit that the participants engage in it "pur joie e pur amistied" (6968) [for joy and for friendship]. He concludes his brief foray into Anglo-Saxon ethnography by commenting that the custom is still observed at important feasts today (6980 ff.).

136. The Germanic origins of the ritual and the appearance of the English lexemes *washeil* and *drincheil* in the French and Latin texts suggest that the scene is rooted in the English tradition and is not the common inheritance of all three poets. Aside from proper or place names, these are among the only demonstrably English words to appear in either the *Roman* or the *Historia*.

137. We should note, however, that while the ritual always has a positive outcome in Old English poetry, it does not guarantee that the bond it reaffirms (or establishes) will necessarily last. We never see the ritual fail, but we can infer that it would be subject to the same types of pressure that attend the related, and more important, ritual practice of using marriage to establish (or reinforce) intertribal ties. To take just two examples from Old English poetry, the bond created through Hildeburh's marriage to Finn does not prevent either political discord or awful violence and, as Sklute, "*Freoðuwebbe*," 206, notes, Beowulf himself "is openly wary of the value" of marrying women off as a means of securing peaceful political alliances: "Oft seldan hwær / æfter leodhryre   lytle hwile / bongar bugeð,   þeah seo bryd duge" (2029b–31b) [often the deadly spear will rest only a little while under such a circumstance, though the bride be good].

138. [D]edit illi per quendam familiarem suum uenenum potare꞉ quem innumerabilibus donariis corruperat (374).

139. Quod cum hausisset inclitus bellator ille꞉ subita infirmitate grauatus est ita ut nullam spem uiuendi haberet (374).

140. Ringbom, *Studies in the Narrative Technique*, 87.

141. Ibid.

142. *Horn* is extant in three manuscripts: Cambridge, University Library, Gg. 4. 27. 2; Oxford, Bodleian Library, Laud Misc. 108; and London, British Library, Harley 2253.

The first two date to the late thirteenth or very early fourteenth century, while the latter dates from the early to mid–fourteenth century. See further Allen, *King Horn,* 3–15, and Hall, *King Horn,* vii–x.

FOUR.   The Tradition in Flux: Fragmentation and Survival

1. See Ong, *Orality and Literacy,* 31–77.

2. 1 Cor. 13.12, 1611, King James version.

3. The expanded lexical system becomes most apparent in the later medieval period, where poets habitually employ doublets in which one element is native and the other imported, chiefly from French, Latin, or Scandinavian. See further Serjeantson, *History of Foreign Words.*

4. Hahn, "Early Middle English," 81.

5. The prose works that survive from the early Middle English period, such as the *Ancrene Wisse, Seinte Katerine,* and *Hali Meiðhed,* to cite just three, show a similar indebtedness to the Anglo-Saxon prose tradition.

6. Chaucer, *Canterbury Tales,* Parson's Prologue, X, 42–43; I cite from Benson's edition (*Riverside Chaucer*).

7. Ibid., General Prologue, 1 [A] 682.

8. For discussions of the so-called Alliterative Revival of the fourteenth century, see the essays collected in Levy and Szarmach, *Alliterative Tradition,* and Lawton, *Middle English Alliterative Poetry.* See further Turville-Petre, *Alliterative Revival;* Everett, "Alliterative Revival"; Salter, "Alliterative Revival" and "Alliterative Modes and Affiliations"; Lawton, "Unity of Middle English Alliterative Poetry"; and Scattergood, *Lost Tradition.*

9. Chambers, *On the Continuity,* lxvi, comments wryly that "[t]he displacement of an English by a Norman ruling class cannot have tended towards the careful preservation of manuscripts in Anglo-Saxon; then for centuries before the Dissolution of the Monasteries they must have been useless curiosities, which a competent monastic librarian would eject; and at the Dissolution whole libraries, like those of Glastonbury or Malmesbury or Crowland, vanished almost utterly." However, Old English prose texts, including Ælfric's homilies, Wulfstan's sermons, and saints' lives, were rewritten or copied early in the post-Conquest period. Cf. Swan and Treharne, *Rewriting Old English.* For a list of texts that survive from this period, see Roseborough, *Outline of Middle English Grammar,* chart following 109.

10. On the international nature of life in western Europe in the years following the Norman Conquest, see Salter, *English and International,* 1–100.

11. Salter, *Fourteenth-Century English Poetry,* 119. Of course, we must bear in mind that Anglo-Saxon poetics was also able to accommodate non-native material, as

evidenced by the frequent use Anglo-Saxon poets make of learned Latin material. But when they do incorporate nontraditional material into their verse, they make the imported matter conform to the demands of their poetics, as the seamless interweaving of Latin and Old English in the traditional, alliterative, macaronic verses that conclude the *Phoenix* testifies. See Heffernan, "Old English *Phoenix*"; Irvine, "Cynewulf's Use of Psychomachia Allegory"; and Calder, "Vision of Paradise."

12. On the Scandinavian and French impact on the English lexicon, see Serjeantson, *History of Foreign Words,* 61–103, 104–69; and Baugh and Cable, *History of the English Language,* 90–103 and 165–73.

13. Although we will focus on individual lexemes in what follows, we must bear in mind that they occur within a phraseology and that often it is an entire phrase, and not just a single lexeme, that functions as a metonymic trigger for traditional, inherent meaning. See further Foley's discussion of traditional Old English phraseology in *Traditional Oral Epic,* 207–39.

14. Bosworth and Toller, *Anglo-Saxon Dictionary,* s.v.

15. On traditional epithets in Old English verse, see Foley, *Immanent Art,* 195–214. DeGregorio, "Theorizing Irony," offers a different view of how such phrases operate in the tradition.

16. The OED, s.v., cites examples of *helm* in the sense of "helmet" and "the top or summit of something" occurring as late as the late eighteenth century.

17. OED, s.v. In a few instances its concrete referentiality is metonymically extended to soldiers wearing helmets.

18. MED, s.v. (c).

19. Ibid., s.v. *helmet.*

20. OED, s.v.

21. The MED dates the first example of *protectour* to 1390. It gives a slightly earlier date, 1350, for the first attestation of the related and similarly French-derived noun *proteccioun.*

22. The same cannot be said of the word's meaning, as *æglæca* remains a much discussed term. The substantial scholarship devoted to it includes Kuhn, "Old English *aglæca*"; Mezger, "Goth. aglaiti 'unchastity'"; Olsen, "Aglæca"; Duncan, "Epitaphs for Æglæcan"; Nicholls, "Bede 'Awe-inspiring' not 'Monstrous'"; Mizuno, "Beowulf as a Terrible Stranger"; and, most recently, Roberts, "Hrothgar's Admirable Courage." In offering the firmly neutral gloss that they do, the editors of the DOE commendably depart from the long-standing and widely endorsed practice of defining *aglæca* as "miserable being, wretch, miscreant, monster" when it refers to a monstrous figure and as "fierce combatant" when it refers to a human such as Beowulf or Sigemund. See Bosworth and Toller, *Anglo-Saxon Dictionary,* s.v., and, more recently, the on-line MED, http://ets. umdl.umich.edu/m/med/, which, in the spring of 2004 defined *egleche* as "Brave, fearless," and offered the following: "Cp. OE *æglæcea* warrior, hero, monster."

23. In addition to the instances cited above, the lexeme refers to Grendel ten more times and the dragon three more times. Although the matter is not clear, it may also refer to Beowulf twice more as well (1512a; 646b). See further the commentary on these lines in the editions of Sedgefield, Wrenn, Klaeber, Dobbie (*ASPR*, IV), and Mitchell and Robinson.

24. The lexeme is also used to describe the immensely powerful whale ("þone aglæcan" [52a]), a creature that we earlier learn is "frecne ond ferðgrim" (5a) [dangerous and savage]. I cite the *Whale* from *ASPR*, III.

25. When the *Beowulf*-poet uses *aglæca* to refer to Sigemund and Beowulf, he does not invert, through irony or any other rhetorical strategy, the lexeme's primary meaning. Far from distancing the heroes from the many other unambiguously evil *aglæcan* who populate Old English poetry, this lexeme problematizes the heroes by linking them closely to their more clearly monstrous brethren. Sigemund and Beowulf may enjoy far more positive reputations than *aglæcan* normally do, but they fit surprisingly comfortably under the term's semantic umbrella. Sigemund is a renowned hero who successfully kills a dragon, but as we learn from the *Völsungasaga,* our chief source of information about him, he is a shape-shifter and also incestuously (if unknowingly) fathers Fitela, with whom he later roams the woods robbing and killing the men unfortunate enough to cross their path while they are in their wolf shapes. While Beowulf never overtly engages in such socially unsanctioned behavior, his actions often lead him to straddle the line between socially acceptable and socially threatening behavior. Both against the monsters and even against some of his human foes (cf. his killing of Dæghrefn), Beowulf's behavior on occasion seems to be less than human, as, for example, when he stands enraged and roaring before the dragon's cave (2550–52a) or when he stands in the damaged hall still distended with rage as he clutches the enormous arm and shoulder he has just brutally torn off the monster Grendel.

26. We may also wish to include two adverbial variants of the term, *aȝly,* found in *Cleanness,* a poem generally accepted as having been produced by the same poet who wrote the other poems that appear in London, British Library, Cotton Nero A. x with it: *Sir Gawain, Pearl,* and *Patience.* See the comment on *aȝleȝ* later in this section.

27. I cite the Trinity B. 14. 52 homilies from Morris, *Homilies of the Twelfth Century,* by page number, as this edition contains no line numbers.

28. Morris, *Homilies and Homiletic Treatises,* p. 177, line 281.

29. I cite the Peterborough Chronicle here from Clark's edition of MS E, Laud Misc. 636.

30. *Ancrene Wisse,* Tolkien's edition (*English Text*) of the version contained in Cambridge, Corpus Christi College, 402. The text is cited throughout by reference first to the page numbers of Tolkien's edition and then to the corresponding line numbers on those pages.

31. Salu, *Ancrene Riwle,* 24.

32. Morton, *Nun's Rule,* 44; H. White, *Ancrene Wisse,* 30.

33. Morris edited both these versions of the *Poema* in, respectively, *Homilies of the Twelfth Century* and *Homilies and Homiletic Treatises.*

34. Oxford, Bodleian Library, Laud 108.

35. These versions are contained in Cambridge, Trinity College B. 14. 39, and Oxford, Jesus College, 29. The three transcripts of another version of the *Proverbs*, the one found in London, British Library, Cotton Galba A. xix, suggests that the lexeme appeared as well in this now fragmentary manuscript, since all three transcribers, James, Wanley, and Spelman, include it. Cf. Arngart, *Proverbs of Alfred*, 11–25. The acephalic nature of Maidstone A. 13 prevents us from knowing whether it appeared in that version as well.

36. *Sir Gawain* survives in London, British Library, Cotton Nero A. x, and the *Parlement* in London, British Library, Additional 31042, and London, British Library, Additional 33994 (the Ware manuscript).

37. All citations to the *South-English Legendary* are from Horstmann's edition.

38. For reasons that he does not explain, Horstmann prefers *was* in line 157 to the alternate reading *wax*. Because *wax* focuses our attention on the changing nature of Mary's character, something essential to this narrative, there is sound reason for accepting it in this instance, as I have silently done.

39. The proof the childless prince wants is for his wife to get pregnant, something that occurs the very night he makes his request of Mary.

40. On the semantics of the Old English words for *courage* and *bravery,* see Bately, "Bravery."

41. Gollancz may have been the first to suggest this etymology for *aghlich,* but we cannot be sure because the critical and glossarial apparatus to his 1897 revision of Morris's text (the apparatus to which Gollancz notes is "still at press" in 1912) does not finally appear until 1940.

42. Benson, *Art and Tradition,* 59.

43. Borroff, *Sir Gawain,* 108.

44. Davis, in his appendix to the revised second edition of Tolkien and Gordon's *Sir Gawain,* notes, 150–51, that "[w]ords beginning with *h* very commonly alliterate with words beginning with a vowel."

45. Borroff, *Sir Gawain,* 112.

46. See Cable, *English Alliterative Tradition,* 66–113.

47. Its related adverbial form, *aȝly,* similarly bears alliterative stress when it occurs in *Sir Gawain* ("Armed, ful aȝlez: in hert hit hym lykez" [2335] [armed, full *aȝlez:* it pleased him in his heart]) and *Cleanness* ("Þat aȝly hurled in his ereȝ her harloteȝ speche" [874] [that *aȝly* hurled her harlot's words into his ears]; "Þe aungeleȝ hasted þise oþer & aȝly hem þratten" [937] [the angels pressed upon these others and *aȝly* urged them on]). Unless otherwise noted, all citations to *Sir Gawain* are from Tolkien and Gordon's revised second edition. I cite *Cleanness* here from J. Anderson's edition. Even in a poem with such loose metrics as the *Poema Morale,* the lexeme continues to allit-

erate, although without bearing stress: "Þer buð ateliche fend. and eisliche wihte" (Lambeth, 281); "Þat beð ateliche fiend and Eiseliche wihten" (Trinity, 285) [there/that is the terrible fiend and *eisliche* creature].

48. Curiously, immediately after establishing the character's monstrosity by connecting him so explicitly to the nonhuman race of *eotenas* [giants], the poet hastens to add, "Bot mon most I algate mynn hym to bene" (141) [but a very large man I at any rate declare him to be], a maneuver that allows him to mitigate the character's alterity by shifting attention to his wonderful and unmistakably human attributes, features that serve to anchor him to the human world as "þe myriest in his muckel þat myȝt ride" (142) [the (?)strongest in his size of any who might ride]. For this sense of *myriest*, cf. MED, s.v. *mirie*, 7.b.

49. During the Christmas feast in Camelot he "hales in at þe halle dor" (136) [comes in at the door] on horseback and rides right up to the high table, where, among other things, he insults Arthur and impugns the still-fledgling but nonetheless precious reputation of Camelot and its knights.

50. While a number of modern translators prove themselves sensitive to the lexeme's traditional affective dynamics and translate it accordingly as "awesome" (Barron), "frightening" (J. Rosenberg), and even "ungodly" (Gardner, *Complete Works*), many others do not and so skew the Green Knight's presentation and subsequent reception. Among the many translations that largely ignore *aghlich*'s etymology and so largely fail to capture even a hint of its traditional referentiality, we find "unknown" (Borroff), "haughty" (Finch, *Complete Works*), "appalling" (Stone), and, rather surprisingly, "ugly" (Moorman, *Works of the Gawain-Poet*).

51. See esp. Hill, *Cultural World*, 108–40.

52. London, British Library, Additional 31042. Unless otherwise noted, all citations to the *Parlement* are from Offord's edition. *Egheliche* may have appeared in the only other surviving version of the *Parlement*, Additional 33994, but because this version is acephalic, we have no way of knowing whether it did.

53. Wright, *Metrical Chronicle*, xliii.

54. As Offord, *Parlement*, 38, notes, a *sowre* is a fourth-year male that an old stag trains "to act as a kind of squire, watching out for danger and providing a decoy when the chase is on."

55. I am grateful to Dr. Lawrence Schek for pointing out to me in conversation that while continental European elk are known for their aggressiveness, the species of deer in question would have used its impressive hardware solely for mating purposes or in self-defense only when cornered.

56. The dragon's physicality in *Beowulf* is so terrible even in death that the Geats immediately tip its carcass into the sea. The severed body parts of Grendel that are publicly displayed in Heorot—his shoulder, arm, hand, and head—remain powerful reminders both of the terror that the Grendelkin visited upon Denmark for so many years and of the Danes' helplessness in the face of their repeated attacks. Although the

Green Knight does not die as a result of the beheading blow he receives in Camelot, his body, both with and without its head attached to it, remains a wondrous and fearful object throughout the poem.

57. The *Parlement* is generally thought to have been composed somewhere between 1352–53 and 1390. Offord, *Parlement*, xxxvi, advocates a date between 1352–53 and 1370, while Pearsall, *Old and Middle English Poetry*, 297, dates it to c. 1390. *Sir Gawain* is thought to have been composed at some point in the same period, with Pearsall favoring a date c. 1390. Cf. Gollancz, *Pearl, Cleanness*, 7–9, and *Sir Gawain*, ix–xiii, and Tolkien and Gordon, *Sir Gawain*, xi–xii.

58. I cite the *Metrical Chronicle* from Wright's edition. The lines cited can be found in appendix xx, vol. II, pp. 838–77 and are taken from the version of the poem found in Cambridge, Trinity College, R. 4. 26.

59. Healey and Venezky's *Microfiche Concordance to Old English* lists approximately 125 occurrences of *beot* and its derivatives in Old English prose and poetry.

60. Bosworth and Toller, *Anglo-Saxon Dictionary*. For a complete list of Old English synonyms for NE *promise* and *oath*, see Roberts and Kay, *Thesaurus of Old English* (12.07.02.01, 12.07.02.01.01, 12.07.02.01.01.01).

61. According to Bessinger and Smith's *Concordance*, the breakdown is as follows: *beot* (11), *beotast* (1), *beote* (1), *beotedan* (1), *beotode* (1), *beotum* (1), *beotwordum* (1), *gebeot* (1), *gebeotedon* (2), *wordbeot* (2), *wordbeotunga* (1).

62. I cite the *Wanderer* from *ASPR*, III.

63. All citations to *Beowulf* are from Klaeber's edition unless otherwise noted. The importance of the vows the Danish warriors have made (and failed to keep) is further underscored in this passage by Hrothgar's labeling his now deceased men *oretmecgas*, a word that Robinson, *Beowulf and the Appositive Style*, 67, suggests means "man of the ultimate vow." Bjork, "Speech as Gift," 1005, accepts both Robinson's definition and the etymology he proposes, but see Brady, "'Warriors' in *Beowulf*" (cited in Robinson, *Beowulf and the Appositive Style*, 67, and Bjork, "Speech as Gift," 1005n55), who takes *oretmecgas* to have the less charged meaning of "a man who calls out a challenge, a challenger." The lexeme's specialized meaning was not stressed earlier. Cf. Bosworth and Toller, *Anglo-Saxon Dictionary*, who gloss *oretmæcg* as "a combatant, warrior, champion" and Wyatt and Sedgefield, who both translate it as "warrior." Sedgefield adopts this reading and cites not only the proto-Germanic form *or-hat* that Sievers, *Grammar of Old English*, § 43n4, does but the OHG cognate *ur-heiz* [challenge] as well, as does Klaeber. Heyne does not include the word in his glossary.

64. I cite *Genesis A* from *ASPR*, I. On the nature of speech acts, see Austin, *How to Do Things*, and Searle, *Speech Acts* and *Expression and Meaning*.

65. For a variety of reasons, such as the more complete state of Caligula and its decidedly greater artistic achievement, it has garnered far more critical attention than has Otho. Madden, for example, argues, in *Laȝamons Brut*, I, xxxvi, that the Otho version must be "regarded as an abbreviated recension" of the poem and notes, "It would

appear also, from some passages, that this copy must have been partially written from recitation" (I, xxxviii). Otho has recently been the focus of renewed interest. See Cannon, "Style and Authorship," and Bryan, *Collaborative Meaning*.

66. *Beotlice* occurs in the *Holy Rood* (Napier's edition [*History of the Holy Rood-Tree*]) on p. 26, line 3, where Napier translates it loosely as "exultingly" (p. 27, line 33). For Donoghue, "Laȝamon's Ambivalence," 551–54, *beot* is not a dynamic part of Laȝamon's poetics but rather one of the poem's many "archaic-sounding poeticisms" (522).

67. All citations to *Brut* are from Brook and Leslie's edition unless otherwise noted.

68. See, for example, *Brut*, 3830, where it appropriately describes the vows the French make to fight against Julius Caesar (3821–28); 10651, where it is used by Arthur to characterize Childric's earlier declarations that Arthur "ne dærst in nare [st]ude: his ræsses abiden. / no on uelde no on wude: no nauere nane stude. / 7 ȝif þu him abidest: he þe wule binden. / quellen þine leoden: and þi lond aȝen" (10166–69) [does not dare in any place await his attacks, not in the field, the wood, or in any place; and if you wait for him, he will bind you, kill your people, and conquer your land]; and 12441, where Cador uses *beot* to describe the statements the Romans have been making about coming to England, conquering it, and carrying Arthur as a prisoner to Rome. Among the examples found in Old English poetry, the *Beowulf*-poet's announcement that "Beowulf maðelode,   beotwordum spræc / niehstan siðe" (2510–11a) [Beowulf spoke, he spoke boasting words for the final time] stands out as perhaps the most dramatic.

69. Something similar occurs in *Beowulf* when the poet, not Beowulf, marks the speech the hero gives before fighting the dragon as being spoken in "beotwordum" (2510b). Beowulf articulates a powerful *beot* in this speech, though he does not identify it as a formal *beot*.

70. In one of these instances we can surmise with some certainty that the Otho-redactor omitted *beot* once again because even though the damage to line 13952 is severe, much of the line is still readable, and we can therefore see that the poet replaces Caligula's reading "And seoððen he his beot makede" [and afterwards he made his *beot*] with the phrase "and þar-in wonie" [and dwelt therein]. Despite the damage to the second half of the line in Otho, we can see that the redactor apparently copied the second half of Caligula's line because Otho has "[. . .]te some come" where Caligula reads "a sumere þat he wolde."

71. The Otho-redactor omits *beot* and the line in which it appears six times (Caligula lines 8153, 10239, 10651, 11819, 13124, and 14073), while he substitutes different words for it seven other times (Otho lines 3830, 10238, 10493, 10814, 12441, 12526, and 13885). The evidence of line 13952 suggests that he omits it in one other instance, so that the number of omissions and substitutions comes to seven each.

72. See Cannon, "Style and Authorship," 193, who contends that the "Otho writer is attempting, albeit tentatively, to reorientate the *Brut* away from its strong association with the English writing of the past, and, in order to make this change, he must

not only modernize the language of the *Brut* but must eject as much of the antiquarian colouring from the text as he safely can."

73. Madden, *Laȝamons Brut*, III, 498, similarly suggests that *broc* "is the modern term *brag*, the meaning of which was originally the same with *threat*. Gavin Douglas writes it *braik*. The verb in Mhd. is *brogen*, which is connected with A.-S. *bregan*, *broga*, etc." Skeat, *Etymological Dictionary*, s.v. *brag*, makes no mention of the lexeme's meaning "threat" but notes as analogues "MDan. *brage*, to crack, also to speak great words . . .; Norw. *braka*, to snap, also to prate, chatter . . .; Icel. *braka*, to creak. Cf. Jutland *brag*, a noise . . .; AS. *gebræc*, a crash, noise."

74. Lexical clustering may be partially responsible for the redactor's use of this term in this section of the poem, one in which *beot* appears three times in the space of only seven lines in Caligula. In only one other spot in the *Brut*'s approximately sixteen thousand lines do two occurrences of *beot* appear in such close proximity to each other, and the Otho-redactor handles matters very differently then. In line 10238 he substitutes the phrase "mid word seide" for Caligula's *beot* and then omits Caligula line 10239, a line containing the past participle *beoteden*.

75. *Duȝeðe* and its compounds appear some ninety-five times in Caligula. In Otho, it appears eight times, is omitted thirty-seven times, and is replaced by another lexeme forty-four times (with *cnihtes* [nineteen times] and *folk* [nine times] occurring most frequently). In the remaining instances in which *beot* appears in Caligula, damage to the Otho manuscript has made it impossible to determine whether the lexeme was used, omitted, or replaced by the redactor.

76. The terms that are used as substitutes for *doȝeþe* more than once are, in order of descending frequency of occurrence, *cnihtes*, *folk*, *leod* [people], *men*, and *ferde* [troop]. The remaining ones, all of which are used as substitutes for *duȝeþe* one time each, are *world*, *somme* [united], *(ȝong)e* [young], *hii* [they], *feue* [few], *monie* [many], and *king*. In addition, the phrase "hii alle" [they all] is used one time.

77. *Beot* and *duȝeðe* are not the only terms the Otho-redactor handles in this fashion. See Donoghue, "Laȝamon's Ambivalence"; Cannon, "Style and Authorship'; Bryan, *Collaborative Meaning;* and Keith, "Layamon's *Brut*."

78. We must not lose sight, after all, of the fact that Otho contains what appears to be *beot*'s final occurrence in the Middle English written records. On the dating of the Caligula A. ix and Otho C. xiii manuscripts, see above, chapter 3, note 39.

79. Lord, *Singer of Tales*, 68.

80. For the purposes of this study, this global tradition is the Indo-European one, although oral traditions from other parts of the world would trace their roots back to different sources. To cite just one of the many possible examples of the cross-cultural and cross-linguistic transmission of traditional thematics, Renoir demonstrates in "Oral Theme and Written Texts" that two Old English poems, the *Dream of the Rood* and the *Husband's Message*, share a traditional theme with Catullus's *Poem IV*. See further Renoir, "Hero on the Beach" and "Oral-Formulaic Context." Olsen, "Proteus in Latin,"

considers the ways in which vernacular poetics and Latin stylistics intersect during the Anglo-Saxon period in the Bonifatian correspondence edited by Tangl (*Die Briefe*).

81. Lord, *Singer of Tales*, 69. He expands on this definition and more fully addresses the multiformity of traditional themes in "Theme of the Withdrawn Hero." See also Lord, "Theme in Anglo-Saxon Poetry."

82. Renoir, *Key to Old Poems*, 117–56.

83. Ibid., 123.

84. Ibid., 118.

85. Lord, "Theme of the Withdrawn Hero," 18.

86. Translators, of course, are able to provide very serviceable and often eloquent equivalents for formulaic phrases, but they cannot infuse their translated formulas or formulaic epithets with any of the inherent meaning they possessed in their original languages. For any such transference to take place, the two traditions would have to be so closely aligned as to be nearly indistinguishable from one another. See chapter 5, the section "Oral Poetics and Post-Traditional Texts." The degree to which scholars were, until fairly recently, stymied by the formulaic character of many earlier poetic traditions illuminates the point here. Because they did not grasp the very different process through which formulaic language conveys meaning within the expressive economy of oral poetics, scholars quite logically approached it as if it were produced by poets whose aesthetics and compositional practices mirrored their own. When viewed from such a perspective, formulaic language does appear to be, as it was long mistakenly thought to be, mechanistic, limiting, and aesthetically barren.

87. See Foley, *Traditional Oral Epic*, 331–32, and M. Edwards, "Homer and Oral Tradition." The shared themes and story patterns are not equally important in the different traditions. For example, in the ancient Greek and contemporary South Slavic traditions, the pattern first identified by Lord as the Return Song is a far more important and far more central narrative element than it is in the medieval English tradition.

88. For example, feasts in *Beowulf* are almost always used positively to reinforce existing social bonds or to establish new ones, as we can see in the feast held before Beowulf's fight with Grendel and the one that Hygelac holds for him upon his return to Geatland after successfully defeating Grendel and his dam. In the *Iliad* feasts are not only events during which the Trojans and Greeks celebrate and honor their dead and living members but also such crucial components of the larger *communitas* that encompasses both Trojan and Greek culture that Priam's refusal of Achilleus's hospitality threatens the very fabric of the poem's social world. It is only after Priam acquiesces and shares a feast with his son's killer that the threat dissipates. See further Foley, *Immanent Art*, 135–89.

89. Cf. lines 2304, 2331, 2401, and 2550.

90. The total changes if we accept the first of the MED's definitions for the *hapax wandliche*: "?Quick to anger, ill-tempered; ?wicked." The Otho-redactor substitutes

ohte, a commonly occurring adjective that the MED glosses as "mighty, worthy" and "worthy in warfare or other dangerous situations" (s.v. *ought* adj. 1 [a] and [b], respectively). This gloss is, however, only partially applicable here, ignoring as it does the sense "fear, terror" that the noun *oht* carries with it in Old English. Cf. Bosworth and Toller, *Anglo-Saxon Dictionary*, s.v.

91. For the former, see, for example, Ælfric's life of St. Martin in Skeat, *Ælfric's Lives of Saints*, II, 506 ff., and for the latter, see Pope, *Homilies of Ælfric*, II, 17, 241 ff.

92. Although beyond the scope of the current discussion, ME *aweden* and its descendants (chiefly *wod* [mad]) come increasingly to do the work that OE *gebelgan* did, although not so exclusively nor so entirely, as we can see from the list of meanings for *aweden* cited in the MED, s.v.: "(a) To become enraged; grow insane or beside oneself; behave foolishly; ... (b) *ppl. awed(de*, enraged, rabid; insane, senseless; as *noun:* a lunatic." In Old English, *wod* appears in a variety of forms, chief among which are the adjectives *wod* and *wodlic* [mad, furious], the adverb *wodlice* [madly, furiously], and the nouns *woda* [madman], *wodness* [madness, fury], *wodscipe* [madness, fury], and *wodþrag* [mad fit, madness]. The only one of these forms to appear in the poetry is *wod*, which appears a total of ten times. When *wod* does appear in the poetry, however, it is always the preterite indicative of the verb *wadan* [to go] and is not linked to the various terms for madness and insanity.

93. All quotations to the Anglo-Norman *Boeve* are from Stimming's edition (*Der Anglonorman-nosche Boeve*).

94. Boefs uses his sword to decapitate the boar ("le chef li va couper" [447]), but the actual breaking of the sword is neither presented in nor accounted for in the Anglo-Norman text. One moment Boefs is quite logically using his sword to behead his fallen enemy, and the next moment he is putting the severed head on the "tronsoun" of his inexplicably broken blade.

95. I cite *Beues* from Kölbing's edition (*Romance of Sir Beues*).

96. Despite his tendency to depart frequently and freely from his source, the *Beues*-poet is often seen as a little more than the slavish, untalented translator. Crane, *Insular Romance*, 54, offers an important corrective to this view when she argues that Middle English and Anglo-Norman versions should be seen as "related works whose differences may be more accurately understood in terms of insular generic and historical developments than in terms of textual revision."

97. See chapter 2, the section "Oral Poetics and a Narrative Complex."

98. In her "retelling" of the English romance, Hibbard relates that Bevis's lance breaks, but she completely effaces the sword's failure. In her version, *Three Middle English Romances*, 103, Bevis does not carry the boar's head back on his broken sword but more logically "stick[s] it on his spear handle."

99. Baugh identifies Bevis's Christmas Day fight against a band of fifty Saracens (585–738) and his pitched battle with the inhabitants of London (4287–538) as the *Beues*-poet's two other major additions to his source material. See further Baugh, "Making

252 — Notes to Pages 166–171

of *Beves*" and "Improvisation," 430–37. Weiss, "Major Interpolations," does not count the Christmas battle as a "major" interpolation.

100. Even in Best's "Villains and Monsters," a study whose announced focus is the text's monsters, the boar fight receives little attention: Best mentions the boar in passing only in her essay's first sentence.

101. Weiss, "Major Interpolations," 72.

102. Crane, *Insular Romance*, 60. On dragon fights in hagiographic texts, see Rauer, *Beowulf and the Dragon*, 52–86.

103. Pearsall, *Old and Middle English Poetry*, 147.

104. Not all of these details will be shared among all three episodes, something that poses little problem once we recall that the traditional thematics upon which they are founded does not depend upon or demand a set presentation of predetermined narrative events. As a result, Morpidus's fight with the beast is no less traditional than the other two heroes' battles because his takes place in a single encounter, and not the bi- or tripartite ones we discover, respectively, in the boar fight in *Beues* and the dragon fight in *Beowulf*.

105. The *Beues*-poet elsewhere employs just such a strategy. During the boar fight, the poet first relates that Bevis's spear "barst to pises þore" (790) [burst into pieces there] and three lines later repeats that "al to-borste is Beues spere" (793) [Bevis's spear is shattered]. Bevis also has a spear break on him during his battle with Ascopard (Bevis's "spere al to-fliȝ" [2536] after hitting the giant's shoulder), but, tellingly, its failure plays virtually no part within the scene's affective dynamics. In fact, not only does the spear (again) do no damage, but the seriocomic narrative event that follows it— Ascopard swings so mightily at Bevis that he slips and finds himself suddenly in danger of being beheaded—immediately and completely obscures it.

106. *Wod* occurs one other time within the broader compass of the dragon episode, as opposed to the narrower one of the actual dragon fight.

107. Much the same is true in another episode, in which Bevis becomes *wod* during a fight with two nonhuman antagonists, in this case two lions. The lions rend his armor, wound Bevis terribly, and generally cause him "grete distresse" (2430). Bevis suffers a wound in his thigh that so greatly shames him that he begins to fight "As he were wood" (2443) [as if he were enraged]. As in the case in the dragon fight, though, Bevis's anger is not pivotal to the scene and does not prevent him from suffering a further wound: the lion manages to get under Bevis's shield "And with his teeþ with sory happe / He kitte a pece of his lappe" (2455–56) [and with his teeth with sorry chance, he cut off a piece of his shirt], something that causes the hero to fall "For anguysse . . . to þe grounde" (2458) [for anguish . . . to the ground]. Nor does his being *wod* lead to the quick dispatching of his foes. He kills the lion not after becoming *wod* but rather after becoming "greuyd in his hert" (2460) [aggrieved in his heart].

108. The etymology of *berserkr* has long been contested, but there is general agreement, as Vigfusson, *Icelandic-English Dictionary*. s.v., notes, that in "battle the

berserkers were subject to fits of frenzy, . . . when they howled like wild beasts, foamed at the mouth, and gnawed the iron rim of their shields."

109. Related to ME *tenen*, "1. To do (sb. or sth.) harm; harass (sb. an animal), annoy, oppress . . . 4. (a) To anger (sb.), enrage; vex (sb.), irritate; *ppl.* tened, enraged, angered," and descended from OE *teonian*, "to vex, irritate," Bosworth and Toller, *Anglo-Saxon Dictionary*, s.v., *atened* is yet another lexeme without roots in oral poetics that is injected into traditional thematics in the post-Conquest period. Its Old English ancestor is a relatively rare lexeme, one that, moreover, occurs almost entirely in the prose. The only form of *teonian* extant in the poetic records is the adverb *teonlice*, which appears just three times in the entire Anglo-Saxon poetic corpus, in the *Phoenix* (407a) and in Psalms 103.27 and 104.26. Its meaning, "in a manner that causes harm or trouble, grievously, miserably," Bosworth and Toller, *Anglo-Saxon Dictionary*, s.v., is even further removed from *gebelgan* than is ME *wod*.

110. See Crane, *Insular Romance*, 62n22, and Zupitza, *Romance of Guy*, i–xv.

111. These are the "second or 15th-century Version" that survives in Cambridge, University Library, Ff. 2. 38 (edited by Zupitza [*Romance of Guy*]) and the version attributed to John Lydgate found in Oxford, Bodleian Library, Misc. 683 (edited by Mac-Cracken [*Minor Poems*]).

112. Unless otherwise noted, all quotations from *Guy* are from Zupitza's edition of the Auchinleck version found in his *Romance of Guy: 14th Century Version*. Where a second set of line references are included, the reader is directed to the equivalent lines in the CUL manuscript. Some of the details in CUL differ from those in Auchinleck and Caius—for example, the boar kills only twenty hounds, instead of one hundred—but for the most part they are minor, and I pass silently over them.

113. The author of the CUL version does not explicitly mention Guy's fear here but tells us only that "He was in a farre cuntre / All aloone fro hys meyne, / And, as he openyd there the boore, / Euyr he blewe more and more" (6463–66) [he was in a distant country all alone from him men, and as he opened the boar there, he blew ever more and more]. The Auchinleck episode follows very closely the version found in the Anglo-Norman *Gui* (6812–66).

114. In *Sir Gawain*, Bertilak similarly dispatches the boar with a single thrust of his sword, but the context in which he does so is narratively more charged and its affective dynamics more decidedly traditional.

115. Auchinleck and CUL contain fuller versions of the second dragon episode than does Caius, which often compresses or omits much that the other versions take directly from the Anglo-Norman *Gui*.

116. Cf. MED, s.v. 1.a and 2.a.

117. Responding perhaps to what he may have perceived to be a deficiency in his source at this point, the poet or scribe responsible for the CUL version attempts to clarify the issue by adding that Guy told the three knights "That none were so hardye / To come to hym, þogh he schulde dye" (6871–72) [that no one should be so brave

(?foolhardy) as to come to him, even though he should die]. As a result of this addition, CUL more fully emphasizes the hero's physical risk and the possibly dire consequences that Guy faces than do the other versions of *Guy,* but the affective impact of this addition is minor and localized.

118. Once again, the poet/scribe responsible for the CUL version distinguishes himself from his cohort by incorporating into his text an element from medieval English oral poetics. After bearing, without injury, Guy's initial attack, the dragon "To Gye . . . starte, as he wolde wede / And smote hym downe and hys stede" (6883–84) [toward Guy . . . jumped as if he would go mad and struck down him and his steed]. But despite this parallel, this episode remains far more closely aligned to a post-traditional rather than traditional poetics because after receiving this fearsome blow, one that "stonyed [him] sore" (6885) [sorely stunned him], Guy, apparently none the worse for the wear, "starte vp and lay not longe" (6887) [jumped up and did not lie there long].

119. I take the term *draconitas* from Irving, *Rereading Beowulf.* Cf. his important discussion of the dragon, esp. 100–132.

120. The specific ways in which various traditions channel meaning vary widely, of course, but one of the few things that oral traditions have in common is that the expressive economies through which they are articulated communicate meaning in very similar ways. See further Foley, *Singer of Tales in Performance,* 1–59.

FIVE. Continuations

1. A variety of arguments have been put forward to explain the genesis of the Revival. See esp. Pearsall, "Origins of the Alliterative Revival"; Moorman, "Origins of the Alliterative Revival"; Levy and Szarmach, *Alliterative Tradition;* Lawton, *Middle English Alliterative Poetry* and "Unity of Middle English Alliterative Poetry"; Turville-Petre, *Alliterative Revival;* Everett, "Alliterative Revival"; Salter, "Alliterative Revival" and "Alliterative Modes and Affiliations"; and Scattergood, *Lost Tradition.*

2. Chambers, *On the Continuity,* lxvi–lxvii. Chambers is not alone in this view. Cf., for example, Andrew and Waldron, *Poems of the Pearl Manuscript,* 46, who assert that the "long lines of *Cl[eanness], Pat[ience], and [Sir] G[awain]* are composed in the alliterative metre which was inherited, through Old English poetry, from the prehistoric Germanic period."

3. Cable, *English Alliterative Tradition,* 3.

4. The four poems of Cotton Nero A. x nevertheless witness the formal diversity of fourteenth-century alliterative verse. For example, *Sir Gawain* is written in unrhymed, alliterative long lines in stanzas of varying length (from twelve to thirty-seven lines), all of which end with a bob containing a single stressed syllable that is preceded by one or perhaps two unstressed ones and a rhyming *and* alliterating quatrain of three-stress lines known as the wheel, while *Pearl* is written in a very different style.

Its stanzas are each twelve lines long—with one notable exception—and its short lines not only alliterate but also follow, as Gordon, *Pearl*, xxxvi, notes, "an elaborate rhyme-scheme combined with stanza-linking by echo and refrain."

5. Approaching the Homeric epics, *Beowulf*, or any other work of traditional verbal art solely from the perspective of a literate-based aesthetics will, finally, prove no more productive or illuminating than faulting Homer, as Swift's modern, "True Critick[s]" do in *Tale of a Tub*, 128, for his failure to mention "that useful Instrument a *Save-all*" or for his "gross Ignorance in the *Common Laws of this Realm*, and in the Doctrine as well as Discipline of the Church of *England*." Applying a literate aesthetics to the narrative structure of *Beowulf* or using the same aesthetics to demonstrate that Homer occasionally "nods" in the *Iliad* or *Odyssey* is not so very far removed from arguing that Homer's *opera* cannot possibly be the "compleat Body of all Knowledge Human, Divine, Political, and Mechanick" that Swift tells us Xenophon had claimed it to be (*Homerus omnes res humanas Poematis complexus est*. Xenoph. in conviv.) because it contains "many gross Errors" and, more importantly, fails to take into account recent eighteenth-century developments in history, philosophy, and science (127). I cite Guthkelch and Smith's edition of Swift's text.

6. The same holds true of our other senses as well, all of which are able to detect only a small percentage of the world's many different smells, tastes, and physical sensations.

7. Smith and de Selincourt, *Spenser*, lxi.

8. Ibid., lxii.

9. Sidney, *Defence of Poetry*, 64. I cite Van Dorsten's edition of Sidney's text.

10. An exception to this trend is Davidson, "Did Spenser Consciously Use Archaic English?"

11. Compare, for example, the language spoken by the inhabitants of Camelot in Twain's *A Connecticut Yankee in King Arthur's Court*, or the fading, but still present, "ye olde" signs that Stanley points to in "Laʒamons Antiquarian Sentiments."

12. Stock's distinction between "traditional" and "traditionalistic" behavior does much to illuminate the issue here. See further his discussion in *Listening for the Text*, 159–71.

13. Heaney, *Beowulf*, xxvi. I cite Heaney's introduction to the Faber and Faber edition of his *Beowulf* throughout. In writing about his poetic making, Heaney has on numerous occasions displayed his awareness of the metonymic, associative power of the specialized lexemes he frequently includes in his verse. See, for example, his introduction to his translation/reworking of *Beowulf*, esp. xxii–xxvii, and *Crediting Poetry*. I am indebted to Rachel Becker for the latter reference.

14. On several occasions, including over dinner in Poughkeepsie in the fall of 2000, Heaney has remarked that his translation is two-thirds *Beowulf* and one-third Heaney, although these percentages perhaps ought to be reversed.

15. Heaney, *Beowulf*, xxvi.

16. Ibid., xxv.

17. Ibid.

18. These lexemes are included in the two-volume *Shorter OED,* the full twenty-two-volume standard version of the dictionary, and the on-line version, www. dictionary.oed.com/entrance.dtl.

19. For example, a search undertaken in the spring of 2001 for these terms in the on-line *Merriam-Webster Dictionary,* www.merriamwebster.com, resulted in the following message: "The word you've entered isn't in the dictionary. Click on a spelling suggestion below or try again using the dictionary search box to the right." The same search in the summer of 2003 reveals that *thole* is now included in this dictionary but that the other two terms remain outside its lexicon.

20. For example, a translator's note in David, *Norton Anthology,* 43n4, explains that the word *bawn* (523) refers to a "[f]ortified outwork of a court or a castle. The word was used by English planters in Ulster to describe fortified dwellings they erected on lands confiscated from the Irish." In contrast, no explanation of *hirpling* (975) is offered.

21. *Thole* and its related forms are well attested in the Middle English period, but none more so than the verb *tholen,* which the MED cites as late as the *Destruction of Troy,* a text the dictionary's editors date to "c1540 (?a1400)."

22. Although in his youth he habitually thought of "English and Irish as adversarial tongues," *Beowulf,* xxiv, Heaney came to discover that certain lexemes served as linguistic/cultural "loophole[s]" through which he was able to gain entry "into some unpartitioned linguistic country, a region where one's language would not be simply a badge of ethnicity or a matter of cultural preference or even an official imposition, but an entry into further language" (xxv). It is perhaps more to this striving for "further language" than to any overtly political program that we should attribute his "scullion speech."

23. What makes Heaney's text more challenging than one such as Eliot's *Waste Land*—a poem famous for its difficult and often cryptic intertextual allusions—is that the hermeneutic tools that have developed and that work so well to help us unpack the *Waste Land*'s world of networked meanings can take us only partially into the rich lexical world of Heaney's poetic register. If Heaney had chosen to remain silent on the genesis of his "scullion speech," we would not even be able to see into it in the limited manner that we now do.

24. Renoir, *Key to Old Poems,* 169–74.

25. All citations to *Sir Gawain* are from Tolkien and Gordon's revised second edition.

26. I mark "expected" with a question mark and place it within parentheses here and below in this chapter to indicate that it is possible that the fourteenth-century poet and audience may not have expected bloodshed in the way that poets and audiences for whom oral poetics was the way of creating and receiving poetry would have.

27. To cite just several of the very many instances in which a shining object is mentioned in a martial context or is used to mark a character's or setting's liminality, we can consider the firelight that shines brightly in the underwater dwelling of Grendel's mother (1516b–16), Bevis's shining helmet (2818), the brightness associated with the fairy castle in *Sir Orfeo* (358), the cloak Emaré wears when she is set adrift in a boat to die (265 ff.), and Bertilak's castle in *Sir Gawain* (772). The beasts of battle type scene also survives—or at least remnants of it survive—into the postmedieval period in texts as varied as Milton's *Paradise Lost* (X. 272–78) and Tolkien's *The Hobbit* (243). I cite Rickert's edition of *Romance of Emaré* and Bliss's edition of the version of *Sir Orfeo* found in Edinburgh, Scottish National Library, Advocates' MS 19. 2. 1 (the Auchinleck Manuscript).

28. For example, in describing the moments before the troop departs for the attack on Helm's Deep in the *Two Towers*, Tolkien's prose, as it so often does, falls into a rhythm highly reminiscent of Old English poetry: "The trumpets sounded. The horses reared and neighed. Spear clashed on shield" (153).

29. To get an idea of just how deeply Tolkien's fiction is indebted to Old English, see D. Anderson, *Annotated Hobbit*. Of course, the traditional thematics he employs is available not only to authors trained as medievalists. An example in which the thematics of a shining object is successfully and traditionally deployed can be found near the end of Phillip Pullman's novel *The Amber Spyglass*. In the midst of the most protracted and extensive battle depicted in the novel, we learn at one point that "the enemy's ground forces waited: machines *glinting brightly,* flags astir with color, regiments drawn up, waiting" (390; emphasis added). Shortly thereafter, Pullman again employs the same thematics: "Behind [Lyra] the sun was still shining, so that every grove and every single tree between her and the storm *blazed* ardent and vivid, little frail things defying the dark with leaf and twig and fruit and flower" (391; emphasis added).

30. Yeats, in "Easter 1916" (*Collected Poems*) ruminates upon the events of the Easter Rebellion, ponders the price that was paid by the rebel leaders, many of whom were killed by firing squad, and concludes that from their actions "A terrible beauty is born" (80).

31. Foley, *Traditional Oral Epic*, 368.

32. Lord, "Theme of the Withdrawn Hero," 19, draws attention to the pan-Indo-European nature of this story pattern when he explains why he employs Homeric parallels to illustrate his argument concerning the pattern's role in South Slavic epics: "Although I introduce Homeric parallels chiefly in illustration . . . it is nevertheless with the conviction that in the Homeric songs I am dealing with simply an older stratum of one and the same Indo-European oral tradition, in its Balkan and Near Eastern forms." The most comprehensive consideration of comparative Indo-European poetics to date is Watkins, *How to Kill a Dragon*. Foley has recently advanced the important and promising argument that certain features of oral poetics can circulate between and among genres in *How to Read*, 188–218, and "How Genres Leak."

33. Although he discusses it in *Singer of Tales,* Lord first schematizes this pattern in "Theme of the Withdrawn Hero." See further Foley, *Traditional Oral Epic,* 359–87, *Singer of Tales in Performance,* 175–80, and *Homer's Traditional Art,* 115–67. Cf. also Nagler, *Spontaneity and Tradition,* 131–76; Peabody, *Winged Word,* 216–72; and Feldman, "Two Performances."

34. I cite Hall's edition of *King Horn.*

35. Kane's assessment of the narrative is fairly representative of the ways in which it is frequently viewed. The poem, he asserts in *Middle English Literature,* 48, "has almost no technical merit, for its author had very little notion of trying for an effect but was sufficiently occupied with the exigencies of simply moving his story on."

36. McLaughlin, "Return Song," discusses the presence of this story pattern in *King Horn, Sir Orfeo,* and several later ballads from the oral-formulaic perspective.

37. I cite Bliss's edition of *Sir Orfeo.*

38. On the traditional narrative patterning of *Sir Gawain,* see Camargo, "Oral Traditional Structure," and Suzuki, "Oral-Formulaic Theme Survival."

39. On the problematics of Gawain's return, see Amodio, "Tradition, Modernity," 58–63.

40. What is perhaps the clearest example of this sort of shift occurs during the dragon fight in *Beowulf,* where, as Foley argues in *Immanent Art,* 239, the hero Beowulf becomes the "substitute who must die in the process of the hero's—that is, *another* hero's*—eventual triumph" (emphasis in original).

41. To take an obvious example, within the genre of the western, significant information about a character is often transmitted through the clothes he wears. The "good guys" are frequently marked by their white hats, bad guys by their black ones, and new arrivals from the East by their inappropriate dress. Like all artists, filmmakers are free to deviate from this pattern and often do so that white and black hats do not necessarily function as simple, traditional signifiers but can, on occasion, serve as more ambiguous or even inverted ones.

42. Lyrics by Ned Washington, music by Dimitri Tiomkin. This is my transcription of the lyrics from the collector's edition DVD, released by Artisan (Fox Video), 22 October 2002.

43. The marshal knows that fleeing, in addition to contravening his heroic code, will only buy him a brief respite because the outlaws will track him wherever he goes.

Bibliography

Primary Sources, Editions, Translations, and Reference Works

Allen, Rosamund, ed. *King Horn: An Edition Based on Cambridge University Library MS. Gg. 4.27(2)*. New York: Garland Press, 1984.

Anderson, Douglas A. *The Annotated Hobbit*. London: Unwin Hyman, 1989.

Anderson, J. J., ed. *Cleanness*. Manchester: Manchester University Press, 1977.

Andrew, Malcolm, and Ronald Waldron, eds. *The Poems of the Pearl Manuscript*. 1978. Rev. ed. Exeter: University of Exeter Press, 1996.

Arngart, Olof S., ed. *The Leningrad Bede: An Eighth Century Manuscript of the Venerable Bede's Historia Ecclesiastica Gentis Anglorum in the Public Library, Leningrad*. EEMF 2. Copenhagen: Rosenkilde and Bagger, 1952.

———, ed. *The Proverbs of Alfred*. 2 vols. Lund: Gleerup, 1942, 1955.

Arnold, Ivor, ed. *Le roman de Brut de Wace*. 2 vols. 1938, 1940. Reprint, Paris: Société des Anciens Textes Français, 1983.

Baker, Peter S., ed. *The Anglo-Saxon Chronicle: MS F*. Vol. 8 of *The Anglo-Saxon Chronicle: A Collaborative Edition*. Cambridge: D. S. Brewer, 2000.

Barron, W. R. J., trans. *Sir Gawain and the Green Knight*. Manchester: Manchester University Press, 1974.

Bately, Janet M., ed. *The Anglo-Saxon Chronicle: A Collaborative Edition*. Vol. 3, *MS A*. Cambridge: D. S. Brewer, 1986.

———, ed. *The Tanner Bede: the Old English Version of Bede's Historia ecclesiastica, Oxford Bodleian Library Tanner 10, Together with the Mediaeval Binding Leaves, Oxford Bodleian Library Tanner 10* and the Domitian Extracts,*

London, British Library, Cotton Domitian A. ix Fol. 11. EEMF 24. Copenhagen: Rosenkilde and Bagger, 1992.

Bennett, J. A. W., and G. V. Smithers, eds. *Early Middle English Verse and Prose.* 1966. 2nd ed. Oxford: Clarendon Press, 1968.

Benson, Larry D., gen. ed. *The Riverside Chaucer.* 3rd ed. Boston: Houghton Mifflin, 1987.

Berger, Sidney. "A Concordance to Layamon's *Brut:* Part 1, A–F." Ph.D. diss., University of Iowa, 1971.

Bessinger, Jess B., Jr., ed., and Philip H. Smith, pgmr. *A Concordance to the Anglo-Saxon Poetic Records.* Ithaca, N.Y.: Cornell University Press, 1978.

Bliss, Alan J., ed. *Sir Orfeo.* 1954. 2nd ed. Oxford: Clarendon Press, 1966.

Bloom, Allan, trans. *The Republic of Plato.* New York: Basic Books, 1968.

Borroff, Marie, trans. *Sir Gawain and the Green Knight, Patience, Pearl: Verse Translations.* New York: W. W. Norton, 2001.

Bosworth, Joseph, and T. Northcote Toller, eds. *An Anglo-Saxon Dictionary Based on the Manuscript Collections of the Late Joseph Bosworth.* 1898. Reprint, London: Oxford University Press, 1983.

Brook, George L., ed. *Selections from Laȝamon's Brut.* 1963. Rev. ed. Exeter: Exeter University Press, 1983.

Brook, George L., and Roy F. Leslie, eds. *Laȝamon: Brut.* 2 vols. EETS os 263, 277. London: Oxford University Press, 1963 (for 1961), 1978.

Burrow, J. A., and Thorlac Turville-Petre, eds. *A Book of Middle English.* 1991. 2nd ed. Oxford: Blackwell, 1996.

Campbell, Alistair. *Old English Grammar.* 1959. Reprint, Oxford: Oxford University Press, 1987.

Clark, Cecily, ed. *The Peterborough Chronicle 1070–1154.* 1957. 2nd ed. Oxford: Clarendon Press, 1970.

Colgrave, Bertram, and R. A. B. Mynors, eds. *Bede's Ecclesiastical History of the English People.* 1969. Reprint, Oxford: Clarendon Press, 1979.

Conlee, John W., ed. *Middle English Debate Poetry: A Critical Anthology.* East Lansing, Mich.: Colleagues Press, 1991.

Conybeare, J. J. *Illustrations of Anglo-Saxon Poetry.* Edited by W. D. Conybeare. 1826. Reprint, New York: Haskell House, 1964.

Cubbin, G. P., ed. *The Anglo-Saxon Chronicle: A Collaborative Edition.* Vol. 6, *MS D.* Cambridge: D. S. Brewer, 1996.

David, Alfred, ed. *The Norton Anthology of English Literature.* Vol. 1A. *The Middle Ages.* New York: W. W. Norton, 2000.

Dickins, Bruce, and R. M. Wilson, eds. *Early Middle English Texts.* Cambridge: Bowes and Bowes, 1951.

Dobbie, Elliot Van Kirk, ed. *The Manuscripts of Cædmon's Hymn and Bede's Death Song, with a Critical Text of the Epistola Cuthberti de Obitu Bedæ.* New York: Columbia University Press, 1937.

Doyle, Roddy. *A Star Called Henry*. New York: Penguin, 1999.

Eliot, T. S. *Collected Poems, 1909–1935*. 1936. Reprint, New York: Harcourt Brace, 1958.

Evans, G. Blakemore, ed. *The Riverside Shakespeare*. 1974. 2nd ed. Boston: Houghton Mifflin, 1997.

Evans, Sebastian, trans. *History of the Kings of Britain by Geoffrey of Monmouth*. 1912. Revised by Charles W. Dunn. New York: Dutton, 1958.

Finch, Casey, trans. *The Complete Works of the Pearl Poet*. Berkeley and Los Angeles: University of California Press, 1993.

Foley, John Miles, ed. *Oral-Formulaic Theory and Research: An Introduction and Annotated Bibliography*. New York: Garland Press, 1985.

Furneaux, Henry, ed. *Germania*, by Tacitus. Oxford: Clarendon Press, 1894.

Gardner, John, trans. *The Complete Works of the Gawain-Poet: In a Modern English Version with a Critical Introduction*. 1965. Reprint, Chicago: University of Chicago Press, 1970.

Gneuss, Helmut. *Handlist of Anglo-Saxon Manuscripts: A List of Manuscripts and Manuscript Fragments Written or Owned in England up to 1100*. Tempe, Ariz.: ACMRS, 2001.

Gollancz, Sir Israel, ed. *Pearl, Cleanness, Patience and Sir Gawain, Reproduced in Facsimile from the Unique MS. Cotton Nero A.X in the British Museum*. EETS os 162. 1923. Reprint, London: Oxford University Press, 1955.

———. *Sir Gawain and the Green Knight: Re-edited from MS. Cotton Nero A.X., in the British Museum*. EETS os 210. 1940. Reprint, London: Oxford University Press, 1966.

Gordon, E. V., ed. *Pearl*. 1953. Reprint, Oxford: Clarendon Press, 1980.

Griscom, Acton, ed. *The Historia Regum Britanniæ of Geoffrey of Monmouth*. New York: Longmans, Green, 1929.

Guthkelch, A. C., and D. Nichol Smith, eds. *A Tale of a Tub*. 1958. 2nd ed. Oxford: Clarendon Press, 1973.

Hall, Joseph, ed. *King Horn*. 1901. Reprint, Oxford: Clarendon Press, 1976.

Hall, Joseph, and K. S. B. Keats-Rohan, eds. *Metalogicon* by John of Salisbury. Turnhout: Brepols, 1991.

Hamilton, N. E. S. A., ed. *Willelmi Malmesbiriensis Monachi De Gestis Pontificum Anglorum, Libri Quinque*. London: Longman, 1870.

Healey, Antonette diPaolo, et al., eds. *Dictionary of Old English*. Toronto: Pontifical Institute of Mediaeval Studies, 1986 (*D*), 1988 (*C*), 1991 (*B*), 1992 (*Æ, Beon*), 1994 (*A*), 1996 (*E*). Revised electronic versions of fascicles A through E and the first release of F published on CD-ROM as *Dictionary of Old English: A to F*. Toronto: Pontifical Institute of Mediaeval Studies, 2003.

Healey, Antonette diPaolo, and Richard L. Venezky, eds. *A Microfiche Concordance to Old English*. Toronto: University of Toronto Press, 1980.

Heaney, Seamus. *Crediting Poetry*. Loughcrew: Gallery Press, 1995.

————, trans. *Beowulf.* London: Faber and Faber, 1999.

————, trans. *Beowulf.* New York: Norton, 2000.

Heyne, Moritz, ed. *Beowulf.* Paderborn: Ferdinand Schöningh, 1898.

Hibbard, Laura A., trans. *Three Middle English Romances.* London: David Nutt, 1911.

Horstmann, Carl, ed. *The Early South-English Legendary or Lives of Saints I. MS Laud, 108, in the Bodleian Library.* EETS os 87. 1887. Millwood, N.Y.: Kraus Reprint, 1987.

Hudson, Anne, ed. *Selections from English Wycliffite Writings.* Cambridge: Cambridge University Press, 1978.

Hughes, Merrit Y., ed. *John Milton: Complete Poems and Prose.* Reprint, Indianapolis: Hackett Publishing 2003.

Ker, N. R. *Catalogue of Manuscripts Containing Anglo-Saxon.* 1957. Reprint, Oxford: Clarendon Press, 1990.

————. "A Supplement to *Catalogue of Manuscripts Containing Anglo-Saxon.*" *ASE* 5 (1976): 121–31.

Keynes, Simon, and Michael Lapidge, eds. *Alfred the Great: Asser's Life of King Alfred and Other Contemporary Sources.* New York: Penguin, 1983.

Kiernan, Kevin S., et al., eds. *The Electronic Beowulf.* London and Ann Arbor: British Library and University of Michigan, 1999.

Klaeber, Friedrich, ed. *Beowulf and the Fight at Finnsburg.* 1922. 3rd ed. Lexington, Mass.: D. C. Heath, 1950.

Kölbing, Eugen, ed. *The Romance of Sir Beues of Hamtoun.* 1885, 1886, 1894. EETS os 46, 48, 65. 3 vols. in 2, 1894. Reprint, 3 vols. in 1, edited with an appendix by Carl Schmirgel. Millwood, N.Y.: Kraus Reprints, 1987.

Krapp, George Philip, and Elliott Van Kirk Dobbie, eds. *The Anglo-Saxon Poetic Records.* 6 vols. New York: Columbia University Press, 1931–53. [I. *The Junius Manuscript,* ed. Krapp. II. *The Vercelli Book,* ed. Krapp. III. *The Exeter Book,* ed. Krapp and Dobbie. IV. *Beowulf and Judith,* ed. Dobbie. V. *The Paris Psalter and the Meters of Boethius,* ed. Krapp. VI. *The Anglo-Saxon Minor Poems,* ed. Dobbie.]

Lapidge, Michael, and Michael Herren, trans. *Aldhelm: The Prose Works.* Cambridge: D. S. Brewer, 1979.

Lapidge, Michael and Richard Sharpe, eds. *A Bibliography of Celtic–Latin Literature, 400–1200.* Dublin: Royal Irish Academy, 1985.

Leonard, William Ellery, trans. *Beowulf.* New York: Random House, 1932.

MacCracken, Henry Noble, ed. *The Minor Poems of John Lydgate.* 2 vols. 1911, 1934. EETS es 107, os 192. Reprint, London: Oxford University Press, 1961.

Macrae-Gibson, O. Duncan, ed. *The Old English Riming Poem.* Woodbridge, England: D. S. Brewer, 1983.

Madden, Sir Frederic, ed. *Laȝamons Brut.* 3 vols. London: Society of Antiquaries, 1847.

————, ed. *Syr Gawayne; A Collection of Ancient Romance-Poems by Scotish and English Authors, Relating to That Celebrated Knight of the Round Table.* 1839. Reprint, London: Taylor, 1978.

Miller, Thomas, ed. *The Old English Version of Bede's Ecclesiastical History of the English People.* EETS os 95, 96, 110, 111. 4 vols. in 2. 1890–98. Reprint, London: Oxford University Press, 1997.

Mitchell, Bruce. *Old English Syntax.* 2 vols. Oxford: Clarendon Press, 1985.

Mitchell, Bruce, and Fred C. Robinson, eds. *Beowulf: An Edition with Relevant Shorter Texts.* Oxford: Blackwell, 1998.

Moffat, Douglas, ed. *The Soul's Address to the Body: The Worcester Fragments.* East Lansing, Mich.: Colleagues Press, 1987.

Moorman, Charles, ed. *The Works of the Gawain-Poet.* Jackson: University of Mississippi Press, 1977.

Morris, Richard, ed. *Early English Alliterative Poems in the West-Midland Dialect of the Fourteenth Century.* EETS os 1. 1864. 2nd ed. 1869. Reprint, London: Oxford University Press, 1965.

———, ed. *Old English Homilies and Homiletic Treatises (Sawles Warde, and þe Wohunge of Ure Lauerd: Ureisuns of Ure Louerd and of Ure Lefdi &c.) of the Twelfth and Thirteenth Centuries.* EETS os 29. 1868. Reprint, Millwood, N.Y.: Kraus Reprints, 1988.

———, ed. *Old English Homilies of the Twelfth Century from the Unique MS. B. 14. 52 in the Library of Trinity College, Cambridge.* EETS os 53. 1873. Reprint, Woodbridge, England: Boydell and Brewer, 1998.

———, ed. *Sir Gawayne and The Green Knight: An Alliterative Romance-Poem (AB. 1360 A.D.).* EETS os 4. 1864. 2nd ed. 1869. Reprint, London: Trübner, 1969.

Morton, James, trans. *The Nun's Rule: Being the Ancren Riwle Modernised.* 1905. Reprint, London: Chatto and Windus, 1990.

Napier, Arthur S., ed. *History of the Holy Rood-Tree, A Twelfth Century Version of the Cross-Legend, with Notes on the Orthography of the Ormulum (with a Facsimile) and a Middle English Compassio Mariae.* EETS os 103. 1894. Reprint, Woodbridge, England: Boydell and Brewer, 1998.

O'Brien O'Keeffe, Katherine, ed. *The Anglo-Saxon Chronicle: A Collaborative Edition.* Vol. 5, *MS C.* Cambridge: D. S. Brewer, 2001.

Offord, M. Y., ed. *The Parlement of the Thre Ages.* EETS os 249. 1959. Reprint, Woodbridge, England: Boydell and Brewer, 1997.

Orwell, George. *1984: A Novel.* 1949. Reprint, New York: Harcourt Brace, 2000.

Oxford English Dictionary, 2nd ed. 20 vols. New York: Oxford University Press, 1989.

Plummer, Charles, ed. *Two of the Saxon Chronicles Parallel.* 2 vols. 1892–99. Reissued with a bibliographical note by Dorothy Whitelock, 1952. Reprint, Oxford: Clarendon Press, 1972.

Pope, John C., ed. *Homilies of Ælfric: A Supplementary Collection.* 2 vols. EETS os 259, 260. London: Oxford University Press, 1967, 1968.

Pullman, Philip. *The Amber Spyglass.* New York: Knopf, 2000.

Quinn, Karen J., and Kenneth P. Quinn, eds. *A Manual of Old English Prose*. New York: Garland, 1990.

Rickert, Edith, ed. *The Romance of Emaré*. EETS es 99. 1906. Reprint, London: Oxford University Press, 1958.

Roberts, Jane, and Christian Kay, comps. *A Thesaurus of Old English*. 2 vols. KCLMS 11. King's College London: Centre for Late Antique and Medieval Studies, 1995.

Robinson, Fred C., and E. G. Stanley, eds. *Old English Verse Texts from Many Sources: A Comprehensive Collection*. EEMF 23. Copenhagen: Rosenkilde and Bagger, 1991.

Roseborough, Margaret M. *An Outline of Middle English Grammar*. 1938. Reprint, Norwood, England: Norwood Editions, 1978.

Rosenberg, James L., trans. *Sir Gawain and the Green Knight*. Edited with an introduction by James R. Kreuzer. 1959. Reprint, New York: Holt, Rinehart and Winston, 1961.

Salu, M. B., trans. *The Ancrene Riwle*. Notre Dame, Ind.: University of Notre Dame Press, 1955.

Scragg, Donald, ed. *The Battle of Maldon*. Manchester: Manchester University Press, 1981.

———, ed. and trans. *The Battle of Maldon A.D. 991*. Oxford: Blackwell, 1991.

Sedgefield, Walter J., ed. *Beowulf*. 1910. 3rd ed., rev. and partly rewritten. Manchester: University of Manchester Press, 1935.

Sievers, Eduard. *Grammar of Old English*. 1885. Translated and edited by Albert S. Cook. 3rd ed., 1903. Reprint, Boston: Ginn, 1983.

Skeat, Walter W., ed. *Aelfric's Lives of Saints*. 4 vols. EETS os 76, 82, 94, 114. 1881–1900. Reprint, 4 vols. in 2, London: Oxford University Press, 1966.

———, ed. *An Etymological Dictionary of the English Language*. 1881. 3rd ed., rev. and enl., 1910. Reprint, Oxford: Clarendon Press, 1995.

Smith, J. C., and E. de Selincourt, eds. *Spenser: Poetical Works*. 1912. Reprint, London: Oxford University Press, 1970.

Smithers, G. V., ed. *Kyng Alisaunder*. 2 vols. EETS os 227, 237. 1952 (for 1947) and 1957 (for 1953). Reprint, London: Oxford University Press, 1983.

Stanley, Eric G., ed. *The Owl and the Nightingale*. London: Nelson, 1960.

Stillinger, Jack, ed. *Selected Poems and Prefaces*, by William Wordsworth. Boston: Houghton Mifflin, 1965.

Stimming, Albert, ed. *Der Anglonormannische Boeve de Haumtone*. Bibliotheca Normannica VII. Halle: Niemeyer, 1899.

Stone, Brian, trans. *Sir Gawain and the Green Knight*. 1959. 2nd ed. Harmondsworth, England: Penguin Books, 1981.

Stratmann, Francis Henry, ed. *A Middle-English Dictionary: Containing Words Used by English Writers from the Twelfth to the Fifteenth Century*. New ed., rearranged, revised, and enlarged by Henry Bradley, 1891. Reprint, Oxford: Oxford University Press, 1995.

Tangl, M., ed. *Die Briefe des heiligen Bonifatius und Lullus*. Monumenta Germania Historica. Epistolae Selectae 1. 2nd ed. Berlin: Weidmann, 1955.

Taylor, Simon, ed. *The Anglo-Saxon Chronicle: A Collaborative Edition*. Vol. 4, *MS B*. Cambridge: D. S. Brewer, 1983.

Tolkien, J. R. R. *The Hobbit or There and Back Again*. 1937. Rev. ed. New York: Ballantine Books, 1966.

———. *The Two Towers*. 1954. Reprint, New York: Ballantine, 1973.

———, ed. *The English Text of the Ancrene Riwle: Ancrene Wisse. Edited from MS Corpus Christi College, Cambridge 402*. EETS os 249. London: Oxford University Press, 1962 (for 1960).

Tolkien, J. R. R., and E. V. Gordon, eds. *Sir Gawain and the Green Knight*. 1925. 2nd ed., revised by Norman Davis. Oxford: Clarendon Press, 1967.

Toller, T. Northcote, ed. *An Anglo-Saxon Dictionary: Supplement*. 1921. Rev. and enlarged by Alistair Campbell, 1955. Reprint, Oxford: Oxford University Press, 1980.

Van Dorsten, J. A., ed. *A Defence of Poetry*, by Sir Philip Sidney. 1966. Reprint, London: Oxford University Press, 1997.

Vigfusson, Gudbrand, ed. *Icelandic–English Dictionary, Based on the MS. Collections of the Late Richard Cleasby*. 1876. Reprint, Oxford: Clarendon Press, 1957.

White, Hugh, trans. *Ancrene Wisse: Guide for Anchoresses*. New York: Penguin, 1993.

White, Robert M., ed. *The Ormulum*. 2 vols. Oxford: Oxford University Press, 1852.

Whitelock, Dorothy, ed. *English Historical Documents c. 500–1042*. Vol. 1. 1955. 2nd ed., 1979. Reprint, London: Routledge, 1996.

———, ed. *The Peterborough Chronicle (The Bodleian Manuscript Laud Misc. 636)*. EEMF 4. Copenhagen: Rosenkilde and Bagger, 1954.

Wrenn, Charles Leslie, ed. *Beowulf: With the Finnsburg Fragment*. 1953. 3rd ed. Revised by Whitney F. Bolton. London: Harrap, 1973.

Wright, William Aldis, ed. *The Metrical Chronicle of Robert of Gloucester*. Rerum Britannicarum Medii Ævi Scriptores 86. 2 vols. 1887. Reprint, London: Eyre and Spottiswoode, 1970.

Wyatt, Alfred J., ed. *Beowulf with the Finnsburg Fragment*. 1894. New ed. with introduction and notes by R. W. Chambers, 1914. Reprint, Cambridge: Cambridge University Press, 1988.

Yeats, W. B. *Collected Poems*. 1933. Reprint, London: Vintage, 1992.

Yolen, Jane. *Commander Toad in Space*. 1980. Reprint, New York: Scholastic Books, 1993.

Zupitza, Julius, ed. *The Romance of Guy of Warwick: The First or 14th-Century Version from the Auchinleck MS and the Caius MS I, II, III*. 3 vols. 1883, 1887, 1891. EETS es 42, 49, 59. Reprint, 3 vols. in 1, London: Oxford University Press, 1966.

———, ed. *The Romance of Guy of Warwick: The Second or 15th-Century Version*. 2 vols. 1875, 1876. EETS es 25, 26. Reprint, London: Oxford University Press, 1966.

Zupitza, Julius, and Norman Davis, eds. *Beowulf Reproduced in Facsimile from the Unique Manuscript British Museum MS. Cotton Vitellius A. XV*. 1882. 2nd ed. EETS os 245. London: Oxford University Press, 1959 (for 1958).

Secondary Sources

Aers, David. "A Whisper in the Ear of Early Modernists." In *Culture and History 1350–1600,* edited by David Aers, 177–202. Detroit: Wayne State University Press, 1992.

Amodio, Mark C. "Affective Criticism, Oral Poetics, and Beowulf's Fight with the Dragon." *OT* 10 (1995): 54–90.

———. "Contemporary Critical Approaches and Studies in Oral Tradition." In *Teaching Oral Traditions,* edited by John Miles Foley, 95–105. New York: Modern Language Association, 1998.

———. "Laȝamon's Anglo-Saxon Lexicon and Diction." *Poetica* 28 (1988): 48–59.

———. "Old-English Oral-Formulaic Tradition and Middle-English Verse." In *De Gustibus: Essays for Alain Renoir,* edited by John Miles Foley, 1–20. New York: Garland, 1992.

———. "Res(is)ting the Singer: Towards a Non-Performative Anglo-Saxon Oral Poetics." In *New Directions in Oral Theory,* edited by Mark C. Amodio. Tempe, Ariz.: MRTS, in press.

———. "Some Notes on Laȝamon's Use of the Synthetic Genitive." *SN* 59 (1987): 187–94.

———. "Tradition, Modernity, and the Emergence of the Self in *Sir Gawain and the Green Knight.*" *Assays* 8 (1995): 47–68.

———. "Tradition, Performance, and Poetics in Early Middle English Poetry." OT 15 (2000): 191–214.

Amos, Ashley Crandell. *Linguistic Means of Determining the Dates of Old English Literary Texts.* Cambridge, Mass.: Medieval Academy of America, 1980.

Andersen, Flemming G. *Commonplace and Creativity: The Role of Formulaic Diction in Anglo-Scottish Traditional Balladry.* Odense: Odense University Press, 1985.

Anderson, Earl R. "*The Battle of Maldon:* A Reappraisal of Possible Sources, Date, and Theme." In *Modes of Interpretation in Old English Literature: Essays in Honour of Stanley B. Greenfield,* edited by Phyllis R. Brown, Georgia R. Crampton, and Fred C. Robinson, 247–72. Toronto: University of Toronto Press, 1986.

———. *Cynewulf: Structure, Style, and Theme in His Poetry.* Rutherford, N.J.: Fairleigh Dickinson University Press, 1983.

———. "The Treasure Trove in *Beowulf:* A Legal View of the Dragon's Hoard." *Mediaevalia* 3 (1977): 141–64.

Andersson, Theodore M. "The Thief in *Beowulf.*" *Speculum* 59 (1984): 493–508.

———. "Tradition and Design in *Beowulf.*" In *Old English Literature in Context: Ten Essays,* edited by John D. Niles, 90–106. Cambridge: D. S. Brewer, 1980.

Austin, John L. *How to Do Things with Words: The William James Lectures Delivered at Harvard University in 1955.* Edited by J. O. Urmson. 1962. 2nd ed., 1975. Reprint, New York: Oxford University Press, 1986.

Bately, Janet. "Bravery and the Vocabulary of Bravery in *Beowulf* and the *Battle of Maldon.*" In *Unlocking the Wordhord: Anglo-Saxon Studies in Memory of Edward B. Irving, Jr.*, edited by Mark C. Amodio and Katherine O'Brien O'Keeffe, 274–301. Toronto: University of Toronto Press, 2003.

Baugh, Albert C. "Improvisation in the Middle English Romance." *PAPS* 103 (1959): 418–54.

———. "The Making of *Beves of Hampton.*" In *Bibliographical Studies in Honor of Rudolf Hirsch*, edited by William E. Miller and Thomas G. Waldman, 15–37. Philadelphia: Friends of the University of Pennsylvania Library, 1975.

———. "The Middle English Romance: Some Questions of Creation, Presentation, and Preservation." *Speculum* 42 (1967): 1–31.

Baugh, Albert C., and Thomas Cable. *A History of the English Language.* 1957. 4th ed. Englewood Cliffs, N.J.: Simon and Schuster, 1993.

Bäuml, Franz. "The Unmaking of the Hero: Some Critical Implications of the Transition from Oral to Written Epic." In *The Epic in Medieval Society*, edited by Harald Scholler, 86–99. Tübingen: Niemeyer, 1977.

———. "Varieties and Consequences of Medieval Literacy and Illiteracy." *Speculum* 55 (1980): 237–65.

Bennett, J. A. W. *Middle English Literature.* Edited and completed by Douglas Gray. 1986. Reprint, Oxford: Clarendon Press, 1990.

Benson, Larry D. *Art and Tradition in Sir Gawain and the Green Knight.* New Brunswick, N.J.: Rutgers University Press, 1965.

———. "The Literary Character of Anglo-Saxon Formulaic Poetry." *PMLA* 81 (1966): 334–41.

———. "The Originality of *Beowulf.*" *Harvard Studies in English* 1 (1970): 1–43.

Best, Debra E. "Villains and Monsters: Enacting Evil in *Beves of Hamptoun.*" *Medieval Perspectives* 13 (1998): 56–68.

Bjork, Robert E. "Speech as Gift in *Beowulf.*" *Speculum* 69 (1994): 993–1022.

Blake, Norman F. "The Dating of Old English Poetry." In *An English Miscellany presented to W. S. Mackie*, edited by Brian S. Lee, 14–27. London: Oxford University Press, 1977.

———. "Manuscript to Print." In *Book Production and Publishing in Britain 1375–1475*, edited by Jeremy Griffiths and Derek Pearsall, 403–32. Cambridge: Cambridge University Press, 1989.

———. "Rhythmical Alliteration." *MP* 67 (1969): 118–24.

Bliss, Alan J. *An Introduction to Old English Metre.* Introduction by Daniel Donoghue. OEN Subsidia, 20. Bighamton, N.Y.: Center for Medieval and Renaissance Studies, 1993.

———. "The Origin and Structure of the Old English Hypermetric Line." *NQ* ns 19 (1972): 242–48.

Bonjour, Adrien. "*Beowulf* and the Beasts of Battle." *PMLA* 72 (1957): 563–73.

―――. "Monsters Crouching and Critics Rampant: Or the *Beowulf* Dragon Debated." *PMLA* 68 (1953): 304–12.

Borroff, Marie. *Sir Gawain and the Green Knight: A Stylistic and Metrical Survey.* 1962. Reprint, Hamden, Conn.: Archon Books, 1973.

Bowra, Cecil M. *Greek Lyric Poetry From Alcman to Simonides.* 1935. 2nd ed. Oxford: Clarendon Press, 1961.

Boyarin, Jonathan, ed. *The Ethnography of Reading.* Berkeley and Los Angeles: University of California Press, 1993.

Bradbury, Nancy Mason. "Literacy, Orality, and the Poetics of Middle English Romance." In *Oral Poetics in Middle English Literature,* edited by Mark C. Amodio, 39–69. New York: Garland Press, 1994.

―――. *Writing Aloud: Storytelling in Late Medieval England.* Urbana: University of Illinois Press, 1998.

Brady, Caroline. "'Warriors' in *Beowulf:* An Analysis of the Nominal Compounds and an Evaluation of the Poet's Use of Them." With an *index locutionum* by Jonathan Wilcox. *ASE* 11 (1983): 199–246.

Brehe, Stephen K. "Reassembling the *First Worcester Fragment*." *Speculum* 65 (1990): 521–36.

―――. "'Rhythmical Alliteration': Ælfric's Prose and the Origins of Laȝamon's Metre." In *The Text and Tradition of Laȝamon's Brut,* edited by Françoise Le Saux, 65–87. Cambridge: D. S. Brewer, 1994.

Brewer, Derek. "The Paradox of the Archaic and the Modern in Laȝamon's *Brut*." In *From Anglo-Saxon to Early Middle English: Studies Presented to E. G. Stanley,* edited by Malcolm Godden, Douglas Gray, and Terry Hoad, 188–205. Oxford: Clarendon Press, 1994.

Bridges, Margaret. "The King, the Foreigner, and the Lady with a Mead Cup: Variations on a Theme of Cross-Cultural Contact." *Multilingua* 18 (1999): 185–207.

Brodeur, Arthur G. *The Art of Beowulf.* 1959. Reprint, Berkeley and Los Angeles: University of California Press, 1969.

Brown, Carleton. "A Thirteenth-Century Manuscript at Maidstone." *MLR* 21 (1926): 1–12, 249–60.

Brown, George H. "The Dynamics of Literacy in Anglo-Saxon England." *BJRL* 77 (1995): 109–42.

Bryan, Elizabeth J. *Collaborative Meaning in Medieval Scribal Culture: The Otho Layamon.* Ann Arbor: University of Michigan Press, 1999.

Bullough, Donald A. "What Has Ingeld to Do with Lindisfarne?" *ASE* 22 (1993): 93–125.

Burchfield, Robert. "Line-End Hyphens in the *Ormulum* Manuscript (MS Junius 1)." In *From Anglo-Saxon to Early Middle English: Studies Presented to E. G. Stanley,* edited by Malcolm Godden, Douglas Gray, and Terry Hoad, 182–87. Oxford: Clarendon Press, 1994.

Byock, Jesse. *Feud in the Icelandic Saga*. Berkeley and Los Angeles: University of California Press, 1982.

Cable, Thomas. *The English Alliterative Tradition*. Philadelphia: University of Philadelphia Press, 1991.

Calder, Daniel G. *Cynewulf*. Boston: Twayne, 1981.

———. "The Vision of Paradise: A Symbolic Reading of the Old English *Phoenix*." *ASE* 1 (1972): 167–81.

Camargo, Martin. "Oral Traditional Structure in *Sir Gawain and the Green Knight*." In *Comparative Research on Oral Traditions: A Memorial for Milman Parry*, edited by John Miles Foley, 121–37. Columbus, Oh.: Slavica, 1987.

Campbell, Jackson J. "Oral Poetry in the *Seafarer*." *Speculum* 35 (1960): 87–96.

Campbell, James, ed. *The Anglo-Saxons*. 1982. Reprint, New York: Penguin, 1991.

Cannon, Christopher. "The Style and Authorship of the Otho Revision of Laȝamon's *Brut*." *MÆ* 62 (1993): 187–209.

Carr, Charles T. *Nominal Compounds in Germanic*. London: Oxford University Press, 1939.

Carruthers, Mary. *The Book of Memory: A Study of Memory in Medieval Culture*. Cambridge: Cambridge University Press, 1990.

Cassidy, Brendan, ed. *The Ruthwell Cross: Papers from the Colloquium Sponsored by the Index of Christian Art, Princeton University, 8 December 1989*. Princeton, N.J.: Princeton University Press, 1992.

Cassidy, Frederic G. "How Free Was the Anglo-Saxon Scop?" In *Franciplegius: Medieval and Linguistic Studies in Honor of Francis Peabody Magoun, Jr.*, edited by Jess B. Bessinger Jr. and Robert P. Creed, 75–85. New York: New York University Press, 1965.

Chambers, R. W. *Beowulf: An Introduction to the Study of the Poem with a Discussion of the Stories of Offa and Finn*. 1921. 3rd ed., 1959, with a supplement by C. L. Wrenn. Reprint, Cambridge: Cambridge University Press, 1972.

———. *On the Continuity of English Prose from Alfred to More and His School*. 1932. EETS os 191a. Reprint, London: Oxford University Press, 1966.

Chance, Jane. *Woman as Hero in Old English Literature*. Syracuse, N.Y.: Syracuse University Press, 1986.

Clanchy, M. T. *From Memory to Written Record: England 1066–1307*. 1979. 2nd ed. Oxford: Blackwell, 1993.

Clark, Cecily. "On Dating *The Battle of Maldon*: Certain Evidence Reviewed." *NMS* 27 (1983): 1–22.

Clover, Carol J. "The Germanic Context of the Unferþ Episode." *Speculum* 55 (1980): 444–68.

Coleman, Janet. *Medieval Readers and Writers, 1350–1400*. New York: Columbia University Press, 1981.

Coleman, Joyce. *Public Reading and the Reading Public in Late Medieval England and France.* Cambridge: Cambridge University Press, 1996.

Cramp, Rosemary. "The Hall in *Beowulf* and Archeology." In *Heroic Poetry in the Anglo-Saxon Period: Studies in Honor of Jess B. Bessinger, Jr.,* edited by Helen Damico and John Leyerle, 331–46. Kalamazoo, Mich.: Medieval Institute Publications, 1993.

Crane, Susan. *Insular Romance: Politics, Faith, and Culture in Anglo-Norman and Middle English Literature.* Berkeley and Los Angeles: University of California Press, 1986.

Creed, Robert P. "The Making of an Anglo-Saxon Poem." *ELH* 26 (1959): 445–54. Reprinted with additional remarks in *The Beowulf Poet: A Collection of Critical Essays,* edited by Donald K. Fry, 141–53. Englewood Cliffs, N.J.: Prentice Hall, 1968.

———. "On the Possibility of Criticizing Old English Poetry." *TSLL* 3 (1961): 97–106.

———. "The Remaking of *Beowulf.*" In *Oral Tradition in Literature,* edited by John Miles Foley, 136–46. Columbia: University of Missouri Press, 1986.

Crosby, Ruth. "Chaucer and the Custom of Oral Delivery." *Speculum* 13 (1938): 413–32.

———. "Oral Delivery in the Middle Ages." *Speculum* 11 (1936): 88–110.

Crowne, David K. "The Hero on the Beach: An Example of Composition by Theme in Anglo-Saxon Poetry." *NM* 61 (1960): 362–72.

Curschmann, Michael. "The Prologue of Þiðreks Saga: Thirteenth-Century Reflections on Oral Traditional Literature." *SS* 56 (1984): 140–51.

Dagenais, John. "That Bothersome Residue: Toward a Theory of the Physical Text." In *Vox Intexta: Orality and Textuality in the Middle Ages,* edited by A. N. Doane and Carol Braun Pasternack, 246–59. Madison: University of Wisconsin Press, 1991.

Davidson, Mary Catherine. "Did Shakespeare Consciously Use Archaic English?" *Early Modern Literary Studies* Special Issue 1 (1997): 4.1–14. http://purl.oclc.org/emls/si-01/si-01davidson.html.

DeGregorio, Scott. "Theorizing Irony in *Beowulf:* The Case of Hrothgar." *Exemplaria* 11 (1999): 309–43.

Derrida, Jacques. *Of Grammatology.* Translated by Gayatri Spivak. Baltimore: Johns Hopkins University Press, 1976.

Doane, A. N. "The Ethnography of Scribal Writing and Anglo-Saxon Poetry: Scribe as Performer." *OT* 9 (1994): 420–39.

———. "Introduction." In *Vox Intexta: Orality and Textuality in the Middle Ages,* edited by A. N. Doane and Carol Braun Pasternack, xi–xiv. Madison: University of Wisconsin Press, 1991.

———. "Oral Texts, Intertexts, and the Editor." In *Influence and Intertextuality in Literary History,* edited by Eric Rothstein and Jay Clayton, 75–113. Madison: University of Wisconsin Press, 1991.

Donahue, Dennis P. *Lawman's Brut, An Early Arthurian Poem: A Study of Middle English Formulaic Composition.* Lewiston, N.Y.: Edwin Mellen Press, 1991.

Donoghue, Daniel. "Laȝamon's Ambivalence." *Speculum* 65 (1990): 537–63.

———. *Style in Old English Poetry: The Test of the Auxiliary.* New Haven, Conn.: Yale University Press, 1987.

Dronke, Peter. *Poetic Individuality in the Middle Ages: New Departures in Poetry.* 1979. Reprint, London: Westfield College, University of London Committee for Medieval Studies, 1986.

DuBois, Arthur E. "The Dragon in *Beowulf*." *PMLA* 72 (1957): 819–22.

Duncan, Ian. "Epitaphs for Æglæcan: Narrative Strife." In *Modern Critical Interpretation: Beowulf,* edited by Harold Bloom, 111–30. New York: Chelsea House Publishers, 1987.

Earl, James W. "*Beowulf* and the Origins of Civilization." In *Speaking Two Languages: Traditional Disciplines and Contemporary Theory in Medieval Studies,* edited by Allen Frantzen, 65–89. Albany: State University of New York Press, 1991.

———. "The Role of the Men's Hall in the Development of the Anglo-Saxon Superego." *Psychiatry* 46 (1983): 139–60.

Edmonson, Munro E. *Lore: An Introduction to the Science of Folklore and Literature.* New York: Holt, Rinehart and Winston, 1971.

Edwards, A. S. G., and Derek Pearsall. "The Manuscripts of the Major English Poetic Texts." In *Book Production and Publishing in Britain 1375–1475,* edited by Jeremy J. Griffiths and Derek Pearsall, 257–78. Cambridge: Cambridge University Press, 1983.

Edwards, Mark W. "Homer and Oral Tradition: The Type-Scene." *OT* 7 (1992): 284–330.

Eisenstein, Elizabeth L. *The Printing Press as an Agent of Change: Communications and Cultural Transformations in Early-Modern Europe.* 2 vols. 1979. Reprint, Cambridge: Cambridge University Press, 1997.

Ellis, John. *Against Deconstruction.* Princeton, N.J.: Princeton University Press, 1989.

Enright, Michael J. *Lady with a Mead Cup: Ritual, Prophecy, and Lordship in the European Warband from La Tène to the Viking Age.* Dublin: Four Courts Press, 1996.

Evans, Stephen S. *The Lords of Battle: Image and Reality of the Comitatus in Dark Age Britain.* Suffolk: Boydell and Brewer, 2000.

Everett, Dorothy. "The Alliterative Revival." In her *Essays on Middle English Literature,* edited by Patricia Kean, 46–96. Oxford: Clarendon Press, 1955.

———. "Laȝamon and the Earliest Middle English Alliterative Verse." In her *Essays on Middle English Literature,* edited by Patricia Kean, 23–45. Oxford: Clarendon Press, 1955.

Fanning, Steven. "Bede, *Imperium,* and the Bretwaldas." *Speculum* 66 (1991): 1–26.

Feldman, Walter. "Two Performances of the 'Return of Alpamiṣ': Current Performance-Practice in the Uzbek Oral Epic of the Sherabad School." *OT* 12 (1997): 323–53.

Finnegan, Ruth H. *Literacy and Orality: Studies in the Technology of Communication.* Oxford: Blackwell, 1988.

———. *Oral Poetry: Its Nature, Significance and Social Context.* 1977. Reprint, Bloomington: Indiana University Press, 1992.

Fish, Stanley. "Interpreting the *Variorum*." *CI* 3 (1976): 183–90. Reprinted in his *Is There a Text in This Class?* 147–80. Cambridge, Mass.: Harvard University Press, 1980.

———. "Introduction, or How I Stopped Worrying and Learned to Love Interpretation." In his *Is There a Text in This Class?* 1–17. Cambridge, Mass.: Harvard University Press, 1980.

Foley, John Miles. "Formula and Theme in Old English Poetry." In *Oral Literature and the Formula,* edited by Benjamin A. Stoltz and Richard S. Shannon, 207–32. Ann Arbor: Center for the Coordination of Ancient and Modern Studies, University of Michigan, 1976.

———. *Homer's Traditional Art.* University Park: Pennsylvania State University Press, 1999.

———. "How Genres Leak in Traditional Verse." In *Unlocking the Wordhord: Anglo-Saxon Studies in Memory of Edward B. Irving, Jr.,* edited by Mark C. Amodio and Katherine O'Brien O'Keeffe, 76–108. Toronto: University of Toronto Press, 2003.

———. *How to Read an Oral Poem.* Urbana: University of Illinois Press, 2002.

———. *Immanent Art: From Structure to Meaning in Traditional Oral Epic.* Bloomington: Indiana University Press, 1991.

———. "Orality, Textuality, and Interpretation." In *Vox Intexta: Orality and Textuality in the Middle Ages,* edited by A. N. Doane and Carol Braun Pasternack, 34–45. Madison: University of Wisconsin Press, 1991.

———. *The Singer of Tales in Performance.* Bloomington: Indiana University Press, 1995.

———. "Texts That Speak to Readers Who Hear: Old English Poetry and the Languages of Oral Tradition." In *Speaking Two Languages: Traditional Disciplines and Contemporary Theory in Medieval Studies,* edited by Allen J. Frantzen, 141–56. Albany: State University of New York Press, 1991.

———. *The Theory of Oral Composition: History and Methodology.* Bloomington: Indiana University Press, 1988.

———. "The Traditional Oral Audience." *Balkan Studies* 18 (1977): 145–54.

———. *Traditional Oral Epic: The Odyssey, Beowulf, and the Serbo-Croatian Return Song.* 1990. Reprint, Berkeley and Los Angeles: University of California Press, 1993.

———. "Word-Power, Performance, and Tradition." *JAF* 105 (1992): 275–301.

Foote, Sarah. "The Making of *Angelcynn:* English Identity before the Norman Conquest." *TRHS* 6th ser. 6 (1996): 25–49.

Frank, Roberta. "*The Battle of Maldon* and Heroic Literature." In *The Battle of Maldon AD 991,* edited by Donald Scragg, 196–207. Oxford: Blackwell, 1991.

———. "Did Anglo-Saxon Audiences Have a Skaldic Tooth?" *SS* 59 (1987): 338–55. Reprinted in *Anglo-Scandinavian England: Norse-English Relations in the Period before the Conquest,* edited by John D. Niles and Mark Amodio, 53–68. Lanham, Md.: University Press of America, 1989.

————. "Germanic Legend in Old English Literature." In *The Cambridge Companion to Old English Literature*, edited by Malcolm Godden and Michael Lapidge, 88–106. Cambridge: Cambridge University Press, 1991.

————. "The Ideal of Men Dying with Their Lord in *The Battle of Maldon:* Anachronism or *Nouvelle Vague.*" In *People and Places in Northern Europe 500–1600: Essays in Honour of Peter Hayes Sawyer*, edited by Ian Wood and Niels Lund, 95–106. Woodbridge, England: Boydell and Brewer, 1991.

————. "The Search for the Anglo-Saxon Oral Poet." *BJRL* 75 (1993): 11–36.

Frantzen, Allen J. *Desire for Origins: New Language, Old English, and Teaching the Tradition.* New Brunswick, N.J.: Rutgers University Press, 1990.

Fritz, Donald W. "Cædmon: A Traditional Christian Poet." *Medieval Studies* 31 (1969): 334–37.

Fry, Donald K. "Cædmon as a Formulaic Poet." In *Oral Literature: Seven Essays*, edited by Joseph J. Duggan, 41–61. New York: Barnes and Noble, 1975.

————. "The Hero on the Beach in *Finnsburh.*" *NM* 67 (1966): 27–31.

————. "The Heroine on the Beach in *Judith.*" *NM* 68 (1967): 168–84.

————. "Old English Formulaic Statistics." *In Geardagum* 3 (1979): 1–6.

————. "Old English Formulas and Systems." *ES* 48 (1967): 193–204.

————. "Some Aesthetic Implications of a New Definition of the Formula." *NM* 69 (1968): 516–22.

————. "Themes and Type-Scenes in *Elene* 1–113." *Speculum* 44 (1969): 35–45.

Fulk, R. D. "Cynewulf: Canon, Dialect, and Date." In *Cynewulf: Basic Readings*, edited by Robert E. Bjork, 3–21. New York: Garland Press, 1996.

————. *A History of Old English Meter.* Philadelphia: University of Pennsylvania Press, 1992.

Gang, T. M. "Approaches to *Beowulf.*" *RES* ns 3 (1952): 1–12.

Garbáty, Thomas Jay. "The Fallible Sword: Inception of a Motif." *JAF* 75 (1962): 58–59.

Glosecki, Stephen O. *Shamanism and Old English Poetry.* New York: Garland Press, 1989.

Goldsmith, Margaret E. *The Mode and Meaning of Beowulf.* London: Athlone Press, 1970.

Greenfield, Stanley B. "The Formulaic Expression of the Theme of 'Exile' in Anglo-Saxon Poetry." *Speculum* 30 (1955): 200–206.

————. "Grendel's Approach to Heorot: Syntax and Poetry." In *Old English Poetry: Fifteen Essays*, edited by Robert P. Creed, 275–84. Providence, R.I.: Brown University Press, 1967.

————. *The Interpretation of Old English Poems.* London: Routledge and Kegan Paul, 1972.

————. "A Touch of the Monstrous in the Hero, or Beowulf Re-Marvellized." *ES* 63 (1982): 294–307.

Greenfield, Stanley B., and Daniel G. Calder. *A New Critical History of Old English Literature.* New York: New York University Press, 1986.

Griffith, Mark S. "Convention and Originality in the Old English 'Beasts of Battle' Typescene." *ASE* 23 (1993): 179–99.

Griffiths, Jeremy, and Derek Pearsall, eds. *Book Production and Publishing in Britain 1375–1475.* Cambridge: Cambridge University Press, 1989.

Grudin, Michaela Paasche. *Chaucer and the Politics of Discourse.* Columbia: University of South Carolina Press, 1996.

Gwara, Scott. *Aldhelmi Malmesbiriensis Prosa de Virginitate.* Corpus Christianorum Series Latina 124. Turnhout: Brepols, 2001.

Hahn, Thomas. "Early Middle English." In *The Cambridge History of Medieval English Literature,* edited by David Wallace, 61–91. Cambridge: Cambridge University Press, 1999.

Haring, Lee C., ed. *African Oral Traditions* [special issue]. *OT* 9 (1994).

Harris, Joseph, ed. *The Ballad and Oral Literature.* Cambridge, Mass.: Harvard University Press, 1991.

Harwood, Britton J. "The Alliterative *Morte Arthure* as a Witness to Epic." In *Oral Poetics in Middle English Poetry,* edited by Mark C. Amodio, 241–86. New York: Garland Press, 1994.

Hasenohr, Geneviève. "Discours vernaculaire et autorités latines." In *Mise en page et mise en texte du livre manuscrit,* edited by Henri-Jean Martin and Jean Vezin, 289–315. Paris: Éditions du Cercle de la Librairie-Promodis, 1990.

Havelock, Eric A. "The Alphabetization of Homer." In *Communication Arts in the Ancient World,* edited by Eric A. Havelock and Jackson P. Hershbell, 3–21. New York: Hastings House, 1978.

———. *The Literate Revolution in Greece and Its Cultural Consequences.* Princeton, N.J.: Princeton University Press, 1982.

———. *Preface to Plato.* Cambridge, Mass.: Harvard University Press, 1963.

———. "The Preliteracy of the Greeks." *NLH* 8 (1976–77): 369–91. Reprinted in his *The Literate Revolution in Greece and Its Cultural Consequences,* 185–207. Princeton, N.J.: Princeton University Press, 1982.

Heffernan, Carol. "The Old English *Phoenix:* A Reconsideration." *NM* 83 (1982): 239–54.

Hieatt, Constance B. "Alliterative Patterns in the Hypermetric Lines of Old English Verse." *MP* 71 (1974): 237–42.

Hill, John M. *The Cultural World in Beowulf.* Toronto: University of Toronto Press, 1995.

Hoffman, Elizabeth A. "Exploring the Literate Blindspot: Alexander Pope's *Homer* in Light of Milman Parry." *OT* 1 (1986): 381–97.

Horvath, Richard. "The Romance of Authorship in Late Middle English Poetry (Geoffrey Chaucer, Thomas Hoccleve)." Ph.D. diss., Stanford University, 1996.

Houck, Margaret. *Sources of the Roman de Brut of Wace.* Berkeley: University of California Press, 1941.

Houston, Rab A. *Literacy in Early Modern Europe: Culture and Education 1500–1800.* London: Longman, 1988.

Howe, Nicholas. *Migration and Mythmaking in Anglo-Saxon England.* New Haven, Conn.: Yale University Press, 1989. Reprint, Notre Dame, Ind.: University of Notre Dame Press, 2001.

Howlett, David R. *The Celtic Latin Tradition of Biblical Style.* Dublin: Four Courts Press, 1995.

Hume, Kathryn. "The Concept of the Hall in Old English Poetry." *ASE* 3 (1974): 63–74.

Illich, Ivan. *In the Vineyard of the Text: A Commentary to Hugh's Didascalicon.* Chicago: University of Chicago Press, 1984.

Irvine, Martin. "Bede the Grammarian and the Scope of Grammatical Studies in Eighth-Century Northumbria." *ASE* 15 (1986): 15–44.

———. "Cynewulf's Use of Psychomachia Allegory: The Latin Sources of Some 'Interpolated' Passages." In *Allegory, Myth, and Symbol,* edited by Morton W. Bloomfield, 39–62. Cambridge, Mass.: Harvard University Press, 1981.

———. *The Making of Textual Culture: "Grammatica" and Literary Theory, 350–1100.* CSML 19. Cambridge: Cambridge University Press, 1994.

———. "Medieval Textuality and the Archaeology of Textual Culture." In *Speaking Two Languages: Traditional Disciplines and Contemporary Theory in Medieval Studies,* edited by Allen J. Frantzen, 181–210. Albany: State University of New York Press, 1991.

Irving, Edward B., Jr. "The Nature of Christianity in *Beowulf.*" *ASE* 13 (1984): 7–21.

———. *A Reading of Beowulf.* 1968. Reprint, Provo: Chaucer Studio, 1999.

———. *Rereading Beowulf.* 1989. Reprint, Philadelphia: University of Pennsylvania Press, 1992.

Jabbour, Alan. "Memorial Transmission in Old English Poetry." *CR* 3 (1969): 174–90.

Jager, Eric. "Speech and the Chest in Old English Poetry: Orality or Pectorality?" *Speculum* 65 (1990): 845–59.

Joyce, Michael. "No One Tells You This: Secondary Orality and Hypertextuality." *OT* 17 (2002): 325–45.

Jurasinski, Stefan. "The Rime of King William and Its Analogues." *Neophilologus* 88 (2004): 131–44.

Kahrl, Stanley. "Feuds in *Beowulf*: A Tragic Necessity?" *MP* 69 (1972): 189–98.

Kane, George. *Middle English Literature: A Critical Study of the Romances, the Religious Lyrics, Piers Plowman.* 1951. 3rd ed. Reprint, Westport, Conn.: Greenwood Press, 1979.

Kaske, Robert E. "*Beowulf.*" In *Critical Approaches to Six Major English Works,* edited by R. M. Lumiansky and Herschel Baker, 3–40. Philadelphia: University of Pennsylvania Press, 1968.

Keefer, Sarah Larratt, and Katherine O'Brien O'Keeffe, eds. *New Approaches to Editing Old English Verse.* Cambridge: D. S. Brewer, 1998.

Keith, W. T. "Layamon's *Brut:* The Literary Differences between the Two Texts." *MÆ* 29 (1960): 161–72.

Kellogg, Robert. "Oral Literature." *NLH* 5 (1973): 55–66.

Kelly, Susan. "Anglo-Saxon Lay Society and the Written Word." In *The Uses of Literacy in Early Medieval Europe,* edited by Rosamond McKitterick, 36–62. Cambridge: Cambridge University Press, 1990.

Kendall, Calvin. *The Metrical Grammar of Beowulf.* CSASE 5. Cambridge: Cambridge University Press, 1991.

Kiernan, Kevin. *Beowulf and the Beowulf Manuscript.* New Brunswick, N.J.: Rutgers University Press, 1981. 2nd ed., with a foreword by Katherine O'Brien O'Keeffe. Ann Arbor: University of Michigan Press, 1996.

———. "Old English Manuscripts: The Scribal Deconstruction of 'Early' Northumbrian." *ANQ* 3 (1990): 48–55.

———. "Reading Cædmon's 'Hymn' with Someone Else's Glosses." *Representations* 32 (1990): 157–74.

Kirk, G. S. *Homer and the Oral Tradition.* Cambridge: Cambridge University Press, 1976.

Kliman, Bernice. "Women in Early English Literature, *Beowulf* to the *Ancrene Wisse.*" *NMS* 21 (1977): 32–49.

Knight, S. T. "The Oral Transmission of *Sir Launfal.*" *MÆ* 38 (1969): 164–70.

Kristeva, Julia. "Word, Dialogue and Novel." In *The Kristeva Reader,* edited by Toril Moi, 34–61. New York: Columbia University Press, 1986.

Kuhn, Sherman M. "Old English *aglǣca*—Middle Irish *oclach.*" In *Linguistic Method: Essays in Honor of Herbert Penzel,* edited by Irmengard Rauch and Gerald F. Carr, 213–30. The Hague: Mouton, 1979. Reprinted in his *Studies in the Language and Poetics of Anglo-Saxon England,* 213–30. Ann Arbor, Mich.: Karoma Publishers, 1984.

Lapidge, Michael. "Aldhelm's Latin Poetry and Old English Verse." *CL* 31 (1979): 209–31.

———. "The Anglo-Latin Background." In *A New Critical History of Old English Literature,* edited by Stanley B. Greenfield and Daniel G. Calder, 5–37. New York: New York University Press, 1986.

———. "*Beowulf* and the Psychology of Terror." In *Heroic Poetry in the Anglo-Saxon Period: Studies in Honor of Jess B. Bessinger, Jr.,* edited by Helen Damico and John Leyerle, 373–402. Kalamazoo, Mich.: Medieval Institute Publications, 1993.

Lawton, David A., ed. *Middle English Alliterative Poetry and Its Literary Background.* Cambridge: D. S. Brewer 1982.

———. "The Unity of Middle English Alliterative Poetry." *Speculum* 58 (1983): 72–94.

Le Saux, Françoise. *Laʒamon's Brut: The Poem and Its Sources.* Cambridge: D. S. Brewer, 1989.

Lee, Alvin. *The Guest-Hall of Eden: Four Essays on the Design of Old English Poetry.* New Haven, Conn.: Yale University Press, 1972.

Lerer, Seth. *Chaucer and His Readers: Imagining the Author in Late-Medieval England.* Princeton, N.J.: Princeton University Press, 1993.

———. *Literacy and Power in Anglo-Saxon Literature.* Lincoln: University of Nebraska Press, 1991.

———. "Old English and Its Afterlife." In *The Cambridge History of Medieval English Literature,* edited by David Wallace, 7–34. Cambridge: Cambridge University Press, 1999.

Levy, Bernard S., and Paul E. Szarmach, eds. *The Alliterative Tradition in the Fourteenth Century.* Kent, Oh.: Kent State University Press, 1981.

Lewis, C. S. "The Genesis of a Medieval Book." In his *Studies in Medieval and Renaissance Literature,* 18–40. Collected by Walter Hooper, 1966. Reprint, Cambridge: Cambridge University Press, 1998.

Leyerle, John. "Beowulf the Hero and the King." *MÆ* 34 (1965): 89–102.

Liestøl, Aslak. "Correspondence in Runes." *Medieval Scandinavia* 1 (1968): 17–27.

Lindow, John. *Comitatus, Individual and Honor: Studies in North Germanic Institutional Vocabulary.* University of California Publications in Linguistics 83. Berkeley and Los Angeles: University of California Press, 1976.

Lord, Albert B. "Composition by Theme in Homer and Southslavic Epos." *TAPA* 82 (1951): 71–80.

———. "Homer as an Oral-Traditional Poet." In his *Epic Singers and Oral Tradition,* 72–103. Ithaca, N.Y.: Cornell University Press, 1991.

———. "The Merging of Two Worlds: Oral and Written Poetry as Carriers of Ancient Values." In *Oral Tradition in Literature,* edited by John Miles Foley, 313–49. Columbia: University of Missouri Press, 1986.

———. *The Singer of Tales.* 1960. Harvard Studies in Comparative Literature 24. 2nd ed. Edited by Stephen Mitchell and Gregory Nagy. Cambridge, Mass.: Harvard University Press, 2000.

———. "The Theme in Anglo-Saxon Poetry." In his *The Singer Resumes the Tale,* edited by Mary Louise Lord, 137–66. Ithaca, N.Y.: Cornell University Press, 1995.

———. "The Theme of the Withdrawn Hero in Serbo-Croatian Oral Epic." *Prilozi za književnost, jezik, istoriju i folklor* 35 (1969): 18–30.

Lyons, John. *Semantics.* 2 vols. 1977. Reprint, Cambridge: Cambridge University Press, 1984.

Machan, Tim William. "Editing, Orality, and Late Middle English Texts." In *Vox Intexta: Orality and Textuality in the Middle Ages,* edited by A. N. Doane and Carol Braun Pasternack, 229–45. Madison: University of Wisconsin Press, 1991.

Magoun, Francis Peabody, Jr. "Bede's Story of Cædmon: The Case History of an Anglo-Saxon Oral Singer." *Speculum* 30 (1955): 49–63.

———. "The Oral-Formulaic Character of Anglo-Saxon Narrative Poetry." *Speculum* 28 (1953): 446–67. Reprinted in *An Anthology of Beowulf Criticism,* edited by Lewis E. Nicholson, 189–221. Notre Dame, Ind.: University of Notre Dame Press, 1963.

———. "The Theme of the Beasts of Battle in Anglo-Saxon Poetry." *NM* 56 (1955): 81–90.

McGillivray, Murray. *Memorization in the Transmission of the Middle English Romance.* New York: Garland Press, 1990.

McKinnell, J. "On the Date of *The Battle of Maldon.*" *MÆ* 44 (1975): 121–36.

McKitterick, Rosamond. "Introduction." In *The Uses of Literacy in Early Medieval Europe,* edited by Rosamond McKitterick, 1–10. Cambridge: Cambridge University Press, 1990.

McLaughlin, John. "The Return Song in Medieval Romance and Ballad: King Horn and King Orfeo." *JAF* 88 (1975): 304–7.

McNelis, James, III. "Laȝamon as Auctor." In *The Text and Tradition of Laȝamon's Brut,* edited by Françoise Le Saux, 253–72. Cambridge: D. S. Brewer, 1994.

Mendoza, Kenneth. *Talking Books: Ethnopoetics, Translation, Text.* Columbia, S.C.: Camden House, 1993.

Metcalf, Allan A. "Ten Natural Animals in *Beowulf.*" *NM* 64 (1963): 378–89.

Mezger, F. "Goth. aglaiti 'unchastity', OE aglæc 'distress.'" *Word* 2 (1946): 66–71.

Miller, William Ian. "Choosing the Avenger: Some Aspects of the Bloodfeud in Medieval Iceland and England." *Law and History Review* 1 (1983): 159–204.

Mizuno, Tomoaki. "Beowulf as a Terrible Stranger." *Journal of Indo-European Studies* 17 (1989): 1–46.

Moffat, Douglas. "Anglo-Saxon Scribes and Old English Verse." *Speculum* 67 (1992): 805–27.

Monroe, Benton S. "French Words in Laȝamon." *MP* 4 (1907): 559–67.

Moorman, Charles. "The Origins of the Alliterative Revival." *Southern Quarterly* 7 (1969): 345–71.

Nagler, Michael N. *Spontaneity and Tradition: A Study in the Oral Art of Homer.* Berkeley and Los Angeles: University of California Press, 1974.

Nicholls, Alex. "Bede 'Awe-Inspiring' not 'Monstrous': Some Problems with Old English *Aglæca.*" *NQ* 236 (1991): 147–48.

Niles, John D. *Beowulf: The Poem and Its Tradition.* Cambridge, Mass.: Harvard University Press, 1983.

———. *Homo Narrans: The Poetics and Anthropology of Oral Literature.* Philadelphia: University of Pennsylvania Press, 1999.

———. "Ring Composition and the Structure of *Beowulf.*" *PMLA* 94 (1979): 924–35.

Noble, James E. "Laȝamon's 'Ambivalence' Reconsidered." In *The Text and Tradition of Laȝamon's Brut,* edited by Françoise Le Saux, 171–82. Cambridge: D. S. Brewer, 1994.

———. "Layamon's *Brut* and the Continuity of the Alliterative Tradition." Ph.D. diss., University of Western Ontario, 1981.

Oakden, J. P. *Alliterative Poetry in Middle English: A Survey of the Traditions.* 2 vols. 1930, 1935. Reprint, 2 vols. in 1, Hamden, Conn.: Archon Books, 1968.

O'Brien O'Keeffe, Katherine. "*Beowulf,* Lines 702b–836: Transformations and the Limits of the Human." *TSLL* 23 (1981): 484–94.

———. "Deaths and Transformations: Thinking through the 'End' of Old English Verse." In *New Directions in Oral Theory*, edited by Mark C. Amodio. Tempe, Ariz.: MRTS, in press.

———. "The Performing Body on the Oral-Literate Continuum: Old English Poetry." In *Teaching Oral Traditions*, edited by John Miles Foley, 46–58. New York: Modern Language Association, 1998.

———. *Visible Song: Transitional Literacy in Old English Verse*. CSASE 4. Cambridge: Cambridge University Press, 1990.

Ólason, Vésteinn. "Literary Backgrounds of the Scandinavian Ballad." In *The Ballad and Oral Literature*, edited by Joseph Harris, 116–38. Cambridge, Mass.: Harvard University Press, 1991.

Olsen, Alexandra Hennessey. "The Aesthetics of *Andreas:* The Contexts of Oral Tradition and Patristic Latin Poetry." In *De Gustibus: Essays for Alain Renoir*, edited by John Miles Foley, 388–410. New York: Garland Press, 1992.

———. "The *Aglæca* and the Law." *ANQ* 20 (1981): 66–68.

———. "Old English Poetry and Latin Prose: The Reverse Context." *Classica et Medievalia* 34 (1983): 273–82.

———. "Proteus in Latin: Vernacular Tradition and the Boniface Collection." In *New Directions in Oral Theory*, edited by Mark C. Amodio. Tempe, Ariz.: MRTS, in press.

———. *Speech, Song, and Poetic Craft: The Artistry of the Cynewulf Canon*. New York: Lang, 1984.

Ong, Walter, J., S.J. *Orality and Literacy: The Technologizing of the Word*. London: Methuen, 1982.

———. "Orality, Literacy, and Medieval Textualization." *NLH* 16 (1984): 1–12.

———. "Writing Is a Technology That Restructures Thought." In *The Written Word: Literacy in Transition*, edited by Gerd Baumann, 23–50. Oxford: Clarendon Press, 1986.

Opland, Jeff. *Anglo-Saxon Oral Poetry: A Study of the Traditions*. New Haven, Conn.: Yale University Press, 1980.

———. "From Horseback to Monastic Cell: The Impact on English Literature of the Introduction of Writing." In *Old English Literature in Context: Ten Essays*, edited by John D. Niles, 30–43. Cambridge: D. S. Brewer, 1980.

———. "*Scop* and *Imbongi:* Anglo-Saxon and Bantu Oral Poets." *English Studies in Africa* 14 (1971): 161–78.

———. *Xhosa Oral Poetry: Aspects of a Black South African Tradition*. Cambridge: Cambridge University Press, 1983.

Orchard, Andy. "Both Style and Substance: The Case for Cynewulf." In *Anglo-Saxon Styles*, edited by Catherine Karkov and George H. Brown, 271–306. Albany: State University of New York Press, 2003.

———. *A Critical Companion to Beowulf*. Cambridge: D. S. Brewer, 2003.

————. *The Poetic Art of Aldhelm.* CSASE 8. Cambridge: Cambridge University Press, 1994.

Orwell, George. "Politics and the English Language." In *George Orwell: A Collection of Essays,* 156–71. 1946. Reprint, San Diego: Harcourt Brace, 1993.

Parkes, M. B. "The Contribution of Insular Scribes of the Seventh and Eighth Centuries to the 'Grammar of Legibility.'" In his *Scribes, Scripts, and Readers: Studies in the Communication, Presentation, and Dissemination of Medieval Texts,* 1–18. London: Hambledon Press, 1991.

————. "On the Presumed Date and Possible Origin of the Manuscript of the *Orrmulum*: Oxford, Bodleian Library, MS Junius 1." In his *Scribes, Scripts, and Readers: Studies in the Communication, Presentation, and Dissemination of Medieval Texts,* 187–200. London: Hambledon Press, 1991.

————. *Pause and Effect: An Introduction to the History of Punctuation in the West.* Berkeley and Los Angeles: University of California Press, 1993.

————. "The Scriptorium of Wearmouth-Jarrow." Jarrow Lecture, 1982. Reprinted in his *Scribes, Scripts, and Readers: Studies in the Communication, Presentation, and Dissemination of Medieval Texts,* 93–119. London: Hambledon Press, 1991.

Parks, Ward. "The Oral-Formulaic Theory in Middle English Studies." *OT* 1 (1986): 636–94.

————. "Song, Text, and Cassette: Why We Need Authoritative Audio Editions of Medieval Literary Works." *OT* 7 (1992): 102–15.

————. "The Textualization of Orality in Literary Criticism." In *Vox Intexta: Orality and Textuality in the Middle Ages,* edited by A. N. Doane and Carol Braun Pasternack, 46–61. Madison: University of Wisconsin Press, 1991.

————. "The Traditional Narrator and the 'I Heard' Formulas in Old English Poetry." *ASE* 16 (1987): 45–66.

Parry, Milman. "The Epithet and the Formula I: The Usage of the Fixed Epithet." In *The Making of Homeric Verse: The Collected Papers of Milman Parry,* edited by Adam Parry, 37–117. 1971. Reprint, Oxford: Oxford University Press, 1987.

————. "Studies in the Epic Technique of Oral Verse-Making. I. Homer and Homeric Style." In *The Making of Homeric Verse: The Collected Papers of Milman Parry,* edited by Adam Parry, 266–324. 1971. Reprint, Oxford: Oxford University Press, 1987.

————. "The Traditional Epithet in Homer." In *The Making of Homeric Verse: The Collected Papers of Milman Parry,* edited by Adam Parry, 2–23. 1971. Reprint, Oxford: Oxford University Press, 1987.

Parsons, David N. *Recasting the Runes: The Reform of the Anglo-Saxon Futhorc.* Runrön. Runologiska bidrag utgivna av Institutionen för nordiska språk vid Uppsala universitet 14. Uppsala: Reklam and Katalogtryck, 1999.

Pasternack, Carol Braun. *The Textuality of Old English Poetry.* CSASE 13. Cambridge: Cambridge University Press, 1995.

Patterson, Lee. *Negotiating the Past: The Historical Understanding of Medieval Literature.* Madison: University of Wisconsin Press, 1987.

———. "On the Margin: Postmodernism, Ironic History, and Medieval Studies." *Speculum* 65 (1990): 87–108.

Peabody, Berkley. *The Winged Word: A Study in the Technique of Ancient Greek Oral Composition as Seen Principally through Hesiod's Works and Days.* Albany: State University of New York Press, 1975.

Pearsall, Derek. *Old and Middle English Poetry.* London: Routledge and Kegan Paul, 1977.

———. "The Origins of the Alliterative Revival." In *The Alliterative Tradition in the Fourteenth Century,* edited by Bernard S. Levy and Paul E. Szarmach, 1–24. Kent, Oh.: Kent State University Press, 1981.

———. "The *Troilus* Frontispiece and Chaucer's Audience." *YES* 7 (1977): 68–74.

Quinn, William A., and Audley S. Hall. *Jongleur: A Modified Theory of Oral Improvisation and Its Effects on the Performance and Transmission of Middle English Romance.* Washington, D.C.: University Press of America, 1982.

Rauer, Christine. *Beowulf and the Dragon: Parallels and Analogues.* Cambridge: D. S. Brewer, 2000.

Reames, Sherry L. "*Mouvance* and Interpretation in Late-Medieval Latin: The Legend of St. Cecilia in British Breviaries." In *Medieval Literature: Texts and Interpretation,* edited by Tim William Machan, 159–89. Binghamton, N.Y.: MRTS, 1991.

Renoir, Alain. "Crist Ihesu's Beasts of Battle: A Note on Oral-Formulaic Theme Survival." *Neophilologus* 60 (1976): 455–59.

———. "The Hero on the Beach: Germanic Theme and Indo-European Origin." *NM* 90 (1989): 111–16.

———. "*Judith* and the Limits of Poetry." *ES* 43 (1962): 145–55.

———. *A Key to Old Poems: The Oral-Formulaic Approach to the Interpretation of West-Germanic Verse.* University Park: Pennsylvania State University Press, 1988.

———. "Oral-Formulaic Context: Implications for the Comparative Criticism of Mediaeval Texts." In *Oral Traditional Literature: A Festschrift for Albert Bates Lord,* edited by John Miles Foley, 416–39. Columbus, Oh.: Slavica, 1981.

———. "Oral-Formulaic Rhetoric and the Interpretation of Literary Texts." In *Oral Tradition in Literature: Interpretation in Context,* edited by John Miles Foley, 103–35. Columbia: University of Missouri Press, 1986.

———. "Oral-Formulaic Theme Survival: A Possible Instance in the *Nibelungenlied.*" *NM* 65 (1964): 70–75.

———. "Oral Theme and Written Texts." *NM* 77 (1976): 337–46.

———. "Point of View and Design for Terror in *Beowulf*." *NM* 63 (1962): 154–67. Reprinted in *The Beowulf Poet: A Collection of Critical Essays*, edited by Donald K. Fry, 154–66. Englewood Cliffs, N.J.: Prentice Hall, 1968.

Riedinger, Anita. "The Formulaic Relationship between *Beowulf* and *Andreas*." In *Heroic Poetry in the Anglo-Saxon Period: Studies in Honor of Jess B. Bessinger, Jr.*, edited by Helen Damico and John Leyerle, 283–312. Kalamazoo, Mich.: Medieval Institute Publications, 1993.

———. "The Old English Formula in Context." *Speculum* 60 (1985): 294–317.

Ringbom, Håkon. *Studies in the Narrative Technique of Beowulf and Lawman's Brut.* Åbo: Åbo Akademi, 1968.

Roberts, Jane. "Hrothgar's Admirable Courage." In *Unlocking the Wordhord: Anglo-Saxon Studies in Memory of Edward B. Irving, Jr.*, edited by Mark C. Amodio and Katherine O'Brien O'Keeffe, 240–51. Toronto: University of Toronto Press, 2003.

———. "A Preliminary Note on British Library, Cotton MS Caligula A.ix." In *The Text and Tradition of Laʒamon's Brut*, edited by Françoise Le Saux, 1–14. Cambridge: D. S. Brewer, 1994.

Robinson, Fred C. "The Afterlife of Old English: A Brief History of Composition in Old English after the Close of the Anglo-Saxon Period." In his *The Tomb of Beowulf and Other Essays on Old English*, 275–303. Oxford: Blackwell, 1993.

———. *Beowulf and the Appositive Style.* Knoxville: University of Tennessee Press, 1985.

———. *The Editing of Old English.* Oxford: Blackwell, 1994.

———. "Elements of the Marvelous in the Characterization of Beowulf: A Reconsideration of Textual Evidence." In *Old English Studies in Honour of John C. Pope*, edited by Robert B. Burlin and Edward B. Irving, Jr., 119–37. Toronto: University of Toronto Press, 1974. Reprinted with an afterword in his *The Tomb of Beowulf and Other Essays on Old English*, 20–35. Oxford: Blackwell, 1993.

———. "*Medieval*, the *Middle Ages*." *Speculum* 59 (1984): 745–56. Reprinted in his *The Tomb of Beowulf and Other Essays on Old English*, 304–15. Oxford: Blackwell, 1993.

Rogers, H. L. "Beowulf's Three Great Fights." *RES* ns 6 (1955): 339–55.

Rosenberg, Bruce A. *Folklore and Literature: Rival Siblings.* Knoxville: University of Tennessee Press, 1991.

Rosenthal, Joel T. "Bede's *Ecclesiastical History* and the Material Conditions of Anglo-Saxon Life." *Journal of British Studies* 19 (1979): 1–17.

Saenger, Paul. "Silent Reading: Its Impact on Late Medieval Script and Society." *Viator* 13 (1982): 367–414.

———. *The Space between Words: The Origins of Silent Reading.* Stanford, Calif.: Stanford University Press, 1997.

Salter, Elizabeth. "Alliterative Modes and Affiliations in the Fourteenth Century." *NM* 79 (1978): 25–35. Reprinted in her *English and International: Studies in the Lit-*

erature, Art and Patronage of Medieval England, edited by Derek Pearsall and Nicolette Zeeman, 170–79. Cambridge: Cambridge University Press, 1988.

———. "The Alliterative Revival." *MP* 64 (1966): 146–50, 233–37. Reprinted in her *English and International: Studies in the Literature, Art and Patronage of Medieval England,* edited by Derek Pearsall and Nicolette Zeeman, 101–10. Cambridge: Cambridge University Press, 1988.

———. *English and International: Studies in the Literature, Art and Patronage of Medieval England,* edited by Derek Pearsall and Nicolette Zeeman. Cambridge: Cambridge University Press, 1988.

———. *Fourteenth-Century English Poetry: Contents and Readings.* 1983. Reprint, Oxford: Clarendon Press, 1984.

Scattergood, V. J. *The Lost Tradition: Essays on Middle English Alliterative Poetry.* Dublin: Four Courts Press, 2000.

Schaar, Claes. "On a New Theory of Old English Poetic Diction." *Neophilologus* 40 (1956): 301–5.

Schaefer, Ursula. "Alterities: On Methodology in Medieval Literary Studies." *OT* 8 (1993): 187–214.

———. "Hearing from Books: The Rise of Fictionality in Old English Poetry." In *Vox Intexta: Orality and Textuality in the Middle Ages,* edited by A. N. Doane and Carol Braun Pasternack, 117–36. Madison: University of Wisconsin Press, 1991.

Searle, John. *Expression and Meaning: Studies in the Theory of Speech Acts.* 1979. Reprint, Cambridge: Cambridge University Press, 1993.

———. *Speech Acts: An Essay in the Philosophy of Language.* 1969. Reprint, Cambridge: Cambridge University Press, 1988.

Serjeantson, Mary. *A History of Foreign Words in English.* 1935. Reprint, London: Routledge and Kegan Paul, 1968.

Shilton, Howard. "The Nature of Beowulf's Dragon Fight." *BJRL* 79 (1997): 67–77.

Sisam, Kenneth. "Beowulf's Fight with the Dragon." *RES* ns 9 (1958): 129–40.

———. "Dialect Origins of the Earlier Old English Verse." In his *Studies in the History of Old English Literature,* 119–39. Oxford: Clarendon Press, 1953.

———. "Notes on OE Poetry." *RES* 22 (1946): 257–68. Reprinted as "The Authority of Old English Poetical Manuscripts" in his *Studies in the History of Old English Literature,* 29–44. Oxford: Clarendon Press, 1953.

Sklute, L. John [Larry M.]. "*Freoðuwebbe* in Old English Poetry." *NM* 71 (1970): 534–71. Reprinted in *New Readings on Women in Old English Poetry,* edited by Helen Damico and Alexandra Hennessey Olsen, 201–10. Bloomington: Indiana University Press, 1990.

Sorrell, Paul. "The Approach to the Dragon-Fight in *Beowulf,* Aldhelm, and the '*traditions folkloriques*' of Jacques Le Goff." *Parergon* ns 12 (1994): 57–87.

———. "Oral Poetry and the World of *Beowulf.*" *OT* 7 (1992): 28–65.

Stanley, Eric G. "The Date of Laȝamon's 'Brut.'" *NQ* ns 15 (1968): 85–88.

———. "Laȝamon's Antiquarian Sentiments." *MÆ* 38 (1969): 23–37.

———. "Laȝamon's Un-Anglo-Saxon Syntax." In *The Text and Tradition of Laȝamon's Brut,* edited by Françoise Le Saux, 47–56. Cambridge: D. S. Brewer, 1994.

———. "Linguistic Self-Awareness at Various Times in the History of English from Old English Onwards." In *Lexis and Texts in Early English: Studies Presented to Jane Roberts,* edited by Christian J. Kay and Louise M. Sylvester, 237–53. Costerus New Series 133. Amsterdam: Editions Rodopoi, 2001.

———. "Rhymes in English Medieval Verse: From Old English to Middle English." In *Medieval Studies Presented to George Kane,* edited by Edward D. Kennedy, Ronald Waldron, and Joseph S. Wittig, 19–54. Wolfeboro, N.H.: D. S. Brewer, 1988.

———. "Unideal Principles of Editing Old English Verse." *PBA* 70 (1985 for 1984): 231–73.

Stenton, F. M. *Anglo-Saxon England.* 1943. 3rd ed. London: Oxford University Press, 1971.

Stitt, J. Michael. *Beowulf and the Bear's Son: Epic, Saga, and Fairytale in Northern Germanic Tradition.* New York: Garland Press, 1992.

Stock, Brian. *The Implications of Literacy: Written Language and Models of Interpretation in the Eleventh and Twelfth Centuries.* Princeton, N.J.: Princeton University Press, 1983.

———. *Listening for the Text: On the Uses of the Past.* Baltimore: Johns Hopkins University Press, 1990.

Stoltz, Benjamin A. "On Two Serbo-Croatian Oral Epic Verses: The *Bugarštica* and the *Deseterac.*" In *Poetic Theory/Poetic Practice,* edited by Robert Scholes, 153–64. Iowa City: Midwest Modern Language Association, 1969.

Stoltz, Benjamin A., and Richard S. Shannon, eds. *Oral Literature and the Formula.* Ann Arbor: Center for the Coordination of Ancient and Modern Studies, University of Michigan, 1976.

Storms, G. "Grendel the Terrible." *NM* 73 (1972): 427–36.

Suzuki, Eiichi. "Oral-Formulaic Theme Survival: Two Possible Instances and Their Significance in *Sir Gawain and the Green Knight.*" *Studies in English Literature* 162 (1972): 15–31.

Swan, Mary, and Elaine Treharne, eds. *Rewriting Old English in the Twelfth Century.* CSASE 30. Cambridge: Cambridge University Press, 2000.

Tatlock, J. S. P. *The Legendary History of Britain: Geoffrey of Monmouth's Historia Regum Britanniae and Its Early Vernacular Versions.* Berkeley and Los Angeles: University of California Press, 1950.

Thomas, Rosalind. *Literacy and Orality in Ancient Greece.* Cambridge: Cambridge University Press, 1992.

————. *Oral Tradition and Written Record in Classical Athens.* Cambridge: Cambridge University Press, 1989.

Thomas, Russell. "Syntactical Processes Involved in the Development of the Adnominal Genitive in the English Language." Ph.D. diss., University of Michigan, 1932.

Tolkien, J. R. R. "*Beowulf:* The Monsters and the Critics." *PBA* 22 (1936): 245–95. Reprinted in *Interpretations of Beowulf: A Critical Anthology,* edited by R. D. Fulk, 14–44. Bloomington: Indiana University Press, 1991.

Turville-Petre, Thorlac. *The Alliterative Revival.* Cambridge: D. S. Brewer, 1977.

Waldron, Ronald. "Oral-Formulaic Technique and Middle English Alliterative Poetry." *Speculum* 32 (1957): 792–804.

Watkins, Calvert. *How to Kill a Dragon: Aspects of Indo-European Poetics.* Oxford: Oxford University Press, 1995.

Watts, Ann Chalmers. *The Lyre and the Harp: A Comparative Reconsideration of Oral Tradition in Homer and Old English Epic Poetry.* New Haven, Conn.: Yale University Press, 1969.

Weiss, Judith. "The Major Interpolations in *Sir Beues of Hamtoun.*" *MÆ* 48 (1979): 71–76.

Wenzel, Seigfried. *Macaronic Sermons: Bilingualism and Preaching in Late-Medieval England.* Ann Arbor: University of Michigan Press, 1994.

West, M. L. *Greek Metre.* Oxford: Clarendon Press, 1982.

Whallon, William. *Formula, Character, and Context: Studies in Homeric, Old English, and Old Testament Poetry.* Cambridge, Mass.: Harvard University Press, 1969.

White, Stephen D. "Kinship and Lordship in Early Medieval England: The Story of Sigeberht, Cynewulf, and Cyneheard." *Viator* 20 (1989): 1–18.

Woolf, Rosemary. "The Ideal of Men Dying with Their Lord in the *Germania* and in *The Battle of Maldon.*" *ASE* 5 (1976): 63–81.

Wormald, Patrick. "Anglo-Saxon Society and Its Literature." In *The Cambridge Companion to Old English Literature,* edited by Malcolm Godden and Michael Lapidge, 1–22. Cambridge: Cambridge University Press, 1991.

————. "*Engla lond:* The Making of an Allegiance." *Journal of Historical Sociology* 7 (1994): 1–24.

Würzbach, Natascha. "Tradition and Innovation: The Influence of Child Ballads on the Anglo-American Literary Ballad." In *The Ballad and Oral Literature,* edited by Joseph Harris, 171–92. Cambridge, Mass.: Harvard University Press, 1991.

Wyld, Henry Cecil. "Laȝamon as an English Poet." *RES* 6 (1930): 1–30.

————. "Studies in the Diction of Layamon's *Brut.*" *Language* 19 (1933): 171–91.

Ziolkowski, Jan. "Cultural Diglossia and the Nature of Medieval Latin Literature." In *The Ballad and Oral Literature,* edited by Joseph Harris, 193–213. Cambridge, Mass.: Harvard University Press, 1991.

————. "Oral-Formulaic Tradition and the Composition of Latin Poetry from Antiquity through the Twelfth Century." In *New Directions in Oral Theory*, edited by Mark C. Amodio. Tempe, Ariz: MRTS, in press.

Zumthor, Paul. "The Impossible Closure of the Oral Text." *Yale French Studies* 67 (1984): 25–42.

————. *La lettre et la voix de la littérature médiévale.* Paris: Éditions du Seuil, 1987.

Index

MARK C. AMODIO is professor of English at Vassar College.